War and Compromise Between Nations and States

Egbert Jahn

War and Compromise Between Nations and States

Political Issues Under Debate – Vol. 4

Translated by Anna Güttel-Bellert

Egbert Jahn
University of Mannheim
Mannheim, Baden-Württemberg, Germany

Translated by
Anna Güttel-Bellert
Berlin, Germany

ISBN 978-3-030-34133-6   ISBN 978-3-030-34131-2 (eBook)
https://doi.org/10.1007/978-3-030-34131-2

Translation from the German language edition:
"Politische Streitfragen - Band 5: Krieg und Kompromiss zwischen Nationen und Staaten"
by Egbert Jahn, © Springer VS 2019

© Springer Nature Switzerland AG 2020

This work is subject to copyright. All rights are reserved by the Publisher, whether the whole or part of the material is concerned, specifically the rights of translation, reprinting, reuse of illustrations, recitation, broadcasting, reproduction on microfilms or in any other physical way, and transmission or information storage and retrieval, electronic adaptation, computer software, or by similar or dissimilar methodology now known or hereafter developed.

The use of general descriptive names, registered names, trademarks, service marks, etc. in this publication does not imply, even in the absence of a specific statement, that such names are exempt from the relevant protective laws and regulations and therefore free for general use.

The publisher, the authors, and the editors are safe to assume that the advice and information in this book are believed to be true and accurate at the date of publication. Neither the publisher nor the authors or the editors give a warranty, express or implied, with respect to the material contained herein or for any errors or omissions that may have been made. The publisher remains neutral with regard to jurisdictional claims in published maps and institutional affiliations.

This Springer imprint is published by the registered company Springer Nature Switzerland AG.
The registered company address is: Gewerbestrasse 11, 6330 Cham, Switzerland

Preface

This is the fourth volume in the series "Political Issues Under Debate". The first three volumes *International Politics*, *German Domestic and Foreign Policy* and *World Political Challenges* were published in 2015. This new volume focuses on "War and Compromise Between Nations and States". Here, the term "states" refers to the 193 member states of the United Nations, which mutually recognise each other as sovereign (nation) states, and the small number of de facto states that are not internationally recognised. "Nations" here refers to large societal groups, usually consisting of between more than ten thousand and one billion people, among whom either majority aspire to an existing state or who wish to form or reinstate their own nation state. Accordingly, a differentiation should be made between state nations and stateless nations. The desire for nation statehood can also be limited to the establishment of a member state in a federal state or an autonomous territory and in rare cases also to a personal-cultural corporation. In such cases, nations exist in a (federal) nation, in the same way as there are also (member) states within (federal) states.

The creation of nation states after the US American and French revolutions at the end of the eighteenth century, in which the (national) sovereignty of the people forged the legitimisation for the modern state, has involved numerous, often extremely bloody and barbaric, wars. They split populations of polyethnic empires into enemy nations while at the same time also welding them together. Thus, war simultaneously has a disintegrative and an integrative function. Peace often takes the form of a peace through victory, and is thus the result of a diktat, achieved through military action, by one warring party over the other, who has suffered a heavy military defeat. In some cases, however, nation sates can separate peacefully from pre-nation or federal nation sates, as was the case with Norway, Slovakia, the Union republics of the Soviet Union and Montenegro. In such cases, peace is the result of negotiations that have led to a political compromise between the disputing nations.

Currently, the aspiration among stateless nations for a state of their own and national conflicts over territories are still playing a significant role and create the potential for war. Peace and conflict researchers are searching for opportunities for a peaceful compromise between the conflicting parties, ideally before a potential war breaks out. However, this approach is also applied after such a war, since frequently after such a war has come to an end, preparations are already made for the next one, in order to revoke the unsatisfactory, unsatisfying result of the previous one. After all, peace through victory rarely creates a lasting peace. Real peace cannot be secured until a political compromise has been achieved.

This volume focuses on the two aspects of this problem. On the one hand, it looks at the issue of guilt in wars of aggression and incidents of mass murder (Chap. 1) and anti-terrorist violence (Chap. 2), while on the other, it discusses several specific national conflicts, such as the dispute surrounding islands and smaller land features in the South China Sea that have the potential to escalate into a world war (Chap. 3) and the wars in Ukraine (Chaps. 7 and 8) and in Syria (Chap. 10). It remains uncertain whether efforts to attain national independence in Catalonia and the insistence by Spain on centralist statehood will lead to extensive violence (Chap. 14). Against this background, it makes sense to examine in greater detail the way in which other states handle national and linguistic-cultural conflicts in a peaceful manner. In this volume, Switzerland (Chap. 15) and Canada (Chap. 13) serve as examples. Here, complex compromises have been achieved, which from time to time have been adapted to new requirements over the centuries.

The twentieth century was dominated by the east–west conflict, i.e. between the socio-political, liberal democratic capitalist and socialist-bureaucratic communist orders, both of which claimed the sole right to representation of mankind on the global political stage. Both orders competed with each other when it came to integration. They had their most powerful protagonists in the USA (Chap. 4) and in the Soviet Union. In this volume, their fundamental concept of peace will be examined in greater detail and in the case of the Soviet Union also the ideas for a "solution to the national questions" within and between the states (Chap. 9).

While for many contemporaries, the European Union had long been considered an alternative to the nation state, it is increasingly evident today that European politics still has no consistent answer to the wide range of national issues. These include migration between the EU states and migration from outside the EU into the Union, which is discussed in the sections on Brexit (Chap. 12) and the German and European refugee policy (Chap. 11, which has been published already in: МИРОВАЯ ЭКОНОМИКА И МЕЖДУНАРОДНЫЕ ОТНОШЕНИЯ 2016 том 60 № 9 and № 10). There is much to suggest that the EU will only survive in the future as a union of ever more closely cooperating nation sates and national citizens, and not as a union of purely EU citizens without a nation state base.

The volume is rounded off by two articles on the fundamental policy of non-violence, the most important inspiration for which came from Mohandas K. Gandhi. One article focuses on the role of Gandhi in the struggle for Indian national independence (Chap. 5) and the other on his universal importance (Chap. 6). This goes far beyond peace policies between nations as a form of diplomatic compromise by state leaderships and leads to questions regarding the opportunities and limitations of peace policies in civil society. As already suggested in Volume 4, the studies presented indicate that peace policies that have the potential to succeed, and which aspire to long-term world peace, should be regarded as a multidimensional process that combines strictly non-violent civil society movements with low-level violent state policies, which both must attempt to find ways of regulating conflicts between the nations and states.

Preface

The texts in this volume were written in preparation for lectures which I have been regularly giving since May 2004, in other words, towards the end of my regular professional activity, under the heading "Controversial Political Issues from the Perspective of Contemporary History" (*Politische Streitfragen in zeitgeschichtlicher Perspektive*). After fifteen years, sixty-six lectures on hotly debated political topics from all over the world are now available in print. All have been published in German, almost all in English and many also in Russian. Until December 2009, these lectures were given at the University of Mannheim, where I held the professorship for Political Science and Contemporary History from 1993 to 2005, and from October 2009 onwards at the Johann Wolfgang Goethe University in Frankfurt-Main, where I am still a lecturer today. There, I was Professor for Political Science and Political Sociology from 1975 to 1993, and from 1971 to 1990 also worked as an academic specialist and then research director at the Peace Research Institute Frankfurt (*Hessische Stiftung Friedens- und Konfliktforschung*). These lectures are attended by both regular students and many senior citizens from the "University of the Third Age", as this most worthy establishment is rather euphemistically known.

I understand political science as being a study of politics that is not really able to be unbiased and impartial, since all the key elements of this field of science inevitably invoke value judgement. However, one can and should be very cautious when it comes to expressing political value judgements and using strongly biased and emotional language. To the extent that political recommendations are given, they should expressly be identified as such, so that an analysis of the past and a prognosis of what is possible and probable in the future on the one hand and normative statements on the other can remain clearly separate from each other. In my view, contemporary historical science is an essential branch of political science, and was also undisputedly so when after 1945 political science was established at German universities as a science of democracy.

Contemporary history as history that extends into the future is, I believe, a global history of the era of the sovereignty of the people as a concept that is gradually being asserted. Until now, it has been divided into three time periods: the "long century" from 1176/1789 to 1917, in which the forces for forming modern liberal and social democracy slowly unfolded; the "short century" from 1917 to 1991, which was characterised by antagonism between liberal democracies and their communist and National Socialist/fascist antipodes; and the new century that began in 1991. During this latter century, it is clear that new, serious challenges such as the Islamist-theocratic one have emerged for the democracies. Over the coming decades, they are certain to be joined by others. Violent, belligerent politics will not disappear from the scene, and will time and again raise questions about the possibilities for peaceful politics. It remains an objective of peace and conflict research to explore possible answers to these questions.

Of all forms of rule, democracy is the one that requires independently judging and responsible political citizens. The citizen who regards him or herself as being apolitical is unavoidably political in the sense that they support the current political rulers by declining to give their vote for a better alternative. For democracy, it is more true than for all other forms of rule that the population of every country has the government that it deserves; if a population wishes to see improvements in government, it must first improve itself. What is meant by this is that it must improve its power of political judgement and its political activity. In a democracy, every citizen of age represents one vote in elections and referenda that is non-transferable.

As someone who has had the privilege of being able to study politics and its socio-historical background and origins for almost all my life, I hope that I now have a certain ability to critically examine current events and to procure background information that enables others to train their power of political judgement, regardless of their nationality or fundamental political convictions. For this reason, I also permit myself to address topics about which I have not conducted my own thorough research. With a brief analysis with a contemporary historical reference point, my aim is to enable the audience and readers of my lectures to further develop their own political judgement grounded in their previous knowledge, their value premises and interests and inevitably also their unrecognised and unconscious prejudices, by clarifying the requisites, contexts and possible consequences of this or that political decision. The lectures would fail in their spirit and purpose if they were to be judged according to the conclusions at which I arrive more or less clearly and decisively with regard to the debated issue in question at the end of the lecture. To a far greater extent, what matters is whether the listeners and readers can profit from my observations in that they are able to recognise new dimensions, requisites and possible consequences of the subject under dispute, and of the dispute itself, of which they had not previously been aware. Some of the reactions I have received from listeners and readers have confirmed that this has succeeded in some cases, and this gives me encouragement to continue with the experiment.

A scientist should not misuse their lectern for political sermons and confessions of faith, but should illuminate a conflict from all possible and useful political sides, analyse it carefully in terms of its elements and the reasons why it emerged and then represent and explain it in terms of its social and historical development. Consequently, five-sixths of the lecture consists of scientific analysis: a closer definition of the subject of dispute, the citing of the most important positions held in the public sphere in relation to it, an explanation of the historical background to the dispute and a presentation of the likely consequences that the realisation of the one or other political position might have.

During my time teaching at university, students would occasionally ask me about my personal political views on issues and current affairs and were not satisfied with only hearing a scientific analysis. I was open about my political opinion as a citizen on the matter in question, not only in personal conversations but also in the lecture hall or seminar room. During the lectures on political issues under debate, I now express my own ideas from the start. In a separate fifth section, I give a brief outline of how in my view the issue in question might be dealt with in a peaceful political way, which I would recommend to politicians or political activists if they were to seek my advice or read my lecture scripts, as has occasionally been the case.

In order to make the considerable amount of work required to cover each topic more worthwhile, I produce a text of strictly limited length which I then make available on the Internet. However, I always give the lecture freely, since a lecture should not be simply read out from a written document. As a result, there is a clear difference between the manuscript that I have created and the more precise and detailed oral presentation of the issues under debate. Quite frequently, current events from the same week or month, and sometimes even from the same morning, have an impact on the topic of the lecture. I therefore sometimes make direct associations in the lecture with current developments, which are not included in the written version.

For my lectures, I am able to draw on a rich source of material and experiences gathered from over forty years of research activity on issues relating to east–west relations and sociopolitical developments in the former communist-ruled countries of Europe, as well as on national movements, nationalism and the formation of nation states. However, I also permit myself to approach topics about which I have not formerly conducted any research of my own, for which I draw solely on secondary literature and current newspaper reports and documents. In order to check my findings and opinions on the different positions in the dispute, I send the manuscript of each lecture to specialist colleagues with specific expertise in the relevant country and subject of the lecture and ask for their critical feedback. I wish to offer my heartfelt thanks to all these friends and colleagues, all of whom I cannot name here, for their ideas and objections. I would also like to thank the listeners who gave me some valuable suggestions and who with their useful questions and intelligent criticism contributed to the final text. The gratifying level of interest during the course of the past ten years and the informed questions and critical comments offered by my listeners and readers encourages me to continue the experiment of the 50 lectures that I have given to date on the ongoing subject of "Controversial Political Issues from the Perspective of Contemporary History" in the future.

My particular thanks go to Anna Güttel-Bellert for her meticulous translation and excellent cooperation in the sometimes difficult process of rendering specialist political terminology, which is loaded with bias, from German into English. Once again, my heartfelt thanks go to the publishing company and its staff, in particular Mr. Johannes Glaeser. They have shown great understanding for a project by a political scientist and peace and conflict researcher who wishes to tackle controversial current political issues with expert socio-historical arguments.

As with the first volumes, I would again like to invite readers to voice their critical objections, comments and questions. I can be contacted directly at the following email address: streitfragen@uni-mannheim.de or e.jahn@soz.uni-frankfurt.de

Mannheim and Frankfurt/Main   Egbert Jahn
July 2019

Contents

1 Guilt in Wars of Aggression and Mass Murders: Who Is the Perpetrator, Who Is Responsible? 1
    1.1   On the Difference Between Legal and Political-Moral Guilt 2
    1.2   Responsibility for Political Acts of Violence as Merit or as Guilt 6
    1.3   The Slow Historical Process of the Delegitimisation of Foreign Rule, War and Political Mass Murder 8
    1.4   The Tentative Admission of Guilt in Wars and Acts of Mass Murder 12
    1.5   Future-Oriented Awareness of One's Own Potential Guilty Behaviour, Instead of the Predominant Demand for Punishment and Compensation for the Guilt of Others 16
    1.6   Yet in Most Cases, It Is the Others Who Are Still Regarded as Being Guilty 17
    References 18

2 On the Impossibility of Remaining Innocent When an Aeroplane Is Hijacked by Terrorists 21
    2.1   The Killing of Innocents as the Lesser Evil in the Face of Potential Mass Murder 22
    2.2   The Prohibition Issued by the Federal Constitutional Court on Killing Innocent People in Order to Prevent Mass Murder as the Focus of Criticism 24
    2.3   On the Difference Between the Play and the Real-Life Events of 11 September 2001 27
    2.4   "Support for Terror" Versus "Emergency Beyond the Law" ... 31
    2.5   On the Difference Between Legal and Moral Guilt 34
    2.6   The Potential Impact of the TV Film 37
    References 38

3	**Islands in the South China Sea as a Centre of Conflict for a Potential Third World War**	**41**
	3.1 The Spectrum of the Centres of Conflict	42
	3.2 Disputed Political Positions and the Situation in International Law	45
	3.3 The Convoluted History of Political Facts and Claims	49
	3.4 Scenarios for an Escalation of the Conflict into a Third World War	52
	3.5 Options for a Policy of Détente	53
	3.6 The Prospect of Repeated Conflict Escalations	56
	References	57
4	**World Peace—Even Through War: The Role of the USA in Preserving Security in the International System**	**61**
	4.1 The Ambiguous Nature of Peace and War as Concepts	62
	4.2 Ambivalences in US American Global Policy	65
	4.3 Security Structures in the International Systems Since the Eighteenth Century	67
	4.4 The Rise and Fall of the USA as a Global Power	72
	4.5 Opportunities for the Growing Importance of Peaceful Means for Preserving and Changing World Peace	74
	4.6 Cycles of the Willingness to Wage War in the USA	76
	References	77
5	**The Fatal Glorification of Mohandas K. Gandhi as a Saint: His Role in the National Independence Movement in India**	**79**
	5.1 The International Mystification of Mohandas K. Gandhi the Politician	80
	5.2 The Theory of the Singularity of the Success of Non-violent Policy in the Indian National Movement	82
	5.3 The Discussion Surrounding the Methods of Combat of the Indian Movement to Reform British Colonial Rule in South Africa	83
	5.4 Gandhi's Role in the Indian National Independence Movement	88
	5.5 Turning Points at Which the Non-violent Movement for an Independent India Failed	92
	5.6 The Favourable Historical Constellation for Gandhi's Partial Political Successes	94
	References	95

6	Is the Policy of Non-violence of Mohandas K. Gandhi a Unique Phenomenon, or Is It of Universal Significance?	97
	6.1 The Global Inspiration of Non-violent Political Movements Arising from the Intellectual Stimuli and the Successes of Mohandas K. Gandhi	98
	6.2 Gandhi's Concept of Religion and Politics and Fundamental Objections to It	99
	6.3 Gandhi's Strong Impact on Civil Rights and Freedom Movements and His Low Degree of Influence on International Politics	103
	6.4 Contentious Basic Assumptions with Regard to Gandhi's Political Understanding	105
	6.5 The Limited but Not Fully Exploited Scope for Action of Non-violent Policies, Now and in the Near Future	109
	6.6 Unavoidable Setbacks of Non-violent Policies	112
	References	113
7	Putin "Understanders" and Putin Critics: The Intense Controversy Surrounding German and Western Policy Towards Russia	117
	7.1 The Escalation of Socio-political and International Controversies Regarding Western Policy Towards Russia	118
	7.2 The Rapprochement of the Established Parties in Their Criticism of Putin and the Creation of a Left-Right Alliance of "Putin Understanders"	120
	7.3 Stages of Intensification and Moderation in Western Policy Towards Russia	123
	7.4 The Risks of a Confrontational and the Dangers of a Submissive Policy Towards Russia	126
	7.5 Different Functions of Government Policy and a Critically Thinking, Liberal and Democratic Public	128
	7.6 Contradictory Tendencies Towards Conflict Escalation and Limited Cooperation Between the West and Russia	131
	References	132
8	The Impact of the October Revolution on International and Inter-Ethnonational Relations	135
	8.1 Controversial Interpretations of the October Revolution	136
	8.2 Social vs. International Causes of the October Revolution	138
	8.3 The Prospect of the International Soviet Republic	139
	8.4 From Soviet Inner-State to Inter-State Internationalism	142
	8.5 Inter-Ethnonational Federalism as an Alternative to Internationalism, Which Was Perverted to Become Russian Great Power Nationalism	149
	8.6 On the Unlikelihood of a Communist Renaissance and on the Possibility of a Socialist One	150
	References	151

9	**International Involvement in the Civil War in Syria**............	155
	9.1 The Internationalisation of the Syrian Civil War...........	156
	9.2 The Shift in the Debate from Toppling Assad to Forging Peace with Him.....................................	159
	9.3 The Weak Nation Statehood of Syria....................	161
	9.4 The Unlikelihood of Peace Through Victory in Syria........	167
	9.5 Creating a National Balance Through Ethnic-Confessional Federalisation......................................	169
	9.6 Limited Prospects for a Russian-Western and Sunni-Shiite Peace for the Purpose of Presenting a Common Front Against Islamic State.................................	171
	References...	172
10	**We Will (Not) Succeed! The Helplessness of German and European Refugee Policy**................................	175
	10.1 The Increase in the Number of Refugees Arriving in Europe...	176
	10.2 Unlimited or Limited Acceptance of Refugees.............	179
	10.2.1 Various Welcome Positions.....................	180
	10.2.2 Numerous Positions Designed to Limit the Number of Refugees Accepted.........................	181
	10.3 The Globalisation of Refugee Movements..................	184
	10.4 The Current Mass Movement of Refugees................	186
	10.5 The Legal Status of Refugees...........................	188
	10.6 Refugees in Germany and Other European Countries.........	191
	10.7 The Increase in Right-Wing Nationalism Following the Large-Scale Acceptance of Refugees from Other Cultures..	192
	10.8 Fundamental Traits of a Global-Humane Refugee Policy.....	194
	10.9 A Recommendation to the German Government............	199
	10.10 The Establishment of European Refugee Settlements: "Refuges" (Refugium)................................	200
	10.11 The Simultaneous Nature of National and European Refusal to Accept Refugees..................................	204
	References...	204
11	**Brexit: A Preliminary Step Towards the Exit, or the Harbinger of Deeper Integration Within the European Union?**.............	207
	11.1 The Uncertain Consequences of Brexit....................	208
	11.2 Brexit as a Driver for Hopes for an End to—or Reform of—the EU..	210
	11.3 Britain's Half-Hearted Membership of the EU..............	212
	11.4 Possible Economic and Political Consequences of Brexit.....	215
	11.5 The Need to Adapt European Integration to the Changeable Willingness to Integrate Among EU Citizens..............	219

	11.6	The Fatal Strengthening of German Influence in the EU as a Result of Brexit.................................. 222
	References... 223
12	**The Catalan Independence Movement: A Challenge That Spain and the EU Have Chosen to Suppress**........................ 225
	12.1	The Speechless Political Stalemate Between the Central Spanish Government and the Catalan Independence Movement... 226
	12.2	The Dispute Surrounding the Legal and Political Concept of the Nation as the Intellectual Core of the Differences Between Spanish and Catalan Nationalism................ 229
	12.3	Stricter Legalism and Status Quo, More Autonomy, Federalisation in Spain or an Independent Catalonia......... 232
	12.4	Historical Reference Points for Catalan Independence....... 236
	12.5	Concepts of a Federalisation of Spain and of a European Unification and Separation Law....................... 238
	12.6	Spanish and European Indecision in the Fatal Process of "Muddling Through"............................... 241
	References... 242
13	**Switzerland: A Model for the Regulation of Relations Between Ethnic and National Groups in Multilingual States?**............ 245
	13.1	Switzerland: Model for Multilingual and Polyethnic States or Special Case?..................................... 246
	13.2	"Swissification" as a Model or as a Risk for Ethnonational Policies.. 248
	13.3	The Laborious Development of the Multi-lingual Nation State and Multi-cantonal Federal State.................. 250
	13.4	The Non-nationalisation of the Language Groups as the Key to Language Tolerance..................... 255
	13.5	Astute Language Policy as a Condition for Language Peace... 262
	13.6	Concordance Democracy as a Means to the Social Integration of a Linguistically Heterogeneous Society................ 268
	13.7	Using the Multi-lingual and Multi-cantonal Swiss Structures Not as a Model to Be Emulated, But as an Impulse for Independent Nationalities Policies.................... 271
	13.8	The Persistence of the Linguistic-Ethnic Assimilatory Nation State Versus Proposals for Decentralisation and Federalisation.................................. 273
	References... 274

Table of Contents for Volumes 1, 2 and 3........................ 277

Guilt in Wars of Aggression and Mass Murders: Who Is the Perpetrator, Who Is Responsible?

Abstract

The word "guilt" has not been used by sociologists and historians since 1945, and is almost never mentioned in publications, even though in the everyday social context, people, ways of behaviour and circumstances are accused of being guilty of undesirable acts and events that are considered to be damaging. Blaming others is, however, far more common that acknowledging one's own guilt. For many years, the major works by historians on the origins of the First World War have avoided any reflection about war guilt, preferring to talk about responsibility for the war. The two most important German-language, systematic, academic studies on the concept of guilt appeared in Switzerland in the field of political philosophy. In this text, the focus is above all on political-moral guilt in wars of aggression and mass murder, the increasing awareness of which interacts with the development of standards in criminal and international law that prohibits acts of aggression, genocide and severe violations of human rights.

For wars of aggression, only the narrowest band of political, military and economic state leadership needs to be brought to account, whereas when it comes to mass murders, the people who carry them out should be brought before a court, alongside those who order them. There continues to be a vast discrepancy between the codification of the norms and their application in court, since generally, governments and their henchmen can only be punished after they have been toppled politically and have suffered a military defeat. Political-moral guilt in both major crimes is not justiciable, differs extremely widely among individuals, and is graded according to the degree of knowledge, the potential level of knowledge and social position. It arises from both actions taken and the failure to act. Since the Second World War, a certain socio-political learning process, albeit a limited one, has been taking place with regard to the condemnation of wars of aggression and mass murder, although even now, there are still more monuments dedicated to peace-breakers and mass murderers than

---

Lecture given on 13.5.2019.

© Springer Nature Switzerland AG 2020
E. Jahn, *War and Compromise Between Nations and States*,
https://doi.org/10.1007/978-3-030-34131-2_1

there have been sentences pronounced against them in court and characterisations as criminals in the politics of commemoration.

The purpose of a public debate about political-moral guilt is not to blame another due to their behaviour that enables past major crimes, but to raise awareness of the ways in which future wars of aggression and mass murder can be facilitated by one's own erroneous political behaviour, since in the age of the sovereignty of the people, non-political behaviour is no longer possible. Only a stronger sense of responsibility in civil society, in the state and among the world's citizens, can prevent future major crimes.

1.1 On the Difference Between Legal and Political-Moral Guilt

In the words of Gesine Schwan, referring in 1997 to the general tendency to refrain from mentioning guilt, "It seems absurd to make guilt the subject of discussion in the political sciences, let alone analysis".[1] In 1987, Ralph Giordano said that in Germany, guilt was an "emotive word that is frowned upon".[2] In the two decades that followed, nothing changed in this respect, although it is certainly common in public political debate to speak of guilt, albeit usually the guilt of others rather than one's own. According to Schwan, the question of guilt in politics plays an important role "particularly for the establishment and maintenance of democracy after the collapse of dictatorships".[3] However, even in established and consolidated democracies, guilt is frequently spoken of in relation to all kinds of disasters, such as climate change, global social suffering and poverty or environmental destruction. Here, the focus will be solely on guilt in wars of aggression and mass murder, even if several conclusions can be made from this for other social and political questions of guilt. Between 1900 and 1987, 34 million people were killed in armed battles in wars, while 169 million were killed in acts of mass murder, many of which took place in times of peace.[4]

---

[1] Schwan (1997, p. 10).
[2] Giordano (1998, p. 18).
[3] Giordano (1998, p. 13).
[4] Rummel (1994, p. 6). Rummel provides no figures for the number of unarmed people (civilians and prisoners of war) who have been killed or exposed to the risk of death during inter-state and civil wars.

1.1 On the Difference Between Legal and Political-Moral Guilt

The question here is: who bears guilt[5] for a war of aggression or a political mass murder (democide, i.e. the killing of a population), genocide (the killing of a particular people), sociocide (murder of a social group, class murder) or politicide (murder of actual or alleged political opponents)?[6] The highest-ranking holders of political power and commanders? The entire group of leaders? The ruling or oppositional social elite, the political party that starts a civil war and that makes mass murder possible? The entire people, the majority of which elected or tolerated as their representatives those who conduct a war of aggression or order an act of mass murder? Those who provoke a war of aggression by another state[7] or an opposing political party? Or also those who are decidedly against wars of aggression and mass murder but who do not do everything in their power to prevent or terminate them?

Below, mass murder is classified only as the politically motivated mass murder of between dozens and countless millions of people, not the mass murder perpetrated by common criminals against their own. Additionally, it should not be forgotten that mass murder and war mean not only the killing of people, but also torture, physical and psychological injury, robbery, the withdrawal of food supplies, humiliation in many different forms, and the destruction of social and political orders, particularly also democracies.

In order to find answers to these questions, a differentiation must be made between four dimensions of this issue. First, there is the predominant principle according to international law in different countries and regions, second the court practice in individual countries and in international courts, and the regard in most cases of the legal norms, third the critical literature on both forms of violence in the fields of sociology and history, and fourth, public opinion with its different nuances in the politics of remembrance and commemoration, the media and private views.

While attempts were already made in antiquity to limit the right to wage war to cases of justified war, in the modern age, until the First World War, state sovereignty included the right to start wars when they appeared to serve the state ("national")

---

[5]"For legal experts, guilt means being culpable. A person is guilty when the accusation is correct that they have behaved in an illegal manner, although they were capable of behaving legally... The everyday use of the term "guilt" differs from the legalistic one in just one aspect: the accusation relates to both actions and failures to act that conflict with the norms of the valid law, and to behaviour that violates other norms, norms of religion, morals, tact, convention and the functioning of communication and interaction." "The moral issue is the issue which behaviour is correct and which is incorrect, and the issue of guilt is the issue of the existence and non-existence of responsibility" Schlink (2007, pp. 11–12 and 128).

[6]For an introduction to the concept, see Jahn (2005, p. 199). See also Jahn (1990). For initial thoughts on this subject, see Jahn (1987).

[7]The principle according to international law with regard to wars of aggression deals only with inter-state wars, the number of which has declined dramatically since 1945, while the involvement by other states in civil wars—be it on the side of the government or the opposition—has increased, see Petterson and Wallensteen (2015). Strangely enough, there is no discussion in the specialist literature as to whether support for an opposing civil war party should be classified as aggression by another state.

interest, however that might be defined. It was only after 1918 that the prohibition on wars of aggression came into being through a series of small steps, along with the right to prosecute as criminals those responsible for an act of aggression.[8] To date, there is still not even a name for persons who are deemed guilty of a "crime against peace" or a war of aggression. War criminals are merely those people who commit crimes in a war, not those who start a war. Aggressors are generally regarded as being states, not individuals. Since July 2018, the International Criminal Tribunal can in principle pass judgement, according to a complex procedure involving the UN Security Council, on the "crime of aggression" due to an "act of aggression".[9] Wars of aggression can only be conducted by states, not individuals. For them, while states or state peoples can be made responsible, only the small group of individuals in the state leadership[10] can be found guilty of and sentenced for the crime of aggression by a national or international court. In the legal sense, there is only one guilt on the part of the individual, never for a group. Thus, an entire people cannot bear guilt for a war of aggression.

All the many soldiers and other individuals who implement order to start a war of aggression are not guilty in the legal sense, unless they conduct war crimes, in other words, violate the international law of war. States that are defeated in war, regardless of whether they have conducted a war of aggression or a war of defence, can under certain circumstances lose territory, be obliged to pay reparations and limit their armament, but not as a penalty in the legal sense and following a court judgement against a people, but as a result of peace accords between states. With civil wars, no differentiation is made between wars of aggression and wars of defence; instead, the victorious warring party is adjudged and sentenced according to other legal norms.

The term "act of aggression" is consciously broader in scope than that of "war of aggression" (which will continue to be used below according to the standard linguistic use), although its meaning is narrower than that of a skirmish or border incident. It includes armed attacks that are not met with a military response.[11] Additionally, it does not cover wars of intervention that only lead to a political change or the toppling of a regime, in that "act of aggression" means "the use of armed force by a State against the sovereignty, territorial integrity or political

---

[8] Schabas (2005).

[9] However, this would only be possible in the 37 states (including Germany) that signed this part of the Statute.

[10] A person is considered to be a member of a state leadership when they are "in a position effectively to exercise control over or to direct the political or military action of a State", International Criminal Court (2011) Article 8bis Paragraph 1.

[11] In this spirit, the older international law also regarded a war of aggression as being the occupation and annexation of other states without more severe armed fighting (such as that of Luxembourg and Denmark by the German Reich in 1940), see Werle and Jeßberger (2016, pp. 681–719).

independence of another State, or in any other manner inconsistent with the Charter of the United Nations."[12]

Parallel to the illegalisation of wars of aggression, and in a far more reticent manner, steps towards prohibiting genocide were taken, as well as towards legal punishment of perpetrators of genocide,[13] i.e. of murders of other ethnic, national, racial or religious groups. The mass murder of members of one's own people (politicide, sociocide) is still not penalised explicitly in international and state law, but there is a prohibition on it as a "crime against humanity"[14] from the universal human rights.

In contrast to wars of aggression, for mass murders, not only the leaders who issue the order for the mass murder are regarded as being responsible before the law, but also those individuals who carry out the killing. In individual cases, people also appeared in court who merely guarded the German concentration camps, without actually killing anyone themselves.[15] Others who are accessories to mass murder, such as in the National Socialist German Reich, such as the drivers of the trains transporting Jews and others to the death camps, or those who organised these transports, were not prosecuted.

Since the end of the First World War, many small steps have been taken in international law until it has now been quite clearly determined that wars of aggression and mass murder[16] are illegal and that it has also been very clear for several years what these two crimes are understood to mean, despite all the contentious questions surrounding the detail, which will not be discussed here. Here, the law has reacted to the changing legal awareness among large parts of the global population following the millions of atrocities committed during both world wars and the genocide and mass murder during the National Socialist period, as the development of legal norms has made a small contribution towards changing awareness of the law within society.

In most cases, what can actually be classified during the course of real-life political events as being a war of aggression or mass murder remains highly contentious in most cases in the minds of the public, regardless of court judgements inside and between the nations. Accordingly, there is only an awareness of a political-moral guilt among more or less large swathes of the population in states

---

[12] International Criminal Court (2011) Article 8^{bis,} Paragraph 2. On the previous debate surrounding the concept of aggression, see several contributions in: Politi and Nesi (2005, pp. 55–117), Werle and Jeßberger (2016, pp. 681–719), Hummrich (2001). On incorporation into the German Code of Crimes against International Law see Hoven (2014).

[13] United Nations (1948).

[14] According to more recent law, they are directed against any identifiable group for political, racial, national, ethnic, cultural, religious, gender-specific or other reasons, International Criminal Court (2011) Article 7, Paragraph 1 (h).

[15] Cramer (2011).

[16] The literature on human rights directly or indirectly discusses mass murder in all its three dimensions, but otherwise, there is almost no juristic literature on sociocide and politicide, although this does not apply to genocide see e.g. Schabas (2009), Volkmann (2009), and von Lingen (2018).

that have waged a war of aggression or in which mass murder has been conducted, while the victims of both crimes tend to assign broad or even collective political-moral guilt to the people of the state that is responsible for the crimes. However, what is the purpose in general of talking of political-moral guilt of individuals, groups or peoples when there is not even any punishment designed to penalise this guilt? Should it lead to financial compensation (reparations), loss of assets and territory, restrictions on armament, limitations on state sovereignty, or public gestures of humiliation? Or is the aim solely a recognition and confession of guilt?

1.2 Responsibility for Political Acts of Violence as Merit or as Guilt

Wars of aggression are frequently interpreted as wars of defence or defensive prevention of a war of aggression.[17] Mass murders are usually either entirely denied by the political party that commits them—as covertly as possible—or defined as individual, unfortunate attacks, or as understandable retribution for a previous injustice.[18] They and wars of aggression are frequently only tried before a court after a military defeat and a regime change. For this reason, a crime of aggression, a war crime or a crime against humanity is only relatively rarely also brought before national or international courts; those who are mainly responsible are either given the death penalty or a long prison sentence. Over the last century, the number of persons found guilty of wars of aggression worldwide has been no more than a few dozen, while those found guilty of mass murder have numbered several thousands. Following successful wars of aggression, state leaders do not have to fear judgement from national or international courts.

For large parts of global public awareness and among large numbers of sociologists and historians, there is a far higher number of criminals, originators of wars of aggression and mass murders than those who have been designated as such, either officially or by the majority of the population from which the perpetrators originate. More monuments have been erected worldwide for leading mass murderers and wagers of wars of aggression than judgements have been made against them or those who have carried out the mass murders. Many of the prominent mass murderers and perpetrators of aggression were regarded as heroes during their

---

[17]A preventive war, which is now regarded as being illegal in international law, is understood as being the beginning of a war months or years before the anticipated attack by an enemy. By contrast, a pre-emptive war, which is started directly (a few hours) before the imminent attack of an enemy, is justified in international law as being a legitimate form of defence, Kimminich (1997, p. 275).

[18]On the German (and Austrian) response to the National Socialist mass murders, which has fluctuated since 1933, see Giordano (1998). The author introduced the term "second guilt" (p. 10), i.e. the widespread guilt of denying and suppressing the Jewish and non-Jewish Holocaust after 1945 (pp. 133, 194, 210). Kittel (1993, pp. 11, 385) accuses Giordano's school of thought as being "judgement that has almost no empirical foundation" by the "suppression theoreticians".

lifetimes and are still often honoured as such today. Only in a few cases is there a predominant view worldwide that certain people bear the guilt for one or more wars of aggression or mass murders. They include Adolf Hitler and his closest collaborators in the leadership of the German Reich and the National Socialist Party, as well as hundreds of thousands who were directly or indirectly involved in the mass murders.[19]

As mentioned above, global outrage over the two major crimes perpetrated by Germany was an important impetus for the development of norms in criminal and international law for the conviction of wars of aggression and mass murders, and facilitated an awareness of guilt in Germany over the course of decades, even though this entailed a long learning process. This in turn promoted an awareness of guilt for colonial and imperial crimes in many western European countries and in America, as well as an awareness within society for war crimes and wars that are in contravention of international law, as the huge international protest movements against the Vietnam war and the Iraq war of 2003 showed. Overall, there is still a huge gap between the development of state and international legal norms relating to the prohibition of wars of aggression and mass murder on the one hand and legal punishment and disapproval of such crimes in society on the other.

In his famous document "Die Schuldfrage" ("The Question of German Guilt"),[20] published in 1946, Karl Jaspers specified three other forms of guilt, aside from the legal, criminal guilt that follows from the violation of laws: political, moral and metaphysical guilt. He understood the latter as being guilt before God: "There exists a solidarity men as human beings that makes each co-responsible for every wrong and every injustice in the world, especially for crimes committed in his presence or with his knowledge. If I fail to do whatever I can to prevent them, I too am guilty."[21] This is reminiscent of the Christian concept of sin, according to which no person can be innocent by their nature or being, which is why every Christian asks God to forgive them their sins when they recite the Lord's Prayer. This idea of guilt is of no help in the debate surrounding specific guilt in wars of aggression and mass murders.

Jaspers regards political guilt as being the co-responsibility borne by every citizen for the way in which they are ruled, in other words, also for illegal actions by the state leadership. Jurisdiction when determining guilt rests with "the power and the will of the victor, in both domestic and foreign politics. Success decides."[22] From political guilt follows the liability for actions taken by the statesmen, which can lead, for example, to loss of territory, reparations and armament restrictions. Jaspers wished to use this argumentation to reinforce the willingness among Germans to

---

[19] According to estimates, several hundred thousand Germans and Austrians, and a few hundred thousand citizens of occupied and allied states were involved in the murder of the European Jews, Pohl (2003, p. 29).

[20] Jaspers (1946).

[21] Jaspers (1946, p. 11; in English: 2009, p. 26). Buber calls this the "Urschuld des Menschengeschlechts", Buber (2008, p. 127).

[22] Jaspers (1946, p. 10).

accept the decisions made by the Allies regarding the occupation of Germany as being a consequence of the German war of aggression and destruction. Jaspers does not discuss the fact that a people must also be liable for the loss of a war of defence or capitulation without a fight. He also does not develop standards for judging political guilt and its conditions for liability as being lawful or arbitrarily repressive. His term "political guilt" is also inappropriate for the many cases of a victorious war of aggression.

According to Jaspers, moral guilt arises from the actions of the individual, including their political and military actions. "It is never simply true that 'orders are orders'." There can only be mitigating circumstances "depending on the degree of danger, blackmail and terrorism". Jurisdiction for this type of guilt rests with "my conscience, and in communication with my friends and intimates who are lovingly concerned about my soul."[23] For Jaspers, moral guilt can be linked to political guilt. "Every human being is fated to be enmeshed in the power relations he lives by. This is the inevitable guilt of all, the guilt of human existence. It is counteracted by supporting the power that achieves what is right, the rights of man. Failure to collaborate in organizing power relations, in the struggle for power for the sake of serving the right, creates basic political and moral guilt at the same time."[24] What Jaspers means is the guilt of the responsible citizen who is of age, and who bears responsibility for "organizing power relations" and for exerting power in the service of what is right, namely in their own state, and not all over the world.

Below, the discussion will focus on political-moral guilt in relation to the two major crimes; in other words, guilt that cannot be punished by courts. This guilt also exists when the war of aggression is successful and the regime that perpetrates the mass murder remains in power. It remains in the widespread social memory, particularly of the victims of the two major crimes. Jurisdiction for political-moral guilt by no means rests only with one's own conscience and in communication with friends and one's closest loved ones, but in a public debate about the guilty effectuation of the morally wrong behaviour. Conscience has a connection with knowledge (*sciens*), and is therefore modifiable during the course of the societal learning process.

1.3 The Slow Historical Process of the Delegitimisation of Foreign Rule, War and Political Mass Murder

The historical prerequisites for legal and socio-political condemnation of wars of aggression and mass murder include several contradictory developments and factors. One central factor is the creation of the modern nation state, particularly in the form of the democratic constitutional state and the state governed by the rule of law, although sometimes also in the form of an autocratic dictatorship, since the end of

---

[23] Jaspers (1946).

[24] Jaspers (1946, p. 13, see also p. 54; in English: p. 28).

the eighteenth century. During a decades-long process, it replaced the corporative state and the dynastic imperial state, which were no longer regarded as being legitimate. There were no generally recognised criteria and procedures regarding the affiliation of the individual people to a nation forged by the political will of its people and to a specific space, so that frequently, national wars and acts of genocide were conducted in order to produce and create boundaries for the nation states. At the same time, with the sovereignty of the people, the notion of a permanent order of world peace between the nationally constituted, equal nations, which became widespread in particular among the lower social strata, which suffered particularly severely from war and mass murder.[25] After the atrocities of the First World War, this notion was expressed through the formation of the League of Nations and in the further development of international law as the right to peace, whereby wars of aggression gradually became subject to legal condemnation,[26] and human rights were expanded and reinforced.

Important stages in this historical process are: the statute of the League of Nations of 1919, in which wars of aggression are declared a matter to be dealt with jointly by the community of states,[27] the prohibition on biological and chemical weapons of 1925,[28] the Briand-Kellogg Pact of 1928,[29] which was signed by a large number of states, in which wars of aggression were condemned (although it failed to provide for sanctions in cases of violation of the pact), the Charter of the United Nations of 1945, in which violence was declared illegal with the exception of individual and collective state defensive wars and war authorised by the UN Security Council to restore world peace and international security, and human rights were declared as being the express purpose of the association of states.[30] These were specifically set out in the Universal Declaration of Human Rights of 1948[31] and in the two human rights covenants of 1966.[32]

While frequently in history, peoples and their leaders have been punished for actual or alleged wars of aggression and mass murders after their military defeat, the jurisdiction of national and international courts is a very recent historical phenomenon when it comes to wars of aggression and genocide and other forms of mass murder. The first time that individuals were sentenced in court for genocide, the

---

[25] See also the lectures Jahn (2015b).

[26] Hummrich (2001, pp. 19–29).

[27] League of Nations (1919) "The Members of the League undertake to respect and preserve as against external aggression the territorial integrity and existing political independence of all Members of the League" (Article 10). "Any war or threat of war, whether immediately affecting any of the Members of the League or not, is hereby declared a matter of concern to the whole League, and the League shall take any action that may be deemed wise and effectual to safeguard the peace of nations" (Article 11).

[28] Geneva Protocol (1925).

[29] Lillian Goldman Law Library (2008).

[30] United Nations (1945, Articles 1, 2, 42, 51).

[31] United Nations General Assembly (1948).

[32] United Nations (1966).

"crime of crimes"[33] was following the murder of many hundreds of thousands of Armenians in the Ottoman Empire. The defendants were several members of the "Unity and Progress" party (İttihat ve Terakki) who held the main positions of responsibility, who were accused of "attacks against Armenians and other ethnic groups" in June 1919. 17 people were sentenced to death (some in absentia; those who were mainly responsible had fled to Germany), while three were executed.[34] Due to disagreements between Britain and France, no international tribunal was held.

The former German Kaiser, Wilhelm II, was also never brought to trial "for the most serious infringement of international moral law", for which provision was made in Art. 227 of the Treaty of Versailles,[35] since the Netherlands refused to extradite him. By contrast, Art. 231, which attributed responsibility for a war of aggression to Germany and the Central Powers, and which held their peoples accountable for its consequences, had significant practical repercussions, with loss of territory, the payment of reparations and armament restrictions.[36]

It was not until after the Second World War that an international military court of justice in Nuremberg sentenced 12 people to death for crimes including waging a war of aggression[37] and crimes against humanity, while 7 others were given prison terms.[38] In 12 subsequent trials before a US American military court, by April 1949, a further 24 people were sentenced to death and 108 were sent to prison. In Tokyo, death sentences were handed out in November 1948 to 7 individuals, while 18 were given prison sentences.[39] In several other countries, a few of those responsible for mass murders under the Nazi regime were sentenced to death and executed. However, it was not until 9 December 1948 that a UN Convention on the Prevention and Punishment of the Crime of Genocide was signed.[40]

A further step in international jurisdiction over mass murderers was only made after the end of the East-West conflict in Europe. In 1993, an International Criminal

---

[33] The expression was used by the International Court of Justice for Rwanda, Schabas (2009, p. 11). For the murder of a people ("Völkermord"), the Latinised form, "genocide", was not used until after 1948.

[34] Akçam (1996, pp. 353–364). See the lecture Jahn (2015a).

[35] Wikisource (2018).

[36] "The Allied and Associated Governments affirm and Germany accepts the responsibility of Germany and her allies for causing all the loss and damage to which the Allied and Associated Governments and their nationals have been subjected as a consequence of the war imposed upon them by the aggression of Germany and her allies" Wikisource (2018, Art. 231).

[37] The International Military Tribunal demanded e.g. responsibility for "Crimes against peace: namely, planning, preparation, initiation or waging of war of aggression, or a war in violation of international treaties, agreement or assurances, or participation in a common plan or conspiracy for thee accomplishment of any of the foregoing" (Article 6a), Charter of the International Military Tribunal (1945).

[38] Darnstädt (2015).

[39] Osten (2003) and Buruma (1994).

[40] United Nations (1948).

1.3 The Slow Historical Process of the Delegitimisation of Foreign Rule, War...

Court was used for trials relating to the former Yugoslavia,[41] and for Rwanda[42] in 1996. It was not until 1998 that the Rome Statute of the International Criminal Court was able to be passed in the Hague,[43] which came into force in 2002.[44] However, only 123 member states have ratified the Statute. These do not include the USA, Russia, China, India, Turkey and Israel. 27 other states have signed the Statute but not ratified it. Following an amendment to the Statute, which has been in force since July 2018, the crime of aggression was also included as a criminal offence,[45] albeit only for the 30 states that signed the amendment. The international juridification of the prohibition on wars of aggression and mass murders and the jurisdiction regarding these two crimes is making historical progress, but only extremely slowly. Not every war begun in violation of international law is classified as a war of aggression, but only those that are initiated for the purpose of annexing (parts of) a state or the subjugation of a state.

In 2002, Germany passed international criminal legislation[46] that names genocide (§ 6) and, in a modified version, also the crime of aggression (§ 13), as being criminal acts. In 1949, the Federal Republic of Germany had already added an Article 26 to its Basic Law; Paragraph 1 states that: "Acts tending to and undertaken with intent to disturb the peaceful relations between nations, especially to prepare for a war of aggression, shall be unconstitutional. They shall be criminalised."[47]

For a very long time, the concept of aggression (of a war of aggression) was contentious. In 1974, aggression was first defined by the United Nations General Assembly as "Aggression is the use of armed force by a State against the sovereignty, territorial integrity or political independence of another State, or in any other manner inconsistent with the Charter of the United Nations, as set out in this Definition".[48] In the modified Rome Statute of the International Criminal Court, the following is stated in Article 8bis: "For the purpose of this Statute, 'crime of aggression' means the planning, preparation, initiation or execution, by a person in a position effectively to exercise control over or to direct the political or military action of a State, of an act of aggression which, by its character, gravity and scale, constitutes a manifest violation of the Charter of the United Nations."[49]

The question that is the subject of intense debate worldwide, as to whether a war of intervention to protect human rights ("humanitarian intervention"), as expressly

---

[41] Bienk-Koolman (2009) and Roggemann (1998, pp. 60–126).
[42] Strizek (2015) and Fall (2017).
[43] Vesper-Gräske (2016), Kersten (2016), Steinberger-Fraunhofer (2008), Schabas (2011, pp. 146–155), and Heilmann (2006, pp. 149–162).
[44] International Criminal Court (2011). The Court passed its first sentence with a jail term lasting many years against a Congolese militia leader, in July 2012.
[45] International Criminal Court (2011) Article 8bis.
[46] Bundesgesetzblatt (2016).
[47] German Bundestag (2017), Article 26, Paragraph 1.
[48] United Nations General Assembly (1974).
[49] International Criminal Court (2011) Article 8bis.

legitimised since 2005 following the resolution passed by the UN General Assembly on the "responsibility to protect", should be regarded as illegal under international law when it has not been decided by the UN Security Council, was the topic of a previous lecture.[50]

1.4 The Tentative Admission of Guilt in Wars and Acts of Mass Murder

Recently, historians have been inclined to no longer speak of guilt, for example with regard to the start of the First World War, but of responsibility. They only write in more detail about the question of guilt in connection with the Second World War and the National Socialist mass murder of Jews and others.[51] And yet: "Since the publication of Karl Jaspers' 'The Question of German Guilt', no attempt has been made for nearly sixty years among German-speaking philosophers to bring systematic clarity to the problem of guilt for historical wrongdoings."[52] While guilt may be linked to the notion of a reprehensible act that is to be avoided or prevented—an act or a failure to act—the term "responsibility" means several different things. Responsibility for a person or an event means as much as bearing responsibility and having the power to make decisions. This responsibility may or may not be borne excellently and commendably by parents over their children, or politicians over their voters. It is only when it is not borne that they are guilty. It is an extenuation to speak of responsibility for a war of aggression or mass murder, instead of guilt.

What is the purpose of speaking of political-moral guilt beyond the scope of punishable behaviour? Individuals or entire groups and peoples can be accused of being guilty with the aim of generating a bad conscience and to oblige them to pay compensation, and in some cases also to accept loss of territory and restrictions on sovereignty and armament. However, a bad conscience for guilty, reprehensible behaviour (acts or the failure to act) does not require external pronouncements of guilt, but can also arise through one's own, self-critical reflection, and can result in a change in one's behaviour on one's own impetus, as well as remorse, grief, atonement,[53] conversion or repentance, in the Christian language. Thus, in Germany after 1945, an awareness gradually emerged of political-moral guilt, not only of involvement in the crimes of the war of aggression and mass murder, but above all for enabling the National Socialist party to take power and to hold onto power for so long. In many people's eyes, this learning process took far too long, and was

---

[50]Jahn (2015c).

[51]Gudrun Kämper regards Jaspers' "The Question of German Guilt" as being "the most important contribution to the very many contemporary analyses of guilt" in Germany, Kämper (2007, p. 302).

[52]Schefczyk (2012, p. 1).

[53]For a detailed discussion on the moral intergenerational obligation to recompense the victims of major crimes and their descendants, see Schefczyk (2012, pp. 263–368).

1.4 The Tentative Admission of Guilt in Wars and Acts of Mass Murder

inadequate,[54] while others regarded it as being impressive and sufficient, while others still saw it as being humiliating and over-excessive. For many contemporaries, it is a model for Japan, the post-Stalinist countries and the former colonial powers, where a broader awareness of guilt has not yet developed.

In the age of the nation state, political-moral guilt is primarily guilt that is limited along nation state lines, as the guilt of state citizens, since it is the state that conducts a war of aggression against another state. The major acts of mass murder are planned, implemented or tolerated by state leaders. While most citizens of a country do not want the crimes planned or committed in their name by their government, do not know about them or attempt to bury their head in the sand, they do bring the criminal governments to power, or tolerate their seizure of power. This is where they are guilty—not of the crime itself. Even the opponents and the surviving victims of mass murders sometimes rightly ask themselves whether they could have done more to prevent a takeover of power by the criminals.[55]

States do not exist in a vacuum, but are connected in many ways with other states; they are dependent on the international environment and are influenced by the behaviour of states and by social processes from this environment. While this does nothing to change the sovereignty and responsibility of citizens for the behaviour of their state, it does constitute complicity in enabling and tolerating the major crimes of other states and thus indirectly also of their citizens.[56] Thus, the UN member states have assumed responsibility for preventing and stopping aggressive force and the UN General Secretary has admitted that it was a failure of the United Nations not to have prevented or stopped the genocide in Rwanda.

Blanket assignment of guilt to entire peoples, social classes, elites, parties and even state leaderships are specious. Political-moral guilt is also the guilt of individuals, and differs considerably from one individual to another. Usually, the discussion focuses solely on the contrast between guilt and non-guilt or innocence. However, it is helpful to make a clear differentiation between one form of guilt and another, and also between one point in time at which guilt occurs and another.

Thus, it appears to make sense to create a hierarchy for the offence of political-moral guilt for wars of aggression and mass murder:

(a) punishable guilt according to state and international legal norms[57] for the perpetration of a major crime and active involvement in it, regardless of whether the case is taken to court or not (because the criminal dies prior to proceedings, commits suicide or is celebrated as a national hero long after their death);

---

[54] As an example of both positions, see Giordano (1998) and Kittel (1993).

[55] For example Neumann (1977, p. 669).

[56] However, the problem of excessive demands on citizens of the world arises, for example with regard to the atrocities in Bosnia-Herzegovina, Enzensberger (1993).

[57] According to Michael Schefczyk, in an unconvincing way, it is possible to also use natural justice norms as a yardstick for responsible action, depending on the first point in time that they were mentioned, Schefczyk (2012, p. 71).

(b) the guilt that is usually not punished of assisting the perpetration of the major crime, such as construction of concentration camps, building crematoria, arresting and transporting the people to be killed, tortured and humiliated, the production of weapons, barracks and uniforms for the war of aggression, and all activities without which the major crime cannot take place;
(c) the guilt of the express or tacit approval of the major crimes, in some circumstances also decades after they have been committed;
(d) the guilt of denying, despite better knowledge for which evidence has been provided;
(e) the not wishing to know, even though information about atrocities is available, for very different reasons such as fear of one's own compassion for the people who are suffering, of punishment for revealing public secrets, or a worsening of relationships with those who are involved in the major crimes;
(f) the not wishing to believe information about the planned, ongoing or past major crimes and qualifying such information as propaganda and lies;
(g) the failure to contradict in one's mind all one's own thoughts and all ideas received from others, which suppress and justify the wrongdoing;
(h) the failure to speak out against the preparations for the major crimes at a time at which this is still possible with very low risk to oneself;
(i) the failure to put up political opposition in the form of commitment to an oppositional organisation and a movement that has an impact on public awareness, particularly at a time in which these were still operating legally[58];
(j) enrichment by means of the property of the victims of the major crimes;
(k) some political awareness of guilt relates to the failure to emigrate, desert or defect to the side the warring party defending the law, or even armed resistance or participation in a coup attempt.

Ultimately, it is correct that it is a matter of individual conscience as to what constitutes one's own political-moral guilty behaviour in connection with a war of aggression or mass murder that presents a current threat or that has occurred in the past.[59] However, a general orientation for political-moral behaviour that can be reasonably expected or that is too challenging is certainly possible. The guilt of the large majority of adult Germans before 1945, and their political-moral failure, can therefore be located in the period before 1933 and in gradations until 1939, and not after the start of the war and the murder of millions of Jews, Sinti and Roma, Slavs and others, in which hundreds of thousands, but not countless millions, of

---

[58]Gesine Schwan emphasises the high degree of importance of joint action as encouragement for individuals and as a constraint on the excessive demands on individual responsibility, Schwan (1997, p. 222).

[59]Thus, the Federal President Richard von Weizsäcker said in his famous speech of 8 May 1985: "There is no such thing as the guilt or innocence of an entire nation. Guilt is, like innocence, not collective but personal. There is discovered or concealed personal guilt. There is guilt which people acknowledge or deny. Everyone who directly experienced that era should today quietly ask himself about his involvement then" Von Weizsäcker (1985).

1.4 The Tentative Admission of Guilt in Wars and Acts of Mass Murder

Germans were involved. After 1939, it was only the officer corps that had real, politically realisable options for putting up resistance and opportunities for avoiding guilt. In the same way, the main guilt of countless millions of communists and citizens in the Soviet Union, China, North Korea, Cambodia and elsewhere in the murder of 110 million people[60] can be pinpointed during the period prior to the establishment of the Communist Party regime that committed the mass murders.

The degree of guilt for politically-morally unjust, reprehensible behaviour depends on the willingness, within what can be reasonably expected, to expose oneself or others to risk, for which it is difficult to find a generally applicable yardstick. Accusations of guilt by others usually come cheaper than the willingness to acknowledge one's own guilt or lack of courage. An appropriate understanding of guilt should not arise from excessive demands made on people. Is there a potential risk to good relationships with one's closest relatives and friends, to one's standing in one's social environment, professional career opportunities or even one's job? Is there even a risk to one's health and life? The guilt of taking action is difficult to balance against the guilt of failing to do so.

Modern life, and not just in the military, is regulated by highly complex social organisation patterns, or chains of command and obeisance. The decisions of companies, clubs, parties and states are only influenced by the individuals who belong to them, if they are modifiable by them. The hierarchies in working society imply different levels of responsibility for behaviour, depending on the individual's position in society and thus their ability to impact events. Accordingly, the degree of guilt resulting from incorrect behaviour is staggered. A manager bears more responsibility than the people under them, although no citizen who is of age is without responsibility for their own behaviour. Thus, certainly, a general bears a larger degree of guilt for the mass murders committed by their troops than a private, and the director of a company that produces Cyclone B for the gas chambers bears more responsibility than the workers who make it. The judge who issues and signs illegal death sentences verging on murder bears a higher level of guilt than the secretary who types it out on the typewriter. A professor is more liable to be guilty than an illiterate unskilled labourer. However, the concept of the responsible citizen implies, however, that they do not allow themselves to be instrumentalised as a tool for the guilty behaviour of the management of their company, their club, their party or their state. Non-cooperation with illegal behaviour is a low-risk strategy in many cases. It has been proven that the refusal to carry out the order to commit murder in the Third Reich did not lead to any significant sanctions, but at most to a transfer.[61]

Responsible behaviour that avoids guilt initially requires knowledge, first about the norm of what behaviour is or is not legally permissible (such as the difference between wars of aggression and defence, or murder and the death penalty), second

---

[60]This figure was calculated from numerous estimates Rummel (1994, p. 3).

[61]Schefczyk (2012, p. 224). The author adds: "The fact that no-one was sanctioned because they decided not to participate in crimes does not necessarily mean, however, that those in question did not participate in the belief in the crimes; otherwise, they would have been punished most severely."

about the actual event, i.e. which state is the aggressor (knowledge that is sometimes difficult to obtain), third, in which manner one can oneself be involved in the criminal activity, either on one's own initiative or by others, and fourth, on the options regarding how to avoid guilty behaviour and the risks involved.

1.5 Future-Oriented Awareness of One's Own Potential Guilty Behaviour, Instead of the Predominant Demand for Punishment and Compensation for the Guilt of Others

What is the purpose of discussing political-moral guilt when this does not lead to criminal proceedings and a court judgement? Human society is not just based on the observance of laws and adherence to court judgements, but on the existence of political-moral norms that are usually abided by, although they are still too frequently violated. A social historical political-moral learning process oriented to a "general state of world citizenship" was not only adopted by philosophers such as Kant,[62] but also really has occurred.[63] Conscience and morality are not inborn, but are acquired and modified during the familiar and social learning process. To this extent, they can also be discussed in society, and are not just a matter for individual decisions to the extent that parts of society do not rigidify in a doctrinaire manner around "truths" from religious or secular teachings.

Conscience is connected to knowledge (*sciens*), and is therefore not the same for all people, regardless of the fact that it is another matter whether one follows one's own conscience or consciously or unconsciously fails to do so. The claiming of moral, religious or secular-based norms can assume the form of accusing others, sometimes in anticipation of compensation payments, gestures of remorse and reticence in asserting interests. However, it can also lead one to examine one's own conscience and to ask for forgiveness from the surviving victims. An acknowledgement of one's own guilt or the anticipation of a response from the injured parties can also be an attempt to liberate oneself from guilt. There is a major difference between awareness of guilt and public admission of guilt, since the latter usually results in demands for compensation. For this reason, many states and parts of their society fail to admit their guilt in wars of aggression and mass murder, even if they may be aware of it.

It does make sense in some respects to talk about guilt for past crimes, for example in order to punish guilty parties in the legal sense and to cause the highest possible compensation to be paid to the victims and their relatives, and to remember the victims with dignity. However, the far more important purpose is to avoid future crimes and to develop political-moral sensitivity for one's own potentially guilty behaviour. For this purpose, it is necessary to differentiate between guilt and guilt, in other words, between very different forms and degrees of guilt and points in time in

---

[62]Kant (1970, p. 47).
[63]Pinker (2011).

which guilt arises. This aspect is far to inadequately discussed, or not discussed at all, in the well-known documents on the question of guilt, such as the publications by Jaspers, Schefczyk, Schwan and Schlink mentioned above. The usual debate surrounding guilt pertains almost exclusively to the issue of guilt or innocence, but hardly ever to a gradation of different degrees of guilt. Here, the purpose cannot be to produce a ranking of guilt and possibilities for mitigating guilt, but to increase the level of awareness of situations in which guilt arises.

The debate surrounding guilt in the two major crimes usually pivots around the point in time that they directly began and their course of progress. This approach ignores the long prehistory in which the emergence of a political movement and government that is preparing for a war of aggression or mass murder can still be prevented with non-heroic, civilian, political-moral commitment. The purpose of a public discussion of guilt is not to encourage people to become heroes, and to offer up resistance at high risk, but forward-looking, responsible political behaviour that thwarts the risk of criminal policies. The first maxim is that in the age of sovereignty of the people, there is no longer any such thing as non-political behaviour.[64] In a democracy, not voting always amounts to supporting the governing party, and a refusal to vote for alternative politics. According to Joseph Marie de Maistre (1753–1821), every people has the government that it deserves, while Mohandas K. Gandhi (1869–1948) added that "Only when we improve can we attain Swaraj (literally: self-mastery, in the sense of self-determination)."[65]

1.6 Yet in Most Cases, It Is the Others Who Are Still Regarded as Being Guilty

There is no doubt that since 1945, a considerable learning process has taken place throughout the world with regard to condemnation of wars of aggression and mass murder, although since then, several hundred wars have been waged, and countless millions of people have been murdered, in Cambodia, Rwanda and elsewhere. However, today's networked global communications make them a globally known and admonished scandal, although autocrats continue to attempt to portray mass murders as being a domestic matter for their respective states. Occasionally, however, there are admissions of one's own guilt in at least failing to assist the victims of genocide, such as on the part of the United Nations in the case of the danger posed to hundreds of thousands of Tutsi in Rwanda in the spring of 1994, which was already foreseeable at an early stage. Yet it is still the case that citizens of a country tend not to be aware of and fail to discuss mass murders initiated by their own state, and to accuse other nations or civil war participants of being guilty of wars. Acknowledging one's own national guilt is frequently denounced still as being unpatriotic.

---

[64]"Failure to collaborate in organizing power relations, in the struggle for power for the sake of serving the right, creates basic political guilt and moral guilt at the same time" Jaspers (1946, p. 19).
[65]Gandhi, Young India, 10 Nov. 1920.

However, the major wars and incidents of mass murder cannot be erased from people's memories. When the Mongolian People's Republic took up diplomatic relations with the Hungarian People's Republic, its ambassador apologised for the atrocities committed by the Mongols in Hungary during the thirteenth century. While human learning processes often take quite a long time, persistent education about state and global political responsibility among citizens cannot avoid holding to account not only those who are guilty of wars of aggression and mass murders in the legal sense, but also creating awareness among the public as a whole for the non-justiciable political-moral guilt within society for past major crimes, in order to prevent such atrocities from occurring again in the future.

References

Akçam T (1996) Armenien und der Völkermord. Die Istanbuler Prozesse und die türkische Nationalbewegung. Hamburger Edition, Hamburg

Bienk-Koolman S (2009) Die Befugnis des Sicherheitsrates der Vereinten Nationen zur Einsetzung von ad hoc-Strafgerichtshöfen. Zur Rechtmäßigkeit der Einsetzung des Internationalen Strafgerichtshofes für das ehemalige Jugoslawien sowie zum nachfolgenden Wandel in Praxis und Rechtsauffassung. Lang, Frankfurt am Main

Buber M (2008) Schuld und Schuldgefühle (1957) (Guilt and guilt feelings). Werkausgabe 10:127–152

Bundesgesetzblatt (2016) Gesetz zur Einführung des Völkerstrafgesetzbuches vom 26. Juni 2002, bgbl102s2254_13757 und Gesetz zur Änderung des Völkerstrafgesetzbuches vom 22. Dezember 2016, bgbl116s3150_74792

Buruma I (1994) The wages of guilt: memories of war in Germany and Japan. Farar Straus Giroux, New York

Charter of the International Military Tribunal (1945). https://www.legal-tools.org/en/doc/64ffdd/

Cramer J (2011) Belsen Trial 1945. Der Lüneburger Prozeß gegen Wachpersonal der Konzentrationslager Auschwitz und Bergen-Belsen. Wallstein, Göttingen

Darnstädt T (2015) Nürnberg. Menschheitsverbrechen vor Gericht 1945. Piper, Munich

Deutscher Bundestag (2017) Grundgesetz. https://www.bundestag.de/grundgesetz

Enzensberger HM (1993) Ausblick auf den Bürgerkrieg. Über den täglichen Massenmord und die überforderte Moral. Der Spiegel, 21 June, p 175

Fall A (2017) Le traitement juridictionnel du crime de génocide et des crimes contre l'humanité commis au Rwanda. L'Harmattan, Paris

Geneva Protocol (1925) Protocol for the prohibition of the use in war of asphyxiating, poisonous or other gases, and of bacteriological methods of warfare. https://www.un.org/disarmament/wmd/bio/1925-geneva-protocol/

Giordano R (1998) Die zweite Schuld oder Von der Last Deutscher zu sein, New edition. Rasch and Röhring, Hamburg

Heilmann D (2006) Die Effektivität des Internationalen Strafgerichtshofs. Die Rolle der Vereinten Nationen und des Weltsicherheitsrates. Nomos, Baden-Baden

Hoven E (2014) Der Tatbestand der Aggression – Wege zur Implementierung der Ergebnisse von Kampala in das Völkerstrafgesetzbuch. In: Safferling C, Kirsch S (eds) Völkerstrafrechtspolitik. Praxis des Völkerstrafrechts. Springer, Heidelberg, pp 339–372

Hummrich M (2001) Der völkerrechtliche Straftatbestand der Aggression. Historische Entwicklung, Geltung und Definition im Hinblick auf das Statut des Internationalen Strafgerichtshofes. Nomos, Baden-Baden

International Criminal Court (2011) Rome Statute of the International Criminal Court. https://www.icc-cpi.int/resourcelibrary/official-journal/rome-statute.aspx

References

Jahn E (1987) Geschichte – Schuld – Frieden. Kolyma, Auschwitz, Hiroshima und der potentielle "nukleare Holocaust". Loccumer Protokolle 66/87:79–115

Jahn E (1990) Zur Phänomenologie der Massenvernichtung. Kolyma, Auschwitz, Hiroshima und der potentielle nukleare Holocaust. Leviathan 18(1):7–38

Jahn E (2005) On the phenomenology of mass extermination in Europe. A comparative perspective on the Holodomor. In: Sapper M, Weichsel V (eds) Sketches of Europe: old lands, new worlds. Berliner Wissenschaftsverlag, Berlin

Jahn E (2015a) Commemoration of genocide as a contemporary political weapon: the example of the ottoman genocide of the Armenians. In: International politics: political issues under debate, vol 1. Springer, Heidelberg, pp 219–235

Jahn E (2015b) The peace congress of the socialist international in Basel, November 24–25, 1912 and a century of wars and striving for peace since the peace congress of Basel in 1912. In: World political challenges: political issues under debate, vol 3. Springer, Heidelberg, pp 55–89

Jahn E (2015c) Kosovo and elsewhere. Military interventions in defence of human rights ('humanitarian interventions'). In: International politics: political issues under debate, vol 1. Springer, Heidelberg, pp 43–57

Jaspers K (1946) Die Schuldfrage (The question of German guilt). Artemis, Zürich

Kämper H (2007) 'Die Schuldfrage' von Karl Jaspers (1946). In: Hermanns F, Holly W (eds) Linguistische Hermeneutik. Theorie und Praxis des Verstehens. Niemeyer, Tübingen, pp 301–322

Kant I (1970) Idee zu einer allgemeinen Geschichte in weltbürgerlicher Absicht (1784). In: Werke, vol 9. Wissenschaftliche Buchgesellschaft, Darmstadt, pp 31–50

Kersten M (2016) Justice in conflict: the effects of the international criminal court's interventions on ending wars and building peace. Oxford University Press, Oxford

Kimminich O (1997) Einführung in das Völkerrecht, 6th edn. A. Francke, Tübingen

Kittel M (1993) Die Legende von der 'zweiten Schuld'. Vergangenheitsbewältigung in der Ära Adenauer. Ullstein, Berlin

League of Nations (1919) Covenant of the League of Nations, 28 April 1919. http://www.unhcr.org/refworld/docid/3dd8b9854.html

Lillian Goldman Law Library (2008) Kellogg-Briand Pact 1928. http://avalon.law.yale.edu/20th_century/kbpact.asp

Neumann F (1977) Behemoth. Struktur und Praxis des Nationalsozialismus 1933–1944. Europäische Verlagsanstalt, Frankfurt am Main

Osten P (2003) Der Tokioter Kriegsverbrecherprozeß und die japanische Rechtswissenschaft. Berliner Wissenschaftsverlag, Berlin

Petterson T, Wallensteen P (2015) Armed conflicts, 1946–2014. J Peace Res 52(4):536–550

Pinker S (2011) The better angels of our nature: why violence has declined. Viking, New York

Pohl D (2003) Verfolgung und Massenmord in der NS-Zeit 1933–1945. Wissenschaftliche Buchgemeinschaft, Darmstadt

Politi M, Nesi G (eds) (2005) The international criminal court and the crime of aggression. Ashgate, Aldershot

Roggemann H (1998) Die internnationalen Strafgerichtshöfe. Einführung, Rechtsgrundlagen, Dokumente, 2nd edn. Berlin-Verlag Arno Spitz, Berlin

Rummel RJ (1994) Power, genocide and mass murder. J Peace Res 31(1):1–10

Schabas WA (2005) Origins of the criminalization of aggression: how crimes against peace became the 'supreme international crime'. In: Politi M, Nesi G (eds) The international criminal court and the crime of aggression. Ashgate, Aldershot, pp 17–32

Schabas WA (2009) Genocide in international law: the crime of crimes, 2nd edn. Cambridge University Press, Cambridge

Schabas W (2011) An introduction to the international criminal court, 4th edn. Cambridge University Press, Cambridge

Schefczyk M (2012) Verantwortung für historisches Unrecht. Eine philosophische Untersuchung. De Gruyter, Berlin

Schlink B (2007) Vergangenheitsschuld. Beiträge zu einem deutschen Thema. Diogenes, Zürich

Schwan G (1997) Politik und Schuld. Die zerstörerische Macht des Schweigens. Fischer, Frankfurt am Main

Steinberger-Fraunhofer T (2008) Internationaler Strafgerichtshof und Drittstaaten. Eine Untersuchung unter besonderer Berücksichtigung der Position der USA. Duncker & Humblot, Berlin

Strizek H (2015) Der Internationale Strafgerichtshof für Ruanda in Arusha – Tansania. Eine politisch-historische Bilanz. Lang, Frankfurt am Main

United Nations (1945) Charter of the United Nations. http://www.un.org/en/sections/un-charter/un-charter-full-text/

United Nations (1948) Convention on the prevention and punishment of the crime of genocide. https://www.ohchr.org/EN/ProfessionalInterest/Pages/CrimeOfGenocide.aspx

United Nations (1966) International covenant on economic, social and cultural rights and international covenant on civil and political rights. https://www.ohchr.org/EN/ProfessionalInterest/Pages/InternationalLaw.aspx

United Nations General Assembly (1948) The universal declaration of human rights. http://www.un.org/en/universal-declaration-human-rights/index.html

United Nations General Assembly (1974) Definition of aggression, A/RES/29/3314. http://www.un-documents.net/a29r3314.htm

Vesper-Gräske M (2016) Zur Hierarchie der Völkerrechtsverbrechen nach dem Statut des Internationalen Strafgerichtshofs. Nomos, Baden-Baden

Volkmann C (2009) Die Strafverfolgung des Völkermordes nach dem Weltrechtsprinzip im internationalen Strafrecht und Völkerstrafrecht. Untersucht am Beispiel der deutschen Rechtsordnung. Lang, Frankfurt am Main

von Lingen K (2018) 'Crimes against Humanity'. Eine Ideengeschichte der Zivilisierung von Kriegsgewalt 1864–1945. Schöningh, Paderborn

Von Weizsäcker R (1985) Commemorative event in the plenary hall of the German Bundestag to mark the 40th anniversary of the end of the Second World War in Europe. https://www.bundespraesident.de/SharedDocs/Downloads/DE/Reden/2015/02/150202-RvW-Rede-8-Mai-1985-englisch.pdf?__blob=publicationFile

Werle G, Jeßberger F (2016) Völkerstrafrecht, 4th edn. Mohr, Tübingen

Wikisource (2018) Treaty of Versailles (1919). https://en.wikisource.org/wiki/Treaty_of_Versailles

On the Impossibility of Remaining Innocent When an Aeroplane Is Hijacked by Terrorists

Abstract

The film "Terror—Ihr Urteil" ("Terror—Your Judgement"), which was broadcast by the German television company ARD on 17 October, based on a play by Ferdinand von Schirach, constructed a threat situation in which an Islamist terrorist hijacked a Lufthansa aircraft in order to fly it towards the Allianz stadium in Munich, where 70,000 people were watching a football match. The inspiration for the play came from the four terrorist acts of 11 September 2001 in the US and the threat on 5 January 2003 issued by a man in a sports plane over the city centre of Frankfurt (Main) to fly into the tower of the European Central Bank. In the film, the major of a quick reaction air defence force receives the order to make contact with the passenger plane and to force it off its course. After he fails to do so, he decides on his own initiative to shoot down the plane with all 164 people on board in order to save tens of thousands of lives in the football stadium—even though he has no permission to do so from the Minister of Defence and his military superiors. In the subsequent court hearing, the prosecution demands that the major be convicted of mass murder, while the defence pleads for his release. The prosecution referred to the decision by the Federal Constitutional Court of February 2006 regarding the air safety act, which described the shooting down of an aeroplane with passengers and crew on board who were not involved in the terrorist activity in order to save the lives of many other people as in contravention of the Basic Law and with human dignity. After the court hearing was broadcast, viewers were asked to adjudge the behaviour of the major as jurors. 86.9% said he was innocent, while 13.1% proclaimed him guilty.

In a subsequent roundtable discussion on the German television programme "hart aber fair" ("hard but fair"), two former ministers, Franz Josef Jung and Gerhart Baum, clashed particularly harshly during the debate. Franz Josef Jung invoked a so-called "emergency beyond the law", in which he as minister of defence would have given the major the order to shoot down the plane. Gerhart

---

Lecture given on 21.11.2016.

Baum, in harmony with the judgement of the Federal Constitutional Court on the Aviation Security Act, regarded this view as being unconstitutional. However, some important questions were not asked during this discussion which will be considered in this lecture. Furthermore, a clear differentiation should be made between circumstances surrounding the threat and the decision made that were constructed in the play on the one hand and the usually far more complex real-life situations on the other, in which decision-makers from the political field, the military and the police can become involved, and in which the key issue is often not guilt or non-guilt in the legal or moral sense, but the weighing of two forms of behaviour that inevitably entail culpability.

2.1 The Killing of Innocents as the Lesser Evil in the Face of Potential Mass Murder

The repeated terror attacks in France in 2015 and 2016 again provided reason to discuss in public the possible courses of action if an aeroplane is hijacked with the aim of perpetrating mass murder, as was the case on 11 September 2001.[1] They aroused the particular interest of 6.9 million viewers of the theatre performance of Ferdinand von Schirach's "Terror. Ein Theaterstück"[2] ("Terror. A play"), and particularly the television film based on it, which was broadcast by the German national television company ARD on 17 October 2016.[3] A court case was shown in which the defendant, Major Koch, had to justify why he as the leader of a quick reaction defence force used two fighter jets to shoot down a Lufthansa plane with 164 passengers and crew on board on a flight from Berlin to Munich, on 16 May 2013 (in the film: 2016). According to the message sent by the pilot, the hijacker wanted to make the plane crash into the Allianz arena in Munich during an international football match between Germany and England, which was filled with a crowd of 70,000. The plane had been hijacked by an Islamist who had forced the pilot to convey his message that he would now kill a large number of people "with the permission of Allah", in revenge for the many Muslim brothers who had died at the hands of the "crusader governments of Germany, Italy, Denmark and England".[4] Then, radio contact was lost. Attempts to force the plane off the course planned by

---

[1] For an overview of events, see Aust and Schnibben (2002). (All Internet texts retrieved on 19.11.2016). Ablauf der Terroranschläge (2001). The following literature was not available for viewing: Greiner (2011), Kucklick (2001), Archangelskij (2005), and Giemulla and van Schyndel (2006).

[2] von Schirach (2016a).

[3] "Terror—Ihr Urteil" ("Terror—Your Judgement"), a film broadcast on 17 October 2016 on the "Erste" ARD TV station by Oliver Berben and Lars Kraume, with Lars Eidinger (as attorney Biegler), Maria Gedeck (as state prosecutor Nelson), Florian David Fitz (as the defendant Major Lars Koch), Burghart Klaußner (as the presiding judge).

[4] von Schirach (2016a, p. 31).

2.1 The Killing of Innocents as the Lesser Evil in the Face of Potential Mass Murder

the terrorist by the two fighter jets, which had been quickly dispatched by the German army, failed, while a warning shot in front of the nose of the plane also had no effect. Three minutes before the target was reached, Major Koch shot down the passenger plane, which crashed onto a potato field, thus leading to no further loss of life other than that of the 165 people on board.

In the court proceedings shown in the play, the state prosecutor accused the pilot of multiple murder, while the defence requested a not guilty verdict, since as a result of his actions, Major Koch had saved the lives of tens of thousands of people. At the end of the play, the 200,000 or so members of the public who attended the play before the television broadcast and then later, the millions of TV viewers, were asked to act as "members of the jury" and adjudge whether the pilot should be found guilty of multiple murder or be acquitted as the saviour of a large number of people. Of the 600,000 and more German TV viewers, 86.9% voted in favour of acquittal, and coincidentally, the same number did so in Austria, while in Switzerland, 84% of viewers who took part in the voting opted for acquittal, while 13.1 and 16% respectively thought that he was guilty.[5] Following the previous theatre performances, the corresponding figures were 60 and 40% respectively.[6]

After the TV film was screened, the former ministers, Franz Josef Jung and Gerhart Baum, disagreed particularly strongly in the "hart aber fair" programme moderated by Frank Plasberg as to whether the shooting down of a passenger plane hijacked by a terrorist, and which was intended for use as a weapon to murder a large number of people, was legally and morally permissible. In September 2007, both ministers had already been the main participants in a vehement dispute over a judgement of the Federal Constitutional Court of 15 February 2006 regarding the Aviation Security Act, which declared a key paragraph in the Aviation Security Act to be unconstitutional and void. Shooting down passenger planes that have been hijacked was, the court claimed, in contravention of the Basic Law, since it was compatible neither with the fundamental right to life, nor with human dignity.

The dispute surrounding the problem, as in the case of the hijacking of a plane that is intended for use as an air-to-ground guided missile against a large number of people in Germany, was triggered by the events of 11 September 2001 in the US and by the occurrence in Frankfurt/Main on 5 January 2003. On that date, the mentally confused pilot of a sports plane circled over the skyscrapers and threatened to crash into the European Central Bank tower.[7] However, the police succeeded in persuading him via radio not to go through with this idea. A clear differentiation should be made between both of these real-life events and the play by Ferdinand von Schirach,

---

[5]The film was simultaneously shown in Slovakia and the Czech Republic.

[6]However, in some theatres, for example in Japan, as well as in Germany, the majority of the audience voted for a verdict of guilty; http://terror.theater/. In the People's Republic of China, a slim majority at two performances returned a not guilty vote, while in three others, the verdict was guilty; red 2017: Das Urteil von Peking, in: Der Spiegel, No. 28, 8 July. The author, Ferdinand von Schirach, would have voted in favour of a guilty verdict, although he only said so indirectly in an interview: Schirach (2016b).

[7]FAZ (2003) and Spiegel (2003).

which for dramaturgical reasons clearly inserted several uncertainties into the sequence of events. In so doing, the author cleverly generated a considerable degree of suspense and a changing emotional response among the audience.

On subsequent reading of the play, it emerges that the author ascribed several implausible patterns of behaviour to the protagonists involved in the events in order to make it more difficult to pass judgement as to the guilt or innocence of Major Koch.

2.2 The Prohibition Issued by the Federal Constitutional Court on Killing Innocent People in Order to Prevent Mass Murder as the Focus of Criticism

On 11 January 2005, the German parliament passed the Aviation Security Act with the votes of the government coalition consisting of the SPD and Bündnis 90/the Green Party.[8] According to § 14, para. 3, "Direct intervention by force of arms is only permissible when under the prevailing circumstances it can be assumed that the aeroplane is intended for use against the life of people, and that this is the sole means of providing defence against this present danger."[9] The CDU/CSU voted against the measure, since they wanted a further change to be made to the Basic Law, which was intended to also regulate the use of the German Federal Army within the Federal Republic. They did not understand why the Federal Army should be sent out "for all possible duties, all around the world", while at the same time "its deployment to protect our own population is not permitted."[10] Furthermore, the decision-making process that they envisaged, according to which the police of a federal state would be requested to provide administrative assistance by the German Federal Army, would take up valuable time in the case of an acute threat. The FDP and the PDS rejected the law, with a basic objection against empowering the Federal Ministry of Defence to order a passenger plane that had been hijacked by a criminal or terrorist to be shot down. In public, and clearly also among legal scholars, there was agreement with this law, however; only a few left-wing liberal individuals expressed the view that the law was unconstitutional.[11]

The former Federal Minister of the Interior, Gerhart Baum (1978–1982) from the FDP, his fellow party member, the former interior minister of North Rhine-Westphalia (1975–1980) and vice-president of the German parliament (1994–1998) Burkhard Hirsch and four others, including a professional pilot, submitted a constitutional complaint. This was permitted, since as frequent flyers, the persons submitting it could be personally affected by the impact of the law.

---

[8] Deutscher Bundestag (2004)—15th electoral period—115th session, Berlin, Friday, 18 June 2004, http://dipbt.bundestag.de/doc/btp/15/15115.pdf#P.10536, pp. 10536–10545.
[9] Bundesministerium der Justiz und für Verbraucherschutz (2005).
[10] Binninger (2014).
[11] Schlink (2005).

2.2 The Prohibition Issued by the Federal Constitutional Court on Killing...

On 15 February 2006, the First Senate of the Federal Constitutional Court decided that § 14, para. 3 of the Aviation Security Act was in contravention of the fundamental right to life (Art. 2, para. 2 of the Basic Law) and against human dignity (Art. 1 of the Basic Law), and was therefore unconstitutional and void.[12] Only the shooting down of an unmanned plane, or one that is solely occupied by terrorists, was deemed to be permissible. According to the judgement, the state has no right to degrade people to the status of reified objects and a means of achieving its aims, as the terrorists do. The right to life and human dignity also applies directly prior to a foreseeable death as a result of a terror attack.[13] Furthermore, the judgement stated that: "Human life and human dignity enjoy the same constitutional protection, regardless of the duration of the physical existence of the individual person." ... "The state may not kill people because they are fewer in number than those it wishes to save through killing them." Therefore, the state may not turn people into mere objects of its rescue operation in order to protect other people.[14] A relativisation of the right to life of the passengers can also not be justified on the grounds that these people are regarded as being a part of the plane being used as a weapon.

The Federal Constitutional Court thus rejected the argument presented in the statement by the Green Party: if a passenger plane is used as a weapon, the rights of the passengers and the crew to the abstention by the state of an intervention in their right to life should not be subordinate to the obligation to protect those persons on the ground that arises from this right through the targeted downing of the plane. In so doing, it also rejected the argument by the federal government: "Only when the state acts in accordance with § 14, para. 3 of the Aviation Security Act can at least a portion of the lives threatened by saved. This may also occur in such an unusual situation, including to the cost of those who, inseparably connected to the weapon, cannot be saved anyway." Lars Koch, the fighter pilot in the play, also argued entirely along these lines.[15]

In the proceedings in the Federal Constitutional Court in Karlsruhe, the "Vereinigung Cockpit" association particularly emphasised the "uncertain factual basis" of a possible decision to shoot down a plane by the Minister of Defence, as was also emphasised by the state prosecutor in the play. The decision could therefore

---

[12] Bundesverfassungsgericht—Federal Constitutional Court (2006).

[13] In the words of the Court: the Aviation Security Act renders the appellant "the mere object of state action. The value and preservation of their life would be placed at the discretion of the minister of defence, taking into account quantitative considerations and their foreseeable remaining life expectancy 'under the circumstances'. In a case of emergency, they should be sacrificed and intentionally killed, if the minister assumes on the basis of the information available to him that their life will only be of a short duration and thus has no value compared to the other losses that are threatened, or at least, if their life is only of subordinate value" Federal Constitutional Court (2006).

[14] "Due to the fact that they are killed as a means of saving others, they are objectified and at the same time deprived of their rights; when there is single-sided control over their lives on behalf of the state, the passengers, who are themselves victims and are in need of protection, are denied the value due to a person in itself" Federal Constitutional Court (2006).

[15] Schirach (2016a, p. 90).

generally only be made on the basis of suspicion, but not on the basis of certain knowledge. The Federal Constitutional Court agreed with this view by talking of the "uncertainties in reality", as to whether a plane that had been hijacked by terrorists might still be taken back into control by the crew or the passengers. The obligation of the state to provide protection to the likely victims of a terrorist attack should be implemented only with means that were compliant with the Basic Law. It should be stressed that the Federal Constitutional Court expressly did not reach a decision as to how the shooting down of a plane hijacked by terrorists, either by the pilot at their own initiative or on the orders of the Minister of Defence, that is in contravention of the Basic Law, should be adjudged in criminal law.[16]

The most vehement critic of the judgement reached by the Federal Constitutional Court was and remains Franz Josef Jung from the CDU, who a few months after the Aviation Security Act was passed became Federal Minister of Defence (from November 2005 to October 2009). In September 2007, in other words, after the judgement of the Federal Constitutional Court, he declared that in an emergency, he would give the order to shoot down a passenger plane that had been hijacked by terrorists and which was intended for use as a weapon against many other people.[17] As he explained in "hart aber fair" on 17 October, he would also do so if his wife were sitting in the plane, as he had agreed with her if such an emergency occurred. Jung invokes the presence of a so-called "emergency beyond the law", a concept regarded by most legal experts as being incompatible with the valid legislation.[18]

In September 2007, the federal chairman of the association of crew members of jet fighter aircraft ("VBSK"), Thomas Wassmann, immediately spoke out against Jung's opinion, which was evidently also shared by Wolfgang Schäuble.[19] Ex-minister Baum accused Jung of intentional contravention of the constitution.[20] Nothing has changed with regard to the extreme differences of opinion held by both politicians, with Baum supported by the judgement of the Federal Constitutional Court, and Jung by a majority view held by the general public and probably also of the political elite in Germany.

Prominent judges have also expressed their views on the play and the film. The former constitutional judge Udo di Fabio was supportive and appreciative, even

---

[16]"Here, the decision to be made is not how shooting down the plane and the circumstances surrounding it should be adjudged in criminal law" Federal Constitutional Court (2006).

[17]Spiegel (2007a).

[18]However, according to § 34 of the Criminal Code, no emergency situation is recognised in criminal law that would provide justification, but which permits only the use of appropriate means: "Persons taking action in the presence of a risk to life, body, liberty, honour, property or other legally protected right, which cannot otherwise be averted, in order to avert the risk from themselves or others, are not acting illegally if on consideration of the conflicting interests, namely those of the legally protected rights in question and the degree of risk with which they are threatened, the protected interest significantly outweighs that which is affected. However, this only applies if the action is an appropriate means of averting the risk", Bundesministerium (2018a).

[19]Spiegel (2007b). Wassmann responded in 2016 in "hart aber fair".

[20]Spiegel (2007c).

though several factual issues were simplified.[21] However, the federal judge on the Federal Constitutional Court, Thomas Fischer, hurled numerous unveiled insults at the author, the publisher, the broadcaster, the theatre and the audience, making several false claims alongside factually convincing objections.[22] The Bielefeld expert in criminal law, Wolfgang Schild, published a booklet on the play, which accused the "excitingly written" work of proffering an education about the law that was unnecessarily misleading.[23]

2.3 On the Difference Between the Play and the Real-Life Events of 11 September 2001

According to the judgement of the Federal Constitutional Court, the shooting down of the sports plane over Frankfurt would have been legal if it was foreseeable that no other people would be harmed, since the pilot had no people on board who were not involved in the intended crime. In the case of the almost simultaneously hijacked passenger planes in the US on 11 September 2001, it would have been illegal according to German law to shoot them down.

After the first two planes crashed into the World Trade Center (or only half an hour after the fourth plane crashed?), US president George W. Bush issued the order to shoot down any other hijacked planes.[24] However, the coordination of the information and the military chains of command after notification was given of the hijacking of the plane after it had taken off in Boston was so inadequate that the four fighter jets that were launched were not able to come close to the planes that had been hijacked by Al Qaida Islamists fast enough. In all four planes, a hijacker with a pilot's licence obtained in the US took over control after the regular pilots had been overcome. In the fourth plane, which had taken off from Newark, New Jersey, later than its scheduled time, the passengers learned of the two terror attacks in New York via their mobile phones. Some passengers, who now knew that they were not simply hostages who were to play a part in the negotiations with the authorities after a landing announced by the hijackers, as had been the case with earlier plane hijacking operations, but were instead doomed to die, then tried to overcome the hijackers, who were armed with carpet knives and pepper spray, and to enter the cockpit, although they failed to do so. However, as a result, the hijackers no longer believed that they would be able to reach Washington, where they intended to crash the plane

---

[21] Kleber (2016).

[22] Fischer (2016).

[23] Schild (2016, p. 64). In particular, no differentiation is made between the illegality and culpability in criminal law of an action (p. 39). Schild describes the play as a "major mistake in legal terms" (p. 49).

[24] This was claimed in a TV show broadcast on Phönix, "Die Macht hinter dem Präsidenten" ("The power behind the president") on 7 November in relation to the Chief of Staff of the White House. I have no information regarding the probable constitutional debate surrounding this decision in the US.

onto the Capitol (the parliament) or the White House (the seat of the president). They therefore crashed the plane in Shanksville near Philadelphia, onto a patch of ground where by chance no people were present.

The attempt by the passengers to enter the cockpit in order to gain control over the plane is used as an argument—including in von Schirach's play—that it cannot be entirely certain that a plane hijacked by terrorists really will fulfil its intended function as a weapon. Conversely, the fact that the first three planes were successfully used as a weapon of mass murder in New York and in the Pentagon building near Washington is used to argue that the passengers "anyway" only had a few more minutes to live—whether they would be forced to act as a protective shield[25] for the plane that was to be used as a weapon of mass murder or whether they would die from being shot down by a state fighter jet so that hundreds or thousands of others could be saved. In the play, the fighter pilot reckoned that there would be 70,000 victims in the football stadium in Munich.

For dramaturgical reasons, in his play, Ferdinand von Schirach included a greater number of uncertainties in the way he constructed the case than there were in reality on 11 September, at least after the first impact of the first plane in the North Tower of the World Trade Center. Furthermore, with the construct, he operates with several implausible behavioural patterns of the protagonists in the play. Probably, the audience would have adjudged the problem differently if the author had constructed the case in question in another manner, or if the film had not starred such a good-looking actor as Florian David Fitz in the role of Major Koch.

First, Schirach had the Lufthansa plane hijacked but just one terrorist, who is also not capable of taking over at the helm of the plane himself. It is merely stated that he is seen by a fighter pilot approaching the plane as standing between the two regular pilots. It is unclear which weapon was used to threaten the pilots, the other crew and the passengers, so that in the court proceedings, the state prosecutor could say that it was entirely unclear whether the Lufthansa plane really would have crashed into the football stadium. The black box from the cockpit, which was found after the crash, showed that the passengers were in the process of forcing their way into the cockpit. Certainly, it is unlikely that the terrorist would not have shot or stabbed the pilots and several passengers and the plane crash could have been avoided at the last minute. But this would not have occurred over the stadium.

Ultimately, the unspoken assumption in the play (and also throughout the discussion in "hart aber fair") is entirely implausible, namely that the pilot and co-pilot of a hijacked plane would implement the orders of the hijacker until the plane crashed at the intended site. As soon as they would have been convinced of the determination of the hijacker to really make the plane crash into the football stadium, in other words, that they themselves were doomed to die, they would have changed course, even if

---

[25] By contrast, the words used by Lars Koch: "The civilians have in part become a weapon. . . . And I must combat this weapon" (von Schirach 2016a, b, p. 90) do indeed refer to an objectification of people, a concept that was clearly condemned by the Federal Constitutional Court as being unconstitutional.

2.3 On the Difference Between the Play and the Real-Life Events of 11 September 2001

they risked being killed before the plane crashed. The plane would then have crashed outside Munich, in a similar way to the manner in which it was shot down in the play by fighter pilot Koch.

Using the stylistic means of the construct of an unclear situation 3 min before the planned crash into the stadium, in the play, the author enables the state prosecutor to create a wide range of alternative scenarios to that assumed by the fighter pilot (and by Franz Josef Jung in the "hart aber fair" discussion). The construct of the play, that the 60–65 people in the national situation and management centre for security in airspace, which aside from the Ministry of Defence[26] and the federal police was also the responsibility of the Ministry of the Interior and Transport and the Federal Office of Civil Protection and Disaster Assistance, did nothing to evacuate the stadium during the 52 min between the announcement of the planned attack on the stadium by the hijacker and the likely time at which the passenger plane would crash—an operation that would apparently have taken just 15 min to complete—is simply not plausible. With this construct, von Schirach possibly wishes to raise awareness among politicians, the authorities and above all the leaders of the Federal Army, that they are preparing for an adequate response to a terrorist plane hijacking or the pilot running amok. In his play, all the Federal Army members, from the jet pilot to the Duty Controller in the airspace security centre to the Inspector General of the German Air Force, are entirely fixated on imagining a purely military solution to a situation that is by no means as clear as the one in the play (in contrast to 11 September).[27]

A further implausible element is the confusion and helplessness of fighter pilot Koch, who according to his statement had told his friends that he had thoroughly thought through the question of what to do in the case of a planned use of a passenger plane as a weapon by terrorists, when the state prosecutor asked him whether he would also have fired the shot if his wife and small son had been sitting in the plane.[28] It is utterly improbable that he had never asked himself this question before, to which Minister Jung clearly answered in the "hart aber fair" debate that he would also have given the order to shoot, as agreed with his wife.

It would have been interesting if von Schirach or another author had offered several versions of a case construct relating to the problem of a terrorist instrumentalisation of a passenger plane at the same time, shown either in succession in the same theatre, or in different theatres and films. The author would have been able to make his case construct more exciting by placing the wife and son, the parents and several other relatives and close friends of the fighter pilot in the stadium. Would the court then take into consideration § 35 (exculpating emergency)

---

[26] On 26 May 2013, Thomas de Maizière was Federal Minister of Defence. Like the present minister of defence, Ursula van der Leyen, he never publicly issued a statement regarding the play or the fundamental issue.

[27] Clearly an instruction has been given by the superior air force authorities that someone who is not willing to shoot has no place in the cockpit of a fighter jet.

[28] von Schirach (2016a, p. 96).

of the criminal code, according to which: "(1) A person who, faced with an imminent danger to life, limb or freedom which cannot otherwise be averted, commits an unlawful act to avert the danger from himself, a relative or person close to him, acts without guilt...."?[29] At any rate, the Federal Constitutional Court did not consider such an equally unlikely case as the presence of family members of the Minister of Defence or the fighter pilot in the hijacked plane.

For his play, Ferdinand von Schirach formulated two opposing judgements of the court, of which only one is shown, depending on whether the theatre audience (or TV viewers) vote in favour of guilty or not guilty. He would have been able to make viewers think even more deeply if he had presented two contrary sequences of facts with regard to the core issue, in other words, also one in which the fighter pilot does not shoot down the passenger plane, which then crashes into the football stadium and kills tens of thousands of people there, as well as injuring tens of thousands more. This scenario could also be shown in two variants: (1) The fighter pilot follows the order of the Minister of Defence not to shoot down the plane, so that the Minister, above all on the initiative of the relatives of the stadium visitors, possibly faces being prosecuted due to facilitation of a criminal act or due to failure to provide assistance as defined in § 323c of the Penal Code[30]; (2) The fighter pilot disobeys the order issued by the Minister of Defence to shoot down the plane, claiming that this order is in contravention of the constitution, so that he himself would likely appear before a court.[31]

---

[29]Bundesministerium der Justiz und für Verbraucherschutz (2018b) "This does not apply insofar as it could be reasonably expected from the perpetrator that they accept the risk in light of the circumstances, namely because they themselves have been the cause of the risk or because they were in a particular legal relationship; however, the penalty as defined in § 49, para. 1 could be mitigated if the perpetrator should not have accepted the risk in light of a particular legal relationship." In the 2nd paragraph, it is even stated that under certain circumstances, unintentional killing may also go unpunished: "(2) Should the perpetrator assume the existence of incorrect circumstances when taking the action, they would only be subject to penalty if the possibility had existed of avoiding the mistake. The penalty is to be mitigated in accordance with § 49, para. 1." Schild (2016, pp. 26–27) clearly regards such as case as being an illegal but not culpable one. Accordingly, the action should be adjudged entirely differently if the other fighter jet in the emergency operation, who has no close relatives in the stadium, were to shoot down the plane.

[30]"A person who fails to provide assistance in case of accident or risk to the community, even if such action is necessary and can be reasonably expected from them, and is in particular possible without significant risk to themselves and without infringement of other important obligations, shall be punished with imprisonment for up to one year", Federal Ministry (2018d).

[31]The Austrian legal system evidently judges a "failure to prevent an action subject to penalty", according to § 286 of the Criminal Code, far more harshly: "(1) A person who intentionally fails, in the case of an intentional threatened action that is subject to penalty, to prevent its imminent or already initiated implementation, or in cases in which a notification enables a prevention, when the action subject to penalty has at least been attempted and which is subject to penalty of imprisonment exceeding 1 year, shall be punished with imprisonment for up to 2 years. However, the penalty may not be more stringent with regard to its nature and extent than is threatened by the law for the action that was not prevented" Austrian penal code (2018).

In his play, Ferdinand von Schirach has the state prosecutor make an application in her concluding comments that the defendant should be "adjudged guilty of murder on 164 counts", which the court duly did in the film and the theatres in which the majority of the audience voted "guilty".[32] Here, von Schirach uses the colloquial term whereby every act of intentional and lawless killing is described as "murder". As a legal expert, he naturally knows the difference between murder and manslaughter, and refers to this in an another book.[33] Accordingly, it would have been more realistic if he had made the state prosecutor plead in favour of manslaughter. And if the jury had voted guilty, the court would certainly only have passed a verdict of manslaughter. Probably this is the reason why the author refrained from mentioning the severity of the punishment that would have been required in a real-life court case.

According to § 211 (murder) of the Penal Code, a murderer should be punished with life imprisonment. A murder is defined as a person who "kills a person for pleasure, for sexual gratification, out of greed or otherwise base motives, by stealth or cruelty or by means that pose a danger to the public or in order to facilitate or cover up another offence." By contrast, in § 212 (manslaughter), it is stated that: (1) Whosoever kills a person without being a murderer under Section 211 shall be convicted of manslaughter and be liable to imprisonment of not less than 5 years. (2) In especially serious cases, the penalty shall be imprisonment for life. And § 213 even recognises a less severe case of manslaughter.[34]

2.4 "Support for Terror" Versus "Emergency Beyond the Law"

In the play, the justification given by the defendant fighter pilot Lars Koch for his refusal to accept the judgement issued by the Federal Constitutional Court of February 2006 is that he regards this judgement as being incorrect.[35] This "absurd" judgement, he claimed, had rendered the state (in reality, society) "helpless. We are unprotected against the terrorist. The state lays down its arms, and we have given up." After all, now, every terrorist knows that they can "exploit innocent people" in Germany in order to commit mass murder without the state taking effective counteraction.[36]

Koch explained that he had "weighed up against each other" the lives of 164 passengers and those of 70,000 football fans,[37] that "with very large figures",

---

[32] von Schirach (2016a, pp. 123, 134).

[33] von Schirach (2010, pp. 178–179).

[34] "If the manslayer, without themselves being culpable, be rendered angry by maltreatment or grave offence directed against themselves or a member of their family by the individual killed, and as a result felt immediately impelled to take action, or if another less severe case has occurred, the penalty is imprisonment for a period of between one year and ten years." Federal Ministry (2018c).

[35] von Schirach (2016a, p. 82).

[36] von Schirach (2016a, p. 95).

[37] von Schirach (2016a, p. 82).

an exception should be made from the observance of the judgement of the Federal Constitutional Court. When asked by the state prosecutor whether he would have considered a ratio of 1:4 to be sufficient, he answered "No, certainly not."[38] When asked which ratio would have been acceptable, he was unable to provide a response.

The relative figure argumentation suggests that according to Koch's logic, shooting down the two planes that crashed into the World Trade Center on 11 September 2001 would probably have been legitimate, while taking the same action against the third plane, which crashed into the Pentagon (with 125 casualties) with 59 passengers on board would not. These number games are not very convincing in the play. The point is not the weighing up and balancing out of the lives of (a small number of) people against those of (a more or less large number), as is frequently argued in the debate[39] and also in Schirach's play.[40] The point is whether the state has the right to implement one of the terrorists' aims, to kill the passengers on the aeroplane, in order to prevent their other aim, that of killing as many of the 70,000 stadium visitors as possible. The question therefore arises in relation to the play as to whether hypothetically, a maximum of 70,164 people or "only" 164 people have to die within the next 3 min, the latter killed not by the terrorists, however, but by the state, which forestalls the terrorists by 3 min. To this extent, the state becomes the henchman for a part of the murderous aims of the terrorists.[41]

It is not clearly stated in the play whether the minister of defence and the inspector general of the air force have merely not issued an order to shoot to the pilot, or whether they have expressly forbidden him to shoot.[42] By means of this dramaturgical ploy, Schirach avoids discussing the guilt of the higher-level authorities. While in military practice, there may be no difference between the

---

[38] von Schirach (2016a, p. 84).

[39] In the case of the famous railway points scenario, in which a goods carriage the brakes of which no longer function rushes downhill towards a full passenger train can be diverted onto a siding on which five track labourers are currently conducting repair works. Here, a decision must in fact be made as to whether tolerating the unavoidable death of a large number of people by doing nothing is to be preferred over a very different small group of people through an action by the person setting the points. https://de.wikipedia.org/wiki/Trolley-Problem. In the case of the hijacked plane, however, the choice is not between two groups of people threatened with death, but rather, the decision at issue is whether the inevitable death of a small quantity of people may intentionally be brought about, who otherwise are exposed to the risk of death together with another, large quantity. In the comparisons between the validity of the protection of the right to life and human dignity under all circumstances in the case of a plane hijacked by terrorists or criminals, with the prohibition on torture, organ transplantation, assisted dying, abortion, etc., the very different respective case constellations prevail.

[40] von Schirach (2016a, pp. 82, 85).

[41] This is fundamentally different from a situation in which e.g. the police ("the state") inadvertently also shoot hostages alongside terrorists in their attempt to save the hostages. Here, the state enters a risk of intentional killing, while in the case of a plane hijack, it intentionally and unavoidably causes the deaths of the passengers, since only in this way can the deaths of the people in the stadium be prevented.

[42] On page 43, it is stated that the fighter pilot was informed that he "may not shoot", while on page 45, it is stated that after he asked twice, he was informed that no order to shoot had been given.

omission of an order to carry out an action and an express prohibition, but for the judgement of the action of the pilot by the audience, it was probably important to create the impression that he was given no clear instructions by his superiors, and was abandoned by them (as argued by Thomas Wassmann in "hart aber fair"), thus having to make his own decision. This no doubt increases the level of tension in the play and relieves the burden of guilt on the pilot in the eyes of many in the audience.

A serious theoretical question would be whether an anticipated terrorist attack causing mass murder, which is almost certain to occur, or the action of a pilot running amok[43] might lead to greater loss of life (regardless of whether it is just one life or 70,000 lives), or whether a greater degree of uncertainty regarding a forthcoming forced plane crash, which in the view of the "Vereinigung Cockpit" association as well as the Federal Constitutional Court is likely in most specific cases, would only justify shooting down a plane (in the logic of those supporting this action, such as Jung) if a larger number of additional casualties were to be anticipated.

In the play, it is assumed by the state prosecutor, as well as in the judgement of the Federal Constitutional Court, that each human life is of equal value. However, would this assumption really hold true in reality? A case can be constructed in which an aeroplane that has been kidnapped by terrorists, which is being guided by them and which is being effectively controlled with weapons (as was the case on 11 September), which has taken off in the direction of Berlin from a country with lax airport controls, and which is intended to crash into the Reichstag parliament building, for example on the Day of German Unity or on a day to commemorate the victims of Auschwitz. On such a day, parliament would be filled with almost all parliamentary representatives, the government, a large number of federal constitutional judges and possibly also the US president or the prime minister of Israel as guest speakers. In such a case, the terrorists would take over control of the plane in German airspace just before landing in order to divert it from Berlin-Tegel airport to the district of Mitte where parliament is located. They would even clearly announce their intention of crashing the plane into the parliament building, and they would justify their action by claiming to act in retaliation for Germany's involvement in the war against the Islamic State.

And if one takes the constructed case to the extreme in order to clearly illustrate the fundamental problem, the terrorists, who were born and grew up in Germany, would in a radio announcement make a mocking reference to the judgement of the Federal Constitutional Court, by which the German soldiers, who had been trained to obey the authority of the state would undoubtedly abide. They could even cynically allow themselves to fly an extra circuit for the Federal Constitutional Court and

---

[43]On 24 March 2015, a psychiatrically ill co-pilot, Andreas Lubitz, crashed a Germanwings plane with five other members of the crew and 144 passengers on board into the southern French Alps. This was not the first time that a pilot had attempted to crash a passenger plane. The possibility cannot be excluded that a psychiatrically ill pilot might intentionally steer their [besser "gender neutral" sein, da es natürlich auch eine Pilotin sein könnte] plane towards a tall building or a gathering of people.

Gerhart Baum before extinguishing the entire state leadership of Germany. The question arises as to whether repeated acts of terror that are organised and regarded by the "Islamic State" as being acts of war against those states that are fighting this organisation through military intervention in Syria and Iraq, should be classified in the long term as criminal acts that should be dealt with solely by the police and under police law.[44] Imagine that there's a war, and no politician or judge in a position of responsibility wants to label it as such.

In its judgement, the Federal Constitutional Court argued that the kidnapping of a plane in order to implement a terrorist attack is "not defence against attacks intended to extinguish the community and destroy the state legal and liberal order."[45] Would it adjudge a lethal attack on a few hundred individuals who represent the constitutional organs differently to one on tens of thousands of normal citizens or on an atomic power station? If it were to do so, it would abandon its claim to treat all human life equally. Probably, in such an extreme case, the constitutional argumentation would be overturned and the incident would be described as an attack on the legal and liberal order or even as an act of war, instead of as a crime (as in the US and France), in which under certain conditions, civilians may also be killed who have not committed a crime.

2.5 On the Difference Between Legal and Moral Guilt

In my view, the central argument by theologian Petra Bahr in the "hart aber fair" discussion was convincing. She claimed that there was a difference between legal and moral guilt, and that "we (must) accept that the law is evidently not in a position to resolve every moral problem without contradiction."[46] The legal system, she said, could not anticipate and clearly regulate all situations in which people make decisions, as a result of which a differentiation could be made between the legal and moral guilt of the pilot Lars Koch. There were situations in which one might by all accounts bear moral guilt, regardless of whether or not one makes a decision for or against an action. This is fundamentally the classic situation of a tragedy, as already formulated in antiquity. Where Ms. Bahr failed to convince was in her failure to provide an answer to the question as to the nature of the guilt that she would assume as the fighter pilot. To state that one might refrain from taking such a job due to one's unwillingness to expose oneself to situations in which such difficult decisions would have to be made would be to avoid giving a clear answer to a real-life social problem.

A strong argument against assigning predominantly moral guilt or denial of guilt is that concepts of morals are generally individual and are controversial among groups. While they can be more or less precisely determined as being majority or

---

[44]Encke and Ameri-Siemens (2016).
[45]Federal Constitutional Court (2006).
[46]Cf. also Kleber (2016).

2.5 On the Difference Between Legal and Moral Guilt

minority concepts through public opinion surveys, they are not generally binding in society. The strong constitutional state and legal theory argument presented by Gerhard Baum and others is that only the (most democratic possible) constitutional law and the laws subordinate to it may be generally binding, and not the moral requirements and prohibitions to which religious communities or other groups that are part of the state population regard themselves as being bound. In Germany, the Federal Constitutional Court is the highest body that decides over the validity of a law.[47] To this extent, the judgement of the Federal Constitutional Court of February 2006 could not even be altered by a unanimous vote for change to the constitution or by a referendum on such a change (as has been the case in Switzerland), if it were 1 day to be possible to hold one in the Federal Republic of Germany—even if 99% of those eligible to vote were to be in favour of this change. One possibility would be a revolutionary replacement of the Basic Law with a new constitution in which the right to life and human dignity is limited, as is the case in democratic countries with the death penalty. This option could hypothetically be pursued in a non-violent way if the overwhelming majority of the population only wished to alter these two articles in the Basic Law; an entirely improbable scenario. The other option is to change the judgement of the Federal Constitutional Court by means of a different composition of the court itself in the future, which would be willing to accede to the altered legal situation and opinion,[48] such as after a major terrorist attack in Germany on the scale of 11 September or the scenario presented in von Schirach's play.

I did not participate in the audience vote on the film, and I would also not vote in a theatre as to whether Lars Koch is guilty or innocent of murder. I would argue as a member of the jury that according to the law, he should be judged as a manslayer, not as a murderer, albeit only with the most lenient sentence possible of 1 year if it has been clearly ascertained that it is almost certain that the aeroplane would have crashed into the fully occupied stadium 3 min later.[49]

An entirely different question in the role of a member of the jury in a real-life or fictitious court case relating to the shooting down of a hijacked plane is whether one would have shot the plane down oneself, or whether as an advisor to the fighter pilot or the minister of defence one would have recommended that they shoot or not shoot. In general, I never advise anyone how to act in a difficult situation. I always say that

---

[47]This does not exclude the possibility that there is a great deal of contention among legal experts with regard to the judgement of the Federal Constitutional Court regarding the Aviation Security Act. See e.g. a critical viewpoint from Ladiges (2013, p. 30). Above all, Ladiges stresses the right to defence by a state against attacks from non-state actors. The judgement is also supported by many authors, including Bott (2011, pp. 69–74). Bott presents a critical discussion of Ladiges (pp. 60–66).

[48]Thus, the Federal Constitutional Court had already revised its earlier judgements several times, including with reference to the change in the general awareness of the law, cf. also the interview with Udo di Fabios mentioned above.

[49]There, the explosion of the kerosene would probably not have killed all 70,000 people in the stadium, although there would have been around 35,000 casualties and 20,000 with more or less severe injuries, according to the haphazard judgement of Thomas Wassmann, the federal chairman of the VBSK, the Verband der Besatzungen (the flight crew association) in "hart aber fair".

they must find the right decision for themselves, since they, and not me as the person giving the advice, must bear the legal and psychological consequences of that decision. However, whenever possible, I tend to say what I would probably do in the situation of the person asking for advice, while always stressing that I don't know whether in a specific stress situation and with perhaps insufficient information, I really would act in the way that I would rationally plan to do in advance, in a calm and relaxed atmosphere.

Our legal system is designed to adjudge an action more harshly than a failure to act. I belong to the post-war generation for whom the question of guilt through failure to act on a political and moral basis during the Third Reich and the Second World War played an extremely important role, alongside that of illegal or morally wrong actions. The play, and in principle also the events that occurred on 11 September, did not present the question as to whether all the persons responsible for making the decision as to whether to shoot down a passenger plane that had been turned into a weapon were guilty or not guilty. They found themselves in a situation in which they could not fail to be guilty regardless of how they acted. They merely had the choice between one form of guilt and the other, which in Germany—unlike in other countries—is also a constitutional guilt. I assume that I would tell the German minister of defence asking me for advice that in his place, I would give the order to shoot, then resign immediately from office and request that my defence lawyer refrain from submitting a plea for a verdict of not guilty.[50]

If the fighter pilot were to ask for my advice, I would probably tell him that in his place, I would refrain from shooting if the minister of defence and my military superiors had expressly given the order not to shoot. If, as was the case in the play, all my superiors had failed to make a clear decision, I would probably not have tolerated the murder of tens of thousands of people and would have shot down the plane. Then I would immediately have resigned from my post in the German Army and instructed my defence lawyer not to submit a plea for a not guilty verdict in court—out of respect for the constitution and in recognition of the guilt for which I have opted.

Unfortunately, no-one in the "hart aber fair" debate asked Gerhart Baum whether he would have ordered or prohibited the shooting down of the second and third hijacked planes (as well as the fourth plane, if it had got close the Capitol in Washington) on 11 September if the air force fighter jets had been near them, in

---

[50] According to the same principle, Helmut Schmidt as Federal Chancellor had already written his letter of resignation in case the release of the hostages in a passenger plane in Mogadishu on 18 October 1977 led to the death of several hostages, whether by the hand of the terrorists or by the police. However, it should be taken into account that the unintentional shooting of hostages by the police during a rescue operation or as a result of police provocation as a result or a risky or even amateurish rescue operation such as the decision taken in Fürstenfeldbruck on 5 September 1972 differs significantly from the intentional killing of innocent people by state organs, even if the actual consequence for the victims, namely a violent death, is the same. At that time, when two helicopters were stormed that were filled with eight terrorists and nine hostages, members of the Israeli Olympic team, all hostages and one police officer were killed, alongside five terrorists.

2.6 The Potential Impact of the TV Film

other words, at the latest after it had become unequivocally clear that they were intended for use as air-to-ground guided missiles.

What argumentation could the Federal Constitutional Court use to revise its judgement of February 2006, which is indeed in essence a type of carte blanche for terrorists who use other people in aeroplanes, or in buses and cars loaded with explosives, which they plan to turn into weapons, as a protective shield? The human dignity of the hostages is not only violated due to the fact that they are murdered, but also because in their last minutes of life, they are instrumentalised in order to murder other people. This second violation of their human rights could be avoided if the state organs killed them a few minutes before their inevitable death, which neither they themselves nor the state can prevent. In this way, they would be freed from unbearable pangs of guilt in relation to the victims of the terrorists that under certain circumstances may torment them. These people could only be killed because they are allowed to, or must, survive for a few minutes more. Any sensible person would surely demand "assisted dying" from the state in such a situation, so that through the prolongation of their life by 3 min or less, they are not degraded as the involuntary instrument of a mass murderer. The compulsion to live until the terrorists have achieved their main goal, mass murder, can be understood as an intolerable violation of the human dignity of the hostages. With such a legal position, the Federal Constitutional Court would do justice to a tragic situation in which there is no way out without violating the human dignity of hostages. The human dignity of the hostages is not preserved by allowing them to live for 3 min longer so that they can be used as instruments to violate human dignity and kill a large number of other people, who have the chance of being saved.

Such a change in the interpretation of the basic right to human dignity bears a risk, however. It can only apply to situations in which mass murder, as was the case with the second or third terror attack on 11 September, could be prevented to a degree of probability bordering on certainty. The re-interpretation could mean that state organs also decide to shoot down a hijacked passenger plane (or another plane) as a preventive measure as the alleged "lesser evil" even in situations where the degree of probability of mass murder using human shields is less than certain. There is no avoiding entirely the dilemma depicted, in which people can find themselves in situations in which they are guilty whatever choice they make.

2.6 The Potential Impact of the TV Film

The film, with its audience of millions and the clear result of the vote, has probably had a long-lasting impact on public opinion regarding the willingness to agree that shooting down a passenger plane that has been hijacked by terrorists and is being used as a weapon is justified in order to save a large number of likely victims of a terrorist attack. It could therefore certainly mean that any future decision of a minister of defence or a pilot of a quick reaction air defence force might be more inclined to shoot the plane down. However, in a specific case, the assessment of how probable it is that the announced act of destruction really will be carried out or could feasibly be perpetrated would probably play a central role. The not unjustified fear remains, however, that the people making the decision may decide to shoot down the plane in cases of doubt, since they fear that the consequences of omitting to do so would be morally and politically more severe for them than the consequences of shooting the plane down, if this would later transpire as being not necessary on the basis of the information from the cockpit voice recorder—unless they had failed to adequately process all the information about the situation available to them at the time of their decision. No assessment can be made on the basis of the judgement of the Federal Constitutional Court relating to the Aviation Security Act, nor of the literature I have read, as to how a failure to conduct a rescue operation, resulting in the deaths of hundreds or thousands of people, in addition to the dead aeroplane passengers, would be adjudged in court.

References

Ablauf der Terroranschläge am 11. September 2001. https://de.wikipedia.org/wiki/Ablauf_der_Terroranschl%C3%A4ge_am_11._September_2001

Archangelskij A (2005) Das Problem des Lebensnotstandes am Beispiel des Abschusses eines von Terroristen entführten Flugzeuges. Berliner Juristische Universitätsschriften, Berlin

Aust S, Schnibben C (eds) (2002) 11. September 2001. Geschichte eines Terrorangriffs, 3rd edn. DTV, Stuttgart

Binninger C (2014) Deutscher Bundestag. Stenografischer Bericht. 115 Sitzung, Berlin, Freitag den 18. Juni, S. 10538–10539

Bott I (2011) In dubio pro Straffreiheit? Untersuchungen zum Lebensnotstand. C. F. Müller, Heidelberg

Bundesministerium der Justiz und für Verbraucherschutz (2005) Luftsicherheitsgesetz (LuftSiG). http://www.gesetze-im-internet.de/luftsig/__14.html

Bundesministerium der Justiz und für Verbraucherschutz (2018a) § 34 StGB Rechtfertigender Notstand. http://www.gesetze-im-internet.de/stgb/__34.html

Bundesministerium der Justiz und für Verbraucherschutz (2018b) § 35 StGB Entschuldigender Notstand. http://www.gesetze-im-internet.de/stgb/__35.html

Bundesministerium der Justiz und für Verbraucherschutz (2018c) § 213 StGB Minder schwerer Fall des Totschlags. http://www.gesetze-im-internet.de/stgb/__213.html

Bundesministerium der Justiz und für Verbraucherschutz (2018d) § 323c StGB Unterlassene Hilfeleistung; Behinderung von hilfeleistenden Personen. http://www.gesetze-im-internet.de/stgb/__323c.html

Bundesverfassungsgericht (2006) Urteil des Ersten Senats vom 15. Februar – 1 BvR 357/05 – , BVerfGE 115, 119

Deutscher Bundestag – 15. Wahlperiode – 115. Sitzung, Berlin, Freitag, den 18. Juni 2004. http://dipbt.bundestag.de/doc/btp/15/15115.pdf#P.10536, S. 10536–10545

Encke J, Ameri-Siemens A (2016) Die Drohung. Das neue Theaterstück von Ferdinand von Schirach heißt "Terror" – und ist aktueller als geplant: Ein Gespräch mit den ehemaligen Bundespolitikern Gerhart Baum und Burkhard Hirsch über die gefährlichen Konsequenzen. faz.net vom 1. August. http://www.faz.net/aktuell/feuilleton/ferdinand-von-schirach-terror-baum-hirsch-14364755.html?printPagedArticle=true#pageIndex_2

FAZ (2003) Irrflug setzt Frankfurt in Angst und Schrecken. Frankfurter Allgemeine Zeitung vom 5. Januar. http://www.faz.net/aktuell/gesellschaft/flugzeug-entfuehrung-irrflug-versetzt-frankfurt-in-angst-und-schrecken-189977.html

References

Fischer T (2016) 'Terror' – Ferdinand von Schirach auf allen Kanälen! Die Zeit vom 18. Oktober. http://www.zeit.de/gesellschaft/zeitgeschehen/2016-10/ard-fernsehen-terror-ferdinand-von-schirach-fischer-im-recht

Giemulla E, van Schyndel H (2006) Luftsicherheitsgesetz. Luchterhand, Neuwied

Greiner B (2011) 9/11. Der Tag, die Angst, die Folgen. Beck, Munich

Kleber C (2016) Interview im heute-journal des ZDF mit dem ehemaligen Verfassungsrichter Udo di Fabio vom 18. Oktober 2016. https://www.youtube.com/watch?v=27oA0TSNjA0

Kucklick C (2001) 11. September 2001. Der Tag, der die Welt verändert hat. Die Planung, der Ablauf, die Folgen. Alle Hintergründe der Katastrophe. Gruner und Jahr, Hamburg

Ladiges M (2013) Die Bekämpfung nicht-staatlicher Angreifer im Luftraum unter besonderer Berücksichtigung des § 14 Abs. 3 LuftSig und der strafrechtlichen Beurteilung der Tötung von Unbeteiligten, 2nd edn. Duncker und Humblot, Berlin

Schild W (2016) Verwirrende Rechtsbelehrung. Zu Ferdinand von Schirachs 'Terror'. LIT, Berlin, S. 64

Schlink B (2005) An der Grenze des Rechts. Spiegel online vom 17. Januar. http://www.spiegel.de/spiegel/print/d-38998436.html

Spiegel (2003) Entführtes Flugzeug setzte Frankfurt in Angst. Spiegel online vom 5. Januar. http://www.spiegel.de/panorama/luftfahrt-entfuehrtes-flugzeug-versetzte-frankfurt-in-angst-a-229487.html

Spiegel (2007a) Jung würde entführtes Flugzeug abschießen lassen. Spiegel online vom 16. September. http://www.spiegel.de/politik/debatte/berufung-auf-notstand-jung-wuerde-entfuehrtes-flugzeug-abschiessen-lassen-a-505981.html

Spiegel (2007b) Jetpiloten meutern gegen Jung. Spiegel online vom 17. September. http://www.spiegel.de/politik/deutschland/flugzeugabschuss-jetpiloten-meutern-gegen-jung-a-506134.html

Spiegel (2007c) Baum wirft Jung Verfassungsbruch vor. Spiegel online vom 17. September. http://www.spiegel.de/politik/deutschland/terrorabwehr-baum-wirft-jung-verfassungsbruch-vor-a-506118.html

Strafgesetzbuch Österreich 2018 § 286 Unterlassung der Verhinderung einer mit Strafe bedrohten Handlung. https://www.jusline.at/gesetz/stgb/paragraf/286

von Schirach F (2010) Schuld. Stories. Piper, Munich

von Schirach F (2016a) Terror. Ein Theaterstück und eine Rede. btb, Faber & Faber, London, München 2017

von Schirach F (2016b) "Nachdenken, in welchem Staat wir leben wollen". Interview mit dem rbb vom 6. Oktober. http://www.rbb-online.de/kultur/beitrag/2016/10/interview-von-schirach.html

Islands in the South China Sea as a Centre of Conflict for a Potential Third World War

Abstract

Long before the First and Second World War, the territorial centres of conflict—the Balkans respectively Manchuria and eastern central Europe—in which war broke out in 1914 and 1937/1939 were generally well known. Today, too, territorial centres of conflict can be identified in which a Third World War could be triggered. Alongside Kashmir and Korea, these also include Taiwan and several islands in the East China and South China Sea.

The People's Republic of China and the Republic of China are asserting a claim, on historical grounds, for the unification of all of China, including Taiwan and the largest portion of the South China Sea, and the Senkaku/Diaoyu Islands in the East China Sea, which are under Japanese control. In recent decades, the desire for autonomy and state independence in Taiwan has grown continuously, and is a development that Beijing is unwilling to tolerate. Further centres of conflict are the Paracel Islands, the Macclesfield Bank, the Scarborough Reef, the Natuna Islands and in particular, the Spratly Islands. Here, the irreconcilable claims, above all of the two Chinese states, with those of Vietnam and the Philippines, as well as of Malaysia and Brunei, collide. There have already been individual armed disputes between the states bordering the South China Sea. These frequently centre around merely small land elevations, or even nothing more than raised sandbanks and reefs, on which fishing and marine ports and military airfields are built. In recent years, the interest in exploiting the mineral resources on the sea floor around the natural and artificial islands has intensified. Here, the claims to exclusive economic zones, which are legitimate in accordance with the United Nations Convention on the Law of the Sea of 1982, overlap. By contrast, the irreconcilable visions of air space monitoring zones held by several states remain unclarified in international law.

The local conflicts take on their intensity and potential for causing a world war due to the fact that they are embedded in the competition between China, the

---

Lecture given on 15.7.2019.

aspiring world power, and the declining world power that is the USA, which for the present is still acting as an economic, political and military prop for Japan, Taiwan and the smaller states bordering the South China Sea. The stylisation of the disputed islands, land features and waters as essential objects of vital national interest and prestige among the conflicting parties risks causing significant escalation and is a stimulus for intensified armament efforts and air and sea manoeuvres designed to demonstrate power. For this reason, the development of de-escalation strategies in the east and south-east Asia region is advisable, for which several recommendations will be made here.

3.1 The Spectrum of the Centres of Conflict

Long before the First and Second World War, the territorial centres of conflict—the Balkans and then Manchuria and eastern central Europe—where the world wars broke out in 1914[1] and 1937/1939, were generally well known. Today, too, territorial centres of conflict can be identified in which a Third World War could be triggered. Alongside Kashmir[2] and Korea,[3] these also include Taiwan and a large number of islands in the East China and South China Sea.

Most of the islands on the edge of the East China and South China Sea are clearly assigned to one state or another. Some islands and land features, such as atolls, rocks, sandbanks or reefs, are the subject of severe political and legal dispute, however.[4] While they used to be utilised and claimed for civilian purposes, today, they are increasingly being occupied by navy and air forces, both of which repeatedly lead to violent disputes, such as forcing away or ramming ships, arresting fishermen or in extreme cases, even skirmishes.[5] The risk of a larger war grows when the dispute over a land feature or waters, or the initiator of a violent clash, is turned into a focus of national prestige and essential security interests by the media or politicians, in a manner that could justify a limited war. The risk of a world war only arises from an armed conflict or even a regional war, however, when the major powers regard their vital security interests as being involved, including the honouring of a security guarantee for a local party in the conflict. If one or another of them becomes convinced that the irreconcilable nature of these interests must lead to a major war at some time in the future, this party will be inclined to begin it sooner rather than

---

[1]See the lecture by Jahn (2015a).
[2]See the lecture by Jahn (2015b).
[3]See the lecture by Jahn (2015c).
[4]A map clearly showing the disputed island groups in the South China Sea can be found under Nine-Dash Line (2019).
[5]For a list of the numerous violent clashes between 1917 and 2015, see Fels and Vu (2016, pp. 523–537).

later (under less favourable international constellations). Such a situation (as was the case in 1914 and 1939) is currently nowhere to be seen, although it could arise due to the escalation of local conflicts and the worsening of tensions between the major powers, particularly the global powers of the USA and the People's Republic of China.

In former times, islands were important as a settlement and economic space, acting as fishing, trade and marine ports. Today, the sovereignty of states along all coasts of mainland countries and islands extends along a coastal strip of 12 nautical miles, i.e. approx. 22 km, which are known as the territorial waters. Originally, in the early modern age, this strip was only 3 nautical miles wide, in other words, a canon shot wide, or 5.6 km. After the First World War, several states claimed an extension to 12 nautical miles, although this was only affixed in international law with the United Nations Convention on the Law of the Sea (UNCLOS) of 1982, which has been in force since 1994. In addition, since then, extended territorial waters of 200 nautical miles (approx. 370 km) are recognised as an Exclusive Economic Zone (EEZ). This zone can be extended to 350 nautical miles if evidence is found of a continental shelf within this extension. Such claims had to be submitted to the United Nations by 2009. Since the end of the Second World War, the EEZs were also coveted as deposits of mineral resource, particularly crude oil and natural gas, as well as for fishing. Since most EEZs of two or more states overlap, the borders of each EEZ have to be contractually agreed, which frequently involves a dispute. However, a dispute only arises when states claim an EEZ around a small island or an atoll, even though according to a judgement of the Permanent Court of Arbitration at The Hague, only islands that are inhabited or inhabitable in a natural state, with their own freshwater sources, may be recognised as state territory.[6] For such an island, an EEZ of over 431,000 km^2 can be claimed—in other words, an area that is considerably larger than the Federal Republic of Germany.[7] Rocks, sandbanks, or elevations that only lie above the surface of the sea at certain times, as well as artificial islands, do not qualify as the basis for a claim to an EEZ.[8] According to G.B. Poling, 50 land

---

[6] "The Tribunal interpreted Article 121 and concluded that the entitlements of a feature depend on (a) the objective capacity of a feature, (b) in its natural condition, to sustain either (c) a stable community of people or (d) economic activity that is neither dependent on outside resources nor purely extractive in nature." Permanent Court of Arbitration 2016: The South China Sea Arbitration (The Republic of the Philippines v. The People's Republic of China), PH-CN-20160712-Press-Release-No-11-English.

[7] Kreuzer (2016, p. 4). According to other sources, the EEZ around the Falkland Islands covers an area of 550,872 km^2, Raine and Le Mière (2013, p. 31).

[8] In the UNCLOS, it is merely stated that: "An island is a naturally formed area of land, surrounded by water, which is above water at high tide... Rocks which cannot sustain human habitation or economic life of their own shall have no exclusive economic zone or continental shelf." United Nations Convention on the Law of the Sea 1982, article 121, para. 1 and 3, www.un.org/Depts/los/convention_agreements/texts/unclos/unclos_e.pdf

features in the South China Sea can be classified as islands according to the UNCLOS, of which 9 belong to the Paracel Islands, and 30 to the Spratly Islands.[9]

In an EEZ, the fundamental policy of free shipping and air travel for all states applies in principle, in other words, also for navy ships and air forces. However, some states claim control of air traffic in an air defence or air surveillance zone (Air Defense Identification Zone, ADIZ), which are announced unilaterally and without a basis in international law by some states, such as by the USA (1940), Canada (extended in May 2018), South Korea (1951) and Japan (1968). In this zone, aircraft must identify themselves if they intend to fly to the country in question (according to the US interpretation). In November 2013, China also announced such an ADIZ, which incorporates the territory of the Senkaku/Diaoyu Islands and the Socotra Rock below the sea surface, which is a subject of dispute with South Korea. It is intended to also apply to aircraft that even only fly through the ADIZ.[10]

The South China Sea[11] (approx. 3.6 million km^2),[12] which is located between mainland China, Taiwan, the Philippines, the island of Borneo, which belongs to Malaysia, Indonesia and Brunei, Malaysia and Singapore as well as Vietnam, and the Strait of Malacca that leads to the Indian Ocean, is of huge importance to global commercial traffic.[13] It is also an explosive issue at regional political level within the Association of Southeast Asian Nations (ASEAN), with its ten member states: Brunei, Indonesia, Cambodia, Laos, Malaysia, Myanmar, the Philippines, Singapore, Thailand and Vietnam.[14] This sea contains a large number of, mostly uninhabited, islands, atolls (ring-shaped coral reefs around a lagoon), sandbanks and reefs. Some of these atolls or sandbanks have been raised in very recent years, and turned into inhabitable artificial islands, with ports, airports, residential buildings and barracks, which while they are of military relevance do not form the basis for their own EEZ.

---

[9]Poling (2013, pp. 27–28), quoted from Ohnesorge (2016, p. 42). The Court of Arbitration at The Hague did not recognise any of the land features in the Spratly group as being an island, however.

[10]Page (2013).

[11]"South China Sea "is the standard international name for the sea, although it is also referred to by Vietnam as the East Sea, by the China as the South Sea and by the Philippines as the West Philippine Sea.

[12]By comparison, the European Mediterranean covers an area of 2.5 million km^2, and the Baltic Sea an area of just over 0.4 million km^2.

[13]Around 30% of global maritime trade is transported via the South China Sea, Will (2016, p. 475). According to other sources, that figure is 50%, and the vast majority of Japan's, South Korea's and China's energy supply is transported via the sea routes, Kaplan (2011).

[14]The organisation was founded in 1967 by Indonesia, Malaysia, the Philippines, Singapore and Thailand for the purpose of regulating conflicts and cooperating in their economic, political and social relationship. Later, it also focussed on environmental, cultural and security issues, and in 2009 resolved to create a common economic space similar to that of the EU. The ASEAN was preceded by the Association of South-East Asia (ASA) from 1961 to 1967. See Rosenbusch (2002) and Acharya (2012).

3.2 Disputed Political Positions and the Situation in International Law

Eight individual centres of conflict can be identified in the China Seas, in which the two global powers, the People's Republic of China (below: China) and the USA are directly or indirectly involved on the one hand, with the two regional powers, Japan and India, and the adjoining states, the Philippines, Vietnam, Indonesia, Malaysia, Singapore, Brunei and the de-facto state, the Republic of China (below: Taiwan), on the other. These seven states have a population of around 525 million, while China alone has a population of 1.4 billion,[15] and spends around five times more on its military than the Philippines, Indonesia, Vietnam and Taiwan together.[16]

1. Taiwan, the main territory of the Republic of China, is a densely populated island with 23 million inhabitants (2010), which in the view of the People's Republic of China is one of its 23 provinces. 13 percent of its population fled to the island during the Chinese civil war, and after the constitution of the People's Republic on the mainland on 1 October 1949, they decided to remain there. Several small islands also belong to Taiwan (Quemoy/Yinmen and Matsu/Matsu Liedao) situated off the mainland coast, over which the two Chinese states went to war in 1954/1955 and 1958. For decades, the dictatorial government of the Guomindang Party under Chiang Kai-shek (Jiang Jieshi) on Taiwan, which had been forced to abandon its rule over the whole of China, continued to hold fast to the notion of a unified China, and even wanted to reconquer the mainland. However, its attempts to do so were thwarted by the USA, which still supports Taiwan militarily and politically today. After the Guomindang dictatorship was brought to an end in Taiwan, steps were taken towards declaring the country's independence, which led to threats of intervention by the People's Republic.[17] In 1989, 52% of the population still regarded themselves as being Chinese; today, that figure is just 8%.[18] However, a third view themselves as being both. A war between China and Taiwan could escalate into a war between the two global powers. To date, however, both states have adhered to the contentious consensus of 1992, according to which there is only one China, to which Taiwan belongs.
2. The dispute surrounding the Pratas Islands (Dongsha Islands) is closely linked to the fundamental Taiwan problem. This is an atoll located 400 km to the southwest of Taiwan, and 320 km from Hong Kong. Just one small island, with an area of 1.74 km^2, rises up out of this atoll, which houses around 200 Taiwanese soldiers. In 2007, the atoll and the surrounding sea were declared a national park. While China claims ownership of the islands, they are not the subject of any dispute.

---

[15] Löchel (2018, pp. 528–531).
[16] Burgers (2016, p. 84).
[17] FAZ (2019).
[18] Thomas (2018).

3. The Taiwan problem is a clearly separate issue when it comes to the problem of the Senkaku/Diaoyu Islands in the East China Sea,[19] and the problem of several groups of islands in the South China Sea. Both issues are the focus of competing global political interests between the USA and China, as well as Japan, in the eastern Pacific region. The Senkaku (Japanese) or Diaoyu (Chinese) group of islands consists of five small, uninhabited islands and three rock reefs with a total area of 5–6 km². It is located around 150 km to the north of the Japanese Yaeyama Islands, 170 km to the north-east of Taiwan and 330 km from the Chinese mainland, on the Chinese continental shelf, and is administered by Japan as a part of the Ishigaki district. However, the group of islands, whose vicinity is thought to contain large deposits of oil, gas and manganese, have again been claimed by China and Taiwan since 1970/1971.
4. In the South China Sea, numerous other conflicts are taking place aside from the dispute surrounding the Pratas Islands mentioned above. These essentially centre around five land features and the surrounding waters with their rich fish stocks. It is also thought that they contain large deposits of crude oil and natural gas, although estimates issued by the national energy institutions vary widely.[20] However, most secured energy resources are located on the margins of the South China Sea, and not in the Spratly Islands in the middle of the Sea, which are the subject of dispute. The disputed sea territories are the Paracel Islands (Xisha Islands), a group of coral atolls (22 islands, 8 sandbanks, 10 sunken reefs), in particular those located around 330 km to the south-east of the Chinese island of Hainan, and 400 km to the east of Vietnam. The most important island is Woody Island (Yongxing Dao, approx. 2 km²) with 1443 inhabitants (2014).[21] The group of islands is controlled by China, but is also claimed by Taiwan and Vietnam.
5. The Macclesfield, or Great Zhongsha Atoll, which belongs to a huge area of the "Zhongsha Islands" (atolls, sandbanks, reefs and seamounts) is submerged between 9 and 18 m below the water surface and is about the same distance from China, Vietnam and the Philippines. The area is constantly patrolled by the Chinese navy, but is also claimed by Taiwan.
6. Thirdly, there is dispute between China, the Philippines and Taiwan over the Scarborough Reef (Huangyan Dao). This is located 250 km to the west of the Philippines, and 800 km to the south-east of China. It is mostly below the sea surface, with an area of just 0.02 km² rising 3 m above it. There, China, has built an unmanned meteorological station.
7. The Spratly Islands consist of over one hundred reefs, atolls and small islands with a maximum elevation of 4 m. The largest has an area of 0.5 m². Vietnam,

---

[19]There, a dispute is also ongoing between South Korea and the People's Republic of China over the Socotra Rock, which is submerged below sea level, on which South Korea erected a research station with helicopter landing strip in 2001. The two Korean states are also in dispute with Japan over the Liancourt Rock (0.21 km²) in the Sea of Japan.
[20]On the individual estimates, see Ohnesorge (2016, p. 30) and Klare (2015).
[21]FAZ (2016).

3.2 Disputed Political Positions and the Situation in International Law   47

China and Taiwan in particular are in dispute over this group of islands, which are thought to contain deposits of crude oil and natural gas. These three countries are far away from the islands, at a distance of at last 420, 900 and even 1300 km respectively. However, parts of the island group are also claimed by the Philippines, Malaysia and Brunei, since they lie within their EEZs. There are military bases of five of the six conflicting parties mentioned on 40 of these uninhabited islands. Only Brunei does not have one.

Vietnam has soldiers stationed on six islands, which each cover just 1 ha of land. On *Taiping Dao/ItuAba* (46 ha), a large landing strip has been built by Taiwan. Here, 600 troops are stationed. China controls 21 reefs, sandbanks and small islands, and has built up several reefs (e.g. Fiery Cross Reef/*Yongshu Jiao*, Mischief Reef/*Meiji Jiao*, Subi Reef/*Zhubi Jiao*), enabling military planes to land there and ships to dock, and also providing accommodation for fishermen.[22] They are to be secured by artillery and air defence guns. In April 2018, China stationed rockets and cruise missiles on these three artificial islands in order to underscore Chinese claims to ownership. On the island of Thitu (Pagasa) to the north of the island group, the Philippines has settled around 200 civilians and built an airfield. The country has also built military bases on three other islands.

8. The Natuna Islands are a larger group of islands in north-western Borneo, with a land area of 3420 km^2 and 98,000 inhabitants. They are internationally recognised as belonging unequivocally to Indonesia, although China does not recognise parts of the Indonesian EEZ, which lie within the area of the Chinese Nine-Dash Line, and claims fishing rights there.[23]

On the basis of historical arguments,[24] China claims ownership of around 80–90% of the South China Sea and its land features, and underscores these claims with a map submitted to the United Nations in 2009, on which it marked the area around these waters with the "Nine-Dash Line",[25] which had already been postulated by the Republic of China in 1947 based on maps from the 1930s. Since 2012, this area has also been represented in the passports of the People's Republic, thus reinforcing the claim. In so doing, the People's Republic adopted the demands of the Republic of China, but also has an interest in ensuring that Taiwan stands by its claims in order to promote a One-China policy.[26] In this way, the two Chinese states, albeit with differing levels of military clout, reject the claims both of the other states bordering the Sea to an EEZ in these waters, as well as the general position in international law that the Sea beyond the EEZ is a high sea that should be accessible to all states on

---

[22]boj (2014).
[23]Fähnders (2016).
[24]Scheerer and Raszelenberg (2002, pp. 27–28, 223–225).
[25]Originally, it was an Eleven-Dash Line. See also Carpio (2016).
[26]In the literature considered, no references could be found as to whether those who support independence for the Republic of Taiwan wish to uphold the territorial claims in the South China Sea that have been asserted to date beyond the islands that have thus far been occupied.

Earth. Vietnam is also reinforcing its claim to sole sovereignty over several Paracel and Spratly Islands with historical arguments, with a shipping law from June 2012.[27] The attempt by other states to claim an EEZ around remote, uninhabitable land features that are interpreted as national territory also contradicts international law.

To date, only one judgement has been issued by an international court in relation to the territorial disputes in the South China Sea. In January 2013, the Philippines called on an arbitration court at the Permanent Court of Arbitration at The Hague, in order to assert its claims to islands and other land elevations and an EEZ in the South China Sea. In July 2016, the court decided that the EEZ of the Philippines included the Mischief Reef (*Meiji Jiao*) in the Spratly island group, which China had developed in order to build an airforce base, and two sandbanks, but not the Scarborough Reef.[28] Furthermore, it stipulated that Taiping, which was occupied by Taiwan, was not an island, and did not therefore provide grounds for a separate EEZ. China asserted from the start that this was not a matter for the Permanent Court of Arbitration, and declared the judgement to be non-binding.[29] Taiwan, which was not addressed during the arbitration proceedings, and which unlike China as a de-facto state, was not able to sign the Convention on the Law of the Sea in the first place, also does not recognise the judgement.

Thus, a complex conflict situation arises, in which above all, China, the upcoming global power, asserts wide-ranging claims to marine waters over several other border states, which themselves assert claims to territory that in part conflict with each other,[30] rendering them unable to form a clear common opposition to Chinese expansionist goals. All the smaller bordering states and Japan are searching in different ways and with differing degrees of intensity for economic, political and often also military backing from the USA,[31] and in some cases are attempting to also include India, Australia, New Zealand, the United Kingdom and France in their efforts to oppose Chinese expansionism.[32] However, the stronger China's economic and political global power role becomes, and the more the USA signals plans for withdrawal of its security guarantees in the western Pacific region, or itself enters into conflict with regimes in this region for other reasons entirely, which are not related to territorial disputes (such as in relation to human rights issues in the Philippines), the more the smaller bordering states in the South China Sea will attempt to forge a bilateral reconciliation of interests with the People's Republic. Thus, for example, in 2016, the Philippines under its new president, Rodgrigo Duterte, made approaches to China and distanced itself from the USA.[33]

---

[27]Scheerer and Raszelenberg (2002, pp. 189–220).
[28]Permanent Court of Arbitration (2016).
[29]AFP/dpa (2016) and Zhang (2014).
[30]This relates in particular to Vietnam and the Philippines with regard to the eastern Spratly Islands.
[31]Sakaki (2016, pp. 425–440).
[32]Lucena Silva and de Amorim (2016, pp. 441–468).
[33]Kreuzer (2016, p. 2).

3.3 The Convoluted History of Political Facts and Claims

Taiwan was discovered by the Portuguese in 1517 and then colonised by Spain and in particular the Netherlands. It was not essentially settled by Han Chinese until the mid-seventeenth century. Supporters of the Ming Dynasty who fled from the mainland ended Dutch colonial rule in 1662. Taiwan first came under Chinese rule in 1682 during the Qing Dynasty, which assigned it to the province of Fujian. It only became an independent province of China in 1886. From 1895 to 1945, Taiwan was ruled by Japan, and after that, only remained under Chinese rule for 4 years. In 1949, the Guomindang government fled to Taiwan, together with large swathes of the Party and military, and succeeded in preventing Chinese Communist Party troops from conquering the islands. The Spratly island of Taiping Dao was already taken over by Taiwan in 1946, and remains under Taiwanese occupation today.

Until 1971, the Guomindang regime on Taiwan represented China on the United Nations Security Council, before a fundamental political change in the USA led to a recognition of the People's Republic of China as the sole representation of China in the UN, even though the USA continued its military support of the Republic of China, which was no longer diplomatically recognised. Following gradual democratisation from the end of the 1980s onwards, the Guomindang won two more parliamentary and presidential elections, before a new party, the Democratic Progressive Party, won both elections for the first time in 2000 and 2004. However, it was not able to repeat its electoral success until 2016. Unlike the Guomindang, it emphasises the autonomy of Taiwan, although it does not dare to declare formal independence of the country, to be anchored in the constitution. The People's Republic always responds to political statements to this effect with the threat of military intervention. The USA also urges moderation with regard to efforts to attain independence, although it continues to play a key part in upgrading Taiwan's armaments.

The Senkaku/Diaoyu Islands belonged to the Celestial Empire at the latest from the sixteenth century onwards. After the Sino-Japanese War of 1894/1895, Japan took over rule not only over Korea and Taiwan, but also over the Senkaku/Diaoyu Islands, which were purchased by a Japanese businessman who built fish factories there. However, Japan declared that it had occupied the islands independently of the peace accord with China, as land that until that time had not belonged to anyone.[34] After the Second World War, all Japanese islands to the south of the 29th parallel (excluding Taiwan and the Pescadores) were placed under US military administration as regulated in the San Francisco Peace Treaty of 1951. They were only gradually returned to Japan by 1972, including the Senkaku/Diaoyu Islands, where crude oil and natural gas resources had been discovered in 1968/1969. Later, the Japanese state leased the islands before finally purchasing them in 2012. Both the

---

[34]The peace treaty of Shimonoseki in 1895 is still regarded in China today as a humiliatingly unfair agreement, as a result of which the dispute over the Senkaku/Diaoyu Islands involves deep-seated national emotions on both sides. On the different historical legal interpretations by Japan and China, see Kreuzer (2013, pp. 16–17).

People's Republic of China and Taiwan, which were not included in the peace treaty negotiations in 1951, protested against the allocation of the islands to Japan. After 1995, the People's Republic of China began deep drilling for oil near the island, during which Chinese fishing boats were repeatedly seized by the Japanese coastguard. One such operation in 2010 led to a collision between two ships, which triggered significant reprisals on both sides. Here, the USA provided assurance that it would abide by its alliance obligations towards Japan should war break out with China. In response, the Chinese foreign minister said that "every centimetre" of its territory would be defended. Since 1971, both Taiwan and Japan have repeatedly sent fishing and coastguard boats and warships, as well as reconnaissance planes, to the islands, which are occasionally also visited by civilians from both states, and have raised their flags there. Chinese from the People's Republic also set foot on the islands for the first time in 2004. From the end of the 1990s onwards, the People's Republic of China began to mine the mineral deposits on the border of its EEZ.[35]

When asserting their claims to the South China Sea, the two Chinese states invoke archaeological findings from early settlements on some of the islands from the seventh century onwards, and several maps and documents from the Celestial Empire dating from the eleventh century onwards, in which the South China Sea was classified as belonging to the Chinese domain. At that time, the islands were occasionally used above all by fishermen.

In 1816, a Vietnamese emperor also declared the Paracel Islands as belonging to Vietnamese territory. After France conquered Indochina in 1856–1887, a treaty with China in 1887 specified the Sino-Tonkin Delimitation Line, according to which the Paracel and Spratly Islands should belong to China. However, in 1925, France then declared the Paracel Islands as being part of its territory, followed in 1933 by the Spratly Islands, and occupied the former in 1938. After 1956, the French claims were adopted by South Vietnam, and later also North Vietnam. After temporary occupation by Japan during the Second World War, the Republic of China took over sovereignty of the Paracel Islands.[36] Only one island (Pattle Island, *Shanshu Dao*) was occupied by Vietnam in 1956, while the eastern islands were occupied by the People's Republic. Following armed skirmishes, troops from the People's Republic of China also took over the western Paracel Islands in 1974. In 2014, China erected a drilling platform in Vietnam's EEZ, which led to severe, but non-violent disputes between the two countries. Soon afterwards, China relocated the drilling platform to the Chinese island of Hainan, however.[37]

In 1973, South Vietnam declared the Spratly Islands to be part of its territory, and occupied several islands, which were then taken over in 1976 by communist, unified

---

[35]Kreuzer (2013, pp. 13–15).

[36]For a brief overview of the territorial conflicts in the South China Sea, see Kreuzer (2014, pp. 7–20). See also Kleine-Ahlbrandt (2012). A detailed analysis of the interests and positions of all states that are directly and indirectly involved is given in the contributions in Fels and Vu (2016). For a more detailed discussion of the issue: Tønneson (2002, pp. 6–23) and Raine and Le Mière (2013, pp. 29–54).

[37]Fähnders (2014), Bindenagel (2016, p. 510) and Abb (2016, pp. 151–155).

Vietnam. After 1980, China began occupying individual islands.[38] In 1988, this led to a sea battle with Vietnam, in which 70 Vietnamese soldiers died. In 2014, a violent dispute again arose between ships from both countries after the Chinese erected a drilling platform in waters belonging to the EEZ of Vietnam. In 1968, Philippine troops occupied eight of the Spratly Islands for the first time, and in 1978 also declared many other islands as belonging to Philippine territory. Malaysia followed suit on three southern Spratly islands. In April 2012, the first armed disputes occurred between Philippine and Chinese ships, which ended with China taking over control of the Scarborough Reef.[39] Since then, the western Pacific has seen a considerable increase in armaments. As a result of all the conflicts, the USA sent an air carrier off the Vietnamese in October 2012. Since 2012, China has an air carrier. Japan followed suit in 2015 and 2017 with two helicopter carriers. Australia also declared its intention to upgrade its armaments in 2016. India is also involved in the region, where despite protests from China, it purchased rights to oilfields in Vietnam's EEZ, alongside companies from the USA, without having demonstrated any military presence here thus far.

In recent years, US warships have repeatedly demonstratively sailed through the area around the South China Sea island groups, claiming that they are there to defend freedom of shipping outside of territorial waters. 60% of the US fleet is now located in the Pacific, following Barack Obama's pivot towards Asia in 2011.[40] The US Seventh Fleet has been sailing in the eastern Pacific since the Second World War. In January 2016, a US destroyer crossed the waters around the Paracel Islands, which are designated territorial waters by the People's Republic of China. A month later, evidence of Chinese air defence missiles was found on Woody Island. And in May 2018, it was reported that Chinese fighter jets and bombers had landed on the Paracel Islands. A significant build-up of arsenal by many states has therefore occurred in the South China Sea during the course of the new century, which every so often develops into military and paramilitary shows of force. As yet, no clear formal military alliance has been formed in this part of the world. However, it is clear that in terms of foreign policy, the People's Republic of China is fairly isolated in its efforts to expand its military presence in the China Seas, even though it is moving closer to Russia to a certain degree with regard to its military policy, without a solid alliance having been forged to date.[41] The USA is also not attempting to create a multilateral alliance in east and south-east Asia, although it does maintain an extremely differentiated network of bilateral treaties, armament supplies and political and diplomatic support with all states that border the Chinese Seas that feel threatened

---

[38]To be published shortly: Turcsányi (2019).
[39]Geinitz (2014). According to another source, there was a military dispute, China Power Team (2018).
[40]Lanteigne (2016, p. 100).
[41]Möller (2005).

in one way or another by the increase in Chinese economic and military power.[42] At the same time, the USA says that it is neutral when it comes to the territorial claims of the individual states, and emphasises the necessity for resolving these claims in a peaceful way, through bilateral and multilateral negotiations.[43]

3.4 Scenarios for an Escalation of the Conflict into a Third World War

From the analysis of the eight centres of conflict described briefly above, it emerges that no prognosis can be made as to where and when a more serious escalation of conflict may occur, that could lead to an acute risk of a world war. A larger war will only develop from a limited bilateral military dispute between one of the states bordering the South China Sea and China if the USA or Japan come to that state's assistance.[44] As the brief, limited war between the nuclear powers of Pakistan and India showed in 1999, even a war between the major powers can quickly be brought to an end when first the power that strives to change the status quo withdraws its troops, and when both powers wish to avoid a major war. In principle, therefore, not every military dispute between Chinese and US troops necessarily needs to lead to a world war, when the global power that wants to change the local status quo quickly realises that this will not be tolerated by the other global power. The key prerequisite that is likely to lead to a world war when it comes to a war between the upcoming global power that is China and the USA, which is losing influence as a global power, would either be that China, in its forceful expansion of regional power in east Asia, underestimates the willingness by the USA to wage war and US diplomacy fails to announce this willingness at an early stage during the development of the conflict. Allegedly, this is what occurred before Iraq announced its conquest of Kuwait in August 1990. Alternatively, however, the USA reaches the conclusion that as a diminishing global power, it needs to wage a major war, which is considered to be unavoidable, with the upcoming global power sooner rather than later, for which a local expansion on the part of China could serve as suitable grounds.

When the First World War was triggered, such considerations played an important role in the German Reich and in Austria-Hungary, when the murder in Sarajevo of the Habsburg heir to the throne, Archduke Ferdinand, offered a pretext for risking a war against Russia and France that was regarded as being unavoidable.[45] In individual cases, such considerations can also be heard today in the USA. Thus

---

[42]For a detailed discussion of the contradictory challenges faced by US politics, see Raine and Le Mière (2013, pp. 151–178).

[43]Nye (2015).

[44]Several conflict escalation scenarios, albeit not up to those on the brink of conflict scenarios, are presented by Raine and Le Mière (2013, pp. 187–193).

[45]See Jahn (2015a, p. 121). In the literature, many comparisons are made between the escalation of the conflicts and the naval armament process in the South China Sea and those between Britain and the German Reich before 1914.

the former Supreme Commander of the US land forces in Europe, Ben Hodges, stated at a security forum in Warsaw on 25 October 2018 that a war with China in the next 15 years was "not inevitable" but "highly likely".[46] In a comment on the article about this conference in the Frankfurter Allgemeine Zeitung newspaper, one reader expressed the idea of a preventive war against China even more clearly: "If the Chinese continue to grow in this way, the USA will soon be overtaken economically, and consequently also militarily. After all, a strong military requires a strong economy. China is permanently in the black, while America is permanently in the red. That has consequences. If the USA is to wage a war against China, therefore, then it will need to do so soon, before it is too late."[47]

Despite all the speculation surrounding a Third World War, which could result from a major war between the People's Republic of China and the USA, the situation today and in the future is and will be fundamentally different from that of 1914, 1939 and even 1962, when the USA would have been willing to wage a nuclear war with the Soviet Union if it had not revoked its covert stationing of nuclear missiles on Cuba. During the first half of the twentieth century and even as late as 1962, world wars with several tens of millions of war dead could still be won. It has only been since the end of the 1960s that the eradication of all of humanity has been technically possible in a comprehensive nuclear war, making any thought of a winnable Third World War impossible. As a result, such a war is an unlikely prospect, and a flexible escalation of conflict emerges in war scenarios, in which a restoration of the status quo ante or another form of compromise may be sought in the conflict that triggered the war. However, this does not preclude the possibility that military leaders and politicians may decide that winnable wars within a limited geographical area and with a limited use of weapons, and even nuclear wars, are possible in a regional conflict in east Asia. The Second World War was a limited war to the extent that the gas weapons available to both war alliances were not used.

3.5 Options for a Policy of Détente

What approach is likely to promote peace in the difficult, highly conflictual situation in east and south-east Asia?[48] A regulation of the conflicts through arbitration proceedings at the International Court of Justice at The Hague would be helpful, but for the time being, these will not be recognised by China, as its handling of the only arbitration issued so far, in July 2016, has shown. However, attempts should continue to be made to persuade the conflicting parties to agree to such proceedings. Furthermore, there is an urgent need for an international aviation legislation agreement, similar to the Convention on the Law of the Sea of 1982. In contrast to this

---

[46] sth.Ap (2018).

[47] Bert Fischer in response to a report by Hemicker (2018).

[48] For contributions on this subject, see: Kivimäki et al. (2002, pp. 131–164), Ohnesorge (2016, pp. 45–52), Bindenagel (2016, pp. 509–521), and Raine and Le Mière (2013, pp. 202–213).

convention, it would certainly be possible to develop procedures for establishing internationally recognised overlapping ADIZs since here, the issue is not the law relating to the exclusive national exploitation of natural resources, but merely traffic regulations. It appears to be highly feasible for states to commit to an obligation to provide information regarding plans to cross ADIZs by both civilian and military aircraft and missiles. However, it is unlikely that such flight movements can be approved by national authorities, since most states wish to retain the right to free air traffic in air spaces that are not subject to any national sovereignty. China is willing to resolve contentious issues through bilateral negotiations as far as possible. Thus, for example, it was possible to conclude treaties with Vietnam regarding the border and fishing rights in the Gulf of Tonkin, which have been in force, and also respected, since 2004.[49] In 2002, a limited multilateralisation of obligations to take peaceful measures in cases of conflict was made possible in the form of the Declaration on Conduct (DoC) of ASEAN and China in the South China Sea. Numerous international fora in and around south-east Asia, with changing memberships (ASEAN with China, Japan and South Korea, and occasionally also India, Australia, New Zealand and the USA) offer an opportunity for restraint in dealing with conflicts, also to date, almost no conflicts have been resolved as a result.

The policy of détente means that no attempts are made to resolve opposing interpretations of the law regarding the ownership by individual states of islands and land elevations in the China Seas through violence. However, this also means that the occupation of islands and artificial islands with military bases, which are contested bi- or multilaterally, or the settlement of fishermen and civilian authorities, must be effectively accepted if this can also continue to be contested through political and legal means. Since the navy and airforce of the People's Republic of China are being increasingly expanded, and become ever more superior to the competing states of Vietnam, the Philippines and others, a further expansion of Chinese bases can be anticipated through the development of land areas above water on atolls and sandbanks in the South China Sea. Only the USA and Japan, with their high degree of economic power, are in a position to counteract this development by providing political and economic support and military backup to competing island construction projects by the smaller bordering states in a form of dangerous competition for land seizure. This does nothing to alter the fact that political pressure must continue to be applied to all bordering states to recognise each other's existing EEZs, and also that the stipulation in UNCLOS must be observed that no EEZs are created through the construction and settlement of artificial islands. However, it is also possible that conflicts over disputed islands and land features and the waters that surround them could be regulated through a condominium of the states involved in the dispute, as was recommended, for example, by P. Kreuzer for the Senkaku/Diaoyu Islands.[50] The joint economic use of disputed waters can also de-escalate conflicts.

---

[49]Zhang (2014) and Kreuzer (2014, p. 11).
[50]Kreuzer (2013, pp. 22–24).

3.5 Options for a Policy of Détente

However, the problem remains that in the disputed parts of the South China Sea, huge areas are only covered by shallow water, in which it is becoming ever easier to exploit the mineral resources at a reasonable financial cost, in contrast to the high sea with very deep waters. If there is no will to apply the principle of "first come, first served", a regulation for this problem must be found in international law that has also been agreed internationally. One option is to declare the disputed waters as international nature reserves.

The centres of conflict described above in the East China Sea, and above all in the South China Sea will present enormous challenges in the coming decades to the peace and de-escalation diplomacy of all states, particularly the major powers, the regional international organisations and the United Nations. Germany and the EU, which have no direct interests and alliance obligations, but which do have significant trade interests in the region,[51] will have no option but to repeatedly state their position with regard to these challenges in east and south-east Asia. The idea that has been expressed for decades, of first convening a conference and then creating an organisation for security and cooperation in east Asia, with the involvement of the ten ASEAN members, Russia, China, Japan, the two Koreas, India, the USA, Australia and New Zealand, could still be realised today.[52] At the same time, parallel negotiations regarding armament control between these states would also be helpful.

As the experiences in the east-west conflict between 1944 and 1991 show, a climate of international détente has the major advantage, among others, of avoiding evaluating individual, precarious situations such as smaller military skirmishes or illegal flight or ship movements as being indicators of a forthcoming larger-scale aggression, but enabling them instead to be handled in a de-escalatory manner as isolated conflicts. Perhaps the most famous example of this is now the decision made by the Soviet lieutenant colonel Stanislav Petrov on 26 September 1983 in Serpuchovo-15 near Moscow to interpret the report issued by the early warning system on his computer that five US nuclear missiles had been launched as a false alarm, and not to order an early, comprehensive retaliatory Soviet attack, which would probably have been demanded by the Soviet leadership.[53] It is likely that the error in the warning system was caused by a sunbeam deflected by a cloud. In the period of détente that emerged after the missile crisis of 1962, and which remained until the end of the east-west conflict, the Soviet lieutenant colonel, to put it simply, was in a position to think that clearly, it was the computer that had messed up, and not the military and political leadership of the USA. And this was despite the fact that following the Soviet intervention in Afghanistan, the stationing of SS 20 missiles in eastern Europe, and the development by NATO of Pershing II medium-range missiles and cruise missiles, relations had again become more strained than they had

---

[51] Will (2016, pp. 473–474, 487–489).

[52] Currently, this idea has no relevant proponents in east Asia. A more realistic prospect are bilateral contacts between Chinese and US military officials for the purpose of developing mutual trust.

[53] Bidder (2010).

been during the 1970s. In addition, a few days previously, Soviet fighter jets had shot down a Korean civilian plane, which had inadvertently strayed into Soviet airspace.

In a period of mutual threats of war, such as between the North Korean party leader Kim Jong-un and US president Donald Trump at the beginning of 2018, technical failures or random military skirmishes could far more easily trigger a larger war than in a calmer international atmosphere.

3.6 The Prospect of Repeated Conflict Escalations

Local conflict escalations over islands and land features, and the presence of fishing boats, coastguard and marine units, in disputed waters of the South China Sea, which have become more numerous since the 2010s, will probably continue into the next decade. It is likely that they can be closely contained, even if they will lead to an increase in the power of the Chinese navy and airforce in the region. However, China is no less interested than the other bordering states in upholding the freedoms of global commercial shipping in the western Pacific. It is rather unlikely that China will succeed in entirely forcing the military shipping traffic of other states, particularly the USA, out of the South and East China Sea. However, it will considerably expand its island-supported military bases, its aircraft carriers and fleet capacities, and thus limit the military dominance of the USA. An expansion of ASEAN to form a military alliance is unlikely, due to the extremely different perceptions of threat and security interests of its member countries.[54] Thus, China will not feel seriously encircled, even though it continues to feel threatened by the policy of containment by the USA. It depends less on these conflicts themselves than on the general state of political relations between China, the USA and Japan with regard to global trade, the mutual armament process and international organisations, whether individual armed clashes could escalate into a wider military conflict or even war. A war becomes more likely when public opinion in both the states involved is systematically stimulated at state level and the sovereignty over an island or waters is exaggeratedly presented as being of vital national interest, as has been the case for decades with the Kurile Islands between the Soviet Union/Russia and Japan.

A particularly dangerous scenario is one in which a decision is made in parliament and in a referendum to rename the Republic of China the Republic of Taiwan, and in favour of its independence. In such a case, the possibility cannot be excluded that the People's Republic will intervene militarily. The USA would then be faced with the problem of being required to uphold its obligations towards Taiwan,[55] at risk of losing the credibility of its global security and alliance policy in Japan, south-east Asia and in remote regions of the world. In such a case, a world war could only

---

[54]See the observations of an assumption that the inclination among developing countries in general, and in south-east Asia, to firmly commit themselves in terms of their security policy after the east-west conflict, Ciorciari (2010, pp. 240–247).

[55]Taiwan Relations Act (1979) and Six Assurances (2016).

be prevented by a joint declaration by the USA and the community of states not to recognise Taiwan, despite its declaration of independence, and not to accept it as a member of the United Nations so long as there is no change of attitude among the Chinese population.

This notwithstanding, it can be assumed that local shifts in power in the South China Sea at relatively short time intervals will lead to military manoeuvres and diplomatic disputes that will be cause for consternation, and which will cause observers to fear a war between China, the upcoming global power, and the USA. As long as the USA is clearly superior to China militarily, China under the highly rational, calculating regime of the Communist Party, will not risk entering into a war with the USA. A more dangerous scenario is the prospect of emotionally heated public opinion and an unpredictable president in the USA if the disputes described above in one of the centres of conflict in the East and South China Sea do escalate.

The extensive process of armament on all sides throughout east Asia is almost impossible to halt through armament control agreements. At best, this will occur as a result of severe setbacks in the economies of individual states or the entire region. Any large conflict in south-east Asia will further undermine the limitations of Japan's military policy as enshrined in its constitution.

References

Abb P (2016) Punish the Philippines, forgive Vietnam? The South China Sea disputes in the eyes of Chinese experts. In: Fels E, Vu TM (eds) 2016 Power politics in Asia's contested waters. Territorial disputes in the South China Sea. Springer, Heidelberg, pp 139–157

Acharya A (2012) The making of Southeast Asia. International relations of a region. Cornell University Press, Ithaca, NY

AFP/dpa (2016) Südchinesisches Meer. Schiedsgericht weist Chinas Ansprüche zurück. Der Tagesspiegel, 12 July. https://www.tagesspiegel.de/politik/suedchinesisches-meer-schiedsgericht-weist-chinas-ansprueche-ab/13863892.html

Bidder B (2010) Der Mann, der den dritten Weltkrieg verhinderte. Spiegel online, 21 April. http://www.spiegel.de/einestages/vergessener-held-a-948852-druck.html

Bindenagel JD (2016) Pacific community for peace and governance: towards a framework for peace and security in the pacific. In: Fels E, Vu TM (eds) 2016 Power politics in Asia's contested waters. Territorial disputes in the South China Sea. Springer, Heidelberg, pp 509–521

boj (2014) Streit um Rohstoffe. China baut vierte künstliche Insel. Spiegel online, 18 November. http://www.spiegel.de/wissenschaft/technik/china-baut-kuenstliche-insel-im-suedchinesischen-meer-an-spratly-islands-a-1004769.html

Burgers TJ (2016) An unmanned South China Sea? Understanding the risks and implications of the digital and robotic revolution in military affairs in the SCS. In: Fels E, Vu TM (eds) 2016 Power politics in Asia's contested waters. Territorial disputes in the South China Sea. Springer, Heidelberg, pp 77–94

Carpio A (2016) South China Sea/West Philippine Sea. http://maritimereview.ph/2016/03/01/south-china-seawest-philippine-sea-dispute/

China Power Team (2018) Are maritime law enforcement forces destabilizing Asia? https://chinapower.csis.org/maritime-forces-destabilizing-asia/

Ciorciari JD (2010) The limits of alignment. Southeast Asia and the great powers since 1975. Georgetown University Press, Washington, DC

Fähnders T (2014) Südchinesisches Meer: China beendet Ölbohrung in umstrittenen Gewässern. FAZ-Net, 16 July. http://www.faz.net/aktuell/wirtschaft/agenda/suedchinesisches-meer-china-beendet-oelbohrung-in-umstrittenen-gewaessern-13048253.html

Fähnders T (2016) Südchinesisches Meer: Fischereistreit mit Sprengkraft. FAZ-Net, 25 April. http://www.faz.net/aktuell/politik/ausland/asien/fischereistreit-mit-china-indonesien-wehrt-sich-publikumswirksam-14183780.html

FAZ (2016) China verlegt Kampfflugzeuge auf umstrittene Insel. FAZ-Net, 24 February. http://www.faz.net/aktuell/politik/ausland/asien/suedchinesisches-meer-china-verlegt-kampfflugzeuge-auf-umstrittene-insel-14087379.html

FAZ (2019) China schließt Einsatz von Gewalt gegen Taiwan nicht aus. Frankfurter Allgemeine Zeitung, 3 January, p. 2

Fels E, Vu TM (eds) (2016) Power politics in Asia's contested waters. Territorial disputes in the South China Sea. Springer, Heidelberg

Geinitz C (2014) China errichtet künstliche Inseln vor den Philippinen. FAZ-Net, 11 June. http://www.faz.net/aktuell/wirtschaft/agenda/territorialstreit-im-suedchinesischen-meer-china-errichtet-kuenstliche-inseln-vor-den-philippinen-12983649/chinesische-landnahme-12983667.html

Hemicker L (2018) Pekings Weg zur Supermacht. Droht ein Krieg mit China? FAZ-Net, 25 October. http://www.faz.net/aktuell/politik/supermacht-china/pekings-weg-zur-supermacht-droht-ein-krieg-mit-china-15856441.html

Jahn E (2015a) Sarajevo 1914. A century of debate about the Guilt for the first world war. In: World political challenges. Political issues under debate, vol 3. Springer, Heidelberg, pp 91–117

Jahn E (2015b) Kashmir: flashpoint for a nuclear war or even a third world war? In: World political challenges. Political issues under debate, vol 3. Springer, Heidelberg, pp 205–220

Jahn E (2015c) Escalating conflict in Korea due to nuclear armament? Or prospects for national unification. In: Jahn, Egbert 2015: international politics. political issues under debate, vol 1. Springer, Heidelberg, pp 203–218

Kaplan RD (2011) The South China Sea is the future of conflict. Foreign Policy. https://foreignpolicy.com/2011/08/15/the-south-china-sea-is-the-future-of-conflict/

Kivimäki T, Odgaard L, Tønneson S (2002) What could be done? In: Kivimäki T (ed) (2002) War or peace in the South China Sea? NIAS Press, Kopenhagen, pp 131–164

Klare MT (2015) Schatzsuche in tiefsten Gewässern. Le Monde diplomatique, 12 February. http://www.monde-diplomatique.de/pm/2015/02/13/a0049.text

Kleine-Ahlbrandt S (2012) Chinas Expansion ins Meer. Le Monde diplomatique, 9 November. http://www.monde-diplomatique.de/pm/2012/11/09.mondeText1.artikel,a0008.idx,0

Kreuzer P (2013) Chinas Luftverteidigungszone und der Konflikt um die Diaoyu/Senkaku-Inseln. HSFK-Report No. 9. Frankfurt am Main

Kreuzer P (2014) Konfliktherd Südchinesisches Meer. HSFK-Report No. 2. Frankfurt am Main

Kreuzer P (2016) Zwei Regierungswechsel und ein Urteil: Die Philippinen und Taiwan im Konflikt um das Südchinesische Meer. HSFK-Report No. 10. Frankfurt am Main

Lanteigne M (2016) The South China Sea in China's developing maritime strategy. In: Fels E, Vu TM (eds) 2016 Power politics in Asia's contested waters. Territorial disputes in the South China Sea. Springer, Heidelberg, pp 97–115

Löchel C (ed) (2018) Der neue Fischer Weltalmanach 2019. Fischer, Frankfurt am Main

Lucena Silva AH, de Amorim WD (2016) Australia, India and Japan: the three 'worried outsiders' and their strategies towards the South China Sea. In: Fels E, Vu TM (eds) 2016 Power politics in Asia's contested waters. Territorial disputes in the South China Sea. Springer, Heidelberg, pp 441–468

Möller K (2005) Die Außenpolitik der Volksrepublik China 1949–2004. Eine Einführung. Verlag für Sozialwissenschaften, Wiesbaden

Nine-Dash Line (2019) https://en.wikipedia.org/wiki/Nine-Dash_Line

Nye JS (2015) Chinas entschlossener Griff nach Riffs und Inseln. Die Presse, 21 June. https://diepresse.com/home/meinung/gastkommentar/4759658/Chinas-entschlossener-Griff-nach-Riffs-und-Inseln

References

Ohnesorge HW (2016) A sea of troubles: international law and the spitsbergen plus approach to conflict management in the South China Sea. In: Fels E, Vu TM (eds) 2016 Power politics in Asia's contested waters. Territorial disputes in the South China Sea. Springer, Heidelberg, pp 523–537

Page J (2013) The A to Z on China's air defense identification zone. The Wall Street Journal, 27 November. https://blogs.wsj.com/chinarealtime/2013/11/27/the-a-to-z-on-chinas-air-defense-identification-zone

Permanent Court of Arbitration (2016) The South China Sea Arbitration (The Republic of the Philippines v. The People's Republic of China. http://bit.ly/29KQ1gF

Poling GB (2013) The South China Sea in focus: clarifying the limits of maritime dispute. Rowman & Littlefield, Lanham

Raine S, Le Mière C (2013) Regional disorder: the South China Sea disputes. Routledge, Abingdon

Rosenbusch B (2002) Die Bedeutung inner- und zwischenstaatlicher Konflikte für die Kooperation und Integration der ASEAN-Staaten. LIT Verlag, Münster

Sakaki A (2016) Keeping the dragon at bay: the South China Sea dispute in Japan's security strategy. In: Fels E, Vu TM (eds) 2016 Power politics in Asia's contested waters. Territorial disputes in the South China Sea. Springer, Heidelberg, pp 425–440

Scheerer H, Raszelenberg P (2002) China, Vietnam und die Gebietsansprüche im Südchinesischen Meer. Institut für Asienkunde, Hamburg

Six Assurances (2016) H.Con.Res.88 – reaffirming the Taiwan Relations Act and the Six Assurances as cornerstones of United States-Taiwan relations. https://www.congress.gov/bill/114th-congress/house-concurrent-resolution/88/text/eh

sth.Ap (2018) Ex-General warnt vor Krieg zwischen USA und China. Spiegel online, 25 October. http://www.spiegel.de/politik/ausland/usa-ex-general-ben-hodges-warnt-vor-krieg-mit-china-a-1235015.html

Taiwan Relations Act (1979). https://www.ait.org.tw/our-relationship/policy-history/key-u-s-foreign-policy-documents-region/taiwan-relations-act/

Thomas G (2018) Willkommen im Wohnzimmer. Frankfurter Allgemeine Zeitung, 22 November, p 9

Tønneson S (2002) The history of the dispute. In: Kivimäki T (ed) (2002) War or peace in the South China Sea? NIAS Press, Kopenhagen

Turcsányi RQ (2019) Chinese assertiveness in the South China Seas: power sources, domestic politics, and reactive foreign policy (global power shift). Springer, Heidelberg

United Nations (1982) United Nations Convention on the Law of the Sea 1982. www.un.org/Depts/los/convention_agreements/texts/unclos/unclos_e.pdf

Will G (2016) Distant partners: Europe and the South China Sea. In: Fels E, Vu TM (eds) 2016 Power politics in Asia's contested waters. Territorial Disputes in the South China Sea. Springer, Heidelberg, pp 469–191

Zhang H (2014) China's position on the territorial disputes in the South China Sea between China and the Philippines, 3 April. http://ph.china-embassy.org/eng/xwfb/t1143881.htm

World Peace—Even Through War: The Role of the USA in Preserving Security in the International System

Abstract

The various concepts of the global policy of the USA and their assessments are the subject of a great deal of controversy. In the individual countries, differently distributed essentialist pro- and anti-American attitudes predominate. These either emphasise positive elements of this policy, such as the securing of world peace, democracy and human rights in many countries, or negative elements such as war crimes, policies of using force, a cynical violation of human rights and ignorance of the democratic decisions made by other peoples, and render them absolute. However, US global policy is extremely ambivalent and not infrequently fluctuates between the extremes of a liberal-democratic global peace policy, which also does not exclude war as a means of achieving this aim, and an arch-conservative policy of national isolation. As a result, a differentiated analysis and assessment of the achievements of US global policy that have promoted peace and democracy and those actions that have repeatedly led to the loss of hundreds of thousands of lives is necessary with reference to global-human considerations.

The aim of this brief study is first to explain the apparent internal contradiction between the pursuit of a global peace policy through war with clarifications of the concepts involved, in order to then focus on the decisive turning points in US foreign policy since it entered the global stage. This began after the continental expansion of the USA with a brief phase of colonialist imperialism at the end of the nineteenth century, which then mutated into a policy of global opening up of the markets throughout the world to the increasing level of interest in the USA in sales markets and raw materials. During the First World War under Woodrow Wilson, it took on its conceptual form, which remains influential until this day, for which the world has to thank for the creation of the /League of Nations and later the United Nations. However, as well as forming a universal league of states designed to secure peace, promoting liberal-democratic state orders and a

---

Lecture given on 2.2.2015.

© Springer Nature Switzerland AG 2020
E. Jahn, *War and Compromise Between Nations and States*,
https://doi.org/10.1007/978-3-030-34131-2_4

pluralistic global public, also, under certain circumstances, by means of military intervention, it was also aimed at developing a liberal, capitalist global market in which the USA economy could dominate. This "idealism" has, however, repeatedly been shown to be contradictory in the name of the precedence given to American national interests, be it in the name of isolationism or imperialism or with a view to a "political realism" anchored in European traditions. It strives to create an international power balance that also does not exclude the possibility of limited wars.

For an incalculable length of time, the future of global society and of world peace will depend to a highly fundamental degree on the political development of US society, over which other democracies certainly can and also should exert their influence, however minor it may be.

4.1 The Ambiguous Nature of Peace and War as Concepts

For many people, not only in the USA, the United States of America have to a certain degree been the main guarantor of world peace and international security, human rights and democratic values since the early twentieth century and then above all following the collapse of communist party rule in eastern Europe and the end of the east-west conflict. For many others, the USA is the most important imperialist power in world history, which with brutal, bloody force repeatedly strives to assert the interests of its economic and political power elite in all regions of the world, and in so doing, cynically violates human rights and democratic principles in other countries.

The creation of the two international organisations whose influence extends across the world, first the League of Nations (1920–1946) and then the United Nations (since 24 October 1945), which have made the preservation and, if necessary, the restoration of global peace and international security their main aim,[1] is unthinkable without the power political role played by the USA as the driver and initiator of the formation of the new world orders after the First and Second World Wars. At the same time, there has been almost no single year since 1945 in which US troops have not been at war somewhere in the world; and no longer, as before, to defend or expand US territory, but to intervene in other states with the aim of

---

[1] "The high contracting parties, in order to promote international co-operation and to achieve international peace and security by the acceptance of obligations not to resort to war...agree to this Covenant of the League of Nations". "Any war or threat of war...is hereby declared a matter of concern to the whole League, and the League shall take any action that may be deemed wise and effectual to safeguard the peace of nations. Preamble and Art. 11, Covenant (1919). "The Purposes of the United Nations are: 1. To maintain international peace and security, and to that end: to take effective collective measures for the prevention and removal of threats to the peace, and for the suppression of acts of aggression or other breaches of the peace..." Art. 1 Charter (1945).

4.1 The Ambiguous Nature of Peace and War as Concepts

political or regime change. Historians even claim that "Since the thirteen colonies declared their independence from England in 1776 and in a revolutionary war liberated themselves from the yoke of British colonial rule, this country has almost uninterruptedly been embroiled in military conflicts."[2]

How can the innate contradiction be explained of a power promoting global peace which is permanently at war? When making a first attempt at answering this question, the first task is to undertake a thorough discussion of what is generally understood as being "war" and "peace", and what should usefully be understood by these terms from an academic perspective. During the second stage, the political behaviour of the USA should be presented as a contemporary overview and be assessed with regard to its own frequently cited principles of peace, democracy and human rights.

Both words, war and peace, are used in very different ways, depending on the situation and context, and thus mean very different concepts. This must be brought to mind if one wishes to understand the title of this lecture ("World peace—even through war"), which may appear to some people to be a purely polemical play on words with a logical contradiction. At first glance, war and peace are unequivocally contradictory concepts. Peace is brought to an end when war dominates, and conversely, when war is brought to an end, peace returns. In times in which wars were declared and were brought to an end by peace accords, war and peace were clearly separate from each other as two different states, in which different laws applied. After 1918, however, only a small number of wars were formally declared; most were simply started, although they were still frequently brought to an end by a peace accord. However, some wars end only after a ceasefire has been agreed, without a peace accord being signed. This was the case with Germany, which did not sign a peace accord after 1945, while in Korea, there has only been a ceasefire since 1953, but no peace in the legal sense. Some wars are also declared without the warring parties becoming involved in military action against each other.[3] The legal concept of war must therefore also be supplemented by a social-political one.

In the older political thinking, only larger armed conflicts between states or pre-state ruling organisations were considered to be wars, while inner-state armed conflicts were termed revolutions, rebellions, unrest, uprisings or similar, albeit occasionally also civil wars. However, during the twentieth century, longer and more intensive armed conflicts within states increasingly became labelled civil wars, so that attempts were also made to regulate them under international law. They have now become the most frequent form of war, as wars intended to bring about change to the existing regime or national-territorial separation. In many cases, foreign states

---

[2]Emmerich and Gassert (2014, p. 10).

[3]For example, after the declaration of war by Britain and France against the German Reich on 3 September 1939 until March 1940, in the phony war (drôle de guerre), there were almost no armed disputes. Many other states which later declared war against the German Reich did not send any troops to the theatres of war.

are involved in civil wars, with their own troops,[4] without this leading to war on the territory of the intervening state, so that the majority of the people living in this country does not regard themselves as being at war.

War can be described as a form of armed political conflict and thus as separate from metaphorical uses of the term "war" which are sometimes applied to severe conflicts per se, such as those between married couples (marital war) or polemical debates between politicians or academics (war of words). Accordingly, the Cold War of 1945–1962 between the victorious powers of the Second World War was not a war, but a specific form of extremely tense inter-state relations with a permanent readiness to go to war and the threat of a nuclear war.[5]

In the conceptual boundary zone between war and peace, there are armed, deadly activities such as border incidents, skirmishes, coups, political assassinations, terror attacks, uprisings, "covert activities" and many others. Their essential difference is in their intensity, duration and frequently also the actors of wars. In the interim, war statisticians differentiate between "armed conflicts" with relatively few casualties and full wars, in which at least 1000 people are killed every year.[6] Extensive, single-sided killing, as is the case with massacres and mass murders, which can cost far more human lives than a war, is not a special form of war, since fighting and the mutual willingness and ability to kill is an inherent part of war. Extensive armed conflicts between criminal gangs who are not pursuing any political goal, but at most are seeking to secure financial enrichment or the satisfaction of physical aggression, are difficult to define as war.[7] Thus, war can be understood as a "socially organised form of a political fight of longer duration, involving the acceptance of the need to kill a large number of fighters and people who are not directly involved".[8]

The standard definitions of peace are far more varied and contentious than the definitions of war. For most people who are suffering in a war or who still have living memory of a war, peace occurs when war ends. Peace is non-war, regardless of what form peace takes. Often, however, with a greater distance from the last war, it is claimed that peace is more than non-war.[9] The peace researcher Johan Galtung

---

[4]Nine percent of all wars from 1945 to 2000 were civil wars with external participation. Of all civil wars, the ratio between anti-regime wars and autonomy/secession wars from 1945 to 2000 was calculated in a war statistics study as being 35:26%, see Rabehl and Schreiber (2001, p. 16). Before 2009, 241 wars were counted, Schreiber (2011, p. 13). Other figures result from different calculation methods, Heidelberg Institute (2015), The International Institute (2015), Petersson and Themnér (2012).

[5]According to this specific, historical definition of the Cold War, not all inter-state tensions which do not result in any serious threat of nuclear war should be defined as a Cold War, in order to abet non-military containment policy.

[6]Harbom and Wallensteen (2010).

[7]At the same time, some authors subsume these armed conflicts under the term "new wars", Rabehl and Schreiber (2001, p. 39). It is said that the "new wars" are "characterised [by a] blurring of the boundaries between war ..., organised crime ... and massive violations of human rights", Kaldor (2012, p.8).

[8]Jahn, Egbert (2012, pp. 32–33).

[9]Brock (2006, pp. 95–114).

accordingly introduced the differentiation between a "negative peace" (absence of war) and a "positive peace" (absence of personal and "structural violence").[10] However, the "more" is understood in very different ways. For generations of socialists, it was only possible to talk of real peace when all causes of war were removed and people had liberated themselves from exploitation, poverty, suppression and class rule; in other words, when capitalism had been wiped out worldwide and a socialist or communist world order had been established. By contrast, for liberal democrats, real peace is only possible in a prospering capitalist market economy and in a democratic international community in which fundamental human and citizens' rights are respected.

The fatal aspect of any understanding of a positive peace is that it is not only used by pacifists who want to initiate peace through peaceful, non-violent means, but that it is also often used as a legitimisation of wars through which real peace is to be created in the long term. The politically most relevant protagonists of the opposing and incompatible concepts of peace that have dominated world history since 1917 were Thomas Woodrow Wilson (1856–1924) and Vladimir Ilyich Lenin (1870–1924), as a result of which it was possible to speak of an antagonism between Wilsonianism and Leninism.[11] The "final battle" in the hymn of the internationalist socialists and communists was to be the war to end all wars, just like some democratic missionary wars. The slogan "War Against War" not only referred to the non-violent fight against war and perceived causes of war, but a real war that was to bring about lasting peace. In this sense, the title of this lecture, "World peace—also through war", not only plays on a logical contradiction in terms, but also expresses a concept of peace that is widespread throughout the world, which regards some wars as being a means to create peace. This is also the dominant understanding of peace in US society.

4.2 Ambivalences in US American Global Policy

In a sense, US American political thinking[12] is globally political. The declaration of independence of 1776 proclaimed universal human rights and laid a claim to these rights against a British global power that was perceived as being despotic. After independence was achieved, the United States spent the next hundred years focussing mainly on shaping its domestic framework and on territorial expansion in North America. It wanted to maintain a distance from the old world of Europe and Asia, with its despotism, wars, monarchies, nobility and clerical rule and unjust regimes, and to avoid becoming embroiled in its conflicts (isolationism). With the Monroe Doctrine, the USA attempted to both shield the Latin American republics that were

---

[10] Galtung (1969, pp. 167–191). For a critical assessment: Jahn (2012, pp. 37–39).
[11] See: Mayer (1964). The opposing approaches of Wilsonianism and Leninism are also referred to in the extensive literature on Wilson, e.g. Levin (1968, pp. 13–49 et seq).
[12] See: Schwabe (2006, pp. 3–10), Kissinger (2014, pp. 265–311).

liberating themselves from their European colonial rulers in revolutionary wars from the European colonial powers and to gain influence itself over their domestic affairs.

The end of continental westward expansion and the at times highly contentious decision not to expand northwards and southwards to conquer Canada, Mexico and Central America, went hand in hand with the development of the USA into a leading industrial and commercial power in the world, which sought new sales markets and sources of raw materials beyond the continent. At first, this led to a dispute between those who wished to see a shift to a traditional, imperialist policy of conquest and colonial rule and those who wished to satisfy US American foreign trade interests in an anti-colonialist way. At the end of the nineteenth century, the imperialists initially gained the upper hand, and turned the USA into a colonial power, with the conquest of Cuba, Puerto Rico, Hawaii, Guam and the Philippines. Already prior to that, footholds had also been gained in the Pacific (Samoa, etc.) and the Panama Canal zone (to link the trade and war fleets in the Atlantic and Pacific). However, shortly afterwards, the USA abandoned a policy of establishing direct colonial rule over individually segregated territories, and from then on, after intensive internal disputes, pursued an "open door" policy. This was first applied to China in order to thwart the efforts of the European colonial powers to divide up the Chinese Empire among themselves, and to secure an unlimited sales market and sources of raw materials for the USA economy. At the same time, however, a protectionist policy long provided a defence against unwanted foreign competition. The rise of the USA to become an expanding industrial power therefore provided the impetus to expand the western hemisphere policy to become a trans-oceanic global policy,[13] which was to turn the USA into an "informal global empire", as it was sometimes called, and ultimately into a global hegemonial power.[14] This was done in the name of the universal moral mission of the exceptional US American nation to bring freedom and democracy to all of humankind. To this end, not only peaceful, diplomatic and economic means are used, but also military means, which will be the sole topic of discussion below.

As well as the global missionary ideal that still continues to inspire US foreign policy today to conduct crusades in order to promote its understanding of freedom and democracy, the traditional European attitudes, with their categories of power politics and national interest (naturally more precisely defined by the specific interests of the power elites), which since 1648 has tended to recognise an international power balance, has played a huge role in American politics. In the name of political realism, well-known individuals such as Hans Morgenthau,[15] Henry Kissinger[16] or Zbigniew Brzezinski[17] have repeatedly placed the role of the USA

---

[13]Heideking (1999, pp. 227–244), Heideking and Mauch (2008), Sautter (1986, pp. 305–327), Schwabe (2006, pp. 18–42).

[14]On the difference between empire and hegemony see Menzel (2015, pp. 29–65), on the qualification of the USA as a global hegemonial power (pp. 833–1014).

[15]See the basic work of political realism Morgenthau (2005).

[16]Kissinger (2014).

[17]Brzezinski (2012, 2016). On Brezinski's geopolitical concept, see Feiner (2000, pp. 165–211).

as a global power, as well as geopolitical strategy, at the forefront of political thinking, rather than international global peace. "The debate within America is frequently presented as a conflict between idealism and realism. Both America and the rest of the world could one day realise that America must learn to act in both modes—otherwise, it might be that it becomes unable to fulfil its tasks in either of the two modes."[18]

4.3 Security Structures in the International Systems Since the Eighteenth Century

It was not until America was discovered and conquered by Europeans at the end of the fifteenth century that a global system gradually came into being that consists of states and pre-state entities of rule into which the older, partial worlds of humanity were incorporated over time. This process was at all times linked to attempts to form a global system that secured freedom at least temporarily. In 1494, on the initiative of the Roman Catholic pope Alexander VI, the two Iberian colonial empires, Spain and Portugal, divided up the world between them into two hemispheres in the Treaty of Tordesillas. The bizonal world structure was destroyed by the rise of the two Protestant colonial empires of Great Britain and the Netherlands, as well as France. The Thirty Years' War brought to an end the notion of a papal or imperial universal monarchy, at least in Europe, although it still remained alive in the Ottoman caliphate and sultanate and in south and East Asia.

The Westphalian system of sovereign territorial states that was created in 1648 initially remained restricted to Europe, although it spread throughout the world with the expansion of the European colonial powers, whereby the pre-state territories of rule were dissolved. Since then, the territorial state has been the basic element of the modern state system, which from the point of view of the predominance of several states was an inter-imperial system. Within this system, it was possible to mitigate the destructive power of wars, despite new technological developments. Ideas for a "Fürstenbund", or "League of Princes", as an alliance of peace were never realised. However, this system was again fundamentally transformed by nationalism, which began after the American and French revolutions at the end of the eighteenth century to turn the system of territorial states into one of national states (an international system in the proper sense of the word).[19] This process led to a dramatic increase in the number of states[20] after 1878. While in 1900, there were just 50 states in the

---

[18]See recently e.g. Kissinger (2014, p. 375) at the end of the chapter: The United States: an ambivalent superpower.

[19]In the political sciences, the expression "international system" is often reassigned to the order between pre-state and pre-national ruling organisations in previous centuries or even millennia, such as those of Greece and China, Holsti (1994). Usually, the English word "national" is used for the German "staatlich".

[20]For more detail on this subject, see the three lectures on the formation of the nation states in: Jahn (2015, pp. 1–53).

world, since 2011, there have been 193 member states of the United Nations. The federation of the USA, which on 4 July 1789 consisted of 13 states that became independent in 1783, is the first nation state in history.

The bipolar, Spanish-Portuguese imperial system was finally brought to an end after the Spanish war of succession of 1701–1714 by an organically emergent, multipolar system that was not centrally or jointly planned, that was for the first time to be secured by a concept of a balance of power between five major powers. This system was thrown into turmoil by the two proto-world wars of 1756–1763 and 1792–1815, but was consolidated by the treaties of the Congress of Vienna. However, in political and societal terms, it had already been split into two liberal, gradually democratising western major powers—Great Britain and France—and three still mainly autocratic major powers in the east—Austria, Prussia (later the German Reich) and Russia.[21] On the fringes of the European Pentarchy, the Ottoman Empire was also half-heartedly included in the new imperial state order. The Catholic-Protestant-Orthodox Christian Holy Alliance of the three eastern powers, together with the two western powers, were increasingly inclined to view the Ottoman Empire as a type of bankruptcy asset that they would divide up amongst themselves, for which purpose they instrumentalised the demands among the Balkan peoples for their own nation state. Until that point, all security regulations were designed a priori to have a historical time limit. They were adjusted to new power relations through limited wars.

The notion of a permanent world peace order as a state order supported by the peoples or nations (an association of states in the sense of a League of Nations) had already been developed since the Enlightenment and the French Revolution by philosophers such as Jean-Jacques Rousseau (1712–1778) and Immanuel Kant (1724–1804). It has been propagated by a liberal and a socialist peace movement during the nineteenth century. However, it did not become historically significant until the initiative launched by the president of the USA, Thomas Woodrow Wilson (1856–1924). The First World War provided the impulse to turn the idea into reality. During the war, the neutral USA rose to become a global economic power due to its commercial and financial support of the Allies, and in a break with its isolationist tradition to date began to exert an influence over European political relations.

At first, Wilson attempted to achieve a balance between the warring alliances in a peace without victory and annexations, and to propagate a worldwide league of "civilised nations" as a permanent peace alliance. In his worldview, an end to interstate wars appeared to be possible by spreading the democratic principle of governance by the governed (i.e. their elected representatives) as the basis for the legitimacy of state power. This implied the formation of nation states, in other words, states willed by citizens. He also regarded the worldwide respect for human rights and an educated global public as being an important controlling entity of the states, for which purpose secret diplomacy was to be abolished. Free world trade,

---

[21]During the nineteenth century, several versions of the international system emerged from this according to Craig and George (1983).

4.3 Security Structures in the International Systems Since the Eighteenth Century

more developed international law and a process of disarmament, as well as a system of collective security that demanded a general readiness for war if a member of the League of Nations was attacked, were further elements of his concept for global peace. Pacifistic and imperialist opponents of Wilsonianism saw, and still see today, an unacceptable restriction of national sovereignty, particularly with regard to the last aspect, by a political obligation by members of the alliance to wage war in the interest of other countries and peoples. In Wilson's idealistic concept, there were no fundamental contradictions between the national interests of the USA and the human interest in world peace.[22]

When Wilson and his supporters feared in the spring of 1917 that Germany might win the war and become the predominant power on the continent, they saw the ability of the Allies to pay back their huge war loans to the USA as being endangered. The German military power also appeared to be developing into a direct risk to the security of the USA. The discovery of an offer made by Germany to Mexico to form an alliance, which offered it the prospect of re-conquering the south-eastern parts of the USA, possibly even with the support of Japan, was a key factor in changing the neutralist-pacifistic public opinion in the USA.[23] The declaration by Germany in February 1917 that it would return to the use of unlimited submarine warfare gave the final impetus for the USA to enter the war on the side of the Allies.

The liberal-democratic February revolution in Russia made it easier to re-interpret the world war, which until than had been regarded as a war between imperialist powers, and which was now redefined as a democratic crusade against autocracy (Germany and its allies). Wilson now justified entering the war by claiming that the whole world, i.e. Europe in particular, needed to be made safe for democracy and freedom.[24] The war was therefore to help give birth to a permanent world peace order, a war that was to end all wars. From then on, it was no longer a compromise peace between the warring states, but a victory of the Allies in association with the USA[25] that would create the prerequisite for the establishment of a democratic global peace alliance of nation states. The right to self-determination announced simultaneously of the ("civilised", i.e. European) peoples was intended to justify in programmatic terms the destruction of the Habsburg and Ottoman empires. With a

---

[22]For German depictions of Wilson's world peace policy see Schwabe (1971, 2006, pp. 43–77), Heideking (1999, pp. 191–230). On the comprehensive US-American literature, see Rozwenc and Lyons (1965), Ambrosius (2002), Clements (1992), Cooper (2001, 2008), Pierce (2007), Walworth (1986).

[23]Schwabe (2006, p. 57), Rozwenc and Lyons (1965, p. 11).

[24]In his speech before Congress on 2 April 1917, Wilson said: "We are glad ... to fight thus for the ultimate peace of the world and for the liberation of its peoples, the German peoples included: for the rights of nations great and small and the privilege of men everywhere, to choose their way of life and of obedience. The world must be made safe for democracy. Its peace must be planted upon the tested foundations of liberty", Rozwenc and Lyons (1965, p. 15).

[25]Through this, the USA wanted to preserve a certain distance from the western European colonial powers and their imperialist war aims by describing itself not as an ally but as an associate.

great deal of personal effort, Wilson succeeded in having the Covenant of the League of Nations incorporated into the peace accords with the Central Powers. In doing so, he was forced to enter into a large number of compromises with other victorious powers, who adhered firmly to their colonial and annexationist war aims. In the eyes of many, particularly in Germany and China, this rendered his peace policy untrustworthy. His own racist sentiments contributed to the deferment of the prospect of the right to self-determination among the "uncivilised" peoples, who until that time had been ruled by Germany and the Ottoman Empire, and who were first to be educated in self-governance by the whites, until some point in the distant future.

While Wilson succeeded in pushing through his concept for a global political order in Europe and Asia, he failed to do so in his own country, even though the majority of the population sympathised with the League of Nations idea. Wilson was largely able to assert the congruence between the American national interest of a liberal, capitalist global economy, which at the same time appeared to be compatible with US protectionism, with the moral self-identification of the USA as a power with a liberal and democratic global mission. However, he was unable to bring on board either the die-hard imperialists, who thought in categories of state power expansion politics, nor the isolationists, who rejected any limitation of national sovereignty of the USA through military obligations. As a result of strategic errors, Wilson did not achieve the two-thirds majority in the USA Senate needed to ratify the peace accords with the Covenant of the League of Nations.[26] So it was that the League of Nations entered history without the USA, and also without Germany and Soviet Russia and appeared to many contemporaries to be nothing more than a French-British league of victors intent on securing their spoils of war. The Versailles system may have contained the beginnings of a universal peace order, but it remained a particular international system from which large parts of the world were excluded, or which later excluded themselves (Italy, Japan, Germany).

Despite an external relapse into the isolationist rejection of global political obligations and of the League of Nations, in the two decades that followed, the global economic integration of the USA contributed to the continuation of a modified global policy and also of a global power role. In 1928, the USA secretary of state Frank Billing Kellogg, together with the French foreign minister Aristide Briand, drafted an international agreement condemning wars of aggression,[27] which was a milestone on the road to the prohibition of any armed attack in the United Nations Charter, which has now been approved by all states in the world, and also to a de facto reduction in the number of inter-state wars. Furthermore, it seems hardly possible that the United Nations would have been founded without a US president—Franklin D. Roosevelt

---

[26]This clumsiness is explained by both his moral rigorism and his psychological and physical stress, with lecture tours to propagate his League of Nations policy, which led to his physical collapse and a stroke in October 1919, see e.g. Schwabe (2006, pp. 72–77). The Senate particularly objected to Art. 10 of the Covenant of the League of Nations: "The Members of the League undertake to respect and preserve as against external aggression the territorial integrity and existing political independence of all Members of the League."

[27]Zaun (2008), Buchheit (1998).

(1882–1945) who like Wilson had been nominated by the Democratic Party. These developments arose initially from a war alliance. At first, only those states were regarded as being peace-loving that were willing to wage war against the states allied to National Socialist Germany. It was only later that the neutral and vanquished states were also accepted as members of the UN.

The United Nations is not a pacifistic organisation. Maintaining, or where necessary, restoring global peace and international security, also through the means of war (after peaceful means have failed), is its stated goal, even though the United Nations Charter does not use the word "war", but instead refers to "operations", "measures", "coercive measures" and the use of "armed force".[28] For several decades, some UN wars have also been known as "(robust) peace missions". It is one of the well-tended myths of politics, but unfortunately also in the field of political science and studies of international law, and even of peace and conflict research, to speak of a general prohibition on force in the UN Charter, even though according to the wording of this charter, only certain forms of force are forbidden, while others are regarded as being permissible, either implicitly or by a different choice of words. The use of force within a state to maintain the existing legal order is unquestionably legitimate in the understanding of the sovereignty of the member states of the UN. However, this right to apply force by the state on its territory and against its citizens has for several years no longer entailed the right to perpetrate serious violations of human rights, such as mass murder, without going unpunished internationally.[29] Previously, such violations were regarded in international law and in the prevailing international politics as being "internal matters" for sovereign states. Even today, they are still usually treated as such.

In Art. 2, para. 4 of the UN Charter, inter-state force is not prohibited in general, as is frequently claimed, but only such force in international relations (in other words, not in intra-state relations) that is directed "against the territorial integrity or political independence of any state or in any other manner inconsistent with the Purposes of the United Nations." Thus, it is already implied that force used to maintain the territorial integrity or political independence of a state is legitimised. This is also expressly stated in Article 51, in which a war of defence (even if it is merely referred to as "defence") against an attack, in particular against unwanted crossing of the state borders by foreign troops, is described as a natural right, regardless of whether the states use lethal force or only coercion (such as in Czechoslovakia in 1968 or in Crimea in 2014), which is not impaired by any clause in the charter.[30] Additionally, according to Article 42, the UN Security Council

---

[28] See Art. 42-51 Charter of the United Nations.

[29] See the literature on the responsibility to protect, e.g. Schmeer (2010, pp. 44–54), International Commission (2001), United Nations (2005).

[30] Art. 51 contains an apparently logical contradiction in its detail. On the one hand, the right to defend is described as being an "inherent right" (in French: droit naturel), and therefore as being inalienable and permanently valid, while on the other, it is stated that this applies "until the Security Council has taken measures necessary to maintain international peace and security". This apparent contradiction can only be interpreted such that the inherent right should not only be subject to a

"may take such action by air, sea or land forces as may be necessary to maintain or restore international peace and security," as soon as peaceful means of coercion emerge as being insufficient or unsuitable. In other words: war is a means permitted in international law to maintain or restore world peace and to defend the territorial integrity and independence of states. There is no blanket prohibition on the use of force, merely a prohibition on aggression by means of war and military force. Accordingly, the UN has already authorised international war on several occasions, such as in Korea from 1950 to 1953, Iraq in 1991, Afghanistan from 2001 to 2014 and Libya in 2011. World peace through war is therefore a maxim contained in the UN Charter and which conforms to international law. It is not a particular doctrine of the USA, the most powerful and influential member of the United Nations.

4.4 The Rise and Fall of the USA as a Global Power

Towards the end of the nineteenth century, the USA was already on the way to becoming a major economic power as a result of the huge increase in population following mass immigration, as well as the entrepreneurial and technological innovative power of US society. From 1860 to 1900, exports increased from 234 million dollars to 2.5 billion dollars, while the gross national product trebled between 1869 and 1897.[31]

As an important supplier of foodstuffs and armaments to the British and French economies during the First World War,[32] the USA initially profited for years from the self-destruction of the major European powers before throwing its weight behind the Allies on entering the war and thus becoming the determining major power at the peace conference in Paris. While the USA withdrew back into a limited form of global political isolation after its decision not to join the League of Nations, it still remained a leading global economic power, the importance of which was not impaired by the stock exchange crash of October 1929, since this also caused severe damage to its competitors in the capitalist global economy.

Unlike its participation in the First World War, US involvement in the Second World War was not voluntary; rather, the Japanese attack on Pearl Harbour and the declaration of war by Germany that quickly followed it pulled the USA in. The war caused less economic and demographic damage to the USA than to the other major powers, however, and the USA emerged from this war as the clear global economic leader and military dominant world power. However, it also had to accept the rise of the Soviet Union to the position of second-largest military power. After the victory

---

limited period of validity, but that the inherent right also assumed the task of defending the existing state; as a rule, therefore, merely supplementing self-defence. To date, the UN Security Council has never refused a state the right to self-defence.

[31] Heideking (1999, p. 199).

[32] In 1916, the USA exported goods to both countries to a value of 2.65 billion dollars, while only exporting two million dollars'-worth of goods to Germany as a result of the British sea blockade, according to Heideking (1999, p. 261). Cf. Sautter (1986, p. 330).

over the aggressive anti-democratic and anti-communist major powers of Japan, Italy and Germany, and the division of Germany, a new pentarchy in the post-war order emerged. However, the weakening and division of China resulting from a long, bloody civil war, the process of decolonisation of the western European empires and above all, the social-political antagonism between the communist world, in which a third of humanity lived, and the capitalist world in which the democratic major powers dominated quickly transformed the pentarchy into a bipolar international system that survived in significantly modified versions until 1991.

The downfall of communist party rule and the break-up of the multinational communist states, and the transition of the People's Republic of China to a capitalist market economy, as limited as it may still be, gave rise to a new international system that henceforth covered the whole world with a capitalist economic system that became ever more tightly interconnected, at least at a regional level. Within it, the USA became both a leading world economic power and the politically dominant world military power. However, it is a matter of dispute whether this international system will remain a unipolar system in the long term or whether it will again develop into a multipolar system. For the time being, the USA repeatedly lays claim, either together with NATO allies or with just a few states willing to go to war, and if necessary, also alone, to secure or restore world peace not just using diplomatic means but also through war, since the United Nations are incapable or unwilling to fulfil that statutory obligations.

Since 1945, and particularly since 1973, the global dominance of the USA has declined steadily. After 1945, it generated around 60% of the global social product; today, that figure is only around 24%.[33] The resurgence of Japan and Germany to major global power and later the emergence of China as a global economic power and the growing clout of other countries such as India, Brazil and South Africa, which today take their place at the negotiating table to discuss global economic issues at the G20 summits are weakening the dominance of the USA. The unequivocal military superiority of the USA in wars with regular military forces is restricted by the power that enemies of the USA global power position are developing through guerrilla war and transnational terrorism. In political terms, the USA can no longer count on the unquestioning support of its alliance partners in all global political conflicts, as was particularly clearly demonstrated in the third Gulf War of 2003.

The Shanghai Cooperation Organisation demonstrates the interest of China, Russia and other states of again further multipolarising the unpolarised international system. While the USA government under Georg W. Bush had no qualms about pursuing a more or less solo path on the global stage and marginalised the United Nations with contempt, the government of Barack Obama has again focused more strongly on the multilateral tradition of US foreign policy, which places value on the greatest possible support from the community of states and the global public (as was particularly clearly shown in the Cuban Missile Crisis of 1962) without abandoning the USA claim to global political leadership. President Donald J. Trump then

---

[33] Kissinger (2014, p. 315).

conducted another U-turn by propagating an even more radical, national-egoistic global policy and the annulment of numerous international treaties.

4.5 Opportunities for the Growing Importance of Peaceful Means for Preserving and Changing World Peace

Although many global-human concepts such as human rights, liberalism, democracy and the League of Nations have their intellectual roots in Europe, their link to real-life political state power is a unique historical achievement of the USA. At the same time, one cannot ignore the historical fact that repeatedly, narrow-minded major-power nationalism, cynical power politics, the support of dictatorships that promoted the national economic and strategic interests of the USA, and even illegal interventions and wars in the eyes of international law dominate US foreign policy. One of these dark chapters of US policy is the war of aggression against Iraq in 2003. The broad interpretation of 11 September 2001 as an act of war (and not as a criminal act) by the UN and NATO, which was intended to justify a war of defence waged by the USA that continued for over 14 years, should be viewed critically. It remains a contentious issue even today whether in 1999 there were not more peaceful alternatives that complied with international law to a war of intervention in the Federal Republic of Yugoslavia, after the USA had supported the Kosovar uprising under the KLA.

US society, which was liberal and pluralistic from the start, has become increasingly democratised in a process of multiple small steps since the early nineteenth century (extension of voting rights to the dispossessed and women, granting of citizens' rights to former slaves and native Indians). Unlike the self-contained concept of freedom and democracy in Switzerland, that of the USA has from the beginning been a universal, global missionary one that purports to know what is truly in the interests of mankind, and which since 1917 is also willing to assert itself through war. However, in the history of the USA and as an inherent characteristic of its society, the international peace movement and pacifism have had a comparably strong base for two centuries. The organised international peace movement per se has its origins in the protests held by many US American and British citizens against the USA-British war of 1812–1814. At that time, the first peace organisations were created in the two Anglo-Saxon countries, which later gained support in France and in several other western and northern European countries, as well as in Germany and Austria-Hungary, although not until very late in the nineteenth century.[34]

The need for peace among the people living in the USA was one important basis for the victory of Woodrow Wilson in the presidential elections of 1912, when he promised to keep the USA out of the entanglements of the war politics of the European nations. It was only in the face of considerable social resistance that the USA succeeded in joining the war in April 1917. Wilson's policy of establishing the League of Nations as a league of peace was widely supported in US society, even

---

[34]On the history of the peace movement, see Brock (1972), Holl (1988), Krippendorff (1986).

if it did not have a sufficient majority in the Senate. International, humanitarian commitment to support people suffering from war, natural disasters and economic hardship in many countries has repeatedly been met with support among US citizens to a degree that goes beyond the normal global level. This is despite the fact that the majority of society subscribes to a belligerent form of national patriotism, and is in favour of war against real or imagined enemies of the USA and its value concepts, which are often uncritically regarded as being applicable to humankind as a whole. However, time and again, doubt has been cast on the warlike missionary policy by the USA and its attempts to export its model of democracy as a result of failure and disappointment. The anti-Vietnam war movement in the USA in the 1970s may have been inspired by pacifists, but it was by no means primarily supported by those who opposed war on principle, but by opponents of an imperialist policy of intervention of widely differing political motivations. Hardly any other warring state has led to the creation of, or tolerated, such an oppositional peace movement that has found worldwide support. Without it, a breaking off of the Vietnam war would have been almost impossible, and neither would the many years after 1975 during which the USA refrained from initiating new wars. The build-up to the Iraq war in 2003 also brought millions of people onto the street. There continues to be an incomparable potential for peace in US society, which should not be overlooked for all the criticism of the belligerent interventionist policies of many US governments and its wars that unequivocally in breach of international law, such as the aggression against Iraq in 2003.

What is currently lacking is a sensible combination of realistic and idealistic global policy, which adheres to political solidarity with the proponents of liberal democracy and the human rights and freedoms that are in constant need of further development, including in autocracies, while at the same time recognising the limits of a state export policy with regard to these values, and which aspires to achieve pragmatic peace regulations, including with autocracies, via diplomatic means. The rejection of freedom crusades for democracy requires a modified concept of peace, which is based on the one hand on a narrow definition of peace (peace = non-war), while on the other not classifying all non-war as peace, but inhuman living conditions, particularly in autocracies, although sometimes also in democracies, as an absence of peace.[35] A further requirement is that many forms of absence of peace and autocratic rule must be overcome with non-violent, peaceful means, even if this does not occur rapidly in most cases. The fall of many autocratic regimes over recent decades, such as those in southern and Eastern Europe and in Latin America, without a civil war demonstrates that a non-violent peace policy is possible in order to overcome an absence of peace. Therefore, there is an alternative to a world peace policy with war, from the perspective of which clear criticism of some US foreign policy approaches can be voiced.

---

[35] On the development of a differentiated definition of peace, see in greater detail Jahn (2006), see in particular the overview on p. 58.

4.6 Cycles of the Willingness to Wage War in the USA

In the history of US foreign policy, phases of missionary-style world policy and militarily aggressive striding on the world stage have alternated with an attitude of restraint.[36] The brief imperial-colonialist phase of 1898 was followed in 1917–1919 by the actual entry into world politics by the USA with its voluntary participation in the First World War and its involvement in the creation of the Versailles world order. After largely withdrawing from global politics from 1920 to 1940, the USA was forced into joining the Second World War. During the Cold War, it was involved in several wars, in particular the Korean War, usually provoked by autocratic regimes that wanted to change the international status quo. However, there were also attempts to eradicate communist rule through war. After 1975, the debacle of the Vietnam War and a strong US-American and global peace movement led to a period of military restraint. However, the terror attacks by Al-Qaida of 11 September 2001 triggered several years of war by the USA and its allies in Afghanistan and prepared US society, both politically and morally, for the war against Iraq. The Democrat Barack Obama then entered office with the stated aim of ending both wars,[37] although he was confronted with unforeseen consequences of the Iraq war. The ill-judged full disempowerment of the Sunnis in Iraq enabled the rise of a powerful political movement, the "Islamic State", which knows how to combine conventional warfare tactics of territorial conquest with the means of transnational terrorism, and to assert the claim of restoring the Sunni caliphate, in other words a major Islamic power, and in so doing remove the Arab states and borders created by the European colonial powers, France and Britain, from 1916 to 1919. In turn, the USA, albeit with the military and political support of numerous states, is the sole military power that is able and willing to counteract such an upheaval of the international system with intensive use of force, albeit initially restricted to air warfare operations. The expansion of Russian military power in Ukraine and Syria is also increasing the inclination within US society to again use the threat of war and actual warfare to maintain the existing state order with its boundaries in the name of world peace and international security, while at the same time providing military support for liberalisation and democratisation in some countries. It depends above all on learning process in US society whether the opportunities for non-military peace policy will be exploited. Here, initiatives by US alliance partners as well as a broad international peace movement could certainly provide valuable stimuli for such an approach.

---

[36]On the concept of the New World Order of George H. W. Bush, see Czempiel (1993, pp. 90–97). On the theory-guided options of US foreign policy after 1991, see Dembinski et al. (1994, pp. 431–442) and Gärtner (2014, pp. 19–27). On the historical traditions of US foreign policy, see Medick-Krakau et al. (2012, pp. 173–187).

[37]See in particular the introductory piece in: Hagemann et al. (2014, pp. 1–16). On the expectations of the Obama administration at the beginning of its period in office, see Meier-Walser (2009).

References

Ambrosius LE (2002) Wilsonianism. Woodrow Wilson and his legacy in American foreign relations. Palgrave Macmillan, New York

Brock L (2006) Was ist das ‚Mehr' in der Rede, Friede sei mehr als die Abwesenheit von Krieg. In: Sahm A, Sapper M, Weichsel V (eds) Die Zukunft des Friedens, Bd. 1, Eine Bilanz der Friedens- und Konfliktforschung, 2nd edn. VS Verlag für Sozialwissenschaften, Wiesbaden

Brock P (1972) Pacifism in Europe to 1914. Princeton, Princeton University Press

Brzezinski Z (2012) Strategic vision: America and the crisis of global power. Basic Books, New York

Brzezinski Z (2016) The grand chessboard. American primacy and its geostrategic imperatives, 2nd edn. Basic Books, New York

Buchheit E (1998) Der Briand-Kellogg-Pakt von 1928 – Machtpolitik oder Friedensstreben. LIT-Verlag, Münster

Clements KA (1992) The presidency of Woodrow Wilson. University Press of Kansas, Lawrence

Cooper JM Jr (2001) Breaking the heart of the world. Woodrow Wilson and the fight for the league of nations. Cambridge University Press, Cambridge

Cooper JM Jr (2008) Reconsidering Woodrow Wilson. Progressivism, internationalism, war, and peace. Johns Hopkins University Press, Washington/Baltimore

Charter of the United Nations (24 October 1945). http://www.un.org/en/charter-united-nations

Covenant of the League of Nations (28 April 1919). http://www.refworld.org/docid/3dd8b9854.html

Craig GA, George AL (1983) Force and statecraft. Diplomatic problems of our time. Oxford University Press, Oxford/New York

Czempiel EO (1993) Weltpolitik im Umbruch. Das internationale system nach dem Ende des Ost-west-Konflikts. Beck, Munich

Dembinski M, Rudolf P, Wilzewski J (eds) (1994) Amerikanische Weltpolitik nach dem Ost-west-Konflikt. Nomos, Baden-Baden

Emmerich A, Gassert P (2014) Amerikas Kriege. Wissenschaftliche Buchgesellschaft, Darmstadt

Feiner S (2000) Weltordnung durch US-leadership? Die Konzeption Zbigniew Brzezinskis. Westdeutscher Verlag, Wiesbaden

Galtung J (1969) Violence, peace, and peace research. J Peace Res 6(3):167–191

Gärtner H (2014) Die USA und die neue welt. LIT-Verlag, Münster

Hagemann S, Tönnesmann W, Wilzewski J (eds) (2014) Weltmacht vor neuen Herausforderungen. Die Außenpolitik der USA in der Ära Obama. Wissenschaftlicher Verlag, Trier

Harbom L, Wallensteen P (2010) Armed conflicts, 1946–2009. J Peace Res 47(4):501–509

Heideking J (1999) Geschichte der USA, 2nd edn. A. Francke, Tübingen/Basel

Heideking J, Mauch C (2008) Geschichte der USA, 6th edn. A. Francke, Tübingen/Basel

Heidelberg Institute for Conflict Research (2015) Conflict barometer 2014. HIIK, Heidelberg

Holl K (1988) Pazifismus in Deutschland. Suhrkamp, Frankfurt a. M

Holsti KJ (1994) International politics. A framework for analysis, 7th edn. Prentice Hall, Englewood Cliffs, NJ

International Commission on Intervention and State Sovereignty (2001) The responsibility to protect. International Development Research Centre, Ottawa. https://web.archive.org/web/20050513013236/; http://www.iciss.ca/pdf/Commission-Report.pdf

Jahn E (2006) Ein bißchen Frieden im ewigen Krieg? Zu den Aussichten auf einen dauerhaften Weltfrieden am Beginn des 21. Jahrhunderts. In: Sahm A, Sapper M, Weichsel V (eds) Die Zukunft des Friedens, Eine Bilanz der Friedens- und Konfliktforschung, vol 1, 2nd edn. VS Verlag für Sozialwissenschaften, Wiesbaden, pp 51–82

Jahn E (2012) Frieden und Konflikt. VS Verlag für Sozialwissenschaften, Wiesbaden

Jahn E (2015) World political challenges. Political issues under debate, vol 3. Springer, Heidelberg

Kaldor M (2012) New and old wars. Organized violence in a global era, 3rd edn. Wiley, Hoboken, NJ

Kissinger H (2014) World order. Penguin, New York

Krippendorff E (ed) (1986) Pazifismus in den USA, vol 2. Freie Universität, Berlin

Levin NG Jr (1968) Woodrow Wilson and World politics. America's response to war and revolution. Oxford University Press, Oxford/New York

Mayer AJ (1964) Wilson versus Lenin. Political origins of the new diplomacy 1917–1918. Meridian Books, New York

Medick-Krakau M, Brand A, Robel S (2012) Die Außen- und Weltpolitik der USA. In: Staack M (ed) Einführung in die internationale Politik, 5th edn. Studienbuch, Oldenbourg, München

Meier-Walser RC (ed) (2009) Die Außenpolitik der USA. Präsident Obamas neuer Kurs und die Zukunft der transatlantischen Beziehungen. Hanns-Seidel-Stiftung, München

Menzel U (2015) Die Ordnung der welt. Imperium oder Hegemonie in der Hierarchie der Staatenwelt. Suhrkamp, Frankfurt a.M

Morgenthau HJ (2005) Politics among nations (1948), 7th edn. McGraw-Hill Education, New York et al

Petersson T, Themnér L (eds) (2012) States in armed conflict 2011. Universitetstryckeriet, Uppsala

Pierce AR (2007) Woodrow Wilson and Harry Truman. Mission and power in American foreign policy. Transaction, Westport/London

Rabehl T, Schreiber W (eds) (2001) Das Kriegsgeschehen 2000. Daten und Tendenzen der Kriege und bewaffneten Konflikte. Leske + Budrich, Opladen

Rozwenc EC, Lyons T (1965) Realism and idealism in Wilson's peace program. D. C. Heath, Boston et al

Sautter U (1986) Geschichte der Vereinigten Staaten von Amerika. Kröner, Stuttgart

Schmeer E (2010) Responsibility to protect und Wandel von Souveränität. Berliner Wissenschaftsverlag, Berlin

Schreiber W (ed) (2011) Das Kriegsgeschehen 2009. Daten und Tendenzen der Kriege und bewaffneten Konflikte. Leske + Budrich, Opladen

Schwabe K (1971) Woodrow Wilson. Ein Staatsmann zwischen Puritanertum und Liberalismus. Musterschmidt, Göttingen et al.

Schwabe K (2006) Weltmacht und Weltordnung. Amerikanische Außenpolitik von 1898 bis zur Gegenwart. Eine Jahrhundertgeschichte. Schöningh, Paderborn

The International Institute for Strategic Studies (2015) The ISS armed conflict survey. Routledge, Oxford

United Nations (2005) Resolution adopted by the general assembly on 16 September, A/RES/60.1, http://daccess-dds-ny.un.org/doc/UNDOC/GEN/N05/487/60/PDF/N0548760.pdf?OpenElement

Walworth A (1986) Wilson and his peacemakers. American diplomacy at the Paris peace conference, 1919. W. W. Norton, New York/London

Zaun H (2008) Als der Angriffskrieg geächtet wurde. Telepolis, 24 August, http://www.heise.de/tp/artikel/28/28381/1.html

5. The Fatal Glorification of Mohandas K. Gandhi as a Saint: His Role in the National Independence Movement in India

Abstract

Fifty years ago, India and Pakistan became independent states, after decades during which a national movement throughout India, consisting of Hindus and Muslims, had fought, mainly using non-violent means, first for self-government within the British Empire and then for full independence. Undisputedly, the most important political leader of the independence movement was Mohandas Karamchand Gandhi (1869–1948), who early on was already revered and declared a Mahatma (great soul) and as a type of saint. Gandhi only rarely took up official positions in the Indian National Congress, which has been transformed over the course of the years from simply being a movement to the leading political party. However, he enjoyed authority over the masses that mobilised them, however contentious it may have been. Following the declaration of Gandhi as a Mahatma, any objective, rational and critical academic or political discussion of his actual political role, his political thinking and actions, and above all his impact as a role model for non-violent and peaceful movements throughout the world has largely been neglected.

As a lawyer trained in London, Gandhi moved to South Africa in 1893, where he became a representative of the social and legal interests of the Indian minority against the beginnings of the Apartheid laws. It was here, before he returned to India in 1915, that he developed his new style of non-violent combat known as the "Satyagraha", consisting of non-cooperation and civil disobedience. Following the massacre by the British authorities at a peaceful protest rally in Amritsar, for which no retribution was sought, Gandhi abandoned hope for equal rights for India within the British Empire and began several campaigns for the full national independence of India. However, he was unable to prevent India from being split into an Islamic republic of Pakistan and a Hindu-dominated, albeit constitutionally secular, multi-religious Republic of India.

Lecture given on 10.7.2017.

© Springer Nature Switzerland AG 2020
E. Jahn, *War and Compromise Between Nations and States*,
https://doi.org/10.1007/978-3-030-34131-2_5

It is a matter of dispute as to whether the attainment of independence is primarily the result of non-violent actions by the Indians, or of the moderate British colonial policies, albeit ones that were not always in compliance with constitutional norms. In fact, numerous domestic political factors in India and Britain, and above all the weakening of the British Empire as a result of the two world wars, paved the way for the success of the largely non-violent national independence movement. Gandhi's radical socio-political attempts at reform may have provided an important impetus for change in Indian society (such as equal rights for the casteless and for women), but they remain almost entirely unrealised today, or are in many cases regarded as being outmoded.

5.1 The International Mystification of Mohandas K. Gandhi the Politician

Even before Mohandas K. Gandhi began to play a role in the Indian national independence movement, he had become highly famous between 1893 and 1915 as a leading figure in the resistance movement among the Indian minority in British South Africa against the beginnings of the Apartheid system. On his return to India in January 1915, he was welcomed as a Mahatma (or "great soul" in Sanskrit) by the philosopher and winner of the Nobel Prize for literature, Rabindranath Tagore (1861–1941). Not long afterwards, his first name was replaced by "Mahatma". Most non-Indians are unaware of the fact that several other people have also been bestowed with the title "Mahatma", which is approximately the same as the Christian term "saint". The extent to which Gandhi was also honoured outside India was so great that in a book publication of his essays in the "Young India" newspaper, in 1924, John Haynes Holmes (USA) equated him with Christ returned to earth.[1] The declaration of Gandhi as an ahistorical saintly figure[2] not only obscures his real-life political and societal role in achieving the independence of India and Pakistan in August 1947 after decades of non-violent protest, and thus also to the shattering of the British Empire. According to Gandhi's German biographer, Dietmar Rothermund: "However, unfortunately, he tends to be remembered rather as a

---

[1] "If I were to believe in reincarnation, then—with all respect—I would see Christ in Mahatma Gandhi, who had returned to Earth. If I were to believe in the principle of the second coming, I would claim that this event had already occurred in India.... He, too moves us most deeply with his writings, and like Jesus in the gospels, he lifts us to the greatest heights," in the introduction to: Gandhi (1924, pp. XII, XVI).

[2] Gandhi frequently complained about being honoured as a Mahatma, or saint. "I think that word "saint" should be ruled out of present life. It is too sacred a word to be lightly applied to anybody, much less to one like myself, who claims only to be a humble searcher after Truth..." in: Gandhi (1924, p. 71, see also p. 78).

saint who became unwittingly involved in politics, rather than as a politician whose ideas were and still are of relevance to the future."[3]

When analysed through an objective, socio-historical lens, Mohandas K. Gandhi should be regarded as an individual who like no other in global history steered the political behaviour of countless millions of people, without having access to the force and power of a major state or a party, during his lifetime and solely through his charisma, without recourse to violence. No Lenin or Stalin, Mao or Hitler had such personal power during the twentieth century. Only in rare cases was Gandhi's charisma reinforced by the official authority of the President (1924) or by another leading position in the Indian National Congress party (INC). In 1934, he left the INC, although as the party's "advisor", he probably had an even greater influence over it than before. He played a key role in the conversion of the institutional structures of the INC from an elite organisation to a mass organisation of farmers. In independent India, he did not aspire to hold an official office, as a result of which he was never confronted with the problematic issue of having to exert state force.

Even before the partition of British India into the independent states of India and Pakistan, murders between Hindus, Sikhs and Muslims were committed on an extensive scale in the years prior to 1948. Up to one million of people lost their lives as a result; 20 million people were resettled from India and Pakistan, or were driven out or fled from their homes. Before the partition, Gandhi succeeded in ending the acts of violence in several provinces through his personal presence and through hunger strikes. The last British Viceroy, Lord Louis Mountbatten, wrote: "In the Punjab, we have 55,000 soldiers and large-scale rioting on our hands. In Bengal, our forces consist of one man, and there is no rioting. As a serving officer, as well as an administrator, may I be allowed to pay my tribute to the One-Man Boundary Force...".[4]

In the history and society of India, violence plays no less a role than in other countries.[5] The independent Republic of India waged several wars after Gandhi, and has become an atomic power. It can hardly be claimed that Indian society has become less violent than in other countries since Gandhi's historical impact, although smaller groups of Gandhiists continue to exist in India who live according to his teachings. The question therefore arises as to whether this was simply a one-off historical episode, in which—under extremely favourable social and international constellations—a mainly non-violent national independence movement was able to succeed in a decades-long struggle against a major global power at the time. And this with around 8000 political casualties[6] among a population of far more than 300 million. How much bloodier the battles for independence were among other, far smaller groups of people! How was Gandhi able, therefore, to rise to his outstanding political

---

[3]Rothermund (1997, p. 15).
[4]Rothermund (1997, p. 472).
[5]Singh (2017).
[6]I quote these numbers from memory from my earlier lecture, although I am currently unable to find written evidence of this.

role? What were the methods of combat that were in many respects historically new? What was the basis for his authority and ability to assert his demands within Indian society? Why did the British then ultimately allow their empire to be destroyed by a "semi-naked fakir", as the colonial politician Winston Churchill disparagingly described him in the 1930s?

In today's lecture to mark the 70th anniversary of the independence of the two successor states to British India, on 15 August 1947, I will focus exclusively on the role played by Gandhi in the Indian national independence movement. In another lecture, marking the 70th anniversary of his assassination on 30 January 1948, I shall discuss his universal, global historical importance.

5.2 The Theory of the Singularity of the Success of Non-violent Policy in the Indian National Movement

While admirers of Gandhi and the proponents of the principle of non-violent politics[7] throughout the world assume that the Indian resistance movement against British colonial rule is of universal significance and that it acts as a model, in current political thinking, the attitude dominates that the success of the non-violent politics of the Indian national movement was a unique historical event, and that it could not, and cannot, be replicated in other political situations.

Several reasons have been cited for this view. The most fundamental argument is that of Max Weber, that politics is in its essence the leadership or influence of the leadership of a state (in general terms: a political association), whereby the state is a "human community that (successfully) claims the monopoly of the legitimate use of physical force within a given territory".[8] The ethics of non-violence, of "resist not evil with force", is exclusively the way of the saint.[9] However, politics not only consists of leading and influencing a state, in other words, exerting governmental and state power, but is also the process of attaining the power to rule in the state, which in parliamentary democracies is usually a non-violent one. It can also be non-violent or even violence-free when achieving one's own state through a national independence movement, which in 1919, Max Weber had not yet considered as a possibility.

Most authors explain the success of non-violent politics in India in terms of a specific historical constellation of colonial rule and national independence movement. Here, some emphasise that in pre-industrial Indian society, and above all in the Hindu religion, there was a particular inclination among large swathes of the Indian population to be humble followers of a charismatic, non-violent leader.

---

[7]In the German version, Theodor Ebert introduced the difference between non-violence as an avoidance of violent behaviour on principle and non-violence as such an avoidance based on circumstances, in: Ebert (1969, p. 34).

[8]Weber (1988, p. 506).

[9]Weber (1988, p. 550).

Others see the main reason for the development of the leadership role of Gandhi the non-violent politician in the Indian national movement as being a specifically liberal British colonial policy, which became democratically legitimised and controlled over the course of time, and which had become more humane, which began as a movement to reform the Empire, before radicalising to become an independence movement. One proponent of this view was Karl Jaspers, who initially assumed that "in its essence, politics is a way of dealing with violence",[10] while claiming that Gandhi, quite unlike the pacifists, had successfully pursued "supra-political" religious non-violence. "he did not detach himself from the world in solitude, like a saint indifferent to the world. He also did not act alone, but together with the mass of people who believed in him." According to Jaspers, this success was only possible because Britain was not willing to pursue reckless violence: "Only under England and only under this uniquely liberal of rule in the history of empires was Gandhi able to be successful. Such non-violent politics would never have led to such a result in former times, and in the future, it would only be able to be successful under conditions similar to those under England with regard to liberalism, openness and legality. The liberation of India through Gandhi's politics of non-violence is to a far greater extent the consequence of a struggle in England with itself than of an Indian act." And Jaspers concludes that "In a battle with the totalitarian regimes, Gandhi's approach would no longer have been a political path, but a sure route to destruction."

5.3 The Discussion Surrounding the Methods of Combat of the Indian Movement to Reform British Colonial Rule in South Africa

British colonial rule of the Indian sub-continent began with the establishment of the trading centres of the British East India Company on the coasts of India in the early seventeenth century. Later, the trading company, which had been invested with political and military rights by the king of England, took control of the interior of the subcontinent and finally subjugated around half it, with two-thirds of the population, to direct rule, and 562 princely states to supreme British colonial authority. Nominally, India was still ruled by the Muslim Grand Moguls, who in 1526 had conquered the sultanate of Delhi (since 1206), which was also Muslim, but who had lost their power over the course of time to regional rulers, many of them Hindus, and then to the British. In 1857, there was an uprising against British rule among Indian soldiers in the British forces in north-eastern and central India, which was joined by civilians, mostly from poorer castes, and a small number of princes and the Grand Mogul. Shortly before he was deposed in 1858, he assumed the title of Emperor. The British only succeeded in crushing the revolt after 2 years, with the help of allied Indians, and after many atrocities on both sides that led to the deaths of

---

[10]These and the following quotes can be found in the section "The Notion of Non-Violent Politics" in Jaspers (1960, pp. 63, 65, 67, 68).

over 10,000 people. The uprising led the United Kingdom to dissolve the trading company and to assume direct rule over the subcontinent. From that time onwards, the governor-general bore the title of Viceroy. He was assigned command over the executive and legislative council, the members of which were initially only British, although later, they were joined by Indians elected from the upper castes. The territory of British India covered not only today's republic of India, Pakistan and Bangladesh, with a total area of 4.2 million square kilometres (by comparison, the EU currently covers an area of 4.4 million square kilometres), but from 1886 to 1937 also Burma, known today as Myanmar.

From 1856 to 1947, India as a colony of the Crown was the "jewel" of the British Empire, which in 1922 covered a quarter of the land surface of the earth, and a quarter of the world's population. In 1875, 301 million people lived in British India, with just 33 million living in the United Kingdom.[11] The Kingdom succeeded in exerting its rule over the entire subcontinent with just 150,000[12] or so British officials and military personnel, cleverly incorporating numerous princes and the upper-caste Indians into the colonial administrative system. In 1876, Queen Victoria was crowned Empress of the Indian Empire by the British parliament, in response to the establishment of the German Empire.[13]

The Indian National Congress (INC), an organised national movement, was not created until 1885. For a long period of time, only western educated elites, Hindus and Muslims alike, were actively involved, who wanted to participate in the administration of the colony. They attempted to assert liberal citizens' rights and social reforms. After the Hindus had gained the upper hand in the INC, a separate All-India Muslim League was formed in 1906, to which Muhammad Ali Jinnah (1876–1948) was elected President in 1916.

Mohandas Karamchand Gandhi was born on 2 October 1869, far away from the areas of influences of the national movement, in Porbandar, a small coastal town in what is now the federal state of Gujarat in the westernmost region of the Republic of India. At that time, the town was the centre of one of the princely states of British India, most of which were very small. The Gandhi family belonged to the merchant class (Vaishya), which held a great deal of influence in society; the name "Gandhi" means "grocer" in English. At age eight, Gandhi was engaged to Kasturbai

---

[11] Historical population.

[12] I quote these numbers from memory from my earlier lecture, although I am currently unable to find written evidence of this. In 1921, Gandhi wrote of 300 million Indians, including 70 million Muslims, and 100,000 British, in Gandhi (1924, p. 227). In the final decades of the nineteenth century, 140,000 Indians and 70,000 British served in the British-Indian Army, with the British alone occupying the higher officers' positions, according to: Kulke and Rothermund (2006, p. 325).

[13] Austria had already been an empire since 1804 (in response to the proclamation of Napoleon as Emperor of France and in anticipation of the dissolution of the Holy Roman Empire of the German Nation), while Russia had been an empire since 1721 (as a means of increasing its status over the Holy Roman Empire).

5.3 The Discussion Surrounding the Methods of Combat of the Indian Movement to...

Makthaji,[14] who was of the same age, and was married at 13. The couple had four children.

His strictly religious, Hindu mother (who belonged to the group of Hindus who worship the god Vishnu) exerted an important influence on him. In her religion, fasting and the making of vows played a significant role. She was also influenced by Jainism. This religion, which emerged at about the same time as Buddhism, and which with its strong ascetic beliefs has only about four million followers, espouses, among other things, the radical command of "ahimsa", the non-killing and non-injuring of even the smallest life forms; accordingly, the Jains are vegetarians. Another tenet of Jainism is "satya", or truth. "The search for truth was at the centre of Gandhi's life, but this was not the truth that can be founded on methods of critical scholarship. For him, the truth had to be tested in well thought-through action, supported by a vow."[15] As a result, Gandhi was able to understand religiosity not merely as contemplation, but also as something that had to prove its worth through practical deeds, on a personal level as well as for the general good, in other words, in politics. In his politics, Gandhi never referred to religious commands from holy scriptures, but only regarded those writings as being a religious command that appeared to be of sensible use to him. In his public prayer meetings, he recited prayers from all the major religions. Therefore, he had a clearly rational understanding of religion and politics based on his understanding of the truth, which whenever possible excluded violent physical and psychical behaviour.

Mohandas K. Gandhi's father and grandfather were prime ministers in the small princely state of Porpandar. Mohandas, the youngest son, would also follow in their path and for this reason was sent to London to study (1888–1891). There, he received important inspiration for his future life, such as from the non-violent suffragette movement, constitutional thinking, conflict mediation in labour disputes, theosophy and the Sermon on the Mount in the New Testament. Following his return from London, he worked as a lawyer in Mumbai (Bombay) with moderate success. In 1893, he took up an offer to represent the legal interests of a Muslim trader from Gujarat in Durban, in Natal/South Africa.[16] After experiencing the racial discrimination of Indians in person during a train journey from Durban to Pretoria/Transvaal—he was ejected from the train when he refused to leave his reserved seat in the first class carriage following a complaint made to the guard by a white passenger—he was inspired not only to protest against his personal discrimination, but also to mobilise the Indians living in Pretoria to demonstrate against the racial discrimination against them in general.

The British had brought many Indians to their sugar plantations as contract workers. Many of them also remained in South Africa as free workers following

---

[14]Gandhi Arun (1981). Kasturbai Gandhi died before Gandhi, in 1944.

[15]Rothermund (2011, pp. 7–8).

[16]The four British crown colonies of Natal, Transvaal, the Orange Free State and the Cape Colony were not combined to form the South African Union until 1910.

their five-year tenure to the individual plantation owners.[17] Their increasing number led to fears of foreign infiltration among the Boers and British, which engendered the beginnings of the legally underpinned policy of Apartheid. When Gandhi learned just before he was due to return to India that a law was being drafted in Natal that would have depleted all Indians of their voting rights, he organised protest rallies and became Secretary General of a newly founded Natal Indian Congress.

Strongly influenced by the book Unto this Last, by the Calvinist art historian, painter and social reformer John Ruskin (1819–1900), published in 1860,[18] who in his critique of the principles of national economy sharply criticised not only capitalism and industrialisation, but also Marxism, espousing instead a simple life, manual work and an equal wage for all, in 1906, Gandhi converted to a life of frugality, abstinence and harsh discipline. He was also motivated by his experiences, serving the British with a sanitary corps, of the crushing of the Zulu uprising. On a farm outside Durban, he founded a community with the staff of his newspaper, "Indian Opinion", after having decided to leave his lawyer's practice and dedicate himself entirely to political and social work.

Gandhi had no interest in socio-economic and political theories such as capitalism and socialism, parliamentary democracy, realism and liberal institutionalism, and is also difficult to classify politically. Gandhi wrote no systematic, political theory books, and only very few more extensive works overall.[19] The name Gandhi therefore hardly appears at all in political and sociological works, and only occasionally in passing in political-philosophical writings.[20] Even so, his political attitudes and behaviours can be described as being extremely rationally, systematically thought-through concepts within the framework of a theory of non-violent politics.

In 1907, Gandhi read the short essay, "Civil Disobedience",[21] by Henry David Thoreau (1817–1862), in which civil disobedience was propagated, for example through refusal to pay taxes or against unjust laws that justify slavery. The punishment by imprisonment for violating the law should be accepted. Gandhi first called for the law to be broken when he organised a boycott of a new law in Transvaal that required Indians to register themselves. The purpose of this law was to prevent unwanted immigration by more Indians. Due to his refusal to register, he was

---

[17] Evidently, similar working conditions still exist today in Qatar and other Gulf states.

[18] Ruskin (2011). The title refers to the New Testament parable in which the day labourer most recently employed in a vineyard, and who has therefore worked there for the shortest time, is paid the same wage as those who were employed there earlier, see Matthew 20. Gandhi translated Ruskin's book into Gujarat, calling it "Sarvodaya" (the ascent of man).

[19] As well as the autobiography: Satyagraha in South Africa (1924–1925), Gandhi (2017), and Hind Swaraj or Indian Home Rule (1909), Gandhi (2010).

[20] Thus, e.g. Karl Jaspers (1960) occasionally examined Gandhi's political thinking.

[21] Thoreau (2014).

sentenced to 2 months in prison. During the course of his life, Gandhi would spend over 6 years[22] in total in prison.

Gandhi called his new combat strategy by a new name, "satyagraha", i.e. adherence to the truth, whereby the truth must be proven through one's own, non-violent behaviour. Truth therefore emerges through interaction, and is not something that is discovered in itself.[23] In order to consolidate the policy of non-violent resistance, those taking non-violent resistance action, the "satyagrahis", were required to take an oath. Many of them and their families lived with Gandhi on the Tolstoy Farm (a precursor of the later ashrams in India), where they lived a simple, hard-working communal life eating only vegetarian food. When a court declared that only those marriages were valid that were conducted in a Christian church, and which were registered at a registry office, it was the Indian women above all who were outraged, along with their children, who were now declared illegitimate. They mobilised the Indian mineworkers to take part in a long-term strike. When they were subsequently sentenced to forced labour in their mines, solidarity strikes were called among the plantation workers. When the government of South Africa also came under pressure from a railway strike by the whites, it finally relented and passed a law that recognised Indian marriages, which abolished the poll tax on Indians and which permitted the immigration of qualified Indians. Gandhi then felt that his work in South Africa was complete, and left the country for good at the end of 1914. The leader of a minority movement would now become the leading personality of a majority movement.

Already in 1896, when he travelled to India to bring his family to South Africa, Gandhi had become well known for his report about the situation of the Indians in South Africa, and had met the leading members of the INC. The national reformer and professor, Gopal Krishna Gokhale (1866–1915) supported union between Hindus and Muslims, education for ordinary people and public promotion of health, while being against the caste system and discrimination against the "untouchables". The reformers also wanted to implement constitutional reforms in the Crown colony, to abolish child marriages and the immolation of widows. Gokhale, who was just 3 years older than Gandhi, became his most important advisor. Following Gandhi's return to India at the start of 1915, he urged him to first spend a year travelling through India in order to get to know the country that was the size of an entire continent, and while doing so, to refrain from giving political speeches or issuing political statements.

As well as the national reformers, there was also a strong national-revolutionary group, whose key political representative was Bal Gangadhar Tilak (1856–1920). It propagated achieving independence through violence as a prerequisite to social reforms, and encouraged the uprising against British rule. At times, it formed its

---

[22]In total, 2089 days in Indian prisons and 249 days in South African prisons, according to Fischer (1962, p. 147).

[23]Probably the best book about Gandhi is the psychoanalytical study by Erikson (1993). For the religious historical background, see Mühlmann (1950).

own organised wing in the INC. Violence and war certainly played an important role in Indian history and in the history of the national movement. The national-revolutionary group gained the upper hand in the INC during the First World War, and Tilak was elected its president in 1918. However, after his death, it lost a considerable amount of influence when Gandhi rose to become the de-facto leader of the INC, which was increasingly moving away from being a broad movement organisation and towards becoming a political party, alongside which other parties were also emerging, albeit with a lesser degree of influence.

5.4 Gandhi's Role in the Indian National Independence Movement

At the start of the 1920s, after the death of Gokhal and Tilak, Gandhi quickly became the main leader of the Indian national independence movement, which was at the same time a social reform movement. Gandhi already wrote down his ideas for the social and political development of Indian on a journey from London to South Africa in 1909, in the form of a Socractic dialogue with a violent extremist. He called this work "*Hind Swaraj*",[24] or Indian home-rule. This home-rule, he claimed, could only be achieved through the self-discipline of each individual. Simply replacing British rule by force with an Indian equivalent would not bring India freedom. The document contained radical criticism of western civilisation, and in so doing, went far beyond the ideas, in terms of its propagation of comprehensive social reform, of the moderate Indian liberals and the national revolutionaries, who simply attacked British foreign rule.

Apart from Ruskin's book, Gandhi obtained important ideas for his new socio-political thinking from Socrates' Apology[25] and Leo Tolstoy's ideas of how to organise a Christian society.[26] It was more through his successes in South Africa than his writings that Gandhi quickly became an influential figure in India. However, later, his autobiography was received with a great deal of interest, both internationally and in India. In typical fashion, he called it "The Story of my Experiments with Truth", which he understood to be a way of coming closer to the truth of a non-violent individual and societal life explored through his own activity. The autobiography appeared as a sequel to journal articles written from 1925 to 1929, when Gandhi was already aged 46–49.[27] In this book, he discloses his highly personal, even intimate problems and weaknesses, and gives his views on all possible subjects, such as health, children's upbringing, gender relations, and also socio-economic and political events and fundamental questions with which he was engaged. Social classes, nations, humanity and other collective bodies had no

---

[24]Gandhi (2010).
[25]Fuhrmann (1989).
[26]Tolstoy (2017).
[27]Gandhi (1983).

meaning for Gandhi. For him, they were essentially associations of self-responsible individuals in communities and social contexts. He had become a journalist at an early age and had published his own newspapers. And he was a prolific letter writer. His collected works comprised 100 volumes,[28] with 45,000 pages—far more than the works of Marx and Engels, Lenin, or other political thinkers.

Gandhi was not a socialist, and did not reject the concept of private property of means of production in principle. Instead, he regarded owners of capital as being trustees with an obligation to pay a fair wage. He largely rejected industrialisation and advocated a concept of village farmer communities. He became famous when he turned against socially unjust and ethnically discriminatory laws that made life very difficult for farmers, while at the same time also opposing the suppression of workers' strikes. He always stood up for those in a weaker social position, although at the same time, he was willing to reach a compromise with the social and political rulers. The most accurate way to describe Gandhi, with certain constraints, is as an anarchist, who wanted to achieve non-hierarchical social self-organisation, preferably in village communities, although he by no means wanted to do away with the state, the judiciary, the police or the military overall.

Communist contemporaries found it difficult to evaluate Gandhi: "It is, as it were, as though Gandhi embodies two different people, two class truths", even when they also adjudge him harshly: "This same Gandhi is a smooth political entrepreneur, one of the most crafty, slippery, cunning professional politicians, a master of the smooth compromise, the great master of lies and deception... The class countenance of Gandhi is the countenance of the Indian bourgeoisie, the countenance of the civic national movement in India".[29] "The Communist Party and the working class are themselves leading the movement to a higher level, by forcing back the miserable ideology of Gandhiism, exposing Gandhi himself and his counter-revolutionary ideas, clearly revealing the irreconcilable dichotomy of interests of the revolutionary proletariat and the farmers and the interests of the national-reformist block".[30] "Gandhi hoped to provide distraction from the fundamental issues of the agricultural revolution through a pompous rally against the salt monopoly of the government.... The final exposure of the betrayal of the National Congress and its leaders, who flee to the prisons before this exposure, is one of the most important tasks of the Communist Party of India".[31]

Gandhi was by no means a pacifist, and himself volunteered to participate in wars three times, albeit in the unarmed medical service: in the Boer War, during the suppression of the Zulu uprising, and at the start of the First World War. During the First World War, in which 1.3 million Indian soldiers fought on the side of the British,

---

[28]Collected Works of Mahatma Gandhi (CWMG), 100, Delhi: Publications Division. Government of India 1958–1994.

[29]Reissner (1930, p. 1130).

[30]Reissner (1930, p. 1138).

[31]Freier (1930, pp. 953, 955). See also other articles in this journal, which increased in frequency in 1930.

Gandhi campaigned for the recruitment of volunteers, since he expected that the British would grant India self-government as a mark of gratitude for Indian participation in the war. However, while India became a founding member of the League of Nations, it remained under rigid British colonial rule.

As was the case in South Africa, it was both laws perceived to be discriminatory that were imposed by the British crown and the social harassment of farmers and workers by property owners and companies, as well as the British authorities, that motivated Gandhi to conduct several spectacular, non-violent individual and mass actions of non-cooperation and civil disobedience. Here, he often used limited or even unlimited fasting as a means of urging both the authorities and his supporters to accept his demands or to negotiate compromises. Gandhi's demonstrative failure to comply with an existing law or police order often led to his imprisonment. In many cases, his internment led to massive, sometimes also violent, mass protests, as a result of which Gandhi was repeatedly prematurely released from prison, or his imprisonment was avoided by a re-interpretation of the law.

A turning point in the history of the Indian national movement and Gandhi's attitude towards the British Empire came when the Rowlatt Act was passed in March 1919, which aimed to uphold, in an amended form, the emergency war legislation that had been imposed during the First World War. The law made it possible to imprison individuals suspected of being involved in terrorist activity without a prior court trial. Gandhi organised a *hartal*, a traditional religious, one-day general strike in opposition to this law, with fasting and demonstrations, in several parts of India. In Delhi and elsewhere, the government ordered that shots should be fired at the demonstrators, leading to violent conflicts. It was only after the massacre ordered by the British general Reginald Dyer at a large gathering of non-violent demonstrators in Amritsar in the Punjab region, which led to the deaths of around 400[32] people and which went unpunished, that Gandhi became convinced that India must gain independence from British rule. However, after the campaign of civil disobedience degenerated into a series of violent disputes, Gandhi brought it to a halt and admitted committing a "Himalayan blunder", since, unlike previously in South Africa, he had not trained a sufficient number of satyagrahis to take non-violent action in a controlled manner. Later, he placed great value on training disciplined cadres for civil disobedience. He rather tended to call on the population masses to commit acts of legal non-cooperation, which could take on huge dimensions. This began with the return of medals and awards and the refusal to participate in official events, but could also involve boycotting elections and goods or relinquishing official state posts. Occasionally, people were called on to interrupt their studies in colonial administration schools and universities.

In parallel with the campaign against the Rowlatt Act, Gandhi also organised a campaign of solidarity with the Ottoman caliph (caliphate campaign), from whom the British had withdrawn the power of rule over the holy Muslim sites after the war.

---

[32]Rothermund (2002, p. 74). According to other sources, the number of casualties was 600, Mann (2005, p. 87).

This was met with outrage among numerous Indian Muslims, which Gandhi now wanted to exploit for his policies opposing British rule. However, the campaign was brought to a halt by the Turkish Grand National Assembly under Atatürk, who disbanded the caliphate in March 1924.

One of the most famous campaigns was the boycott of English textile goods. In order to avoid exerting excessive pressure on the import traders, Gandhi called on people to publicly burn clothing personally owned by them that had been produced by the British. At the same time, he summoned the population to spin thread for new clothing themselves on simple spinning wheels, and to weave new clothes. From that time on, the membership fee for the INC would have to be paid in the form of self-spun, later also purchased thread. This campaign had a dual impact. On the one hand, it made a severe dent in the British textile industry, leading to the loss of tens of thousands of jobs. On a visit to the centres of the British textile industry, Gandhi was able to gain understanding for his campaign among the textile workers, however. On the other hand, the campaign mobilised many millions of simple Indians, who through their own, legal action not only made a contribution to the weakening of British rule, but at the same time also strengthened their personal and political self-assurance. It was for this reason that the Indian National Congress incorporated a spinning wheel into its flag in 1931. When India gained independence, the spinning wheel was replaced by the old Indian "wheel of the law". However, even today, the flag must still be made of hand-woven thread.

In 1929, the INC passed a resolution demanding Indian independence. Gandhi initiated a campaign of civil disobedience in its support, which would form the basis for his global fame. In the spring of 1930, he organised a salt march, to the west coast of India lasting for several weeks, with a small number of followers (satyagrahis) trained in civil disobedience. He notified the Viceroy in advance of this action. When he arrived at the coast, he and his supporters, in front of the global press, collected several grains of salt from the sea. This was a punishable act, since the British colonial authorities had a monopoly on salt and drew a considerable portion of their funds from the salt tax. Thousands of Indians followed Gandhi's example in different parts of India. During one march to a salt depot, countless satyagrahis were bludgeoned with bamboo rods filled with lead, leading to several fatalities. Tens of thousands were imprisoned. Finally, Gandhi, too, was interned for 9 months. The campaign against the salt tax went hand in hand with a boycott, mainly by women, of shops selling alcohol, in order to achieve a prohibition on alcohol and thus also the loss of the tax on alcohol, which was a considerable source of revenue. When the global economic crisis led to a drastic drop in prices for wheat, millet and rice, a campaign was launched among the farmers of refusal to pay the land tax that placed a severe strain on their resources. When the British Labour government finally declared that it was willing to enter into round-table negotiations with the Indian parties, and in particular with the INC and Gandhi, concerning a reform of the constitution and the economic and other problems in India, Gandhi brought the sweeping campaign of civil disobedience to an end. However, the negotiations in London did not produce a successful result.

Gandhi regarded one of his greatest failures as being his inability to prevent India from splitting apart. Muhammad Ali Jinnah (1876–1948), who was 3 years old than Gandhi, already became his political opponent in the national movement at an early stage. He left the INC in 1920 after being actively involved in the party for two decades. However, many Muslims remained as members of the INC. In 1916, the INC and the Muslim League demanded in a joint declaration, the Lucknow Pact, that India should attain the status of a dominion. In response, the British government agreed to a gradual transition to self-government. In 1909, the British colonial authorities had strengthened the political clout of the Muslims by introducing separate constituencies for Hindus and Muslims for the Viceroys legislative council, in order to weaken the influence of the INC. Without intending do, this paved the way for the partition of India in 1947.

5.5 Turning Points at Which the Non-violent Movement for an Independent India Failed

Looking back, the outstanding role played by Mohandas K. Gandhi and the non-violent strategy in the Indian national independence movement appears to be undisputed. However, there were repeated phases in the history of the Indian national movement after the violent uprising of 1857–1859 in which politicians wanted to apply a strategy implemented in many other countries, including in India, involving the use of force. Additionally, during the course of the following century, there were repeated cases of unrest, with many casualties. In 1907, the INC split into two branches, one of which was led by Bal Gangadhar Tilak, who propagated the national revolutionary uprising. After the death of Tilak, the movement's importance declined and it reunited with the moderate reformist branch. Under Gandhi's influence, this branch became politically radicalised, although it adopted the approach of non-violent mass mobilisation after 1920. Many leading members of the INC, such as Jawaharlal Nehru (1889–1964), who was President of the INC for a time, and who would later become the first prime minister of independent India from 1947 to 1964, followed Gandhi less from fundamental conviction, and rather because his non-violent individual and mass actions were successful.[33]

Several times, there was violent unrest when Gandhi was interned or threatened. This explains why the British avoided arresting him whenever possible, or even released him from prison prematurely, in order to prevent outbreaks of violence. Gandhi was also always willing to enter into dialogue, and was also prepared to compromise on many issues. To this extent, the threat and option of violent protest and resistance was a key factor in the success of non-violent protest among a large minority in Indian society. When Gandhi made compromises, he was frequently deceived by his partners in South Africa and India alike, who broke the agreements they made with him. This repeatedly led to a considerable loss of face for Gandhi and

---

[33] See Rothermund (2010).

gave impetus to politicians within and beyond the INC to take measures that were just as brutal as those employed by the colonial government. Thus, the terrorist Bhagat Singh, who threw a bomb into the parliament in New Delhi, and who was executed in March 1931, was just as popular as Gandhi.[34]

During the Second World War, around two million Indians fought on the British side. However, some of them regarded Germany and Japan as their natural alliance partners in the fight against British colonial rule. Gandhi and the INC were not willing to enter into an alliance with the two dictators, however. Subhas Chandra Bose (1897–1945), who was a long-term supporter of Gandhi, and who was president of the INC in 1937 and 1939, initially founded an "Indian Legion" in Germany, consisting of 3500 prisoners of war. However, they were hardly ever used, due to Hitler's racist prejudice. In 1943, Bose was taken to Japan by submarine, where he founded an "Indian National Army" with 87,000 members, which fought side by side with the Japanese against the British in Burma, and which advanced towards India after the British had conquered Singapore and Malaysia. Bose also formed a government in exile, "Free India" (*Azad Hind*).

In Bengal, a major famine broke out as a result of the war. Under these circumstances, Gandhi pressed for full independence for India, claiming that Japan was unlikely to be interested in conquering India, but was only waging war against the British Empire. For this reason, he caused the INC to pass a Quit India resolution in August 1942, whereupon he was sent to prison for 2 years by the British, together with the entire leadership of the INC. They remained incarcerated until the end of the war.

Soon after the war, the British came to the conclusion that they could no longer maintain their colonial regime in India without risking a costly war against the insurgent Indians. The strong political influence of the Muslim League under Muhammad Ali Jinnah, which since 1940 had taken up the proposal, with its Pakistan Resolution, of partitioning India into two nations, and which now demanded the establishment of a separate Muslim nation state, moved the British to agree to the founding of two independent states of Pakistan and India. For a long time, Gandhi attempted to prevent this from happening; however, ultimately, he was forced to bend to willingness of the INC to see the country divided. In the tense, as yet unresolved political situation of August 1946, the prime minister of Bengal organised a massacre of 5000 Hindus by Muslims in Calcutta, which was then followed by mass murders of Muslims perpetrated by Hindus in those areas in which Muslims were in the minority. While Gandhi travelled to Bengal, where he was able to contain the acts of violence through his speeches and public prayer meetings (which led Viceroy Mountbatten to write the letter quoted at the beginning of this lecture), in other regions, new violent conflicts broke out. These caused the British to withdraw from India and led to the partition of the country after attempts at federalisation failed. When Gandhi voiced his support for a fair separation of the British-Indian state finances between Pakistan and India, he was shot by a Hindu

---

[34]Rothermund (1997, p. 281).

extremist who, like many others, regarded Gandhi as being a traitor to the Hindu cause, since Pakistan was able to use the money received to wage its war against India in Kashmir.

The border between Pakistan and India was not negotiated between the Muslim and Hindu organisation, but was octroyed by the British. The border was drawn on the basis of a religious state map, creating areas with a Muslim and a Hindu majority, without taking the Sikhs into account. The task was assigned by the British to Cyril Radcliffe, who had never been in India and who also had no personal relationship with the country, and who was therefore considered to be non-partisan.[35] The precise course of the border was not announced until the date the two states became independent, a move that contributed significantly to the extreme violence that followed.

5.6 The Favourable Historical Constellation for Gandhi's Partial Political Successes

Shortly before he was assassinated, Gandhi recognised that he had failed to achieve fundamental reform of Indian society in a shared state in a spirit of non-violence and religious plurality and tolerance. He was successful in overcoming British colonial rule, albeit only through the establishment of an Islamic Republic of Pakistan and of a secular, multi-religious Indian state, in which 40 million Muslims remained. There is no doubt that Gandhi also gave important, sustained impetus to the social recognition and equality of both the "Untouchables" (those who belonged to no caste, and who were assigned the lowest tasks) and to women, although they were still a long way from full emancipation. Finally, his historic example still has an impact today on non-violent and peaceful movements throughout the world.

Gandhi's successes and the peaceful national movement must be seen in the light of a historical constellation that was favourable in many respects. First, this was a movement supported by a huge national majority against colonial rule that was upheld only by a relatively small colonial bureaucracy and military. Second, there were only a small number of weapons circulating in Indian society. Third, despite repeated infringements of the law and a brutal use of force, the British rulers abided by fundamental legal norms, and opened up significant educational opportunities and access to the judicial system to an Indian elite. Over time, they created regional and central parliamentary institutions through several constitutional reforms (1909, 1919, 1935). They endeavoured to avoid violent uprisings wherever possible, and were therefore willing to compromise with the INC and Gandhi. Under a totalitarian regime, Gandhi would never have had the opportunity to develop his strategy as he had in South Africa or India, and would very likely have been killed at an early stage in one way or another. Fourth, Britain as a global power had been decisively weakened by two world wars. Fifth, the upcoming global power, the USA, which under President Roosevelt had sent its own troops to India to defend the British

---

[35]On the treatment of the princely states and above all Kashmir, see the Jahn lecture (2015).

Empire against the Japanese, who were advancing into the subcontinent from Burma, exerted pressure on the British to end colonial rule. Finally, sixth, in July 1945, the coalition government led by the Conservatives under Winston Churchill, who had not been willing to give up British colonial rule, was replaced by a Labour government under Clement Attlee,[36] who finally agreed to terminating British colonial rule in India.

References

Ebert T (1969) Gewaltfreier Aufstand. Alternative zum Bürgerkrieg, 2nd edn. Rombach, Freiburg i. B
Erikson EH (1993) Gandhi's truth. On the origin of militant nonviolence (1969). W. W. Norton, New York/London
Fischer L (1962) Mahatma Gandhi. Sein Leben und seine Botschaft an die Welt, Ullstein, Berlin, in English Fischer L (2015) The life of Mahatma Gandhi (1951). Copyrighted Material
Freier (1930) Der revolutionäre Aufschwung in Indien. In: Die Kommunistische Internationale XI, No. 17, pp. 951–955
Fuhrmann M (ed) (1989) Platon: Apologie des Sokrates. Reclam, Stuttgart
Gandhi M (1924) Jung Indien. Aufsätze aus den Jahren 1919 bis 1922. Rotapfel, Erlenbach-Zürich
Gandhi M (1958–1994) Collected works of Mahatma Gandhi (CWMG), 100 volumes. Publications Division, Government of India, Delhi
Gandhi A (1981) Kasturbai und Mahatma Gandhi. Hinder und Deelmann, Gladenbach
Gandhi MK (1983) An autobiography or the story of my experiments with truth (1927/29). Penguin, Harmondsworth
Gandhi MK (2010) Hind Swaraj. Cambridge University Press, Cambridge
Gandhi MK (2017) Satyagraha in South Africa (1928). Indian ebooks, Ahmedabad
Historical Population of United Kingdom, 43 AD to Present, http://chartsbin.com/view/28k
Jahn E (2015) Kashmir: flashpoint for a nuclear war or even a Third World War. In: World political challenges. Political issues under debate, vol 3. Springer, Heidelberg, pp 205–220
Jaspers K (1960) Die Atombombe und die Zukunft des Menschen, 2nd edn. Piper, Munich
Kulke H, Rothermund D (2006) Geschichte Indiens. Von der Induskultur bis heute. Beck, Munich
Mann M (2005) Geschichte Indiens. Vom 18. Bis zum 21. Jahrhundert. Schöningh, Paderborn
Mühlmann WE (1950) Mahatma Gandhi. Der Mann, sein Werk und seine Wirkung. Eine Untersuchung zur Religionssoziologie und politischen Ethik. J.C.B. Mohr, Tübingen
Reissner (1930) Gandhi, der Prophet der indischen Bourgeoisie. In: Die Kommunistische Internationale XI, No. 20, pp 1130–1138
Rothermund D (1997) Mahatma Gandhi. Eine politische Biographie, 2nd edn. Beck, Munich
Rothermund D (2002) Geschichte Indiens. Vom Mittelalter bis zur Gegenwart. Beck, Munich
Rothermund D (2010) Gandhi und Nehru. Zwei Gesichter Indiens. Kohlhammer, Stuttgart
Rothermund D (2011) Gandhi. Der gewaltlose Revolutionär, 2nd edn. Beck, Munich
Ruskin J (2011) Unto this last (1860). Dixie Publishing, Lamar
Singh U (2017) Political violence in ancient India. Harvard University Press, Cambridge, MA
Thoreau HD (2014) Civil disobedience (The resistance to Civil Government 1849), Copyrighted material
Tolstoy L (2017) The kingdom of God is within you. CreateSpace Independent Publishing Platform
Weber M (1988) Politik als Beruf (1919). In: Gesammelte Politische Schriften, 5th edn. J. C. B. Mohr, Tübingen, pp 505–560

---

[36]The British Social Democrats were already inclined during their brief period of rule in 1924 and from 1929 to 1931 to agree to the Indian demands.

Is the Policy of Non-violence of Mohandas K. Gandhi a Unique Phenomenon, or Is It of Universal Significance?

Abstract

Gandhi's political actions and ideas, which were successful in many ways, have already inspired numerous civil rights and national independence movements worldwide, particularly in liberal-democratic states and in states with a certain degree of constitutionality. Non-violent policies are based on the assumption that law abidance and concepts of justice that promote human dignity and essential equality among all people can be mobilised both in a society that has hitherto been passive and to a certain extent also among political opponents, through a dogged commitment to action against injustice and a willingness to suffer in order to achieve a humanisation of social living conditions and the political order.

Since the existing law and the concepts of justice vary widely in time and space, there are numerous elements of Gandhi's ideas and actions that cannot be applied to non-violent policies in other countries and in other times, such as specific Hindu religious practices and social norms (such as the principle of reincarnation, recognition of the main castes, special protection for cows, conventions with regard to forms of communication). However, the basic principles of non-violent social behaviour and Gandhi's policies have universal significance and will probably continue to do so in the future, particularly in liberal democracies and in dictatorships that are losing their legitimacy in the eyes of an increasing proportion of the population, who are suffering from injustice. The dangers that arise from a growing escalation of violence and the means of force employed by many states that to an increasing degree cannot be overcome by violence, appear to be causing social-political movements to increasingly tend to seek non-violent strategies to overcome inhumane living conditions that are becoming unbearable. For them, the study of Gandhi's experiences and ideas remains an essential source of inspiration for their own actions, which are based on self-determination and also self-control.

Lecture given on 29.1.2018.

The core element of Gandhi's way of life is an awareness of one's responsibility not only for one's actions, but also of one's failure to put up resistance against injustice in one's own environment, which varies widely in its scope depending on one's potential social impact. Non-cooperation is the primary legal means of non-violent action. Civil disobedience is a stage of escalation of non-violent policies that requires extremely careful preparation and a consideration of the risks for the common good that it entails. It is implemented against laws that are largely perceived not only individually, but also among the population, as being unjust, which also contradicts the constitutional law that now applies everywhere, as well as international law.

6.1 The Global Inspiration of Non-violent Political Movements Arising from the Intellectual Stimuli and the Successes of Mohandas K. Gandhi

In July last year, a lecture to mark the seventieth anniversary of the creation of the states of India and Pakistan focussed on the role played by Mohandas K. Gandhi in the Indian minority movement in South Africa before the First World War and in the Indian national independence movement.[1] To mark the seventieth anniversary of Gandhi's death, today's lecture looks at his impact worldwide. During the 1920s, his ideas and above all his political successes already inspired civil rights and peace movements throughout the world, including in Germany.[2] In particular, the model of Gandhi's non-violent movement was a key source of inspiration for the Afro-American civil rights movement under Martin Luther King (1929–1968).[3] Structurally, the US civil rights movement, as the movement of an ethnic-racial minority, had more in common with the Indian movement in South Africa against the beginnings of the Boer-English policy of Apartheid from 1894 to 1914 than with the independence movement in India.

The example of the Indian minority movement and the Indian National Congress (INC) was also a major influence on the African National Congress (ANC) and the South African-Indian Congress and its defiance campaign against unjust laws under the leadership of Nelson Mandela (1918–2013) in 1952 and 1953. It ended with the arrest of 8500 activists and trials for high treason against Mandela and others. Mandela was not a supporter of non-violent policies in general, but merely accepted

---

[1] Jahn (2019), Erikson (1993), Mühlmann (1950), Gunturu (1999) and Blume (1987).
[2] Jahn (1993).
[3] As a student, King was fascinated by a lecture or sermon about India and Gandhi, and began to study his activities intensively. King (1968, p. 74), cf. also Oates (1984, p. 50). See also Lewis (1970, p. 34). In 1959, he visited the places where Gandhi campaigned in India. King himself said: "It was in this Gandhian emphasis on love and nonviolence that I discovered the method for social reform that I had been seeking." Carson (2000, p. 24). See also Scott King (1979, p. 54).

it as a tactic, while at times approving of violent unrest: "I do not consider non-violence according to the Gandhian model to be an inviolable principle, but a tactic to be employed depending on the situation. The principle was not so important that one should pursue the strategy even if it was self-destructive, as Gandhi believed."[4]

Lesser known campaigns were inspired by Gandhi, such as that of Danilo Dolci (1924–1997) who initiated a non-violent reformist movement in Sicily.[5] Ibrahim Rugova (1944–2006), the chairman of the Democratic League of Kosovo and then the first president of independent Kosovo from 2002 to 2006, was lauded as the "Gandhi of the Balkans",[6] but did not refer to Gandhi himself in his policies of non-violence and the institutionalisation of a shadow state with numerous functioning underground administration, education and health facilities during the 1990s.[7] Dolci was popularly known as the "Gandhi of Sicily", in the way that the press clearly enjoys recreating new, regional "Gandhis" every so often. The list of leaders of regional and national non-violent civil rights, reformist and independence movements throughout the world who were inspired by Gandhi could be extended even further. The aim here is not to provide a detailed history of the impact of Gandhi's ideas and actions on the policies of non-violence in a very large number of countries. The purpose here is rather to discuss the key reasons for non-violent policies as presented by Gandhi in many scattered texts, most of them newspaper articles and letters, as well as the fundamental objections to these policies. Finally, an assessment will be made of the possible future prospects for success throughout the world of both general non-violent policies in line with Gandhi's thinking and also non-violent, pragmatic-tactical policies that are willing to shift towards limited violence in specific situations.

6.2 Gandhi's Concept of Religion and Politics and Fundamental Objections to It

From Gandhi's statements scattered over the many newspaper articles and letters, and in the few longer works, a systematically reflected, consistent concept of religion and policy, in other words, one with a theoretical foundation, can be discerned, which is based on the ethical norms explicitly referred to by him. Gandhi described

---

[4]Mandela (2013, p. 147, 182). The political context in which Mandela's views changed is discussed by Limb (2008, pp. 33–62, in comparison with Gandhi, p. 50). As an example of the uncritical glorification of Mandela, see also Sharma (2014, pp. 25, 138–142).

[5]Dolci (1969).

[6]Birukoff (2006).

[7]Clearly, the pragmatic consideration that the Albanians were in the minority compared to the Serbs, and that above all, they had no weapons, was a decisive factor in Rugova's policy, as emphasised by Prorok (2004, pp. 93–96). Not possible to access: Ahmeti (2017).

himself as a Hindu[8] who follows the particular orientation of the faith towards the god Vishnu. However, he does not differentiate between various gods, but regards the ideas of god in all religions as being an approach to comprehending the godly, which he also describes as truth. To this extent, it became a matter of course for him to use ritual prayers from all the major religions in his public prayer meetings. Despite his roots in the Hindu tradition, Gandhi generally had a pan-religious, polyreligious outlook, which attempted to learn from all the holy scripts. In his view, there was no holy script that was an exclusive epiphany of god, but that rather, such writings were an attempt by humankind to understand the godly. Therefore, Gandhi clearly did not perceive god to be a male entity, but as a normative principle of truth, love and respect for all life, not just human life. In this sense, for Gandhi, atheists could also be religious.

For Gandhi, truth is not something that one can possess, but one can only strive to achieve it, without ever succeeding. The goal of this striving is non-violence[9] as "a perfect state. It is a goal towards which all mankind moves naturally though unconsciously."[10] In Gandhi's view, a man would not become divine but perhaps simply a true man, whereas in the present state he is only partly man and partly beast because "we deliver blow for blow and develop the measure of anger required for the purpose. We pretend to believe that retaliation is the law of our being, whereas in every scripture we find that retaliation is nowhere obligatory but only permissible... Restraint is the law of our being. For, highest perfection is unattainable without highest restraint. Suffering is thus the badge of the human tribe. The goal ever recedes from us. The greater the progress, the greater the recognition of our unworthiness. Satisfaction lies in the effort, not in the attainment. Full effort is full victory."[11]

For Gandhi, religion is not just a matter of belief, realisation and thought, but above all of behaviour, in other words, action and omission of action with regard to other people and living things. As a result, for Gandhi, religion is naturally and of necessity social and also political. "Those who say that religion has nothing to do with politics do not know what religion means."[12] It cannot be purely contemplative,

---

[8]"It is not the Hindu religion, which I certainly prize above all other religions, but the religion which transcends Hinduism, which changes one's very nature, which binds one indissolubly to the truth within and which ever purifies. It is the permanent element in human nature which counts no cost too great in order to find full expression and which leaves the soul utterly restless until it has found itself, known its Maker and appreciated the true correspondence between the Maker and itself." CWMG (1999, vol. 20, p. 304).

[9]Among the supporters of non-violence, there is general agreement that the negative term is not satisfactory, and can also hardly be replaced by the Sanskrit neologism Satyagraha. Martin Arnold attempts to replace it with the word "Gütekraft" and to prove that it is appropriate across different cultures and worldviews, in different religious and atheistic concepts alike, see Arnold (2011, pp. 89–94, 36–39).

[10]CWMG (1999, vol. 26, p. 292).

[11]CWMG (1999, vol. 26, pp. 262–263).

[12]Gandhi (1983, p. 453).

observing the world; it is expressed through activity in the world, through a life-protecting mode of living that entails loving one's neighbour; it strives to achieve justice, not just for oneself, but also for one's own environment and potential field of impact. To this extent, individuals are not only responsible for their actions, but also for their omissions to act in order to help people in their environment who are being treated unjustly. That is why for Gandhi, religion is always political. For him, the yardstick by which he judges his actions is his "inner voice," as he calls it; in other words, his conscience.[13] This is not present in the form of religious imperatives or prohibitions that he has taken from one holy scripture or another, and to which he refers as the highest authority, for example in relation to secular legislators. He only recognises those religious imperatives that make sense to him, and for which he can provide sensible reasons.[14] There is therefore no fundamental difference between Gandhi's socio-political ideas and any secular, rational, humanistic thought. It should be analysed according to the same measures and adjudged on the basis of its practicability in society and in politics.

Naturally, Gandhi knows that not everyone's conscience tells them the same thing that his does, although he often also deals with people who he assumes are doing something that they themselves regard as being unjust. It is in this latter group of people that he wishes to mobilise the conscience through his non-violent resistance and his suffering, in order to motivate and urge them to change their behaviour. At the same time, for him, suffering to which one consciously submits oneself also means self-purification and examining one's own conscience. Certainly, he acknowledges the decision made by those whose conscience motivates them to behave in a different way from him. And as a politically minded lawyer, he also acknowledges the necessity for restricting the anarchy of individual consciences through an overall, binding law and statutes. As a consequence, he generally recognises the existing statutory law and the legal order (he usually only indirectly considers the hierarchy of constitutional and simple laws) and the state institutions of the legislator, the government and administration and jurisprudence, and in an apparently schizophrenic way proclaims and demands fundamental obeisance of the law on the one hand, while at the same time, in an act of civil disobedience, which he has publicly announced, targetedly and in a controlled manner breaks individual laws that he regards as being unjust. The reconciliation of the contradiction between obeisance of the law and breaking the law emerges from the fact that Gandhi not only accepts the punishments meted out by the court, but even explicitly

---

[13] "The only tyrant I accept in this world is the 'still small voice' within me." CWMG (1999, vol. 26, p. 260).

[14] "For I do not believe in the exclusive divinity of the Vedas. I believe the Bible, the Koran, and the Zend Avesta to be as much divinely inspired as the Vedas. My belief in the Hindu scriptures does not require me to accept every word and every verse as divinely inspired. Nor do I claim to have any first-hand knowledge of these wonderful books. But I do claim to know and feel the truths of the essential teaching of the scriptures. I decline to be bound by any interpretation, however learned it may be, if it is repugnant to reason or moral sense." CWMG (1999, vol. 24, p. 371).

demands them.[15] This requires consciously provocative, active suffering that has been thoroughly mentally prepared, which differs fundamentally from the suffering passively endured by most people. This philosophy of suffering fundamentally differentiates Gandhi's thinking from all common political ideology. It clearly alienates most political theorists from Gandhi's ideas, and may perhaps also require political thinking as a precondition.

Gandhi knew as a matter of course that there are different notions of what is just and unjust. For Gandhi, conscience was not a fixed entity, but the intellectual conclusion drawn from a situation analysed by him, in which he balanced the interests of all involved against each other, and by all means following a communicative process with these people, and above all also with those who opposed his ideas. The inner voice of his conscience was, therefore, not a dogmatic, a priori doctrine that was set in stone, that he had concocted himself or drawn from holy scriptures, but the result of a social process of reflection. Accordingly, he could regard his inner voice as being a voice from the people when he experienced support for his activities from a section of the population that was underpinned by active participation, such as for the Salt March of 1930 or the spinning and weaving of self-made clothing. However, he was repeatedly forced to recognise that he had entirely misjudged the actual response of parts of the population to his campaigns, as a result of which he abandoned them, and did not prolong them with an overblown adherence to what he felt was right and wrong. This communicative understanding of an acknowledgement of the existing legal order and breaking the law repeatedly enabled him to also reach compromises with opponents whom he regarded as being guided by genuine conviction. This also enabled him to recognise his own errors. Gandhi was only dogmatic when it came to his own non-violent behaviour. He was thoroughly aware that most of his supporters only avoided violence for opportunistic reasons, and could also accept that others used violence when they felt that only violent resistance against injustice was possible.

In his view, it was always necessary to differentiate between violence used for a just cause and violence used to implement injustice. For him, violence was not always the same, and neither was war.[16] He declared unequivocally that resistance with violence against an injustice was preferable over tolerance of the injustice out of

---

[15]When Gandhi was sentenced to 6 years' imprisonment in 1922 due to his call in three newspaper articles to join a campaign of non-cooperation and civil disobedience against the existing governmental system, during which terrible acts of violence were committed by Indians against policemen and other representatives of the authorities, he declared that: "The only course open to you, the Judge, is either to resign your post and thus dissociate yourself from evil, if you feel that the law you are called upon to administer is an evil and that in reality I am innocent; or to inflict on me the severest penalty if you believe that the system and the law you are assisting to administer are good for the people of this country and that my activity is, therefore, injurious to the public weal." CWMG (1999, vol. 26, p. 385).

[16]"My non-violence does recognize different species of violence-defensive and offensive. It is true that in the long run the difference is obliterated, but the initial merit persists. A non-violent person is bound, when the occasion arises, to say which side is just. Thus I wished success to the Abyssinians, the Spaniards, the Czechs, the Chinese and the Poles, though in each case I wished that they could

cowardice.[17] So it was that in his view, the armed resistance put up by a large number of Poles against the German expansionist policy was "almost non-violent".[18]

The main argument against a policy of non-violence on principle as opposed to unjust or even illegal, unconstitutional, state or private-societal violence is the pragmatic argument that it is usually unsuccessful. A second frequent argument states that violent behaviour towards people who use violence requires an "inhumane" willingness to suffer and, in extreme cases, even willingness to die, which most people do not have and which should not be demanded of them in the first place. It is natural, so the argument goes, that people should use force to defend themselves against unjust private-societal and also state violence, when other peaceful, legal means have been exhausted.

The neutral, social and historical question relates to the conditions under which politically relevant groups among the population have found the strength to offer non-violent resistance against holders and users of violence, and in some cases have even been successful in their efforts, and under which conditions non-violent resistance collapses and perhaps then transforms into violent resistance, or perhaps does not come into being in the first place. Also, are only religious people, and Hindus in particular, capable of non-violent resistance with a high level of willingness to suffer and die, since they believe in a life after death, or even in reincarnation in another form? Another question relates to the possible indications that non-violent resistance against unjust conditions could play an increasingly important role in global society in the future.

6.3 Gandhi's Strong Impact on Civil Rights and Freedom Movements and His Low Degree of Influence on International Politics

In the introduction, I named several leaders of civil rights movements, mostly from western democracies, who were influenced by Gandhi's historical example, his writings and his actions. However, many activists in these movements and in the

---

have offered non-violent resistance." (Harijan 9.12.1939, https://www.mkgandhi.org/momgandhi/chap29.htm). Quote found in Kraus (1957, p. 266).

[17] "I do believe that where there is only a choice between cowardice and violence, I would advise violence." For this reason, Gandhi advised the following: "I advocate training in arms for those who believe in the method of violence. I would rather have India resort to arms in order to defend her honour than that she should in a cowardly manner become or remain a helpless witness to her own dishonour. But I believe that non-violence is infinitely superior to violence, forgiveness is more manly than punishment." CWMG (1999, vol. 21, p. 133).

[18] "If a man fights with his sword single-handed against a horde of dacoits armed to the teeth, I should say he is fighting almost non-violently... In the same way, for the Poles to stand valiantly against the German hordes vastly superior in numbers, military equipment and strength, was almost non-violence...You must give its full value to the word 'almost'." CWMG (1999, vol. 79, pp. 121–122).

international peace movement felt inspired by Gandhi even though most of them only knew his name at best, and referred to other sources of inspiration for their work, such as directly to holy scriptures and in particular to the Sermon on the Mount in the New Testament,[19] or to Henry David Thoreau (1817–1862).[20]

Gandhi also exerted an indirect, strong influence, first over publications covering non-violent policies, however limited it may be, and second over the generally marginal branch of peace research that aims to develop theoretical and conceptional conclusions from Gandhi's thought and actions, as well as from other historical examples of non-violent policies. In Germany, these authors include, in particular, Theodor Ebert[21] (born 1937) and his former colleagues such as Gernot Jochheim (born 1942),[22] who worked for the journal "Gewaltfreie Aktion" (in English: "Non-Violent Action"; from 1969 to 2010). The most influential person on the international political stage was and remains Gene Sharp (born 1928) from the US, who developed guidelines for non-violent policies based not only on the non-violent movement in India but also on many other historical events.[23] There is evidence that Sharp influenced the civil rights movements in Serbia, Georgia, Ukraine, Kyrgyzstan, Myanmar and Egypt.[24]

Gandhi's influence on non-Indian national independence movements appears to have been fairly weak, although evidence can be found here and there of his impact, for example in Ghana (on the young Kwame Nkrumah 1909–1972),[25] and in other countries in Africa,[26] or in Georgia (at times on Zviad Gamsakhurdia, 1939–1993).[27] This influence was and remains far greater on civil rights movements that demand individual and social freedoms, human rights, the rule of law and liberal democracy. Even under National Socialist rule in Germany, non-violent resistance was successful

---

[19] See e.g. Alt (1983). More than 20 editions had been published by 2000.
[20] Thoreau (2014).
[21] Ebert (1969, 1984). See also Steinweg and Laubenthal (2011).
[22] Jochheim (1984, 1986).
[23] Sharp (1973). Brief instructions for action without any reference to Gandhi are provided by: Sharp (2010). This booklet has been translated into 31 languages.
[24] On these movements, see also the lectures "Der zweite Demokratisierungsversuch, in Serbien, Georgien und der Ukraine", Jahn (2008, pp. 149–165) and "Democratisation or the Restoration of Dictatorship as the Outcome of the Arab Rebellion", Jahn (2015, pp. 171–186).
[25] Hountondji (1983, pp. 135, 146).
[26] See the examples of Julius Nyerere in Tanzania, Kenneth Kaunda in Zambia, Albert Luthuli in South Africa and Sam Nujoma in Namibia. It is noticeable that all these cases occurred in Anglo-Africa and not in Franco- or Ibero-Africa. Kaunda once said that if he were to be forced to select a colonial power, he would choose the British, "because I would be in a position to go to their country and lead a campaign against their own government" Sutherland and Meyer (2000, p. 110).
[27] Gamsachurdia (1995, p. 148).

in some cases, such as against the deportation of the Jewish partners of non-Jews from Rosenstrasse street in Berlin.[28] Attempts were also made to assert non-violent resistance against the conquest and occupation policies of other states, such as in Norway (1940–1945[29]) and in Czechoslovakia in 1968.[30] Gandhi himself considered both the issue of possible non-violent resistance among the Jews against the violent National Socialist rule[31] as well as a non-violent defence of India against Japan and of Britain and Poland against the German Reich, which could not constitute a defence of the border and which required toleration of the military occupation. At the end of his life, he was also concerned with the question of how non-violent resistance could be asserted against the use of atomic weapons.[32]

6.4 Contentious Basic Assumptions with Regard to Gandhi's Political Understanding

Gandhi never claimed that violent resistance against unjust, subjugating violence is illegitimate on principle. He only said that he himself did not wish to use violence, and that he also wished that his fellow political activists and other people in general would waive violent measures in favour of non-violent ones. What was his justification for this stance? And how can sociologists and political scientists explain that non-violent resistance is successful in some cases and not in others, either because it transmogrifies into violent resistance, or because it collapses entirely and a violent regime succeeds in suppressing any form of resistance over a longer period of time?

Gandhi never criticised or combated violence or the use of physical and psychical violence per se. His motivation for taking social and political action was always the experience of social, and later also political, injustice, which led him to protest and resist, either alone or together with other people, in practice nearly always with Indians. He never became involved in resistance campaigns or solidarity campaigns for suppressed people in other countries,[33] but stated when asked by foreigners about possible resistance in other countries on principle that a universal human approach to the issue of resistance against unjust living conditions was possible.

---

[28] Jochheim (2002) and Gruner (2002, 2004).

[29] Mez (1976).

[30] Horský (1975).

[31] Rothermund (1997, pp. 395–397).

[32] See also the Gandhi quote in Erikson (1993, p. 515) and Rothermund (1997, pp. 503–504).

[33] The purpose of the Khilafat, i.e. the caliphate movement, supported by Gandhi from 1919 to 1924, was not primarily to support the Ottoman caliph and his Turkish supporters, but above all to offer solidarity with the Indian Muslims, see in detail Rothermund (1997, pp. 133–140, 182–183).

Non-violent resistance can take two basic forms: a legal one that is in compliance with the law, and an illegal, unlawful one, which both require different disadvantages to be taken into account.[34] Non-cooperation, such as resigning from one's post in the state administration or in a company that offers miserable working conditions or produces unacceptable goods, may entail a drastic reduction in one's own standard of living, while boycotting certain goods, on the other hand, may sometimes only mean doing without certain conveniences. Generally, boycotting certain goods does not have any direct impact on individuals, aside from members of parliament seeking election. However, non-cooperation can lead to a violent response among those who had counted on the individual's continued cooperation. Then, non-cooperation initially entails suffering from acts of violence without responding with violence oneself, even if legal and political means should be used against the perpetrators of the violence.

The most contentious form of non-violent resistance is civil disobedience,[35] in other words, consciously and openly breaking the law and openly announcing this fact to one's opponent. Either a law is broken that is regarded as being unjust, or another law is broken in its place that represents it. The Rowlatt Act of 1919 in India was an emergency law, for example, which could not be disobeyed as long as it was not applied, and which incidentally never was applied in practice. However, Gandhi mobilised his followers to civil disobedience in defiance of it. The systematically organised infringement of the prohibition on privately taking salt from the sea during the famous Salt March in 1930 was not motivated by the fact that this law was perceived as being unjust, but rather, it was chosen by Gandhi as a symbol of foreign rule by the British when he began a campaign for independence, for which he presented eleven specific demands, including amendments to or the abolition of certain laws.[36]

The state can respond in various different ways to a breach of the law. It can ignore it and attempt to undermine the intention of the perpetrators to lead the state to impose repressive measures. It can also impose financial penalties (which only rarely occurred in India, since many of those who broke the law were simply unable to pay them; this approach tended to be applied in Europe), or it can attempt to initiate court proceedings that lead to imprisonment, and finally, it can even use direct, physical force that either causes injury or is fatal. The acceptance of the financial penalty or imprisonment and the tolerance of the use of repressive private or state force without responding in kind with force, but merely with legal and political means, is more deeply embedded in the fundamental acceptance, mentioned above, of the state legal order and the right of the state organs to penalise breaches of the law.

To this extent, the refusal on principle to pay taxes (as opposed to rejecting a particular type of tax) can be only the most extreme means of non-violent policy,

---

[34] Gene Sharp compiled a detailed list of 198 forms or methods of non-violent action, Sharp (1973, vol. 2: The Methods of Nonviolent Action).
[35] Braune (2017).
[36] Rothermund (1997, pp. 248–272).

6.4 Contentious Basic Assumptions with Regard to Gandhi's Political Understanding

which should generally be avoided, since when applied systematically and en masse, it would endanger the existence of the state and thus also the entire legal order. For this reason, unlike Thoreau,[37] Gandhi never propagated this instrument of resistance. The publicly announced, non-violent breach of the law was intended to force the state legislative bodies to abolish or amend the law that was regarded as being unjust. The voluntary willingness to suffer is aimed at making it clear to the holders of state power that the demands for just laws are serious, after petitions and protest rallies (in autocratic systems) or regular, institutional procedures such as claims made before the constitutional court, elections, involvement in the formation of policies by political parties, and demonstrations (in liberal, democratic constitutional states) have all had no impact. Non-violent resistance and a limited willingness to suffer, which is also required in liberal democracies, are an important form of dramatization of necessary legislative policy conflicts that go beyond the calmer forms of parliamentary conflict and court proceedings.

In times of violent conflict and wars, far more suffering is usually involved than when non-violent campaigns are brutally suppressed. However, most people, probably 95% or more, tend to be willing to participate, either actively or with moral support, in civil and state wars when they regard their vital interests as having been violated, or to subjugate themselves to those in power, than to offer non-violent resistance in such cases. There is little to suggest that these attitudes will change within the space of just a few decades, if at all. How else is the greater willingness to suffer in wars than through non-violent resistance to be explained?

On the one hand, there are different reasons for a willingness to suffer, and to suffer in specific ways. While in many wars, a hero's death and the willingness to die in this way is glorified (*dulce et decorum est, pro patria mori* or to die for another just cause), this is not the case when it comes to the non-violent approach. However, the suffering of people who have been severely injured or raped, or who are languishing in prisons and concentration camps, is usually not mentioned, although it is accepted. While it may be regarded as being "sweet and honourable" to die for a just cause, the same does not apply to being beaten and tortured, and lying in a military hospital with severe wounds. By contrast, with the non-violent approach, physical and psychical suffering, which more rarely does not last for life, is addressed in far greater depth and is acknowledged as the price for resistance against injustice. For Gandhi it is also even occasionally regarded as a means of self-purification.

A second difference appears to lie in the fact that one's own suffering and if necessary, one's own death appear more tolerable when one has inflicted a greater suffering, if possible, on one's enemy. Violent heroism in war includes the heroic act of boldly injuring and killing enemies, not just one's own bold death. The exertion of violent power appears to make it easier to countenance one's own powerlessness. The *satyagrahi*, the non-violent resistor, must do without such direct compensation for their own powerlessness. This requires considerable psychical preparation,

---

[37]Thoreau (2014).

training and self-discipline. The non-violent resistor must in the most extreme case be more courageous than a warrior or soldier. For the non-violent resistor, the justification for one's own suffering lies in the fact that their resistance will in the longer or shorter term contribute to a change of attitude among those in power to rectify an injustice. In democracies, this means the holders of legislative power, the courts or the government and administration.

Thus, in the history of the labour movement, hundreds of thousands of workers were willing to accept millions of accumulated years in prison, death, severe injuries and humiliation by participating in non-violent strikes in order to achieve key improvements in their working and living conditions and ultimately also the legal right to strike.

A third difference, as well as the advantages and disadvantages of non-violent resistance mentioned above, is that consistent non-violent resistance, which can lead to civil disobedience, in other words, a violation of the law and the acceptance of the resulting penalties or also the illegal use of force by those in power, is far less frequently implemented than violent resistance and military service. A soldier goes to war and into battle with an awareness of the risk of dying or of returning to peaceful life injured, although one of these scenarios is more or less likely. In most wars, the large majority of soldiers survive. In some battle situations, the chances of survival for the individual soldiers is close to zero, however. The justification for one's own death, for the individual and for the fighting community, is that it possibly contributes to a better life for one's surviving relatives and the political community (of a country, a people, a social class, religious community or party, etc.). Violent battle and war only make sense in terms of their unpredictable character as long as victory or defeat, survival or death are uncertain. If defeat is certain, capitulation in an individual battle or in the entire war and the conclusion of a peace accord with the most tolerable conditions for the vanquished side are advisable. The willingness of soldiers to fight in a war in which their death is certain (kamikaze attack) is an extremely rare exception in all countries and among all peoples, and requires a vast amount of indoctrination, which must usually be supported by alcohol and drugs. In most battle situations, the individual soldier has a chance of survival through their own skill and luck.

By contrast, the *satyagrahi* consciously resists the legal or illegal use of force by their political opponent, be it the state or another societal organisation or group that exerts force, which they do not wish to avoid as a matter of principle, and which they do not wish to prevent through their own use of force or through flight. To this extent, they surrender entirely to the good or bad will of their opponent, thereby displaying elements of doctrinaire self-sacrifice such as are not usually experienced by a soldier. This individual psychical factor, which makes one's own potential, but uncertain suffering appear more tolerable when suffering is also caused to one's opponent could explain why most people tend to be more willing to accept an actual or alleged defensive war with a very large number of casualties and injured than non-violent resistance with far fewer deaths and injuries in society as a whole, which makes individual suffering inevitable and which denies one the satisfaction of having caused suffering to one's opponent.

However, the non-violent resistor attempts to use all possible measures, such as the early announcement of resistance campaigns, negotiations with the opponent, influencing public opinion through the media, and finally also through their public suffering, in order to mitigate the violence inflicted by the opponent or even to motivate or force them to change their behaviour. Ideally, the opponent will realise that they are in the wrong and will change their behaviour or modify the law. In reality, non-violent acts of resistance are also successful when they are widely approved in society and when the holders of power recognise that for them, violent assertion of their interests and their interpretation of the law are costlier to them then simply giving way on the matter. The certainty that massive suppression of the non-violent resistance may under certain circumstances lead to violent unrest and uprising can also contribute to the success of non-violent resistance.

6.5 The Limited but Not Fully Exploited Scope for Action of Non-violent Policies, Now and in the Near Future

Experience since the Second World War and the death of Gandhi has shown that non-violent movements are playing an increasingly important role, both in toppling autocratic regimes and in creating change in democratic societies. Thus, for example, autocratic regimes were overcome by mainly non-violent mass movements in Iran in 1979, in the Philippines in 1986, on repeated occasions in Latin America, in communist Europe from 1989 to 1993 and in several post-communist neo-autocracies in the decades that followed, and also to a certain degree in the Arab uprisings after December 2010.[38] There are evidently two reasons for this. On the one hand, some autocratic regimes may be able to gain broad approval within society under certain conditions, but sooner or later lose this approval due to their arbitrary actions, which even breach the laws they themselves have decreed, and also due to economic ineffectiveness, corruption and extreme social injustice. Autocratic regimes are clearly less able to adjust to changing societal attitudes and socio-economic challenges than most democracies. Secondly, however, the potential for use of force by the police and military, which has grown enormously over the years, acts as a deterrent against violent resistance in many cases.[39] However, massive and determined suppression, particularly of ethno-national groups and their non-violent protests and demonstrations, can still repeatedly lead to a shift from non-violent

---

[38] A comprehensive analysis of the success and failure of 323 non-violent and violent resistance movements from 1900 to 2006 is provided by Chenoweth and Stephan (2013). According to this analysis, during this period, the success rate of non-violent movements has increased, while that of violent ones has declined (pp. 6–7).

[39] Some social-geographical factors such as sparse settlement in mountains and jungles, are doubtless more suited to guerrilla warfare than densely populated locations in urban regions. However, the long civil wars in Beirut, Aleppo and Mosul demonstrate that even in major cities, war can be conducted over a longer period of time.

movements towards movements that are willing to countenance civil war, as was the case for example in Kosovo and Syria in recent decades.

In some non-violent movements, non-violent activists have played an important pioneering role, even though most of their members—as was the case during the Indian independence movement—are not opponents of all application of force on principle. Generally, they support armed defence of the country against foreign aggression and accordingly are in favour of the military preparation that appears to be required for the purpose, in other words, the maintenance of military forces. And all people accept the need in principle for a police force that uses violent measures against criminals within the scope of what is legally permitted.[40]

Therefore, all attempts by a small number of peace researchers during the 1970s, following the spectacular one-week non-violent resistance in Czechoslovakia against the Warsaw Pact intervention troops in 1968, to use the combat methods used by non-violent resistance for systematic, state-organised preparation for non-violent defence of the country against foreign aggressors, without a military, remained entirely unsuccessful,[41] and will probably remain so in the future. At the same time, it is possible that in the future, non-violent resistance will be offered when a country is occupied by an aggressor who is far superior militarily. While this may have almost no chance of direct success, in the long term, the resistive spirit will be encouraged and when changes occur to the international constellation, success can be achieved, as was the case with the inner erosion of the Soviet occupation morale in Eastern Europe at the end of the 1980s.

During the development of the liberal democracies, non-violent resistance also took on an important function for the innovation of the law, which by itself is not sufficiently observed by institutionalised policy formation in the parliaments and democratic parties. Non-violent resistance with narrowly limited violation of the law can, in liberal democracies, express the seriousness of the will to change the law articulated initially by societal minorities. This resistance does not have to invoke extra-statutory religious or other ethical moral requirements, but can often refer to the central constitutional basic rights. Legalisation of civil disobedience cannot by definition be provided for in a legal system. However, a moralistic de-dramatization of the contradictions between the ruling and oppositional, sometimes actually historically innovative, sometimes confusing legal interpretations is certainly possible in the political culture of the liberal democratic constitutional states. Thus, Jürgen Habermas, for example, said: "Every constitutional democracy that is secure in its existence considers civil disobedience as being a normalised, since necessary, part of its political culture." He also wrote that the constitutional state "must protect and

---

[40]Gandhi certainly did have ideas about a police force that acted non-violently on principle, which countered violent crime without applying violence itself. However, these ideas were never put into practice and will probably have no chance of success in the future either. However, it is possible that the methods used by police for non-lethal suppression (water cannon, police truncheons instead of guns) will be further developed, for example the use of stun guns when dealing with dangerous wild animals.

[41]See Roberts (1969), Ebert (1981), and Jochheim (1988).

keep alive mistrust against injustice that occurs in legal forms, even though it cannot adopt an institutionally secured form."[42] The contradictions between individual legal norms and in the legal interpretations in the hierarchy of the courts and in public opinion are, according to Dworkin, signs of a very different way of handling breaches of the law in cases of civil disobedience than for criminals and those who violate civil and human rights.[43] Thus, the fact cannot be overlooked that civil disobedience plays a very important role in achieving key civil rights among the Afro-American population, as it has done in the past in the attainment of suffrage among workers and women and, more recently, in the fight for equal rights for homosexuals and the right to exist for animals and plants threatened with extinction. In many countries, the abolition of the death penalty was also preceded by a non-violent movement. Overall, a historical trend towards the civilisation of conflict behaviour can be observed, at least in the liberal democracies. In recent decades, the arming of the police with guns has been increasingly supplemented with truncheons and water cannon, so that suppressive state force has been able to replace older, lethal, police and military force when dealing with non-violent, or at least low-violence, oppositional movements.

What conclusions can be drawn from these considerations for future global-human peace policy? A one-dimensional peace policy, which focuses only on the dimension of action—such as non-violent action, diplomatic negotiation and military deterrence—does not promise success. Most people will continue to support the readiness for military defence of their country, in other words, a certain degree of military deterrence. This only has a chance of succeeding when it is incorporated into a functioning system of collective security of the United Nations, when an attack against an individual country is likely to lead to the threat of military countermeasures by the UN Security Council and possibly by all other countries. At the same time, this includes the will, particularly in a major power and in a country that is a permanent member of the UN Security Council, to refrain from attempting to create a military change to the territorial and political status quo, and also to prevent such attempts from being made in other countries through all non-military means.

Actions by governments that take responsibility for maintaining peace remain the cornerstone of all global peace policy and cannot be replaced by the oppositional activities of peace movements. Non-violent movements therefore have the task of motivating the majority of society to only bring parties and governments to power that wish to maintain or achieve peace, and to initially combat those parties and governments that do not promote peace with the existing institutional means of attempting policy change available in the respective political system, and if necessary also non-cooperation and civil disobedience. Non-violent resistance forces are therefore no alternative to armies and police units, as was claimed for a long time by

---

[42]Habermas (1985, pp. 81, 87).

[43]Dworkin (1984). Cf. also Dreier (1983) and Rawls (1999, p. 421): "A general willingness to commit acts of civil disobedience brings stability to a well organised or almost just society".

many of their activists and proponents. Instead, they are an important, partially complementary, partially antagonistic, supplement to the traditional instruments and methods of domestic and foreign policy.[44] Accordingly, there is much to suggest that non-violent resistance offers an alternative to civil war, although hardly ever to a willingness to conduct a state defensive war.

6.6 Unavoidable Setbacks of Non-violent Policies

We can be certain that numerous non-violent movements will arise in the future, in which activists who are non-violent on principle play an important, albeit rarely decisive, role. Such movements will in particular play an increasingly important role in toppling autocratic regimes, with the goal of establishing the rule of law, personal freedoms, liberal and social citizens' and human rights, the dismantling of corrupt structures and of democratic institutions and procedures. For several years, the tendencies towards global liberalisation and democratisation have declined, however. It remains to be seen as to what extent non-violent movements contribute to a reverse in developments, which mainly depends on a loss of legitimacy among the autocratic regimes in socio-economic crises. According to the New York-based Freedom House, in 2016, 39% of people out of the total global population (7.4 billion) lived in free states, 25% lived in partially free states, and 36% lived in non-free states. In 2017, of the 195 countries, 87 (45%) were categorised as free states, 59 (30%) as partially free states and 49 (25%) as non-free states.[45] It can be assumed that only a small number of regimes that assert illegitimate, autocratic or imperialist rule will succeed in becoming stabilised over a long period of time. Additionally, the unavoidable increase in problems that can only be regulated internationally, such as climate change, environmental destruction, migration, and terrorism will in the future lead to the creation of global-humane movements that will exert pressure on the states to find a way of solving these problems.

Since the process of formation of new nation states has by no means been completed, even though most larger nations have in the interim achieved their own statehood within multinational federal states or in the form of independent nation states,[46] we can assume that in the future, several non-violent national autonomy and independence movements will be formed against imperial foreign rule, even though—as past examples have shown—they will remain exposed to the risk of adopting violent strategies if they are severely repressed. Only a small number of

---

[44]The difficulty of also practicing non-violent policies as democratically responsible statesmen following attainment of national independence has been very clearly demonstrated by Kenneth Kaunda and Julius Nyerere, Sutherland and Meyer (2000, pp. 95–113, 69–89).

[45]Freedom House 2017: Freedom of the World 2017, https://freedomhouse.org/report/freedom-world/freedom-world-2017. As well as the 193 UN member states, Kosovo and the Republic of China (Taiwan) have also been included in the list of countries by Freedom House.

[46]For more detail, see the three lectures on the relationship between the state and the nation, and on nationalism, Jahn (2015, pp. 13–68).

nations, as was the case with the Norwegian, Slovak and Montenegrin states, will be in a position in the future to establish their own state without bloodshed, thanks to favourable international constellations.

With both liberal-democratic, anti-autocratic and national, anti-imperial ovements, we can repeatedly expect that they will shift towards a position of supporting civil war in the short or long term, following an initial non-violent strategy, if they are combated with ruthless violence by those in power. In Kosovo, this transition took several years following the dissolution of Yugoslavia in 1991, while in Syria, it took just a few months after the first non-violent protest rallies were held in March 2011.

Even in liberal-democratic states, it is likely that an increasing number of oppositional movements will emerge that are not satisfied with the historically achieved degree of liberalisation and democratisation in their societies, and who do not wish to simply accept the existing institutional procedures regarding policy and legislative change. In a secularised world, they will probably invoke religious norms less and less, and will increasingly base their actions on fundamental norms enshrined in the constitution and in international law, which are not met or are even contradicted by many decisions made by governments, major commercial companies and existing laws. As well as the constitutional forms of protest, legal and political influence and demonstrative non-cooperation, it is likely that to an increasing extent, acts of civil disobedience, in other words, politically moderate and controlled infringements of the rules and of the law, will play a role in communicating to the public, and to the parliaments and governments, the urgency of certain political and legislative changes. Even if civil disobedience by definition cannot be legally institutionalised, during the course of further liberalisation and democratisation in many countries, it could become regarded in many countries as being a part of a largely tolerated constitutional reality during the course of further liberalisation and democratisation, and be recognised as an important tool of continuous, dynamic self-correction in liberal-democratic systems when faced with new socio-political problems. Such progress in social policy and constitutional law will inevitably have to overcome severe setbacks in which attempts are made to regulate the respective status quo or even to restore one that has already been historically overcome.

References

Ahmeti Z (2017) Ibrahim Rugova. Ein Leben für Frieden und Freiheit im Kosovo. Tradition, Hamburg

Alt F (1983) Frieden ist möglich. Die Politik der Bergpredigt. Piper, Munich

Arnold M (2011) Gütekraft. Ein Wirkungsmodell aktiver Gewaltfreiheit nach Hildegard Goss-Mayr, Mohandas K. Gandhi und Bart de Ligt. Baden-Baden, Nomos

Birukoff A (2006) Kosovo-Präsident Rugova. Der,Gandhi des Balkans' ist tot. Spiegel-Online vom http://www.spiegel.de/politik/ausland/kosovo-praesident-rugova-der-gandhi-des-balkans-ist-tot-a-396663.html

Blume M (1987) Satyagraha. Wahrheit und Gewaltfreiheit. Yoga und Widerstand bei Gandhi. Hinder & Deelmann, Gladenbach
Braune A (ed) (2017) Ziviler Ungehorsam. Texte von Thoreau bis Occupy. Reclam, Stuttgart
Carson C (ed) (2000) The autobiography of Martin Luther King, Jr. Abacus, London
Chenoweth E, Stephan MJ (2013) Why civil resistance works. The strategic logic of non-violent conflict. Columbia University Press, New York
CWMG (1999) The collected works of Mahatma Gandhi (Electronic Book), 98 vol. Publications Division Government of India, New Delhi
Dolci D (1969) Die Zukunft gewinnen. Gewaltlosigkeit und Entwicklungsplanung. Hinder & Deelmann, Bellnhausen
Dreier R (1983) Widerstandsrecht und ziviler Ungehorsam im Rechtsstaat. In: Glotz P (ed) Ziviler Ungehorsam im Rechtsstaat. Suhrkamp, Frankfurt a.M.
Dworkin R (1984) Bürgerrechte ernstgenommen. Suhrkamp, Frankfurt a.M. (Taking Rights Seriously 1977)
Ebert T (1969) Gewaltfreier Aufstand. Alternative zum Bürgerkrieg, 2nd edn. Rombach, Freiburg iB
Ebert T (1981) Soziale Verteidigung, 2 vol. Waldkircher Verlag, Waldkirch
Ebert T (1984) Ziviler Ungehorsam. Von der APO zur Friedensbewegung. Waldkircher Verlagsgesellschaft, Waldkirch
Erikson EH (1993) Gandhi's truth. On the origin of militant nonviolence (1969). W. W. Norton, New York
Freedom House (2017) Freedom of the World 2017. https://freedomhouse.org/report/freedom-world/freedom-world-2017
Gamsachurdia K (1995) Swiad Gamsachurdia. Dissident – Präsident – Märtyrer. Perseus, Basel
Gandhi MK (1983) An autobiography or the story of my experiments with truth (1927/29). Penguin, Harmondsworth
Gruner W (2002) Die Fabrik-Aktion und die Ereignisse in der Berliner Rosenstraße. Fakten und Fiktionen um den 27. Januar 1943. Jahrb Antisemitismusforschung 11:137–177
Gruner W (2004) Ein Historikerstreit? Die Internierung der Juden aus Mischehen in der Rosenstraße 1943. Das Ereignis, seine Diskussion und seine Geschichte. Z Geschichtswissenschaft 52:5–22
Gunturu V (1999) Mahatma Gandhi. Leben und Werk, Diederichs, Munich
Habermas J (1985) Ziviler Ungehorsam – Testfall für den demokratischen Rechtsstaat. Wider den autoritären Legalismus in der Bundesrepublik. In: Die Neue Unübersichtlichkeit. Suhrkamp, Frankfurt a.M.
Horský V (1975) Prag 1968. Systemveränderung und Systemverteidigung. Klett/Kösel, Stuttgart/München
Hountondji PJ (1983) The end of 'Nhrumaism' and the (re-)birth of Nkrumah. In: African philosophy. Myth and reality. Hutchinson University Library for Africa, London
Jahn B (1993) Politik und moral: Gandhis Herausforderung für die Weimarer Republik. Weber, Zucht, Kassel
Jahn E (2008) Politische Streitfragen. Verlag für Sozialwissenschaften, Wiesbaden
Jahn E (2015) World political challenges. Political issues under debate, vol 3. Springer, Heidelberg
Jahn E (2019) The fatal glorification of Mohandas K. Gandhi as a saint. His role in the national independence movement in India. In: Jahn E (ed) War and compromise between nations and states. Springer, Cham, pp 79–95
Jochheim G (1984) Die gewaltfreie Aktion. Idee und Methoden, Vorbilder und Wirkungen. Rasch und Röhring, Hamburg
Jochheim G (1986) Länger leben als die Gewalt. Der Zivilismus als Idee und Aktion. Weitbrecht, Stuttgart
Jochheim G (ed) (1988) Soziale Verteidigung – Verteidigung mit einem menschlichen Gesicht. Patmos, Düsseldorf
Jochheim G (2002) Frauenprotest in der Rosenstraße Berlin 1943. Hentrich & Hentrich, Berlin
King ML (1968) Freiheit! Der Aufbruch der Neger Nordamerikas. Heyne, Munich (Stride Toward Freedom 1958, Harper, New York)

References

Kraus F (ed) (1957) Vom Geist des Mahatma. Ein Gandhi-Brevier. Schweizer Druck- und Verlagshaus, Zürich
Lewis DL (1970) King. A critical biography. Penguin, Baltimore
Limb P (2008) Nelson Mandela. A biography. Greenwood Press, Westport
Mandela N (2013) Long walk to freedom. Abacus, London
Mez L (1976) Ziviler Widerstand in Norwegen. Haag und Herchen, Frankfurt a.M.
Mühlmann W (1950) Mahatma Gandhi. Der Mann, sein Werk und seine Wirkung. Eine Untersuchung zur Religionssoziologie und politischen Ethik. J.C.B. Mohr, Tübingen
Oates SB (1984) Martin Luther King. Kämpfer für Gewaltlosigkeit. Biographie. Ernst Kabel, Hamburg
Prorok C (2004) Ibrahim Rugovas leadership. Eine Analyse der Politik des kosovarischen Präsidenten. Lang, Frankfurt a.M.
Rawls J (1999) A theory of justice. Harvard University Press, Cambridge
Roberts A (ed) (1969) Civilian resistance as a national defence. Non-violent action against aggression. Penguin, Harmondsworth
Rothermund D (1997) Mahatma Gandhi. Eine politische Biographie, 2nd edn. Beck, Munich
Scott King C (1979) Mein Leben mit Martin Luther King. Mohn, Gütersloh
Sharma G (2014) Nelson Mandela. The African Gandhi. Ruby Press, New Delhi
Sharp G (1973) The politics of nonviolent action, 3 vols. Porter Sargent, Boston
Sharp G (2010) From dictatorship to democracy. A conceptual framework for liberation. The Albert Einstein Institution, 4th edn. Porter Sargent, Boston
Steinweg R, Laubenthal U (ed) (2011) Gewaltfreie Aktion. Erfahrungen und Analysen. Apsel & Brandes, Frankfurt, a.M.
Sutherland B, Meyer M (2000) Guns and Gandhi in Africa. Panafrican insights on non-violence, armed struggle and liberation in Africa. Africa World Press, Trento
Thoreau HD (2014) Civil disobedience (The Resistance to Civil Government 1849), Copyrighted Material

7. Putin "Understanders" and Putin Critics: The Intense Controversy Surrounding German and Western Policy Towards Russia

Abstract

Neither in Germany nor in the west in general has there ever been consensus on the policy towards the new Russia, particularly during the course of the past 25 years. However, since the epochal violation of the territorial status quo of the state order through military force by Russia in 2014, the controversies regarding German and western Russia policy have intensified significantly. They relate both to the internal state order and to Russia's foreign policy, which in the Putin era has increasingly diverged from the notion entertained since 1991, in the west and to a large extent also in Russia, of incorporating Russia into the market economy-oriented, democratic global system.

From the beginning, the eastward expansion of NATO, as well as that of the EU to an increasing degree, was a matter of dispute in the western alliances. However, some shared German-Russian attitudes towards US global policy (military interventions in Iraq and Libya, a rejection of the NATO membership of Georgia and Ukraine, etc.), the construction of the Nordstream Baltic Sea gas pipeline and the strategy of mitigating the conflict in the Ukraine crisis have led to severe disputes. The "understanders" and critics of Russia or Putin with regard to his domestic and foreign policy are at loggerheads when it comes to deciding how to respond to the severe increase in autocratic tendencies to suppress citizens' freedoms and above all, the expansion of Russia in Ukraine, during the third period in office of President V.V. Putin. At the same time, the positions of the established political parties in relation to Russia have changed considerably over the past 10 years. Then there are the surprising accords between the traditional left-wing and the new right-wing populist parties in the west as a whole when it comes to the attitude that should be taken towards Russia.

In this situation, it is advisable to make a clear differentiation between necessary pragmatic cooperation, and to a certain extent also policies of confrontation in some political sectors by the governments and the leaders of government

---

Lecture given on 4.7.2016.

© Springer Nature Switzerland AG 2020
E. Jahn, *War and Compromise Between Nations and States*,
https://doi.org/10.1007/978-3-030-34131-2_7

parties with regard to Russia the global nuclear power on the one hand, and uncompromising criticism by key institutions in western public life (the media, party base organisations, associations and members of civil society) of the infringements of international law and human rights by Russia's power elite on the other. Even if there is little willingness to accept it in large parts of Russian society, this critical attitude in the west makes an important contribution to supporting societies in the countries bordering on Russia, who feel threatened by Moscow's expansive policy under President Putin. Furthermore, it provides encouragement to the liberal and democratic forces within Russia, however long they may remain weakened.

7.1 The Escalation of Socio-political and International Controversies Regarding Western Policy Towards Russia

Neither in the west in general nor in Germany in particular has there ever been consensus regarding which policy to pursue towards Russia, particularly during the course of the past 25 years. However, since the epochal events in 2014, when through military means, Russia violated the territorial status quo of the global state order, which had until then remained largely stable, the controversies surrounding western and German Russia policy have intensified significantly. They relate both to the internal state order and to Russia's foreign policy, which in the Putin era has increasingly diverged from the notion entertained since 1991, in the west and to a large extent also in Russia, of incorporating Russia into the market economy-oriented, democratic global system. Since December 1993, Russia has been pursuing its own socio-political path that has become ever more autocratic, and is increasingly defining its foreign and global policy interests as being contrary to those of the west, particularly the US. If Russia had opted for a liberal-democratic approach, there would no doubt also have been some foreign policy differences with the US as occasionally occurs between the US, France, Germany, Japan, Australia and other democratic powers, which are never enacted using military force. However, there would not have been the serious international political confrontations arising from opposing socio-political interests.

The core of the subject of dispute surrounding western and German Russia policy is therefore the question of how democratic societies and states should shape their relations with Russia, which may be economically weak, but which in military terms is the second most powerful state in the world. This issue is hotly disputed both among the western nations and between the political parties and societal groups in these countries. The broad range of different national and societal and party political positions goes beyond the scope of this lecture. However, an attempt will be made to take a more detailed look at the most important fundamental approaches among them.

7.1 The Escalation of Socio-political and International Controversies...

A central question being asked by many contemporaries is: are the repeated tensions and even threats of war between Russia and the west a result of the domestic socio-political developments within Russia? Or has Russia been forced into isolation and confrontation with the west as a result of western foreign policy, particularly the eastward expansion of NATO and the EU? Is it therefore the case that a misdirected western Russia policy is responsible for the considerable tensions in the northern hemisphere, which cause some contemporaries to warn of the dangers of a new Cold War[1] or even a nuclear world war?

The eastward expansion, not just of NATO but also of the EU, was contentious from the start. However, some shared German-Russian attitudes towards US global policy (military interventions in Iraq and Libya, a rejection of the NATO membership of Georgia and Ukraine, etc.), the construction of the Nordstream Baltic Sea gas pipeline and the strategy of mitigating the conflict in the Ukraine crisis have dominated the new relations between east and west. The annexation of Crimea and the covert aggression in the Donbas region caused all the main political parties in all 34 western alliance members of NATO and the EU to forge a common policy of imposing sanctions against Russia, even if in western societies, criticism of some of the western governments was frequently voiced.

For years, there has been disagreement between politicians, publicists and academics—referred to in simplified terms as Russia or Putin "understanders" and Russia or Putin critics—as to how the west overall, and their respective individual countries in particular, should respond to Russia's foreign and domestic policy. Here, the focus initially was on the curtailing of civic freedoms in Russia, which has increased considerably during the third period of office of President V.V. Putin. However, for a time, the strong criticism by Russia of the eastward expansion of NATO and the western interventions in the Federal Republic of Yugoslavia, Iraq and Libya was also at the centre of debate. During the course of time, the attitudes towards Russia among the established political parties and media have to a certain degree changed considerably, particularly following Russia's military expansion in 2014. At times, opponents of Putin's policies and their sympathisers clashed using rough, derogatory language. For example, at a party to celebrate Gerhard Schröder's 70th birthday in St. Petersburg,[2] there was talk of "smooching with Putin"; elsewhere, Russia critics were accused by Gernot Erler[3] of "moralist acid Russia bashing".

---

[1] If one disregards the trivial use of the term "Cold War" for any significant (inter-state) tensions, the only serious historical Cold War to date, from 1949 to 1962, was a policy "on the edge of the abyss", in other words, a state of continuous political and military readiness to begin a comprehensive nuclear war between two global powers and their alliance partners within a matter of minutes. Such readiness was not present either during what some authors term the "Second Cold War" following the double NATO resolution and the start of Soviet military intervention in December 1979 until around 1987, when tensions between east and west were merely significantly exacerbated, nor is it present today.

[2] Medick (2014).

[3] Erler (2013).

7.2 The Rapprochement of the Established Parties in Their Criticism of Putin and the Creation of a Left-Right Alliance of "Putin Understanders"

The term "Putin understander", which is usually used synonymously with the concept of a "Russia understander", although the latter generally also refers to Russia under President Boris N. Yeltsin,[4] is commonly used as a polemic-derogatory phrase, which has truculently been turned by those that are the subject of criticism into a term of acknowledgement.[5] In this context, "understanding" has taken on a very specific meaning, albeit with variants that differ in important ways. To understand a country, a person or a policy and to have them explained to you is the natural desire of any academic or open-minded citizen who is interested in an issue and who wishes to know what it is about, how and why it came to be and how it will develop. Understanding is a prerequisite for evaluating, agreeing with or criticising the subject of investigation, and possibly also taking action against it, according to standards, such as ethical or political standards, that have been developed along different lines.

This broad academic-educational meaning of "understanding" is not at all what is meant when referring to a Putin or Russia "understander", as the authors to whom this title is given like to claim. To a far greater extent, "understanding" refers to comprehension for the purpose of agreement and sympathy with, the approval or at least the tolerance of the subject under discussion. Thus, on the basis of the term itself, a certain spectrum of understanding for Russia or Putin is set in place. Someone who tolerates something doesn't have to approve of it or welcome it, or to use it as a model for their own thoughts and actions. However, it counters criticism of, or even oppositional action against, the subject of understanding.

Here, understanding Russia does not refer to Russia itself, with its landscapes, climate, inhabitants, literature, music, painting, history, science, philosophy and other culture, but the policies of the government of the new Russia since the election to office of Boris N. Yeltsin in 1990, and particularly Vladimir V. Putin in 2000, in the new post-soviet political system of Russia that is slowly but surely becoming increasingly autocratic. Therefore, this understanding relates to politics, predominantly foreign policy, but also in some cases the domestic policy of the power elite of Russia and the individual at its head.[6] Understanding of Putin as a person is only a marginal issue.

---

[4]However, many Putin understanders are sharp critics of Yeltsin. There is therefore a clear distinction between Russia understanders and Putin understanders.

[5]Bröckers and Schreyer (2014), Krone-Schmalz (2017, 2018), already at an early stage, Rahr (2000). Klaus von Beyme is also of the view that he belongs to this group, although his study differs from the simply factually incorrect claims made by the purely polemical writings of Bröckers and Schreyer, as well as from some grotesque statements and comparisons made by Krone-Schmalz: von Beyme (2016, p. 10).

[6]For the arguments of individual Russia understanders, see Portnov (2014). The attitude of the German Eastern European historians towards the Ukraine crisis is castigated by Wendland (2014).

7.2 The Rapprochement of the Established Parties in Their Criticism of Putin... 121

In the dispute surrounding the current Russia policy, the following positions can be defined. On the side of the Putin "understanders":

1. In many ways, the repressive, autocratic domestic policy of Russia is regarded as a model for their respective countries by many radical right-wing parties throughout Europe (and probably also in the US). Some of these parties also receive financial support from Russia and are happy to provide political and medial support for Putin's policies.
2. Some left-wing, communist or socialist groups still see post-Soviet Russia, which is increasingly praising the virtues of Soviet social policy, as being an antipode to western capitalism. In their eyes, Putin, the former KGB agent and communist, is a guarantee that Russia will not descend entirely down a capitalist path.
3. National policy-motivated critics of their country's membership of NATO and often of the EU, including those who are by all means conservative-democratic, see Putin's Russia as a key player in the creation of a multi-polar international system consisting of unbound nation states, free of US hegemony.
4. Many pacifists and other citizens who are concerned about the preservation of peace are simply terrified of a new Cold War or even a nuclear war, since in their view, NATO and the EU have acted negligently by threatening Russia's essential security interests through their eastward expansion, and are forcing it to take pre-emptive defensive measures in Georgia and eastern Ukraine. This group of Russia understanders from all democratic parties, from the Greens to the Conservatives, which have no sympathy at all for the repressive, autocratic domestic policies in Russia, probably make up the vast majority of Putin understanders, particularly in Germany, where the Second World War is regarded as being a German-Russian war for which Germany bears the blame.[7]

Positions on the side of the Russia critics:

1. In line with general international law and the UN Charter, the west, and in particular, the US and Britain, are obligated to acts as guarantors of the sovereignty, independence and territorial integrity of Ukraine according to the Budapest Memorandum of 5 December 1994, on the basis of which Ukraine, Kazakhstan and Belarus transferred their nuclear weapons to Russia, the military aggression by Russia against Ukraine obligates the west to guarantee that the territorial integrity of Ukraine will be reinstated, including through military means, as was the case with the Iraqi aggression against Kuwait on 2 August 1990. This position is held by just a few marginal figures in the US and other western countries.
2. Some critics of Russia's foreign policy conclude that Russia is taking a fundamental turn towards imperial expansion, to which the west must respond with a

---

[7]On opinion surveys on Russian policy and the Ukraine conflict, see e.g. von Beyme (2016, pp. 9–10).

significant increase in its own military spending and efforts in order to deter Russia from taking similar covert aggressive action against the Baltic states, Poland or Romania, and to demonstrate the willingness to jointly defend all NATO member states. The strongest advocates of this position are in the US and the western neighbouring states of Russia, although it is also supported, at least cautiously, by all other NATO states.

3. A third view envisioned separate, relatively moderate yet palpable political and economic sanctions to be imposed by the EU, NATO and other states, since military countermeasures would have led to disproportionate costs and risks to the lives of countless millions of people. At the same time, disadvantages to the countries' own economies and to political ambitions in some areas of inter-state relations and in global politics were taken into account. Certain sanctions are only to be lifted when the second Minsk Agreement on ending the war in Donbas has been implemented, and the remainder when the annexation of Crimea has been reversed. Since the latter is hardly likely to occur in the foreseeable future, it remains unclear when this portion of the sanctions will be silently abandoned—presumably without much ado.

4. Here, the German Social Democrats and several European governments are of the view that the sanctions should be modified in stages, in line with the progress made in the implementation of the Minsk Agreement, while the official position held by the EU and the US demands the full realisation of the Minsk Agreement as a prerequisite for the lifting of sanctions imposed as a result of the war in the Donbas. In this regard, it remains unclear what should be done if Ukraine fails to fully comply with its obligations arising from the Agreement, particularly those pertaining to a change in its constitution designed to guarantee special autonomy status to the Donbas. No public political debate has been held regarding the termination of the sanctions imposed due to the annexation of Crimea.

5. Even before the Ukraine crisis, there was intense criticism of the anti-reformist, inefficient economic policy (the halting of modernisation initiatives begun during the presidency of Dmitri A. Medvedev)[8] and the autocratic tendencies in Russia's domestic policy (the undermining of the federative constitutional order, the disempowerment of the parliament, election manipulations, suppression of the opposition, unresolved murder cases of critics of the Kremlin, a limitation of the freedoms of national and international non-governmental organisations, the infringement of numerous civic and human rights, an above-average level of corruption, etc.).[9] This would have to be answered with a reduction in economic dependency on the energy supply from Russia and with a wide-ranging, differentiated limitation on fields of cooperation in relations between Russia and the west.[10] Here, too, criticism of Russia was more intense in the US, Poland and the Baltic and Scandinavian countries than it was in Germany, where at times, confrontation occurred between the members of the Green and Christian

---

[8] Erler and Schulze (2012).
[9] See e.g. Schewzowa (2009), Gudkow (2013), and Burkhardt (2013).
[10] See e.g. Stewart (2012), Umland (2013), and Heinemann-Grüder (2013).

Democrat parties on the one hand and Social Democrats on the other (and also between the publicists and academics who sympathised with them).[11]

7.3 Stages of Intensification and Moderation in Western Policy Towards Russia

The following stages in relations between Russia and the west can be observed. In a first stage, the west looked on with a high level of mistrust and consternation as Russia became detached from the Soviet Union in 1990/91 under Boris N. Yeltsin. He generally supported the attempts by Mikhail S. Gorbachev to implement economic and political reforms in the Soviet Union. It was only after the Soviet Union disintegrated in December 1991 that the west accepted the political forces surrounding Yeltsin that wished to pursue reforms within the Russian economy and society, particularly against the highly conservative Communist Party of the Russian Federation (CPRF), even when Yeltsin disempowered the Supreme Soviet through use of force and in December 1993 octroyed a presidial democracy with unusually extensive competencies of the president. However, during the first free parliamentary elections, the liberal-democratic parties only won a third of the votes. (In all the elections that followed, their share of the vote further declined dramatically, so that in Russia, the democrats have to date never been able to influence politics to a significant degree).

After this election, Russia, in a series of many small steps, turned its back on the notion of full socio-political and global political integration into the western liberal-democratic system. Russia was involved in the summits of the leading industrial nations (G8), was a member of the International Monetary Fund and the World Bank and finally also the World Trade Organisation; it took steps towards rapprochement with NATO by participating in the Partnership for Peace, the Euro-Atlantic Partnership Council and the NATO-Russia Council, although from 1993 onwards increasingly stressed the independence of its socio-political system in contrast to the western, pluralist democracy. It also asserted a claim to exert decisive influence in the "near abroad", in other words, the successor states to the Soviet Union and in formerly communist Europe (such as in Yugoslavia). It reluctantly complied with the decision by NATO to accept the membership applications of Poland, the Czech Republic and Hungary (1999) and Slovenia, Slovakia, Bulgaria, Romania, Estonia, Latvia and Lithuania (2004) and finally also Croatia and Albania (2009). It was not until Putin came to power that the government and parliament in Russia criticised this NATO eastward expansion,[12] which was allegedly in breach of a promise, as being a threat to Russia's security interests, and declared that a further enlargement of NATO into the core countries of the former Soviet Union was not acceptable.

---

[11] See e.g. the controversy between Eichwede (2013) and Spanger (2013). Cf. also Schröder (2013) and Vogel (2013).

[12] Creuzberger (2015) and Goldgeier (2016).

Even so, in April 2008, the US and the east-central European countries wanted to include Ukraine and Georgia in the military plan of action for the rapid preparations for full NATO membership. This plan was thwarted when Germany and France objected, saying that the majority of Ukrainians did not want to join NATO, and that Georgia was encumbered with the "frozen conflict" with Abkhazia and South Ossetia.

As well as the fundamental structural issue of the security architecture in Europe, relations between the west and Russia were put under strain several times by individual national-territorial wars. During the two Chechen wars (1994–1996 and 1999–2009), the west consistently emphasised Russia's right to defend its territorial integrity, but also expressed reserved criticism of the disproportionately brutal way in which the Russian military forces waged war in their own country, which triggered concern in Poland and the Baltic states that their countries might be at risk in the future. This concern increased in 2008, and then again in 2014 in particular, to become widespread fear of a policy of military expansionism among the population of the states adjoining Russia. While the South Ossetian war began as a result of an attack by Georgia in August 2008 on South Ossetia and Russian peacekeeping troops in this de-facto state following a longer period of mutual exacerbation of the tensions and threats,[13] in parts of the western public arena and politics, it was interpreted as an expression of Russian imperial expansion, particularly when Russia did not reinstate the status quo ante after the war, but recognised the independence of both republics and concluded military mutual assistance pacts with them.

These military policy steps by Russia should be seen in the context of the worsening relations with the west resulting from other conflicts, however. In Russia's view, NATO's war against the Federal Republic of Yugoslavia in 1999, which was waged without a UN mandate, was a breach of international law and was a negative impact on its influence in the Balkan region, despite the brutal way in which the civil war was conducted by Belgrade in Kosovo and the mass flight of the Albanian Kosovars. When from February 2008 onwards most western states recognised the independence of Kosovo and shortly afterwards, in April, the NATO summit in Bucharest offered Georgia and Ukraine the prospect of future membership (despite the prevention by Germany and France of direct initiation of the acceptance procedures), for Russia, this was a further sign of NATO expansionist policy to which it initially responded with its own expansion of power in the southern Caucasus in August 2008.[14]

However, in the new century in particular, there was an escalation in the competition for integration with regard to social and alliance policy between Brussels (i.e. the EU and NATO) and Moscow, with its numerous but generally unsuccessful

---

[13] For details, see the lecture "The Creation of New Fronts Between Russia and the West in the South Caucasus". In: Jahn (2015a, pp. 160–176).

[14] On the meaning of Russia's aim to attain major power status, see Heller (2013).

7.3 Stages of Intensification and Moderation in Western Policy Towards Russia

integration projects[15] within the framework of the Community of Independent States (CIS), which at times included all twelve post-Soviet states, with the exception of the three Baltic states.[16] Parts of the CIS looked to find a certain degree of independence from Russia, however, such as Georgia, Ukraine, Azerbaijan and Moldova, in the form of the GUAM, which was founded with the assistance of the US in 1997 as an informal organisation and of which Uzbekistan was briefly a member, and which in 2006 was reorganised as the GUAM Organisation for Democracy and Economic Development. With the acceptance of the measures planned by the European neighbourhood policy after 2004, partnership, cooperation or association agreements and the participation in the Eastern Partnership of the EU in 2009, several CIS states responded positively to the offers of rapprochement with the EU. The intention was also to include Russia into this concept of creating a space around the EU that was as constitutional, democratic and market economy-oriented as possible, through the partnership and cooperation agreements of 1997 and the "four common spaces" project (the economy, the judiciary, external security, culture) initiated in 2003.

The competition for integration between Brussels and Moscow is above all a domestic policy debate between those sections of the population who desire a liberalisation and democratisation of their society and accordingly also frequently, if not always, an alliance between their country and the EU and NATO, and others who wish to see an autocratic political-economic order, whichever form it may take in individual cases, and an alliance with Russia. The latter group includes both communists and former communists as well as extreme right-wing conservative, sometimes religious, above all Christian Orthodox sections of the population, which reject western liberalism, individualism and laicism, as well as the western lifestyle. Between these two orientations, both liberal-democratic and autocratic national political forces are at play, which wish to keep their country out of any alliance with the west and with Moscow. In the east, the competition for integration most clearly divided the societies in Ukraine[17] and Moldova after 1991, although the same phenomenon can also be observed in Russia, Belarus, Armenia and Azerbaijan, even if there, it is suppressed by harsh state repression.

---

[15] In 1996, a closer connection was to be created within the Community of Independent States (CIS), with Russia, Belarus, Kazakhstan and Kyrgyzstan, and later also Tajikistan as members. After 1995, Russia and Belarus wanted to create a particularly close connection in a Russian-Belarusian federal state. In 2000, the members of the CIS (without Tajikistan) decided to form a Eurasian Economic Community. This was replaced in 2015 by the Eurasian Economic Union, which Armenia also joined. These six states are also members of the Collective Security Treaty Organisation (CSTO), which has existed since 1994 and 2002; Georgia, Azerbaijan and Uzbekistan were also temporarily members.

[16] Georgia did not become a member of the CIS until 1993, but withdrew again after the South Ossetian war in 2008. Turkmenistan has been only an adjunctive member since 2005, and Ukraine effectively suspended its membership in 2014.

[17] Adomeit (2012).

The status quo with regard to social and alliance policy is primarily endangered by the weak economic and political-moral power of integration in Moscow, which is leading an increasing number of people in the CIS states to rebel against social poverty, electoral manipulation, everyday corruption, arbitrary justice and violence within the police, a lack of rule of law and the curtailment of freedom of expression in the media. Accordingly, the so-called "colour revolutions" in Serbia, Georgia, Ukraine[18] and Kyrgyzstan were also interpreted as being a threat to the power elites in Russia and the other autocratic regimes in the CIS, and repressive countermeasures were initiated. The international non-governmental organisations in particular were the focus of these countermeasures, since several of them had supported the colour revolutions through organisational and financial aid. The Arab Spring in 2011/2012 added fuel to fears of oppositional civic movements among the autocratic power elites in eastern Europe. The freedoms and prosperity in the west frequently served as a model to these movements, which motivated some political oppositional forces to orient themselves to the western states—combined with the hope of political, economic and in some cases also military assistance. In the view of the Kremlin and some Russia "understanders", such movements are nothing more than submissive tools of US imperialist power expansion.

Alongside the national-territorial conflicts in Europe mentioned above, the dispute surrounding the plan to build a missile defence system in Poland and the Czech Republic by the US has poisoned relations between Russia and the west. The plan was first abandoned by President Obama, but was replaced by the NATO missile defence plans. Their first station was declared ready for operation in May 2016, in Deveselu in Romania.[19] This was interpreted by Russia as an infringement of the Intermediate Range Nuclear Forces Treaty of 1987. For its part, it had already installed modern Iskander short-range missiles in the Kaliningrad region in December 2014. Troop deployments by both sides to the borders between NATO and Russia and the associated aggressive military posturing since the start of the Ukraine crisis have been a further expression of the increasing tensions between Brussels and Moscow.

7.4 The Risks of a Confrontational and the Dangers of a Submissive Policy Towards Russia

A very large number of Russia understanders know very little about Russia, about the country and its people, its society or its history, and are often not interested in finding out more. The reason for this is that this understanding of Russia is often nothing more than an expression of fundamental criticism of the continued existence of NATO after 1991 and the global policies of the US (regardless of which

---

[18] See the lecture "Der zweite Demokratisierungsversuch in Serbien, Georgien und der Ukraine". In: Jahn (2008, pp. 149–165).
[19] Thiels (2016).

administration), and sometimes also of the EU and the foreign policy of their own country. Such Russia understanders have shown, or continue to show, great understanding for Chavez' Venezuela, Milosevich's Yugoslavia, Saddam Hussein's Iraq, Assad's Syria, the Islamic Republic of Iran, and the People's Republic of China, in other words, for other countries and regimes that are in conflict with the US or NATO. Russia understanders are usually not Ukraine, Poland, Baltic state or Georgia understanders, and also show no understanding for the liberal, democratic opposition in Russia.

It has been possible to observe significant shifts in attitude among Russia and Putin critics over recent years. Criticism of the policies of Russia and Putin originally focussed very strongly on domestic policy, such as on the policy towards Chechnya, and in particular on the increasingly autocratic way in which the system was developing, a process that had already begun in December 1993, but which accelerated during the Putin era after 2000. At the same time, western criticism of foreign policy, particularly in relation to the "near abroad", i.e. the post-Soviet space, tended to play a subordinate role, since the inclusion of Russia in the NATO-Russia Council appeared to be a suitable means of mitigating and allaying Russian reservations arising from the membership of NATO of the eastern and south-eastern European countries, and then even of the Baltic states. It was not until the war in South Ossetia in 2008 and above all, the annexation of Crimea and the war in eastern Ukraine in 2014, that Putin's foreign policy became a focus of criticism of Russia. These events led to considerable shifts in relations between western critics and understanders of Russia and Putin. Many people, including a large number of German Social Democrats, who until 2014 had shown a great deal of understanding for Putin's policies, and who had attacked Green and Christian Democrat critics of Putin's domestic policy, now joined the Putin critics, albeit the more moderate among them. By contrast, the Putin understanders found numerous new sympathisers among the population who until that point had shown little or no interest in Russia, particularly on the right wing of the political spectrum.

There are many people who are warning of the danger of a new Cold War and a renewed arms race, which in the worst case scenario could lead to a third world war. At least, sanctions and countersanctions over a lengthy period of time would cause severe damage to the economic and societal situation not only in Russia but also in several western countries. This could threaten the stability of the political orders on both sides and lead to the development of unpredictable, violent, right-wing nationalist forces.

According to the counter-argument, flexibility and a policy of appeasement with regard to the policy of expansion and pressure through blackmail by Russia in the southern Caucasus and Ukraine will encourage the Kremlin to take further expansive imperial steps, first in the CIS space and ultimately also against the eastern NATO states, since such a western policy would be interpreted as weakness in Moscow. Putin's goal, they claim, is to split the west, both along national and social lines. Here, the Kremlin not only regards the western political left wing and the peace movements as divisive forces, as was the case in Soviet times, but is increasingly also supporting right-wing nationalist political parties and organisations that wish to see the disintegration of NATO and the EU, and which regard Russia as a partner in the fight against US global hegemony. Therefore, the competition for integration consists not only of opposing social and alliance policy integration options, but also increasingly involves disintegration strategies for undermining the socio-political stability and resilience of the alliance on the other side.

7.5 Different Functions of Government Policy and a Critically Thinking, Liberal and Democratic Public

Behind the polarised dispute between Russia understanders and Russia critics lies the fundamental question of whether, following the unification of Germany in 1990, there were sensible and practicable alternatives to the eastward expansion of NATO and the EU. The argument that most peoples in eastern-central and south-eastern Europe wanted to become members of the EU and NATO is not compelling. The EU and NATO had to decide according to their own interest whether they wished to fulfil this desire or whether they should decide not to do so for the overriding political reason of avoiding potential military conflicts between Russia and its neighbours. Should, therefore, the west have left it to Russia to settle the reorganisation of post-communist Europe with the eastern and south-eastern Europeans, as was repeatedly the case after 1945, when there were uprisings against Soviet rule in 1953, 1956, 1968 and 1981, since the interest in maintaining peace and security outweighed that of democratising the east of Europe? Should, therefore, the Poles, the Baltic peoples, the Ukrainians, Georgians, etc. have waited with their democratisation and involvement in the western state system until Russia itself pursued a second perestroika and took steps along the path to democratisation and westernisation? For a long time, Russia differentiated between the eastward expansion of the EU and that of NATO. It therefore accepted the EU accession of the eastern-central European states, and potentially that of the south-eastern European states, as well as the Baltic states, but rejected the eastward expansion of NATO. It was only when it emerged that the states that wished to join the EU mostly also wanted to join NATO—for whichever reason[20]—and that the deepening of EU integration with EU membership also entails anchoring in its common foreign, security and defence policy, that Russian criticism of the EU eastern European policy and its instruments, the European Neighbourhood Policy (since 2004), the Eastern Partnership (since 2009) and the association agreement with the CIS states, particularly with Ukraine in 2014, intensified.

Two options were discussed as alternatives to the eastward expansion of NATO: the dissolution of NATO or the membership of Russia in NATO (possibly under a

---

[20]For some eastern central and south eastern Europeans, membership of NATO, which was economically cheaper, was simply an entry ticket to membership of the EU, which requires far-reaching social reforms; for others, the security policy argument of a future threat from Russia or from neighbouring states, the possibility of which could not be excluded, was more important.

new name). A dissolution of NATO would entail a return to national, independent military policies, which would probably have significantly increased the risk of war in Europe. One function of NATO that is frequently overlooked, the foreign policy of which can certainly be criticised in individual cases, consists of the important coordination of the armament and military policies, as well as the regulation of conflict among the member states (particularly in the Aegean). The membership of NATO of a large and powerful state, which is becoming increasingly autocratic, would de facto have rendered this alliance system void. Thus, the inclusion of Russia into the NATO system by the Partnership for Peace and particularly by the NATO-Russia Council was a sensible solution, and at the same time an important means of forging trust. The more cooperative the relationship between Russia and the west becomes, and the more Russia progresses along the path to internal democratisation, the more the competencies of the NATO-Russia Council could be expanded to include a greater participation in decision-making by Russia. It is therefore a fundamental error to suspend this NATO-Russia Council, of all times in a crisis in the relationship between Russia and the west, as was the case with the war in Yugoslavia in 1999, the South Ossetian war of 2008 or the war in the Donbas in 2014.[21] Instead, this forum should have met continuously throughout all crisis periods and worked to regulate the conflict.[22]

The notion of a membership of Ukraine, Georgia or Moldova in NATO is unrealisable for the foreseeable future, since NATO would expand into a territory that is partially militarily occupied by Russia, and which is encumbered by unresolved national-territorial conflicts. An end to both the Russian military presence and the national-territorial conflicts can only be achieved through cooperative conflict regulation with Russia. If the west is unwilling to wait for an internal democratisation of Russia, it can only win Russia over to conflict regulation in its immediate vicinity by offering the power elite the opportunity of involvement in a common trade system, yet to be finally negotiated, which covers the northern hemisphere, from Vancouver to Vladivostok. For a time, this may facilitate the stabilisation of the ruling interests of this power elite, but at the same time, in the longer term, it would create the preconditions for a peaceful system change, in which parts of the power elite that have been shown to be open to reform interact with dissatisfied population masses who may put up non-violent resistance, or at least rebel with a low level of violence.

Governments, and to a certain extent also parliamentary majorities, must above all not lose sight of national security and peace policy, as well as essential foreign trade interests. Regardless of how autocratic a powerful country such as Russia may be, or how barbarically its respective government behaves towards its own population, as was the case in Chechnya, peace between states and the energy supply to western Europe can only be secured by working together with this regime. No

---

[21]Russia did so in 1999, while the west did so in 2008, and the west also failed to call a meeting of the NATO-Russia Council after the start of the Ukraine crisis in 2014, waiting until April 2016.

[22]Thus also Wittmann (2015).

government should lose sight of the power political realities and the demands and limitations of pragmatic foreign policy, or be tempted to take actions that have no prospects of success, and which could likely lead to fatal political consequences, whatever their moral basis. Thus, state sanction options often remain restricted to just a few symbolic acts, and criticism of the autocracies must be expressed in a moderate, diplomatic way.

Parliaments can respond far more critically in public than governments and diplomats. This was the case in the German Bundestag on 6 November 2012, for example,[23] when the CDU/CSU, FDP and Greens expressed their "particular concern" over the repressive tendencies in Russia.[24] Political parties, particularly those in opposition, and social organisations have far more opportunities and freedoms to raise awareness of the infringement of international and constitutional law by eastern European governments and powerful social groups, and if necessary to demand that the norms be observed in the requisite harsh tones.

The Russia understanders in Germany like to employ the moral argument that Russia is suffering from the trauma of 27 million victims of the National Socialist German war of conquest and destruction against the Soviet Union,[25] and that like Israel, it has a particularly strong, and understandable, need for security. This argument sets the Soviet Union on a par with Russia[26] without taking the different circumstances into account, and entirely neglects the security interests of Russia's western neighbouring countries, which suffered especially from the German war of conquest and destruction, and which even denies the right to exist of the Ukrainian and Belarusian nations.[27] Gabriele Krone-Schmalz even adopts the manner of speaking of the 25 million Russian "fellow countrymen" in the neighbouring states of Russia, which are citizens of these states and not of Russia, and equates Russia's military concern regarding these "Russians" (in the Donbas and in Crimea) with the provisions made by the US military for the security for the US citizens living in Iraq. She even goes so far as to claim that: "Crimea is land that inherently belongs to Russia. What Putin has done is not seize land, but committed an act of self-defence under pressure of time." She ignores the recognition of the territorial integrity of Ukraine by Russia and the community of states in international law. By no means can a particular "understanding" (in the sense of agreement) of any Russian, or indeed Polish, Ukrainian or Baltic security or even expansionist policy be derived from German moral responsibility. Knowledge about Germany's past

---

[23] Eichwede (2013, p. 92).

[24] The abstention of the SPD triggered an intense dispute over the state fixation of the SPD and the "moralistic spiritual exercise" of the Putin and SPD critics. Wolfgang Eichwede spoke of a "historic error" by the SPD, which was based on an "etatist" approach. Here, highly dubious analogies were made with the eastern and relaxation policy of Willy Brandt and Egon Bahrs. See Eichwede (2013, p. 96), von Studnitz (2013), Erler (2013), Spanger (2013 p. 178).

[25] Cf. the debate in Die ZEIT, Lau (2013), Sandschneider (2013) and Baum (2013).

[26] Eppler (2012), Schmidt (2014), and Jessen (2014). For a critical viewpoint, see Kappeler (2014, 2015).

[27] Particularly stark: Bröckers and Schreyer (2014).

should be the basis for doing everything possible to contribute to a peaceful regulation of conflicts between Poland, Ukraine and Russia, as well as other countries threatened with the prospect of war.[28]

In this sense, the extremely moderate political and economic sanctions policy of the west against the Russian policy regarding Crimea and the Donbas, which hardly touches the core area of east-west economic relations at all, is a necessary, mainly symbolic protest against any further policy of conquest, which while it has economic consequences for both sides is hardly able to force a withdrawal from Crimea or the Donbas by Russia.[29] However, it provides moral support to both the democratic and moral resistance in Russia and its neighbouring states against the policy of violence, and counters the accusation that the west is cynically subjugating itself to the violent dictates of major powers if it serves its economic and some of its diplomatic interests.

7.6 Contradictory Tendencies Towards Conflict Escalation and Limited Cooperation Between the West and Russia

Relations between Russia and the west are more tense now than they have ever been during the past 25 years. Even so, the many areas where limited cooperation does succeed should not be overlooked. Here, it certainly helps that NATO is far superior to Russia militarily, but has absolutely no intention of offering armed resistance to Russian military expansion to the east of NATO's borders.[30] Also, there has been no major armament of Georgia and Ukraine, in the full knowledge that Ukraine and Georgia would be the main victims of any attempt to force Russian troops out of these countries through military means—an attempt that would fail on account of Russia's overwhelming military superiority. On the other hand, no-one in the Russian power elite will doubt that NATO would be willing to prevent a military attack on the new NATO territory (the Baltic states, Poland, Romania), however covert it may be. To this extent, there continues to be an implicit, functioning nuclear and conventional deterrence between NATO and Russia. Above all, however, common interests between the two states are not asserted. The sanctions and counter-sanctions do not negatively impact the core of the mutual economic cooperation in the energy sector, in the automobile industry and in many other industrial sectors. In international politics, there continue to be important areas of common interest in combating Islamist terror, narcotics crime, the functioning of the atomic policy agreement with Iran, the containment of North Korean atomic armament, the achievement of a peaceful compromise in order to end the civil war in Syria, the control of global financial markets and many others. The Obama administration has supported German-French attempts to bring an end to the war in the Donbas and to

---

[28] Alekseenkova (2016). For a recommendation regarding the Ukraine conflict, see Jahn (2015a, b).
[29] Some authors emphasise the excessive economic strain suffered by Russia as a result of its imperialist expansion, e.g. Adomeit (2015, 2016).
[30] Klein and Major (2015).

regulate the conflict between Kiev and Moscow by means of the Minsk Agreement, despite loud calls in the US and eastern central Europe demanding a harsher western stance against Russia in Ukraine. On the other hand, Putin succeeded in forcing back the genies of unification between Russia and "New Russia" (i.e. the entire south and east of Ukraine), which he himself had tolerated and nurtured, back into the bottle of an expansive policy of aggression, without endangering his regime. He has also stopped the further military advance of the Donbas separatists on Mariupol, and through massive military support for Syrian government troops and the offer to the west to join forces to combat the Islamists has substantially diverted international and Russian attention away from the war in Ukraine.

However, the voices in favour of a peaceful compromise, as outlined in the fifth section, remain extremely weak. The possibility cannot be excluded that the uniform western support for sanctions will crumble over the coming months. Within the German policy towards Russia, mild dissent is also growing between the SPD, which demands a loosening of sanctions in stages according to progress made in implementing the Minsk Agreement,[31] and the CDU, which is in favour of full implementation of the Minsk Agreement as a prerequisite for lifting the sanctions. Currently, there is much to suggest that the war in the Donbas and the annexation of Crimea will turn into another long-lasting, "frozen conflict" (alongside the conflicts over Transnistria, Abkhazia, South Ossetia and Nagorno-Karabakh), which keep many eastern states dependent on Russia and which prevents them from achieving domestic peace, as well as any prospect of democratic forces joining the western alliance system. Even if Moscow's power of integration may have further drastically decreased, its disintegration strategy has without doubt been successful.

References

Adomeit H (2012) Integrationskonkurrenz EU-Russland. Belarus und Ukraine als Konfliktfelder. Osteuropa 62(6–8):383–406

Adomeit H (2015) Russlands imperialer Irrweg. Von der Stagnation in den Niedergang. Osteuropa 65(3):67–93

Adomeit H (2016) Imperial overstretch: Germany in Soviet Policy from Stalin to Gorbachev. An analysis based on new archival evidence, memoirs, and interviews, 2nd edn. Nomos, Baden-Baden

Alekseenkova E et al (2016) A shared European Home. The European Union, Russia and the Eastern Partnership. In: Friedrich-Ebert-Stiftung Perspective, May, Berlin

Annen N (2015) Russland. Umgang mit einem schwierigen Partner. In: Friedrich-Ebert-Stiftung Perspektive, July, Berlin

Baum G (2013) Von wegen "Moralecke". Die ZEIT No. 12, March 14, p 5

Bröckers M, Schreyer P (2014) Wir sind die Guten. Ansichten eines Putinverstehers oder wie uns die Medien manipulieren. Westend, Frankfurt am Main

Burkhardt F (2013) Neopatrimonialisierung statt Modernisierung. Dtsch Russlandpolitik plus russischer Otkat, Osteuropa 63(8):95–106

---

[31] Annen (2015).

References

Creuzberger S (2015) Die Legende vom Wortbruch. Russland, der Westen und die NATO-Osterweiterung, Osteuropa 65(3):95–108

Eichwede W (2013) Einmischung tut not! Wider den Selbstbetrug der Putin-Freunde. Osteuropa 63(4):91–100

Eppler E (2012) Bescheidenheit könnte uns nicht schaden, Süddeutsche Zeitung, November 26

Erler G (2013) Schluss mit dem Russland-Bashing! Die ZEIT, May 29

Erler G, Schulze PW (eds) (2012) Die Europäisierung Russlands. Moskau zwischen Modernisierungspartnerschaft und Großmachtrolle. Frankfurt am Main, Campus

Goldgeier J (2016) Promises made, promises broken? What Yeltsin was told about NATO in 1993 and why it matters. https://warontherocks.com/2016/07/promises-made-promises-broken-what-yeltsin-was-told-about-nato-in-1993-and-why-it-matters

Gudkow L (2013) Russland bewegt sich in Richtung Diktatur. Frankfurter Allgemeine Sonntagszeitung, June 2, p 2

Heinemann-Grüder A (2013) Wandel statt Anbiederung. Deutsche Russlandpolitik auf dem Prüfstand, Osteuropa 63(7):179–194

Heller R (2013) Wenn Status zur fixen Idee wird. Russland – Zur Großmacht verdammt? Osteuropa 63(8):45–58

Jahn E (2008) Politische Streitfragen. VS-Verlag für Sozialwissenschaften, Wiesbaden

Jahn E (2015a) International politics. Political issues under debate, vol 3. Springer, Heidelberg

Jahn E (2015b) Neuauflage des Ost-West-Konflikts? Friedenspolitische Herausforderungen durch die neuen Kriege in Europa. Osteuropa 65(3):25–45

Jessen J (2014) Teufelspakt für die Ukraine. Die ZEIT, March 27, p 53

Kappeler A (2014) In Kiew entstand die Nation. Die ZEIT, April 3, p 48

Kappeler A (2015) Im Schatten Russlands, Frankfurter Allgemeine Zeitung, June 9, p 11

Klein M, Major C (2015) Perspektiven der NATO-Russland-Beziehungen. SWP-Aktuell 81, September, Berlin

Krone-Schmalz G (2017) Russland verstehen. Der Kampf um die Ukraine und die Arroganz des Westens. Beck, Munich

Krone-Schmalz G (2018) Eiszeit. Wie Russland dämonisiert wird und warum das so gefährlich ist. Beck, Munich

Lau J (2013) Das bißchen Unterdrückung. Die ZEIT No. 9, February 21, p 7

Medick V (2014) Sanktionen gegen Putin. Schröders Chance. Spiegel Online Politik, July 28. http://www.spiegel.de/politik/deutschland/ukraine-krise-schroeder-muss-putin-die-grenzen-aufzeigen-a-983116.html

Portnov A (2014) Das Mantra der Nicht-Einmischung. Glaubenssätze der Putin-Freunde, Osteuropa 64(9):5–11

Rahr A (2000) Wladimir Putin. Der 'Deutsche' im Kreml. Universitas, Munich

Sandschneider E (2013) Raus aus der Moralecke. Die ZEIT No. 10, February 28, p 13

Schewzowa L (2009) Das System. Wie das Tandem Putin-Medwedjew einigen wenigen Macht und Reichtum sichert und die Zukunft Russlands verspielt Frankfurter Allgemeine Zeitung, September 25

Schmidt H (2014) Putins Vorgehen ist verständlich. Die ZEIT, March 27, p 9

Schröder HH (2013) Russland in Europa. Anmerkungen zur deutschen Russlanddebatte. Osteuropa 63(8):107–114

Spanger HJ (2013) Kooperation tut not! Wider die Blindheit der Putin-Feinde. Osteuropa 63(7):169–178

Stewart S (2012) Prämissen hinterfragen. Plädoyer für eine Neugestaltung der deutschen Russlandpolitik, SWP-Aktuell 50, August, Berlin

Thiels C (2016) Das große Mißtrauen. NATO-Raketenabwehr in Rumänien. Tagesschau, Mai 12. https://www.tagesschau.de/ausland/nato-raketenabwehr-103.html

Umland A (2013) Wir brauchen eine neue Ostpolitik. Frankfurter Allgemeine Sonntagszeitung, June 9, p 11

Vogel H (2013) Stabilität durch Evolution. Russlandpolitik zwischen Konfrontation und Kooperation, Osteuropa 63(8):115–127

von Beyme K (2016) Die Russland-Kontroverse. Eine Analyse des ideologischen Konflikts zwischen Russland-Verstehern und Russland-Kritikern. Springer VS, Wiesbaden

von Studnitz EJ (2013) Konfrontation mit Russland ist nutzlos. Frankfurter Allgemeine Zeitung, May 29

Wendland AV (2014) Hilflos im Dunkeln. 'Experten' in der Ukraine-Krise: eine Polemik. Osteuropa 64(9):13–33

Wittmann K (2015) Deutsche Rußlandpolitik. Der Westen muß selbstkritischer werden. Der Tagesspiegel, October 30. http://www.tagesspiegel.de/themen/debatte-zur-deutschen-russlandpolitik/deutsche-russlandpolitik-der-westen-muss-selbstkritischer-werden/12492678.html

The Impact of the October Revolution on International and Inter-Ethnonational Relations

Abstract

Research into the reasons why during the twentieth century, the rule of the Communist Party, which was guilty of mass murder, was greeted with enthusiasm and led to the mobilisation of countless millions of people for three generations, is far from having been completed and has still not provided satisfactory results. The October Revolution is generally interpreted as a socially motivated event led from below by the suffering lower social orders and by a number of middle-class, property-owning intellectuals and the aristocracy. This view takes insufficient account of the fact that all communist regimes, with the exception of the Cuban regime, were created as a result of military defeats in the two world wars and in several colonial wars. In order for the communist parties to win, the concept of capitalism as the root cause not only of social exploitation, but above all also for war, militarism and nationalism, played a decisive role. The promise of an entirely new way of organising relations between the ethnic nations and the states in the name of internationalism, and not of cosmopolitanism that was without nation or state, was a key factor in the success of the communists.

Lenin was a proponent of a global republic with a centrally administered global economy, a single global corporation and a global office led by a global party. However, for tactical reasons, he propagated the right to self-determination of the people, the dissolution of the large continental and colonial empires and the formation of national republics, to be brought together under one umbrella as federations. In the long term, he anticipated not only a rapprochement between the nations, but their "amalgamation". The multi-national USSR was not intended to act as a successor state to Tsarist Russia, but as an alternative to the capitalist League of Nations, and as the core of the global Union of Socialist Soviet Republics.

After the failure of the global revolution, Stalin developed the concept of socialism in one country, and later of Soviet patriotism. He assumed that in the

---

Lecture given on 6.11.2017.

© Springer Nature Switzerland AG 2020
E. Jahn, *War and Compromise Between Nations and States*,
https://doi.org/10.1007/978-3-030-34131-2_8

future communist global society, humanity would speak just one language, Russian. Accordingly, the non-Russian nations among the Soviet peoples were to "voluntarily" adopt Russian as their second native language. The Communist International as an organisation of the global party, which was separated according to the different nations, was now to act as a tool of Soviet foreign policy. After 1945, the new states that fell under communist rule were not integrated into the USSR, but were rather to form a closed "socialist community of states" with a common foreign policy. In the longer term, the emancipation of the communist nations of Yugoslavia and China was the first step on the road towards the end of communism.

8.1 Controversial Interpretations of the October Revolution

Naturally, the way in which the October Revolution in Tsarist Russia is presented and the explanation of its causes has always been characterised by controversial socio-political interpretations and ways of understanding history, which have taken root in historical study.[1] Communists, socialists, anarchists, social, liberal and conservative democrats, constitutional and absolutist monarchists, nationalists and imperialists still write very different versions of the history of the October Revolution today, which began exactly 100 years ago on tomorrow's date, i.e. on 7 November 1917 (according to the old Julian calendar used in Tsarist Russia: on 25 October). The balance of power between the interpretations of history have shifted dramatically since the collapse of communist party rule in eastern Europe in 1991. Above all, many communists and socialists felt it necessary to significantly alter their understanding of history. Nowadays, only a small number of people agree with the progressive concept of a sequence of historical formations, in which the October Revolution was regarded as the start of the historical period of the communist global social order.[2]

It should be noted that the concept of socialism differs significantly between the communists and the socialists and social democrats. According to the communist understanding, a takeover of power occurs in a proletarian, socialist revolution led by communists, is followed by an initial, relatively short phase of a dictatorship of the proletariat, in which the economic and social conditions are overturned, i.e. private ownership of all key means of production is nationalised (whereby the old, propertied classes no longer exist as such), or is collectivised under state control. On then does the history of socialism begin, of socialist society as the first phase of the communist society with a "state of the entire working people", in which there were still "allied" classes and social orders without opposing interests. This phase was to transition smoothly into a later phase of completed communism, to date not

---

[1] Heinemann-Grüder (2017).
[2] On history schematism see Jahn (1986).

8.1 Controversial Interpretations of the October Revolution

yet achieved anywhere in the world, where there is a classless society with a fading state. In 1961, the party manifesto of the CPSU was still claiming that: "today's generation of Soviet peoples will live in communism".[3] By contrast, in the view of many socialists and social democrats, there never really has been a socialist society in which the means of production have been socialised and democratically administered.

In post-communist Russia, considerable difficulties can be observed on the part of the state leadership,[4] the media and academics[5] as to how to treat the 100th anniversary of the October Revolution. Officially, it is being commemorated in a very muted way, with attempts being made to promote patriotic unity between the "white" (Tsarist) and the "red" (Soviet communist) Russia, and to bring about a "reconciliation" between the supporters of the former civil war parties. The embalmed body of Lenin still lies in the Mausoleum on Red Square in Moscow, while Tsar Nikolai II, who has been proclaimed a saint, is interred in the Peter and Paul fortress in St. Petersburg.

According to the communist and socialist worldview, the bourgeois, liberal-democratic July revolution in France in 1789 was a preliminary historical step towards the October Revolution of 1917. By contrast, in the liberal-democratic interpretation, the October Revolution and the history of communist single-party rule, just like the fascist and National Socialist regimes and other modern dictatorships, are an aberration and a diversion in the global historical development of society towards a global development of liberal democracies and constitutional states, in which human rights have universal validity. According to a positive, progressive, liberal-democratic concept of revolution, the events of November 1917 and the months and years that followed are not revolutionary in character, and instead, should be referred to as a coup, a revolt or similar. By contrast, the overthrow of communist party rule was celebrated as a catch-up revolution in the social liberal-democratic sense,[6] while being branded a counter-revolution by orthodox communists.

It is still a matter of dispute today as to how during the twentieth century, Marxist-Leninist communism[7] attracted countless millions of supporters, managed to rule over a third of the global population, and in some cases was able to retain power over three generations. Also, opinions differ as to why it then surprisingly collapsed, and with comparatively little loss of life—at least compared to the amount of violence

---

[3]Meissner (1962, p. 244).

[4]On the dilemma of the state leadership of not negatively judging Soviet history on the one hand, while on the other avoiding celebrating revolution, see Ibragimova (2017).

[5]See the contributions by Kalinin (2017), Katzer (2017). The attitudes among the population to the October Revolution compared to the February Revolution are discussed by Gudkov and Zorkaja (2017).

[6]Habermas (1990).

[7]Other types of communism, such as anarchistic, religious or monastery communism, which were already conceived and practised here and there in ancient times, are not the subject of discussion here.

involved in achieving and consolidating communist rule. Among the countless millions of communists who often sacrificed their lives and who were more or less convinced of the party ideology in terms of their thoughts and actions, there were numerous world-famous artists, writers, philosophers, journalists and other intellectuals, albeit only temporary ones in some cases. If one wants to understand this phenomenon, it is necessary to study the Marxist concept of society and history in the particular version developed by Vladimir I. Lenin (1870–1924) and Josef V. Stalin (1878–1953). Until the arrival of Mikhail S. Gorbachev (born 1931), this concept was also nurtured by their successors. This worldview is characterised above all by intense criticism of capitalist and pre-capitalist exploitation and living conditions and the imperialist world order that repeatedly led to wars, although it also includes several ideas, often only vaguely expressed, of a future socialist and communist world order.

Another contentious issue is whether the political and legal recognition of the different ethno-nationalities of the citizens of the communist-ruled states, and above all the division of several communist states into ethno-national territorial units (republics, provinces, regional areas, even districts and communities) led to the dissolution of the Soviet Union, Yugoslavia and Czechoslovakia. Would a pure departmentalisation of these states along economic, geographically strategic and population statistics lines, without taking into account the tradition of territorial dominions or ethnic settlement areas, and the introduction of a uniform, generally binding state language in accordance with the French or US models not have prevented the disintegration of polyethnic states after the collapse of Communist Party rule? Therefore, did communism, despite or perhaps even because of its internationalist ideology, unintentionally and contrary to its motives, encourage the nationalism that fragmented the post-communist world in such a lasting way, and which still shakes the region today?

8.2 Social vs. International Causes of the October Revolution

The October Revolution is generally regarded as being a social revolution, and from the communist perspective as a revolution of the labouring social classes and poor farmers.[8] Non-communist historians tend to find it difficult to clearly characterise the events that occurred in October. "What we are talking about has many names, and none of them entirely fits: coup d'état, uprising, overthrow or 'Great Socialist October Revolution', a conspiracy by a minority, or 'Ten Days that Shook the World',[9] an action directed by a handful of highly motivated activists, or the 'Red

---

[8] Thus, for example, "In October 1917, the proletariat of Russia, together with the poor farmers, and under the leadership of the Party of the Bolsheviks, overthrew the dictatorship of the bourgeoisie and established the dictatorship of the proletariat in the form of Soviet power." Berchin (1971), p. 17.

[9] This was the title of the famous depiction of the October events from 1919 by an American journalist, John Reed (1990).

October'—a turning point in the history of the world."[10] Some authors regarded the events as being a "coup" or "putsch" by a number of failed students, which was supported by a minority among the population of Russia after they took power with the aid of a few thousand soldiers and workers in St. Petersburg. The interpretation of the October Revolution as a social revolution, as an upheaval in the social and political conditions in Russia as a result of an uprising by economically exploited and politically suppressed social orders and classes, or by parts of these, falls short of the mark. The revolution did not occur during the course of a cyclical, capitalist economic crisis, as had been assumed in Marxist prognoses, but as the result of a world war that not only dramatically worsened the socio-economic situation of the lower social orders and classes, but which led to the loss of millions of lives and which shattered the Tsarist system of rule.

Fifty years after the October Revolution, it was already ascertained that almost without exception, communist-led revolutions were only successful during and after world wars, and only in those countries that had suffered severe military defeats or had even lost the war. This contrasts with the civilian, liberal and democratic revolutions of 1789, 1830 and 1848/49. The Paris Commune was also created after defeat in the Franco-Prussian war of 1871. However, the two world wars, not only spawned the communist revolutions, but were also the reason why many people, including members of the educated, property-owning orders, were supportive of a transformation of the existing social and state order to create a socialist society, in which all the causes of war were to be removed. This appeared to require not only the overthrow of the elites and classes that had ruled to date, but also a fundamental revolution in the relations between the ethnic groups, nations and states. The causes of war, alongside class rule and militarism, were regarded as being nationalism in particular, which was to be replaced by internationalism within states as well as between them.[11] In other words: the socialist revolution was intended not only as a social revolution, but above all also an international revolution in order to reshape relations between the ethnic groups, nations and states.

8.3 The Prospect of the International Soviet Republic

From August 1914 until the beginning of 1917, Russia's armed forces suffered terrible defeats. The war effort was too great a strain on the economy and the population, whose suffering increased far more greatly during the war than it had during the economic crises in peacetime. Bread, land and peace became the three most important slogans of the Bolsheviks, a branch of the Social Democratic Labour Party of Russia, which did not change its name to the Communist Party (Bolsheviks)

---

[10] Geyer (1985, p. 93). See also Bonwetsch (1991), Hildermeier (1989), Carr (1971), Pipes (1990), Haumann (2007), Furet (1999), Altrichter (2017), Koenen (2017).

[11] For the consensus in principle among all elements of the Socialist Internationale in Basel in 1912, cf. the lectures and literary references in: Jahn (2015, pp. 55–89).

until March 1918. While after the February Revolution, the middle-class parties, the Mensheviks and the Social Revolutionaries, wished to continue fighting alongside the western Allies in the war against the Central Powers, after the October Revolution, the Bolsheviks agreed to the conclusion of a separate peace with Germany, even though this entailed the loss of large parts of the country.

In the eyes of many, the Communist Party, unlike the seemingly toothless, pacifist humanism and cosmopolitanism, appeared to combat the causes of the war and nationalism far more systematically and vehemently than the liberal-democratic and social democratic and socialist parties. While the communists were unable to gain a majority of voters in any country,[12] including Russia, they were willing to use brutal force to establish a minority dictatorship, and then after brief soviet democratic experiments,[13] a party dictatorship. This they succeeded in doing only under favourable international power constellations in Russia, Ukraine, Belarus and the three trans-Caucasian republics, which in 1922 became the Union of Soviet Socialist Republics (USSR), in Mongolia and Tannu Tuva.[14] Without the social democratic movement "Hands off Soviet Russia" in Britain and France, which after the exhaustion suffered by the population as a result of the First World War prevented the expansion of the western Allied war of intervention in Soviet Russia through massive strikes, the Bolshevik regime would hardly have survived between 1918 and 1920. In many other countries, communist attempts at revolution were suppressed.

In 1919, Lenin, like many Bolsheviks, still harboured the hope that the revolution in Russia would become a global revolution within a year, even though in 1915, he had still maintained that socialism could attain victory in one single country.[15] In the minds of the Bolsheviks, the October Revolution was nothing more than an initial spark for the anticipated world revolution, which would take place within a matter of months, particularly in the most highly developed capitalist countries—Germany, France and Britain—which also ruled over vast colonial areas in Africa and Asia. The communists failed to say how the global revolution would then expand to Japan and the whole of America. When after the attack on Soviet Russia by Poland the Red Army advanced as far as Warsaw in August 1920, it appeared to the Bolsheviks to be just a matter of weeks until they would reach Berlin and motivate the German workers to rise up there. At that time, Germany was seen as the centre of the international labour movement, and thus of the global revolution. For a brief period, a Bavarian Soviet Republic was established in Munich (April/May 1919), but all communist uprisings were put down in Germany, as was the Hungarian Soviet Republic (March to August 1919).

1923 marked the end of the phase of repeated communist attempts at uprising in western and central Europe. The acknowledgement of the isolated position of the

---

[12]In the elections to the Constituent Assembly in Russia in November 1917, the Bolsheviks obtained just 22.5% of the votes, Bonwetsch (1991, p. 199).

[13]On the history of the soviets, see Anweiler (1958), Gerlach (1974).

[14]Tannu Tuva was incorporated into the Soviet Union in 1944.

[15]Lenin (1974a, p. 342, 1974b, p. 410), Sinowjew (1919, p. IX).

Soviet Union led Stalin to propagate the notion of "building Socialism in one country" from 1924 onwards, and more intensively in 1925.[16] The result was a re-interpretation of internationalism. Thus, Stalin declared that: "An internationalist is someone who without reservation, without faltering, without setting conditions, is willing to protect the USSR, because the USSR is the basis of the revolutionary movement throughout the world; however, protecting and advancing this revolutionary movement is not possible without protecting the USSR."[17] Thus, the way was paved for the euphemistic reference to Soviet, and soon afterwards, Russian nationalism, as "internationalism". At the beginning of the 1930s, the history of the Russian Tsarist empire was interpreted entirely anew, and was now honoured as the enabler of the multinational Soviet Union,[18] whereas before, it had been blamed for the social suffering of the population, and the political suppression of democracy, the labour movement and the non-Russian peoples in the empire. In 1934, Stalin introduced the term "Soviet patriotism", which used "Soviet" to describe a country and a people, instead of a universal political system. Ultimately, the Soviet people were to adopt the Russian language "voluntarily" as a second language, which is why Russification measures were initiated on a massive scale from the mid-1930s onwards.[19]

Despite the atrocities of the Russian civil war and the communist mass murders during the 1930s, the Second World War, for which the communists and also many socialists made the capitalist economic and social order responsible, became a trigger for a new upswing in the communist global movement and for a vast expansion of communist party rule. This occurred as a result of independent communist revolutions (China, Yugoslavia, Albania) on the one hand, and on the other arose from the takeover of power by communist parties under the umbrella of the Soviet Army (Poland, Czechoslovakia, Hungary, Romania, Bulgaria, the GDR and North Korea). The wars in Indochina until 1975 led to the rise of communist regimes in Vietnam, Laos and Cambodia. Only the Cuban revolution of 1958/59 took place in times of international peace.

Among the ethnic and religious minorities in particular, who had suffered particularly severely under the repressive nationalism within the population majority, communist internationalism presented the prospect of overcoming the repressive nationalism. So far, there has been no comprehensive, global history of a correlation between an ethnic-religious minority situation and the willingness to become actively involved in a communist party, so that this theory can only take many individual examples as references. The outstanding role played by Georgians,

---

[16] In the two publications "Foundations of Leninism" (1924) and "Concerning Questions of Leninism" (1926), Stalin (1971, pp. 37–38, 169–180). On the political context, see Deutscher (1962, p. 173, S. 303–304).

[17] Stalin (1950, p. 45).

[18] Goodman (1960, pp. 86–87, 107–110), Beyrau (2001, p. 227).

[19] Simon (1986, p. 106, 156–157, 174).

Armenians, Jews, Latvians and other minority groups in the Russian Revolution and in the history of the CPSU is likely to be widely known.

Finally, at the beginning of the 1980s, only 16 of 176 countries were under communist party rule and were administered by a central state economic organ; even so, they made up one-third of the world's population and a quarter of the planet's land area. On the European continent, two-thirds of the territory and precisely half the population were subject to communist rule.[20] In nine further countries, a communist or vanguard party took over state power without being able to establish a fully developed communist political and economic system, and thus be recognised by the CPSU as a "socialist country" and part of the "socialist world order".[21] In 1989, in the 80 communist parties and 11 vanguard parties that were politically close to them, 90.5 million people were organised, of whom more than 85 million were organised in the 16 governing communist parties.[22] At this point in time, the communist parties had far more members than all the democratic parties in the world put together. Faced with the communist challenge between 1917 and 1991, the economic and social policy in the capitalist countries found itself forced to make fundamental reforms in order to expand social state institutions, in order to prevent larger parts of the population from being driven into the arms of the communist parties.

Today, there are still a small number of countries with communist single-party rule, but all of them, apart from North Korea, have largely abandoned the central planned and administrative economy and have essentially shifted to capitalist forms of production. Therefore, Marxist-Leninist communism only dominated the global politics and the lives of billions of people in such a decisive way for just three generations.

8.4 From Soviet Inner-State to Inter-State Internationalism

However, what did internationalism mean, first in theory and then also in practice? According to Lenin and the Bolsheviks, the future socialist and later communist world should be organised centrally in a global company and a global bureau, in other words, in a global state with a centrally administered global economy led by the global Communist Party, since only in this way could world peace, social-economic progress and social equality be guaranteed. This goal was not to be achieved through the unification of the existing states, but indirectly through the dismantling of the large continental and colonial empires into nation states. For this

---

[20] This amounted to 6.7 million out of 10.4 million square km in total. 363 million people lived in eastern Europe, with 362 million living in the west in 1988, according to statistical calculations in: Der Fischer Weltalmanach (1989).

[21] These countries included Afghanistan, Angola, Ethiopia, Benin, the Democratic People's Republic of Yemen, the People's Republic of Congo, Mozambique, Nicaragua and Zimbabwe, the ruling parties of which were more or less influenced by the Marxist-Leninist worldview and manifesto.

[22] Staar (1989).

reason, Lenin vehemently propagated the right to self-determination of the peoples, with the right to detach themselves from existing empires, using sharp polemic against socialists such as the Austrian Marxists Karl Renner and Otto Bauer in particular, who wanted to transform the major empires into multinational federal states with personal-cultural autonomy for minorities.[23] He expanded the famous communist slogan of 1848 to: "Proletarians and suppressed peoples, unite!", above all with the goal in mind of smashing the British empire. At the same time, the proletariat in the new nation states were to support the unification of these states in the "international Soviet Republic".

Both sides in the Marxist dispute over nationalities policy, Lenin and Stalin on the one hand and Renner and Bauer on the other, understood internationalism as being a key element for a future multinational large-area state, and ultimately as a prerequisite for unifying humanity. Both also saw the eminent importance of the nations as a structural element of humanity that could not be ignored in the form of non-national cosmopolitanism and global citizenship. The word "internationalism" was an expression of the recognition that global cooperation among people requires their awareness and structure as nations. In Lenin's and Stalin's thinking, the historical character of nations, i.e. not their natural, timeless character, implied far more strongly than was the case with Bauer and Renner that there would be a future of humanity without nations.

Karl Marx and Friedrich Engels only vaguely spoke of the fact that in the classless society, the contradictions between the nations would disappear,[24] although they did not claim that this would also apply to the differences between them or even to their existence. This could be understood as a vision of the future of a continuously cooperative relationship between the nations. They could conceive of a stateless humanity, of a society without a state, but there was never talk of a nationless society or nationless humanity.

The Bolsheviks and also many socialists regarded the liberal-democratic peace concept of the nation states joined together in a League of Nations, the cohesion of which was to be underscored by international law, a liberal, capitalist global economy and a global public that was pluralistic and free, as was particularly espoused by the US president Thomas Woodrow Wilson (1856–1924),[25] as being merely an instrument of rule by a small number of imperialist major powers. These powers would, in their view, intensify global capitalist exploitation, the subjection of most peoples under the colonial yoke, and social suffering, while spurring on nationalist prejudices to instigate new wars.

---

[23] Renner (1918), Bauer (2016).

[24] "National differences and antagonism between peoples are daily more and more vanishing, owing to the development of the bourgeoisie, to freedom of commerce, to the world market, to uniformity in the mode of production and in the conditions of life corresponding thereto... In proportion as the antagonism between classes within the nation vanishes, the hostility of one nation to another will come to an end." (Marx and Engels 1969, pp. 98–137). See Szporluk (1988).

[25] See the lecture in Chap. 4, pp. 61–78.

From these fundamental considerations, Lenin and later also Stalin, inspired by previous ideas published by Karl Marx (1818–1883), particularly with regard to the Paris Commune,[26] developed the fundamental structure of the communist world order, as would be first realised in the dramatically diminished territory of Russia, in the Soviet Union after 1922 and later in the "international Soviet Republic"[27]: the communist global state. In it, the proletarian state would ultimately "die off" to the extent that the global society would succeed in administering itself without the aid of any kind of state power.[28] For many reasons, Soviet democracy was far superior to "bourgeois" parliamentary democracy. All power, be it legislative, administrative or judicial, was to lie in the hands of the people through its elected local, regional, national and global soviet deputies, governments and judges. The peoples' representatives and officials were not permitted to receive any income above that of the average income of the population, and were to be subject to dismissal by the people at all times. From this concept of people's rule, the centralist political and state concept of the communists was born, which they transferred to the international level. In their view, overcoming class rule in the "international Soviet Republic" was designed to remove the contradictions between the nations.

Accordingly, the formation of the USSR in December 1922 was regarded not as a successor state to the Russian Empire, but as the kernel of the global union of all Soviet republics in the world and as a counter-concept to the capitalist League of Nations. Lenin criticised the propagation of the United States of Europe as being a reactionary idea, in place of which the communists set the goal of creating the "United States of the World... So long as the full victory of communism does not lead to the final disappearance of every state, including every democratic state."[29]

Lenin spoke several times of a rapprochement (*zblizhenie*) and amalgamation (*sliyanie*) of the nations,[30] without every explaining what he actually meant by "amalgamation". Stalin was in the first government of Soviet Russia, in the Council of People's Commissioners, responsible for the nationalities policy, and more intensively than Lenin developed the basic framework for the way the communists handled the national issue. In Russian, nation (*natsia*) is traditionally understood as

---

[26] Marx (1973).

[27] The appeal by the Executive Committee of the Communist Internationale on 1 May 1919 stated that: "Im Jahr 1919 wurde die große Kommunistische Internationale geboren. Im Jahr 1920 wird die große Internationale Sowjetrepublik geboren werden." Bibliothek der Kommunistischen Internationale I (Library of the Communist Internationale I.) (1920, p. 91). Other expressions used were the "proletarian" or "socialist world republic". For a fundamental discussion of the topic, still see Goodman (1960, pp. 50–79, 264–284).

[28] Thus Lenin, referring to Friedrich Engels (1974d, p. 396).

[29] Lenin (1974a, p. 342).

[30] "We demand freedom of self-determination ... for the oppressed nations, not because we have dreamt of splitting up the country economically, or of the ideal of small states, but, on the contrary, because we want large states and the closer unity and even fusion of nations ...", Lenin (1974b, pp. 408–409). The CPSU manifesto of 1961 limited the scope of the formula somewhat. Now, the talk was of full unity (*pol'naya edinost'*) instead of amalgamation, but also of the fact that the non-Russians will voluntarily adopt the Russian language as the lingua franca of all peoples living in the USSR, Meissner (1962, pp. 223, 225).

being an ethnic concept. It was in this frame of mind that Stalin developed his concept of the nation, which for decades became binding in global communist policy: "A nation is a historically created stable community of people that is based on a common language, territory, economic life and the psychological type that is reflected in the commonality of the culture".[31] This is an ethnic-territorial understanding of the nation, in contrast to an statist, western definition. For this reason, the citizens of the Soviet Union were not regarded as being a nation, but rather a people, a Soviet people. And just like Russia today, the Soviet Union was consequently categorised politically and constitutionally as a multinational state, not as a nation state, while the USA regards itself as being a multi-state nation in the United Nations (and not in the United States or United Nation States).[32] Stalin's territorialised ethnic concept of the nation was designed among other things to deny Jews membership of any nation, since they played a relatively large, independent role in the labour movement and with the General Jewish Workers' Alliance in Lithuania, Poland and Russia demanded cultural autonomy in a similar way in which it also played a central role in the nationalities policy of the Austromarxists.[33]

Stalin developed more specific ideas about the future of humanity under communism than Lenin when he considered the issue at the heart of national differences, namely language.[34] He was not blind to the fact that languages exert a mutual influence over each other, although in his view, amalgamating and mixing all languages to create a single language for humanity was impossible. To a far greater extent, the smaller peoples would adopt the languages of the large ones, so that after a long period of time, a small number of languages in some zones would assert themselves. A single global language would not come about until a long time in the communist future. In slave-owning society, the predominant language was Latin, in the feudal society, French, in the capitalist society, English, and under global socialism, it would be Russian.[35]

The Leninist and Stalinist concept of a global republic in combination with their ideas of a global party is in itself not one of internationalism, but of anational globalism, a universalism or mondialism, which regards people as global citizens and not as citizens of nation states. In the strict sense of the word, internationalism should be regarded as being a notion of a global society based on the separation of humanity into nations and states as main elements of their structure, and which is oriented to understanding and cooperation between the nations and states.

---

[31] Stalin (1972, p. 272).

[32] At the same time, the communists agreed to describe the organisation of the sovereign state peoples as the *Organizatsia Ob'edinionnych Natsii* (not: *Narodov*) in accordance with the American linguistic usage.

[33] On the historical origin of the different concepts of the nation, see the three lectures on the topic of nationalism, Jahn (2015, pp. 27–29).

[34] Stalin (1972).

[35] Thus, for example, D. Zaslavsky in an article in the Literaturnaya Gazeta of 1 January 1949, according to Goodman (1960, p. 278).

The political practice of the communists was not only determined by theoretical considerations, but often by pragmatic, tactical factors. Internationalism first had to prove its worth as an inner-state internationalism within the Soviet Union. Lenin and his comrades were above all concerned during the initial years of Soviet rule, which was still unsteady, to promote acceptance of communist rule, including among the non-Russian peoples of the former Russian Empire. For this reason, Lenin supported national aspirations among non-Russian peoples for emancipation from the dominance of the Russians, and in particular fought against Russian chauvinism.[36] Although his ideas regarding the party and state were centralist, for tactical reasons, and as an acknowledgement of the nationalism among the peoples living in the Tsarist empire and throughout the world, he supported a federative structure for the Russian Socialist Federative Soviet Republic (RSFSR), and then also for the Union of Soviet Socialist Republics (USSR).[37] In contrast to Lenin's view, Stalin had demanded the incorporation of the non-Russian union republics into the RSFSR, without success.

For these tactical reasons, during the first years following the revolution, the languages of numerous peoples were encouraged or even developed into a written language for the first time. Here, a political decision was made as to whether some ethnic groups should together be classed as a people, while others should be several different peoples. As a result, during the course of the decades, the number of peoples classified as living in the Soviet Union according to the censuses fluctuated by several dozens. Many of the small peoples were recognised as ethnic groups (*narodnost'*), while others and the larger, relatively compact settling nations were granted a state-territorial unit: a community, a district (*raion*), a region (*oblast'*), an Autonomous Republic or a Union Republic. In 1934, in the Soviet Union (and later also in communist Yugoslavia), even the assignment in law of each individual Soviet citizen to a "nationality" (*natsionalnost'*) was introduced, which was noted in passports and other official documents. Nationality was essentially based on origins. For children with parents of different nationalities, the parents, in effect usually the father, decided which nationality the child should have. However, after turning 16, the child had the option of taking on the nationality of the other parent, but not a third nationality based on inclination or language skills. The calculated purpose behind the tactical recognition of national needs among the non-Russian peoples was that among the peoples who were culturally and economically supported, communism would more easily take root than in a Russian-dominated central state.

In the decades that followed the October Revolution, a complex system of national territorial units was created, which was approximately staggered according to the population size of the peoples, with federations within the Soviet Federation

---

[36]Lenin (1974b, pp. 412–413, 1974c).

[37]In the CPR (B) manifesto of March 1919, the "federative unification of the states organised according to the Soviet type" was openly declared as "one of the transitional forms on the path to full unity", Meissner (1962, p. 128). Lenin already wrote in 1914: "We do not advocate preserving small nations at all costs; other conditions being equal, we are decidedly for centralisation and are opposed to the petty-bourgois ideal of federal relationships.", Lenin (1974c, p. 102).

and with autonomous sub-units in the federated republics. At the same time, some territorial units were newly created, while others were dissolved; some were granted higher political status, while others saw their status diminish. This system did not follow a uniform classification principle, but was characterised by numerous situative and tactical political decisions. Although the population size generally played an important role when assigning a state territorial unit,[38] the territory boundaries frequently did not correspond either to older ones that had been passed down, or to the settlement boundaries of the peoples, but often consciously deviated from both in order to keep national differences between them alive. Several peoples were also brought together in binational territorial units such as Kabard-Balkaria, Karachay-Cherkessia or Checheno-Ingushetia, which was intended to promote and intensify the animosities between the respective minority and the majority population. It was not until Khrushchev took over the party leadership that the multinational territorial system of the Soviet Union was consolidated at the end of the 1950s. From then on, the Soviet Union consisted of 15 Union republics, i.e. 14 national Soviet republics and the Russian Socialist Federative Soviet Republic. In five of the Union republics, there were 20 Autonomous Socialist Soviet and 8 Autonomous Regions, while in the RSFSR there were also 10 Autonomous Districts for the small peoples, most of them living in Siberia.[39] The only people that did not have its own national republic and also no communist party of its own in the Soviet Union was the Russian people, which was regarded as the main element of the future, Russian-speaking Soviet people.

The communists even granted the Union republics the status of sovereign state, with the right to leave the Union, although no procedure for claiming this right was determined, since they assumed that the Soviet Union would never be dissolved due to the allegedly internationalist attitude of the proletariat and the socialist peoples; instead, it would simply be expanded to create a global union. In order to render the right to leave plausible, only those republics were recognised as Union republics that had a share of the external border of the USSR. For example, therefore, Tatarstan, which lay within the Soviet Union, was not granted such a right, unlike the Baltic and southern Caucasian republics, which had smaller populations. The status of the Union republics as sovereign states also served to present the USSR as a socialist alternative to the capitalist League of Nations.

After the Second World War, when the Soviet Union decided to join the United Nations, Stalin demanded that all the Union republics—at that time there were 16—be recognised as sovereign nations by the UN. The compromise that was finally reached with the western powers consisted of the fact that alongside the USSR, the Ukrainian and Belarusian SSR were also recognised as members of the United Nations.

On the global political stage, the communists founded the Communist International (Comintern) in March 1919, which as the Third International led to a radical

---

[38] See in detail the list of the peoples and population figures in Jahn (2008, pp. 67–68).
[39] Mark (1989).

break with social democracy and the Second Socialist International.[40] The global party was not intended to take the form of a federation of national parties, but was to be a centralist organisation with only national sections and a headquarters in Moscow. From the start, its executive committee was dominated, and subsequently increasingly so, by representatives of the CPR and later of the CPSU. Initially, the Comintern was designed to promote the revolution in the largest possible number of countries outside Soviet Russia, just as Soviet power and the Red Army were initially regarded as instruments of the global revolution. With the failure of the proletarian revolution on a global scale, the Comintern quickly became a tactical instrument for Soviet foreign policy, which was oriented to the survival of the Soviet state and the exploitation of conflicts of interest between the capitalist states.

While from 1917 until the end of the 1920s, many communists in western and central Europe still believed that their country would soon join the USSR—even in 1942, the communists of Montenegro still decided that their country should become part of the Soviet Union—after 1945, there was no longer any question that the states that had now fallen under communist party rule should join the USSR. The strength of national awareness and the consideration of western fears of Soviet communist world rule were probably responsible for this. The states that fell under communist rule now constituted the "socialist world community" led by the Soviet Union, which then later assumed the role of an international legal body of international organisations in the form of the Council for Mutual Economic Assistance and the Warsaw Pact. Thus, the inner-state inter-ethnonationalism was supplemented by inter-state internationalism, which was intended to achieve the same goals as the former in the long term. For a brief period, the communist states appeared to be a unit in international politics in which the state and party structures aligned with each other and a shared "socialist foreign policy" was pursued.

The standard literature on the subject does not clarify whether the Chinese communists and Mao Zedong ever thought of joining the USSR or whether the Soviet communists and Stalin considered the possibility of incorporating China. Right from the start, Chinese communism had strong national communist traits and from the 1930s onwards, Soviet communism had become decisively Russified, so that the word "Soviet" fundamentally changed its character. A name for a universal political system that was one day to span the entire world became a name for a single, spatially limited state and a state nation, the Soviet people. The Soviet Union, which was originally intended to be a global entity (149 million square km) was reduced in size to greater Russia (22 million square km) which included a republic of Russia (17 million square km) which has now become today's Russian Federation.

However, the three-way split of communism[41] with centres in Moscow, Belgrade and Beijing soon undermined the unity of the Sino-Soviet "eastern bloc". At the party level, the unity of the communist party movement was initially to be bolstered once again by the Communist Information Bureau (Cominform), founded in

---

[40]Weber et al. (2014), Bayerlein (2004), Rees and Thorpe (1998).
[41]Leonhard (1975).

September 1947, the short-lived successor organisation to the Communist International (Comintern), which Stalin had formally dissolved in May 1943 in response to the concerns of his western allies. However, it was avoided by the Chinese communists.[42] National communism outside eastern-central Europe officially won the day after 1963, with the open Sino-Soviet conflict. The "proletarian and socialist internationalism" degenerated entirely into a Moscow-based, Russian-dominated hegemonial ideology.

During the most intensive phase of the Cold War, the idea was still being discussed in Moscow following the start of the Korean War of making the World Peace Council the communist counter-organisation to the United Nations,[43] just as the USSR was conceived in 1922 as a counter-organisation to the capitalist-imperialist League of Nations. However, it clearly quickly emerged as being more advantageous to use the right of veto on the UN Security Council to hobble the United Nations, which were dominated by the western powers, than to build up an opposing inter-state organisation.

8.5 Inter-Ethnonational Federalism as an Alternative to Internationalism, Which Was Perverted to Become Russian Great Power Nationalism

How can the questions asked at the beginning of this essay best be answered? It is beyond dispute that the willingness of the Bolsheviks to end the war at the end of 1917 and the beginning of 1918—the only party to adopt this position—even taking into account the loss of large parts of Russia's territory with over a third of its total population, played a decisive role in gaining and retaining power after the October Revolution. The support of considerable portions of the non-Russian population could only be obtained because the Bolsheviks promised them liberation from Russian rule and their own national republics and autonomous areas within their sphere of power. Neither the forces that defended tsardom nor the middle class and socialist parties would probably have been in a position to retain the unity of the empire. To this extent, the propagation of internationalism and of a federalist organisation of national republics was an important factor in the communists' takeover and retention of power, as well as the indisputably important willingness to use force against political enemies without regard for the consequences.

Another question that is evidently never asked by researchers is why, after consolidating his power, Stalin did not, on the basis of the communist, centralist concept of party and state, dissolve the multinational, federative state order, for

---

[42] Soon after Stalin's death, it was dissolved again in 1956, after it had been decisively weakened by the Cominform conflict with Yugoslavia. After that, only three further world conferences were held, in 1957, 1960 and 1963, in which the contradictions between the national communist parties became increasingly clear.

[43] Schlaga (1991, pp. 82–86).

example when passing the new constitution of December 1936,[44] and replace it with a centralist state structure with administrative units without an ethno-national reference,[45] or remove all elements of the legal recognition of ethnically defined nationality in the interest of forming a uniform, Russian-speaking Soviet people. There is little to suggest that at this time, a nationally motivated rebellion of non-Russians against CPSU rule was to be feared. Apparently, the conviction was sufficient that all ethno-national and federative rights would remain effective only on paper for all time.

At any rate, following the downfall of the Soviet Union, the chairman of the Liberal Democratic Party, Vladimir V. Zhirinovsky, proposed that the ethno-national territories in Russia should be abolished and regional state units should be randomly formed in accordance with the US model. In western research, there were also authors, such as Victor Zaslavsky, who felt that the institutionalisation of individual nationality or ethnicity and the preferential treatment given to certain ethnic groups when creating national territories was one of the main faults of the Soviet nationalities policy.[46] One plausible counter-argument is that it is not the recognition of the ethno-national differences that led to the failure of the Soviet Union as a centralised state, but the entirely inadequate real-life equality granted to the ethnic national groups and the failure to create real federalisation and autonomisation of the territorial units in that vast country, which would only have had a chance of being accepted by all ethno-national groups and by the majority of society, even after democratisation of the state, if the power structures had been decentralised.

8.6 On the Unlikelihood of a Communist Renaissance and on the Possibility of a Socialist One

Will there be a revival of the communist or socialist movement? The capitalist economic and social order, which since the collapse of communist party rule in eastern Europe and of central state economic planning has spanned almost the entire world, has emerged as being considerably open to reform in recent decades, and modifiable through social state institutions—including under the influence of fears of the communist movement, which knew how to exploit social suffering among large parts of the global population in order to win supporters. At the same time, for decades, there has evidently been no sustained, successful fight against the growing social inequality, social suffering, mass flight from socio-economically non-developed countries, the destruction of the environmental balance and the exploitation of natural resources. There is also no evidence of the fact that with the

---

[44]Kriza (2017), Wimberg (1992).

[45]Gerhard Simon mentions such attempts, although without giving or mentioning the sources of such suggestions, Simon (1986, p. 16, 366).

[46]Zaslavsky (1991, pp. 13–14, 19–21).

current power relations, devastating local and regional wars can be prevented. Even the risk of a major or even global war cannot be entirely ruled out.

All this indicates that the fundamental criticism of capitalism will not come to an end. However, it is unlikely that this will lead to a renaissance of communism as a political power, since awareness of the barbarity and mass murders conducted in the name of communism will not disappear from collective memory any more than the crimes perpetrated by the National Socialists. A revival of the illusions for the future propagated by the communists, which alongside their revolutionary willingness to use force were essential for seizing and exerting power by the communist parties, is quite unlikely. At the same time, the fundamental idea developed during the nineteenth century, that the economy and more recently also nature, and not only politics, can and must be the subject of conscious, democratic decisions, is alive and well. This is also occurring today to a certain extent, albeit often under another name than "socialism". The attempts at forging global plans to reduce the climate change created by humans to two degrees by 2100 is nothing other than a small piece of socialism, i.e. the steering and planning of the economy as the result of a political decision, and in some cases even one that is democratically organised.

It remains highly contentious today as to how a social economy, and not just one that is administered by the state, could be organised in a democratic way. Socialist outsiders of differing political orientations have provided important new ideas in this regard. However, in many respects, these have remained unsatisfactory, and have not succeeded in creating mass movements or even majorities among the population. Socialist fundamental principles have been frequently newly presented under different names today, since the occupation of the term "socialism" by the communists has entirely discredited it in the eyes of large parts of the population. It remains to be seen whether this will change in the future. However, it is highly likely that the fundamental principle of an economy and an environment that is socially self-administered in a democratic way will again be of political relevance, and repeatedly so.

References

Altrichter H (2017) Russland 1917. Ein Land auf der Suche nach sich selbst, 2nd edn. Schöningh, Paderborn
Anweiler O (1958) Die Rätebewegung in Russland 1905–1921. Brill, Leiden
Bauer O (2016) Die Nationalitätenfrage und die Sozialdemokratie (1907). Forgotten Books, London
Bayerlein BH (2004) Das neue Babylon. Strukturen und Netzwerke der Kommunistischen Internationale und ihre Klassifizierung, Jahrbuch für Historische Kommunismusforschung. Aufbau-Verlag, Berlin, pp 181–270
Berchin IB (1971) Geschichte der UdSSR 1917–1970. Dietz, Berlin
Beyrau D (2001) Petrograd, 25. Oktober 1917. Die russische Revolution und der Aufstieg des Kommunismus. München, DTV
Bibliothek der Kommunistischen Internationale I (1920) Manifest, Richtlinien, Beschlüsse des Ersten Kongresses. Aufrufe und offene Schreiben des Exekutivkomitees bis zum Zweiten Kongreß. Carl Hoym Nachf, Hamburg

Bonwetsch B (1991) Die russische Revolution 1917. Eine Sozialgeschichte von der Bauernbefreiung 1861 bis zum Oktoberumsturz. Wissenschaftliche Buchgesellschaft, Darmstadt

Carr EH (1971) The Bolshevik revolution 1917–1923, 2 volumes. Penguin, Harmondsworth

Der Fischer Weltalmanach 1990 (1989) Fischer, Frankfurt am Main

Deutscher I (1962) Stalin. Eine politische Biographie. Kohlhammer, Stuttgart

Furet F (1999) The passing of an illusion: the idea of communism in the twentieth century, 2nd edn. The University of Chicago Press, Chicago

Gerlach E (1974) Räte in der Spanischen revolution. Association, Hamburg

Geyer D (1985) Die Russische Revolution. Historische Probleme und Perspektiven, 4th edn. Vandenhoeck & Ruprecht, Göttingen

Goodman ER (1960) The Soviet design for a world state. Columbia University Press, New York

Gudkov L, Zorkaja N (2017) Instrumentalisieren, Klittern, Verdrängen. Russlands unerwünschtes Revolutionsjubiläum. Osteuropa 67(6–8):19–42

Habermas J (1990) Die nachholende revolution. Suhrkamp, Frankfurt am Main, pp 179–204

Haumann H (ed) (2007) Die Russische revolution 1917. Böhlau, Köln/Weimar/Vienna

Heinemann-Grüder A (2017) Zerstörung und Ordnung. Kurze vergleichende Soziologie der Russischen revolution. Osteuropa 67(6–8):68–73

Hildermeier M (1989) Die Russische revolution 1905–1921. Suhrkamp, Frankfurt am Main

Ibragimova E (2017) Neudobnaya revolyutsiya 1917-go, ili tikhij yubilej v Rossii. http://www.dw.com/ru/неудобная-революция-1917-го-или-тихий-юбилей-в-россии/a-412240

Jahn E (1986) Entwicklungsphasen sozialistischer System. In: Nohlen D (ed) Pipers Wörterbuch zur Politik, vol 4. Sozialistische Systeme. Piper, Munich/Zürich, pp 101–106

Jahn E (2008) The state transformation in the East of Europe. 'Second national rebirth', nationalism, national movements, and the formation of nation-states in late and post-communist Europe since 1985. In: Jahn E (ed) Nationalism in late and post-communist Europe, vol 1. Nomos, Baden-Baden

Jahn E (2015) World political challenges. Political issues under debate, vol 3. Springer, Heidelberg

Kalinin I (2017) Antirevolutionäre Revolutionserinnerungspolitik. Russlands Regime und der Geist der Revolution. Osteuropa 67(6–8):7–17

Katzer N (2017) Russlands langer Abschied. Die Revolution als Geschichte und Gegenwart. Osteuropa 67(6–8):43–46

Koenen G (2017) Die Farbe Rot. Ursprünge und Geschichte des Kommunismus. Beck, Munich

Kriza E (2017) From utopia to dystopia? Bukharin and the Soviet Constitution oft 1936. In: Simonsen KM, Kjærgård JR (eds) Discursive framings of human rights. Negotiating agency and victimhood. Routledge, London

Lenin WI (1974a) On the Slogan for a United States of Europe (1915). In: Collected works, vol 21. Progress, Mosow, pp 339–343

Lenin WI (1974b) The revolutionary proletariat and the right of nations to self-determination (1915). In: Collected works, vol 21. Progress, Moscow, pp 407–414, 412–421

Lenin WI (1974c) On the national pride of the Great Russians (1914). In: Collected works, vol 21. Progress, Moscow, pp 102–106

Lenin WI (1974d) The state and revolution. The Marxist theory of the state and the tasks of the proletariat in the revolution (1918). In: Collected works, vol 25. Progress, Moscow, pp 381–492

Leonhard W (1975) Die Dreispaltung des Marxismus. Ursprung und Entwicklung des Sowjetmarxismus, Maoismus und Reformkommunismus. Econ, Düsseldorf

Mark RA (1989) Die Völker der Sowjetunion. Ein Lexikon. Westdeutscher Verlag, Opladen

Marx K (1973) Der Bürgerkrieg in Frankreich. (The Civil War in France) Adresse des Generalrates der Internationalen Arbeiterassoziation (1871). In: Werke, vol 17. Dietz, Berlin, pp 313–365

Marx K, Engels F (1969) Manifesto of the Communist Party (1848). In: Selected works, vol 1. Progress, Moscow, pp 98–137

Meissner B (1962) Das Parteiprogramm der KPdSU 1903 bis 1961. Verlag Wissenschaft und Politik, Cologne

References

Pipes R (1990) The Russian revolution. Knopf, New York

Reed J (1990) Ten days that shook the world. Penguin, Harmondsworth

Rees T, Thorpe A (eds) (1998) International communism and the communist international, 1919–1943. Manchester University Press, Manchester

Renner K (1918) Das Selbstbestimmungsrecht der Nationen, in besonderer Anwendung auf Österreich, I. Teil: Nation und Staat. Deuticke, Leipzig/Wien

Schlaga R (1991) Die Kommunisten in der Friedensbewegung – erfolglos? Die Politik des Weltfriedensrates im Verhältnis zur Außenpolitik der Sowjetunion und zu unabhängigen Friedensbewegungen im Westen (1950–1979). Lit Verlag, Münster/Hamburg

Simon G (1986) Nationalismus und Nationalitätenpolitik in der Sowjetunion. Von der totalitären Diktatur zur nachstalinschen Gesellschaft. Nomos, Baden-Baden

Sinowjew G (1919) Die Perspektiven der proletarischen Revolution, Die Kommunistische Internationale 1(1), p IX

Staar RF (1989) Weltkommunismus 1988/89. Osteuropa 39(11/12):1100–1108

Stalin JW (1950) Die internationale Lage und die Verteidigung der UdSSR (1927). In: Werke, vol 10. Dietz, Berlin

Stalin J (1971) Fragen des Leninismus. Oberbaumverlag, Berlin

Stalin JW (1972) Marxismus und nationale Frage (1913). In: Werke, vol 2. Druck-Verlags-Vertriebs-Kooperative, Frankfurt, pp 266–233

Szporluk R (1988) Communism and nationalism. Karl Marx versus Friedrich List. Oxford University Press, Oxford

Weber H, Drabkin J, Bayerlein BH, Galkin A (2014) Deutschland, Russland, Komintern, 3 volumes. De Gruyter, Berlin/Boston

Wimberg E (1992) Socialism, democratism and criticism: the Soviet press and the national discussion of the 1936 draft constitution. Sov Stud 44(2):313–332

Zaslavsky V (1991) Das russische Imperium unter Gorbatschow. Seine ethnische Struktur und ihre Zukunft. Wagenbach, Berlin

International Involvement in the Civil War in Syria 9

Abstract

The civil war in Syria, which has now lasted for 8 years already, and which has expanded to become a small world war, with military interventions from four major UN powers and soldiers and armed fighters from around 80 countries, is characterised by highly complex, rapidly changing alliances and blurred front lines between numerous military and political participants.

The war in Syria first began during the "Arab Spring" in 2011, and arose from the social-political confrontation between the dictatorial regime of the Baath Party and the Assad clan and heterogeneous, partly pro-west, liberal, potentially democratic oppositional forces, which soon—as was the case in other Arab countries—began to compete with Islamist groups of widely ranging religious and political attitudes. Until the summer of 2013, there was still dispute in the West regarding a military intervention to topple the Assad regime, when the Syrian government also used gas weapons against the civilian population. The dispute over the gas weapons, which was mediated by Russia, largely marked an end to the discussions surrounding western intervention, since Russia made its interest clear in the retention of the Assad regime and its marine base in Tartus, which had been guaranteed by Assad. After that, the Sunni Islamic fighting units in the war against the Assad regime, which received huge material and financial support from Saudi Arabia, Qatar and Turkey, gained greater importance. The Assad regime, meanwhile, increasingly adopted the features of an Alawite regime, and received support from Shiite Iranian and Lebanese fighting units. Finally, with the formation of "Islamic State" (IS), the civil war in Syria became merged with that in Iraq. This in turn triggered the formation of a broad alliance against IS, which was mainly led by the major western powers with the involvement of Sunni states, and which to date has been restricted to air attacks against IS and in part also to the support by Kurdish armed units in northern Iraq and northern Syria. Finally, the Russian air force openly intervened on the side of the

---

Lecture given on 18.4.2016.

© Springer Nature Switzerland AG 2020
E. Jahn, *War and Compromise Between Nations and States*,
https://doi.org/10.1007/978-3-030-34131-2_9

Assad regime in north-western Syria, where the regime is being opposed by a highly tangled web of pro-western, moderate Islamist and extremist al-Qaida groups, as well as local IS units. Despite a dangerous military dispute between Turkey and Russia, to date, this has only opened up limited opportunities for the formation of a new alliance between the Assad regime, the moderate opposition and the entire community of states against IS, which not only aimed to overthrow the internal order of all states, but the entire state system itself. As a result, it will be a long time before real peace returns to the region.

9.1 The Internationalisation of the Syrian Civil War

In 2016, the (Arab) Syrian republic celebrated its 70th day of independence.[1] Three years later, the phase of a parliamentary democracy already came to an end with a military coup, which was followed by others in 1961, 1963 (when the dictatorship of the Baath Party, the "Arab Socialist Renaissance Party" was created), 1966 and 1971. This marked the beginning of the long period of rule by General Hafiz al-Assad (1930–2000) and his son, Bashar al-Assad (born 1965).[2] After the start of the "Arab Spring" or "Arabellion"[3] in December 2010, it appeared to be only a question of time before Syria, too, would experience the end of the era of Arab military dictatorship. One after another, the dictators in Tunisia, Egypt and Yemen were toppled by mass movements.[4] The Iraqi dictator had already fallen from power and been killed as a result of the interventionist war by the USA and its allies, while the Libyan dictator suffered a similar fate with the aid of western air attacks.[5] Some observers saw 2011/2012 as being a fifth wave of global historical democratisation, following those in eastern Europe and Latin America.

With an area of 185,000 km², Syria is around half the size of Germany, although in 2004, it had just 18 million inhabitants, with probably over 21 million by the time the war began. Large parts of the country are covered by desert and are sparsely populated.[6] Most Syrians live in the western parts of the country, in Damascus,

---

[1] However, nearly 5 years previously, it had already been declared independent by the government-in-exile of Charles de Gaulle, and had been a founding member of the United Nations.
[2] Bawey (2016), Gerlach (2015, 2016), Heydemann (2013), Perthes (1990).
[3] See the lecture Jahn (2015a).
[4] Zine el-Abidini Ben Ali (1987 to 14 January 2011) in Tunisia, Muhammad Husni Mubarak in Egypt (1981 to 11 February 2011), and Ali Abdullah Salih (1978 to 22 January 2012) in Yemen.
[5] Saddam Hussein ruled in Iraq from 1979 9 April, and Muammar al-Gaddafi in Libya from 1969 to 20 October 2011.
[6] For useful maps relating to this lecture, see: http://gulf2000.columbia.edu/images/maps/Syria_Population_Demog_lg.png;
 https://de.wikipedia.org/wiki/Datei:Syria_2016_administrative_divisions_-_de_-_colored.svg;
 http://gulf2000.columbia.edu/images/maps/Syria_Ethnic_Detailed_lg.png;

9.1 The Internationalisation of the Syrian Civil War

Aleppo, Homs, Hama, Latakia and on the Euphrates, in Raqqa and Deir az-Zor, which have seen most of the fighting in the civil war. The Syrian population consists of 89% Arabs, approx. 6% Kurds and 2% Armenians, as well as a small number of Circassians, Turkmens and Turks.[7] The confessional groups within the population are also of political importance, with 74% Sunnis, 12% Alawites,[8] 10% Christians and 3% Druze.[9]

The mass protest against the Assad regime began in the south-west of the country on 17 March 2011 in Daraa against the incarceration and maltreatment of a number of children who had sprayed graffiti with political slogans, and spread throughout the country when the state organs used brutal force against demonstrators and shot several people.[10] Just a few days later, some demonstrators also responded with fatal violence, with the result that the mutual use of force quickly escalated into civil war, even though until January 2012, unarmed mass demonstrations were still being held in many towns and cities. At first, the demonstrators demanded freedom, recognition of human dignity, the punishment of state perpetrators of violence, social reforms, an end to corruption and the lifting of the state of emergency that had been imposed since 1963. Soon afterwards, however, they also demanded the dissolution of the Assad regime, after repeated acts of violence by state organs in public places and in the prisons. From the end of July 2011 onwards, a Free Syrian Army was created from the mainly Sunni deserters from the Syrian forces. Initially, it represented secular, liberal, pro-western views, but then also took in Islamic groups and was transformed into a loose umbrella organisation of different political and military groups.

---

https://de.wikipedia.org/wiki/Geschichte_Syriens#/media/File:Sykes-Picot-1916_german.gif;

https://de.wikipedia.org/wiki/Geschichte_Syriens#/media/File:French_Mandate_for_Syria_and_the_Lebanon_map_de.svg;

http://images.google.de/imgres?imgurl=https://niwelt.files.wordpress.com/2015/09/wpid-2000px-syria16.png&imgrefurl=https://niwelt.wordpress.com/2015/09/19/situation-in-syrien-karte/&h=1716&w=1944&tbnid=FrL8tbdKtnrqNM:&tbnh=134&tbnw=152&docid=P2GmZGJsHrfk3M&usg=__aXtNfqGwZxE594HTVSQn1LRzBdE=&sa=X&ved=0ahUKEwiGhMnXlprMAhVDiywKHctcA5kQ9QEIPDAI;

https://de.wikipedia.org/wiki/Rojava;

http://gulf2000.columbia.edu/images/maps/Syria_Federal_Option_sm.png. (All Internet pages retrieved on 17.4.2016 unless otherwise stated.)

[7]Löchel (2015, p. 440).

[8]In Iraq, the Alawites were created as a breakaway group from the Shiite towards the end of the ninth century, and were known for centuries as the Nusayri. During the twelfth century, they settle above all in Syrian coastal areas. It was not until the end of the nineteenth century that they began to call themselves supporters of Ali, or Alawites, in order to avoid discrimination by other Muslims. They should not be confused with the Turkish and Kurdish Alewites, a very undogmatic Shiite faith from the thirteenth/fourteenth century.

[9]The Druze are an independent religious community which developed from the Shiites in Egypt during the eleventh century, with the adoption of religious elements (such as the belief in reincarnation) from other religions.

[10]In an interview with Spiegel magazine, Bashar al-Assad later described this as a mistake, Brinkbäumer and Bednarz (2013).

In the months that followed, the conflict, which was originally mainly socio-political in character, and which intensified enormously as a result of a deep socio-economic crisis and rapid population growth, became a dispute between dozens of fighting units with very different political orientations from the confessional and ethnic groups within Syrian society, in other words, mainly the Alawites, Sunnis, Shiite, Christians and Druze, Arabs and Kurds, as well as secularists and Islamists with very different observances.[11] Occasionally, these political-military fighting units enter into alliances with each other, or silently tolerate each other in the fight against a common enemy, before resuming their fight against each other with full-blown barbarity. All sides fail to observe the law of war to varying degrees, and perpetrate barbaric acts of violence against civilians and prisoners. Overall, according to UN estimates, in the first 5 years, 250,000 people in Syria have lost their lives; according to a Syrian centre for political research, this figure is already as high as 470,000.[12] 6.6 million people of the population of around 20 million have taken flight within the country, while as of October 2018, 5.6 million had fled abroad.[13]

The Syrian civil war would probably never have reached the intensity or have lasted as longwithout the massive international, partly openly declared, partly covert and denied, involvement of numerous other states, with extensive financial means, huge numbers of weapons and many troop units and thousands of individual fighters. In various ways and to varying degrees, four of the five permanent Security Council members were involved in the armed conflict in Syria, as were several Arab states, several other NATO states such as Turkey, and also Iran and Israel,[14] while dozens of states contributed to the financing of the war. Around 30,000 young men and many young women from around 100 states in the world[15] travelled voluntarily to Syria and Iraq, usually via Turkey, to reinforce the armed units of the jihadists and the "Islamic State". Thus, large parts of the world are involved the war that is raging in Syria.

Two fundamental political debates surrounding the Syrian civil war began in succession in the West. Until September 2013, the discussion for and against a western interventionist war to topple the Assad regime dominated the debate, even without legitimisation by the UN Security Council, since the approval of Russia and

---

[11]The transition from socio-political conflict to an increasingly violent civil war with many broken, contradictory confessional-ethnic fault lines, is impressively described by Helberg (2014).

[12]Doppelt so viele Tote wie bisher angenommen (2016). Double the number of fatalities as assumed in 2016. Syrische Beobachtungsstelle für Menschenrechte (2015). According to the Syrian monitoring centre for human rights, by the end of 2015, 261,000 people had died, with fighting over 5 years.

[13]UNO-Flüchtlingshilfe Syrien 2018 (UN Refugee Agency, Syria 2018), Total Registered Syrian Refugees (2018).

[14]Israel, which prefers the Assad regime, despite its support from Iran, to a Sunni Islamic regime in Damascus, is watching the strengthening of Hezbollah with concern and every so often bombs weapons convoys for the Hezbollah in Syria, and also gets involved in brief clashes in the Golan Heights with the Syrian governmental or opposition forces.

[15]The Soufan Group (2015). Among the foreign fighters, there are allegedly 6000 from Tunisia, 2500 from Saudi Arabia, 2400 from Russia, 2100 from Turkey, 2000 from Jordan and 5000 from western Europe, including 760 from Germany.

China was deemed unlikely. Then, a discussion slowly began to unfold over negotiating a peace between the civil warring parties and the numerous states involved in the war, particularly the USA and Russia, Saudi Arabia and Iran, as well as Turkey.[16] The massive military intervention by Russia on the side of the Assad regime from 30 September 2015, which contributed to significant territorial gains by the government troops, meant that ideas in the West and many Arab countries of peace through victory over the Assad regime quickly began to be abandoned. Since then, the notion of a negotiated peace between the supporters of the existing regime and the secular, moderate-Islamist opposition has been the subject of intense discussion. A particularly contentious issue here is whether this should preclude the prospect of a temporary continuation of the presidency of Bashar al-Assad. Another matter of dispute is whether the largest Syrian Kurdish organisation should be involved in the peace negotiations.

Since October 2015, 17 states, the EU, the Arab League and the UN have prepared a conference in Geneva at the Vienna peace talks for Syria, in which the government of Syria and the opposition organisations are to take part in separate talks with the special UN envoy for Syria, Staffan de Mistura, from the end of January 2016. The aim is to create a transition government after 6 months, and initiate parliamentary elections after 18 months. Excluded from the talks are "Islamic State" (*ad-daula al-islāmīya*), the al-Nusra Front ("Support Front") linked to al-Qaida (the "base" of the jihad) and at the urging of Turkey and the USA, the Kurdish people's defence units, the YPG (*Yekîneyên Parastina Gel*), which are connected to the Kurdistan Workers' Party (*Partiya Karkerên Kurdistanê*), even though, like the Iraqi Kurds, they are receiving huge support from the West in their fight against IS. By contrast, Russia wants the Syrian Kurds to take part in the negotiations. Since 27 January 2016, there has been a ceasefire in the west of Syria, which has largely been observed. After just a few weeks, it has already made it easier for the collaborative effort by Russia and the Assad regime, as well as the western powers, the Iraqi Army and the Peshmerga, in their fight against IS in Syria and Iraq.

9.2 The Shift in the Debate from Toppling Assad to Forging Peace with Him

The advocates of western military intervention were of the opinion that the West could not simply stand by and watch while an unscrupulous party and military dictatorship such as that of Assad bloodily suppresses a democratic mass movement. Even when many Syrians abandoned non-violent demonstrations and took up arms, it was claimed that at least no-fly zones enforced by the military should prevent the deployment of the Syrian air force against the insurgents, and above all against the civilian population that sympathised with them. A limited military intervention of

---

[16]At the unsuccessful Geneva Syria conference in January and February 2014, the Syrian opposition, the Arab countries and the USA had not yet rejected involvement by Iran.

this type, which aimed to promote a political compromise between the regime and the opposition, was to be legitimised as far as possible by the UN Security Council, as was the case with Libya. However, in the case of Libya, the western interventionist powers abused the UN resolution to provide de-facto support to the insurgents and to the toppling of the Gaddafi regime in October 2011, with the result that Russia[17] and the People's Republic of China were no longer willing to approve a similar western intervention in Syria.

Some proponents of western military intervention were of the view that regime change could not be achieved through aerial warfare alone. Instead, it would have to be enforced through a massive international ground war, as had been the case in Afghanistan in 2001 or in Iraq in 2003, and then secured by a longer-term occupying regime—something that they claimed insurgent armed groups are not usually capable of doing. In this respect, the fact that Gaddafi was toppled only with the aid of international airstrikes was not an appropriate model, since no stable successor regime emerged as a result. In the USA, some proponents of democratisation by means of military intervention, while legitimising the Iraq intervention in 2003, cited the democratisation of Germany and Japan after 1945 through military occupation as a model for the Middle East. In so doing, they ignored the core difference between the consequences of a defensive war and an interventionist war of aggression.

Opponents on principle of a military intervention in the name of protecting human rights and democratic movements pointed out that such an intervention amounted to a war of aggression, which was prohibited in international law.[18] Some opponents of intervention felt that there was a prospect of legitimisation by the UN Security Council and that it may be conformant with international law, but in the case of Syria, this possibility was precluded due to the veto by Russia and the People's Republic of China, that was foreseeable from the start. Others presented pragmatic military and political arguments. A limited intervention by the air force, as had been the case in Libya, would fail in Syria with its far more extensive population, which was split along ethnic and religious lines (in 2006, the population in Libya was 5.7 million, while Syria had 20.6 million inhabitants); a ground intervention would require more than 100,000 troops. A military occupation of Syria would trigger a guerrilla war and a considerable expansion of Islamist terrorism throughout the western world. However, among the general public and in the governments of the USA and the other NATO states, there was little willingness to commit to military intervention in Syria following the disaster of the Iraq war and the failures of the interventionist policy in Afghanistan and Libya.

Above all, however, it was clear from the start that military intervention in Syria would lead to a major conflict with Russia. For Russia, Syria under the Assad regime is the last reliable alliance partner in the Middle East, after Egypt already began to gradually turn its back on the Soviet Union in terms of foreign policy under Anwar as-Sadat in 1972, and Saddam Hussein had been toppled in Iraq in 2003 and initially

---

[17]Malek (2015, p. 5), Allison (2013, pp. 18–20).
[18]Jahn (2015b).

a pro-western regime had been installed there. Russia has held a small marine base in Tartus since 1971—the only one to exist in the Mediterranean.

The intervention option found new, powerful supporters in the West in 2013, when it became known that the Assad regime had used poison gas (sarin) against the civilian population in March and April of that year, which according to the information publicised led to the deaths of around 1400 people.[19] Britain, France, Turkey and Saudi Arabia demanded military intervention, while the US government under Obama openly threatened it. However, at Russia's initiative, the Assad regime agreed to the destruction of its stocks of gas weapons and the plants that produced them under international monitoring, and to the signing of the Chemical Weapons Convention, which came into force in 1997. In so doing, it undermined the willingness to intervene among the western countries.

However, extremists and particularly violent Sunni Islamists first seized power in north-western Iraq and then also in the east of Syria, and finally, on 29 June 2014, announced the establishment of a caliphate under Abu Bakr al-Baghdadi (born 1971)[20] in a constantly expanding state-like entity[21] known as "Islamic State" (IS), which covered an area of over 20,000 km^2 and six million inhabitants.[22] This led to a renewed willingness for intervention in the West, and with an entirely new objective, since IS not only threatened the existing social-political order, or the one desired by the anti-Assad opposition in Syria, but the entire state order in the Middle East.

9.3 The Weak Nation Statehood of Syria

In order to understand why the conflict that arose in Syria out of the "Arab Spring" was so much bloodier and longer-lasting than those in Egypt, Libya and Tunisia, it is necessary both to consider the internal confessional-ethnic power structure that emerged as a result of French colonial policy and the unstable, weak Syrian nation statehood that was essentially caused by the British-French division of the Arab and Kurdish territories of the Ottoman Empire into extremely haphazardly construed states. Their borders were drawn along geostrategic and economic lines (particularly with regard to the crude oil sources known at the time) without taking the ethno-religious ties into account. Accordingly, four different types of nationalism, i.e. the desire for one's own nation state—are competing with each other.

---

[19] Reuter and Stark (2013), Meier (2013, 2014), Hermann (2015, p. 49).

[20] Caliph "Ibrahim" claims to be of Hashemite origin and with his sobriquet "Abu Bakr" makes reference to the first successor of the Prophet Mohammed. On the creation of IS and its spiritual basis, see Günther (2014).

[21] The entity would only become a de-facto state after a ceasefire with a demarcated territory in which the state power already largely in existence would be exerted over a defined people. However, neither IS nor its enemies are willing to enter into negotiations regarding a ceasefire.

[22] Musharbash (2015), Böhm et al. (2015).

The state nationalism relating to the existing states in the Middle East, which were formed just a few decades ago by the European colonial powers, became the driving factor for the independence of these states, and in recent decades has emerged as the dominant form of mobilising national identity. However, at times, it went hand in hand with a pan-Arab nationalism that promoted an overall, or at least a greater Arab state, and less frequently with pan-Islamic nationalism,[23] the aim of which is to unify the entire Islamic world, or large parts of it, to create a single state. In most cases, the two pan-nationalisms are limited to a certain sympathy and solidarity with the political freedom movements among other Arabs or Muslims. However, they also resulted multiple times in brief mergers between two or three states, without being able to have a long-lasting impact on the formation of a joint Arab or Islamic state.[24] Clearly, there was a lack of a clear hegemonial power that could unify the Arab states, such as Prussia or Sardinia-Piedmont, as was present in the case of German and Italian state unity. Egypt was too weak to be able to assume this role.

Thus, pan-nationalism only became virulent during joint Arab wars against Israel in 1948 and 1967 and in loose state alliances: the Arab League (since 1945) and the Organisation for Islamic Cooperation (since 1969). Otherwise, it remained an important source of legitimisation for many Arab state parties and their state nationalism. Pan-Arabism can be divided into three stages: a monarchist-Hashemite stage that dominated at the end of the First World War and offshoots of which lasted until 1958; an elite, secular, socialist stage of the officer castes from 1958 until around 1977, and recently, the Sunni Islam stage, which is based on de-classed, highly heterogeneous population groups, in part on impoverished lower and middle social classes, in part on the politically marginalised, traditional Sunni tribal groups in the Shiite dominated states of Syria and Iraq, and on dismissed members of Saddam Hussein's military forces in Iraq, as well as tens of thousands of socially marginalised Sunni in Europe and the former Soviet republics. This "basis" (al-Qaida) Islam[25] has been decisively influenced by Salafist and Wahhabiist

---

[23]While Arab (pan-)nationalism plays down the religious differences among the Arabs, pan-Islamism emphasises the low level significance of ethnic and national differences, so that both nationalisms frequently sharply contradict each other.

[24]Like the Arab Federation between the Hashemite monarchies of Jordan and Iraq, which existed for just a few weeks in 1958, and which ended with the overthrow of the Iraqi monarchy, the United Arab Republic, consisting of Egypt and Syria from 1958 to 1961 as a loose association with North Yemen, also failed. After the coup by the Baath parties in Syria and Iraq in 1963, there were renewed attempts at creating an Arab Republic, this time between the "Arab socialist" states of Egypt, Syria and Iraq, which quickly failed due to national reservations regarding the likely predominance of the Egyptians. The subsequent attempts at integration between Syria and Iraq in 1964, Egypt and Iraq in 1964–66, between Egypt, Libya, Sudan and Syria between 1969 and 1977 (the Federation of Arab Republics), between Jordan and Syria in 1975, and between Libya and Syria in 1980, were no less short-lived.

[25]Names such as Islamism and Islamic State are in themselves misleading, since they suggest a unity and solidarity among Muslims that is almost non-existent, since Sunnis, Shiite and the other Islamic confessions frequently make a claim (which is confessionally intolerant) of being the sole true representatives of Islam. Terms such as Sunnitism and Sunni State, and accordingly also Shiism

thinkers. Pan-Islamism and the concept of the caliphate, which resonates particularly among Arabs, are by all means capable, as has been demonstrated by the successes of Islamic State, of fundamentally disturbing both domestic state order and that of the Arab and Islamic world. Initially, IS claims rule over Iraq and "Greater Syria" ("Sham" = Syria, Lebanon, Jordan and the whole of Palestine), and thus wishes to annul the consequences of the Paris Peace Accords in international law, as well as to liberate the holy cities of Mecca and Medina from the "lackeys of US imperialism" (the Saud Dynasty). Finally, the supporters of IS dream of bringing the entire Arab and Islamic world, and ultimately the entire globe, under their rule.

However, the state nationalisms must not only compete with the overarching pan-nationalisms, but also with the individual ethnic (in particular Kurdish) and confessional nationalisms, above all among the Shiites and the Alawites, but also among the Druze and Christians. Alongside Lebanon and Iraq, Syria is a particularly stark example of the clash between highly contradictory state-based loyalties for existing or previous state structures and those projected into the future in an internationalised civil war. Every victory of one of the individual nationalisms or a pan-nationalism in Syria has consequences for the international power balance, which is why there is intensive involvement by a large number of other states in the Syrian civil war.

The instability of the states of Lebanon, Iraq and Syria, and potentially also Bahrain, is connected to the fact that for historical reasons, the power of the ruling elites of these countries was based only in one tribe or clan of the respective religious minorities. In the case of Lebanon, this was the Christians, in Iraq, it was the Sunnis and in Syria, the Alawites. These minorities also produced the officers and a large proportion of the soldiers in their countries, a phenomenon that can be traced back to the tactics used by the ruling colonial powers.

During the First World War, the policy pursued by all the major powers was to stimulate and exploit the national aspirations of many peoples in the enemy empires in order to bind and weaken their military forces through national uprisings.[26] Thus, in 1915/1916, the British promised in correspondence between the High Commissioner Henry McMahon and the Sherif of Mecca, Hussein bin Ali (1853 or 1856–1931; his Hashemite clan, from the Banu Qatada tribe,[27] had ruled over Hejaz on the Red Sea since the tenth century, albeit since 1517 under Ottoman supreme rule) that they would support the establishment of an independent Arab kingdom.[28] However, the boundaries of this kingdom remained unclear. In November, Hussein had himself declared "King of the Arab lands" after invoking an uprising against Ottoman rule in June 1916, although he was only recognised by Britain and France as King of Hejaz. At the same time as reaching an agreement with

---

and the Shiite Republic, would be more accurate to describe the most important forms of political Islam.

[26]Leonhard (2014, pp. 227–236).

[27]The authority of the Hashemites is based on the fact that they are descended from the great grandfather of Mohammed, Hashim ibn Abd Manaf.

[28]For an overview of Arab history, see Halm (2015).

the Arabs, the British foreign secretary, James Balfour, promised a "national home for the Jewish people in Palestine" on 2 November 1917, in a declaration to the British Zionists.

Aside from this, on 16 May 1916, in a secret agreement negotiated between the diplomats Mark Sykes and François Picot, the British and French governments agreed to the division of the North Arabian settlement area. As a result, France received the League of Nations mandate over Lebanon, Syria (with the Sanjak of Alexandretta, which later became the Republic of Hatay[29]) and the United Kingdom, Mesopotamia (Iraq) and Palestine (with what is now Jordan).

Following the abolition of the caliphate[30] by the Turkish National Assembly in March 1924, Hussein declared himself King of Hejaz, the Caliph, but did not find broad recognition among the Arabs. For the Saud Dynasty in Nejd (in the interior of the Arab peninsula, which remained free of Ottoman and British rule), this was cause for conquering Hejaz in the same year, and thus taking over the Wahhabi[31] protectorate over the holy sites in Mecca and Medina. In 1932, it proclaimed the Kingdom of Saudi Arabia. A son of Hussein, Feisal I (1883–1933), who with his brother Abdallah, in cooperation with the British liaison officer T.E. Lawrence, had led the fight against the Ottomans, was proclaimed King of Syria—which was classified as today's Syria, northern Iraq, Jordan, Lebanon and Palestine – by the Syrian National Congress on 7 March 1920 in Damascus. However, since the Supreme War Council of the allied powers (Britain, France and Italy) had finally agreed in San Remo in April to the division of northern Arabia, French troops drove Faisal into British exile following a battle against the Arabs. The British made him King of Iraq (1921–1933) and his brother Abdallah bin al-Hussein I (1882–1951), who had been King of Iraq for several weeks, was made Emir of Transjordan. This country only attained independence as the Kingdom of Jordan in 1946, unlike Iraq, which already became independent in 1930.

---

[29]The Republic of Hatay in the north-west of today's Syria was given to Turkey by the French in 1939 as a means of persuading them not to enter the war against the German Reich. However, they failed to achieve their goal.

[30]The office of Caliph (the successor to the prophet sent by God) was created after the death of Mohammed in 632 by the Muslim leaders for the father-in-law of Mohammed, Abu Bakr, and passed on to Sunni rulers, within just one Arab tribe, the Quaraish. At the beginning of the tenth century, several competing caliphates were also created for several centuries, at times even a Shiite caliphate in Kairuan/Tunisia. In 1517, however, the Ottoman sultans took over the office of Caliph following the conquest of Cairo, which they retained until 1924, when the office was dissolved by the Turkish National Assembly, which had proclaimed the Republic of Turkey 2 years previously.

[31]Muhammad ibn Abd al-Wahhab (1702/1703–1792) founded a strictly orthodox branch of Sunni Islam and in 1744 concluded a pact with the Saudi dynasty in Inner Arabia. Al-Qaida and "Islamic State" adopted key ideological principles from Saudi Wahhabism, so that at times, both received considerable material support from Saudi Arabia and Qatar. This only changed when the two extremist Islamist organisations launched a fundamental ideological attack, as well as terrorist attacks, against the regimes in Saudi Arabia and Qatar due to the alliance with the "infidel" (the USA).

The Sunni ruler of Iraq, a country with a majority Shiite population, preferred to have Sunnis in his military apparatus. The Sunnis account for around 25% of the Arabs in Iraq. In July 1958, a military coup took place against the pro-British position held by the dynasty, and the Republic was proclaimed. Within the military, the Arab-socialist Baath Party gained the upper hand in two further coups in 1963 and 1968. In this way, power was transferred to men from the al-Bu Nasir Sunni tribe in Tikrit, first to Ahmad Hasan al-Bakr (1968–1979), and then Saddam Hussein (1979–2003).

In a similar way, albeit with the converse confessional orientation, the military dictatorship of the Alawite Assad clan from the Kalabiyya tribe in the village of Qardaha in the Syrian coastal mountains, was created in Syria. As poor farmers, the Alawites were unable to buy their release from military service as many Sunni middle-class citizens did, and therefore made up a large proportion of the military. In addition, French colonial policy contributed to the high degree of power held by the Alawites. When it took on the League of Nations mandate in 1922, the French Republic prevented the establishment of a Sunni monarchy under Faisal. Instead, it split Lebanon, which had been dominated by Maronite Christians, off from Syria and initially divided the latter into several federated states: an Alawite state on the Mediterranean coast, a Druze state to the south-east of Damascus, a state of Aleppo and a state of Damascus. The two latter states were united in 1936 to form Syria, to which the Alawite state and the Druze state were annexed. In July 1939, however, autonomy was granted to the Alawites, Druze and Kurds, which was again removed in June 1942.

The French ruling strategy included giving priority to the confessional minorities—the Alawites, Christians and at times also the Druze—when filling posts in the military and administration. This created the basis for enabling the Alawite dynasty of the Assads to seize power after several military coups, a development that led to severe discrimination against the Kurds and which deprived them of their citizenship. The Sunnis were also significantly disadvantaged socially. All this helped create a situation in which no strong Syrian national identity was able to emerge among the citizens of the country, and in which it was not long before the protest against the regime lost its general, liberal-democratic character and quickly assumed traits of an ethnic-confessional conflict.

Roughly speaking, the numerous political-military groupings can be divided into two types: those who are fighting to attain power in the state of Syria and those who wish to eliminate the state of Syria. Four main parties are fighting to control the social order in the state of Syria. The regime of the Baath Party under Bashar al-Assad, which is in principle secular and relatively religiously tolerant, but which during the course of the war has been increasingly limited in terms of the territory under its control to an Alawite core with the support of Christians in western Syria, wishes to retain the power it obtained in 1970. The Syrian military forces, which before the war amounted to 300,000 men, have now shrunk to 80–100,000 men. They are supported by Alawite militias, several thousand Shiite Hezbollah fighters from Lebanon and probably over 10,000 members of the Revolutionary Guard from Iran.[32]

The opposition, which is fighting for a different Syria, consists on the one hand of the originally secular and partly liberal Free Syrian Army, with 45,000 men, which is supported by the USA and the Gulf Cooperation Council. After its initial successes, the Free Syrian Army lost a large amount of territory and disintegrated into a loose umbrella organisation[33] in which more or less moderate Sunni Islamist groups quickly gained influence. On the other, the Islamic Front with around 40,000 men plays an important role. This is an alliance of several militias, such as the Islamic Movement of the Free Men of the Levant (*Ahrar al-Sham*), which is supported by Turkey and Qatar, and the Army of Islam (*Jaysh al-Islam*), supported by Saudi Arabia, with unequivocally Islamist goals. Then, there are other, independent Islamist combat units, also with usually only local or regional reach (around 9000 men). The Islamist combat units have many points of contact with the Support Front (*al-Nusra Front*) that belongs to al-Qaida (around 10,000 men), with which the moderate Islamists sometimes cooperate, and sometimes become embroiled in bloody conflicts.[34]

Two other opposition groups are also calling the existing state order into question. In northern Syria, the Democratic Union PYD (*Partiya Yekitîya Demokrat*), which was founded in 2003 by the Turkish Kurd party, the PKK, together with several other Syrian Kurd parties formed three autonomous cantons,[35] which are intended to form the core of a future "West Kurdistan" (*Rojava*), similar to the autonomous region of Kurdistan ("South Kurdistan") in northern Iraq. In socio-political terms, the Syrian Kurds tend more towards agrarian-socialist, polyethnic and multi-confessional self-administration, however.[36] The People's Protection Units, the YPG, which were created from July 2012 onwards, are said to have 30–50,000 fighters.[37] On 16 March 2016, with the support of Christian Assyrians and several Arabs and Turkmens, they proclaimed the Autonomous Region of Northern Syria.[38] For Syria, the Kurds are clearly aiming to achieve federalisation, and regard the Arab

---

[32]Hermann (2016).

[33]These figures and those that follow from Gutschker (2016).

[34]The constantly changing political umbrella organisations of the opposition, such as the Syrian National Council, the National Coordination Committee for Democratic Change, the National Coalition of Revolutionary and Opposition Forces, and the High Negotiating Committee, cannot be clearly assigned to the military formations.

[35]Afrin/ Efrîn, Ain al-Arab/ Kobanê, al-Hasaka/Cizîrê.

[36]Brauns (2015).

[37]The Christian (Aramaic-Assyrian) militia *Sutoro* (approx. 1000 men) joined forces with them.

[38]Some Kurds certainly also dream of a unification between West Kurdistan and South Kurdistan, and at some point later, also with North Kurdistan (in south-eastern Turkey), in other words, the area that together was a part of the Ottoman Empire. By contrast, so-called "East Kurdistan" (in western Iran) had already been separated from the post-Ottoman Kurdish territories since 1639. See Jahn (2015c), Schmidinger (2014) .

Islamists as being a greater threat than the Assad regime, which has withdrawn its troops from the Kurdish regions without a fight and has revised its laws relating to Kurdish discrimination. While the Kurds hope to achieve a reorganisation and, in the extreme case, the division of Syria, many Sunnis who have joined IS are fighting to unify first Syria and Iraq to create a new Arab caliphate, which will finally seize power throughout the Arab world and far beyond. This "Islamic State" gained power in parts of eastern Syria, western Iraq, and also Libya for a few years.[39] However, by 23 March 2019, it hd lost control of its conquered territories again.

9.4 The Unlikelihood of Peace Through Victory in Syria

For this reason, on 5 September 2014, an International Alliance was formed against Islamic State.[40] After that date, the USA, France and Britain, as well as several other NATO states and the Sunni states of Saudi Arabia, Jordan, Qatar, the United Arab Emirates and Bahrain, began to bomb military positions and crude oil facilities controlled by IS in Iraq and Syria from the air, with the agreement of the government in Baghdad and with the acquiescence—and perhaps also following covert agreement—with the government in Damascus. In the USA, some Republicans criticised the fact that air attacks were not conducted simultaneously against the Assad regime, so that any weakening of IS would lead to a strengthening of the Assad regime. However, as before, willingness in the West among the general public and governments to dispatch ground troops was very low. Instead, a huge amount of support was provided to equip local troops in Iraq, to a greater extent than in Syria, with weapons and other equipment and financial resources. As a result, "Islamic State" again lost territory, particularly in northern Iraq, to the troops (Peshmerga) of the Autonomous Region of Kurdistan, to the Iraqi Army in the areas leading up to Baghdad, and in a particularly spectacular manner in the battle for the city of Kobanê/Ain al-Arab to the Kurdish combat units on the border between Syria and Turkey. However, this notwithstanding, Turkish forces also fired rockets at Kurdish positions in northern Syria, since Kurdish autonomy is regarded by Turkey as being a military and political danger in the longer term, since it could also act as a model for the Kurds living in Turkey, as has already been the case with the Autonomous Region of Kurdistan in Iraq. In January 2018, Turkish troops finally began to occupy the canton of Afrin, which until then had been settled and controlled by the Kurds, with the aim of penetrating into the entire Kurdish border territory in Syria.

The military and political situation in Syria changed significantly once again after 30 September 2015, when Russia began massive bombardment of positions held by

---

[39]Hermann (2015), Neumann (2015), Napoleoni (2015), Todenhöfer (2015), Warrick (2015), Buchta (2015), Cockburn (2015).

[40]Founding members were the USA, Britain, France, Germany, Italy, Poland, Denmark, Turkey, Australia and Canada. The Netherlands and Belgium also took part in the aerial bombardments. The Czech Republic, Hungary and Greece also provided weapons, see Schulte von Drach (2015).

al-Nusra, moderate Islamists and also the Free Syrian Army in the north-west of Syria, and in so doing, enabling the government forces to advance. Previously, Russia, with the agreement of the Assad regime, had established an air base in Latakia, at which between 2000 and 4000 men were to be stationed,[41] before Russia surprisingly withdrew some of them on 15 March. At the same time, Moscow offered the USA and the western European powers the option of joining forces in fighting IS and initiating international peace negotiations with the aim of achieving a compromise between the Assad regime and its secular and moderate Islamist opponents. Iran was also to be involved in the process, which together with Iraq, Syria and the Lebanese Hezbollah forms a Shiite alliance which is supported by Russia for geostrategic and domestic policy reasons, as well as in order to boost arms sales.

In recent years, the USA and the Sunni Arab countries had refused to allow Iran to become involved in the peace negotiations. The success of the Iran nuclear deal framework agreement reached by the West and Russia with Iran on 14 July 2015 was a highly significant contributing factor towards acceptance by the West of Iran as a negotiating partner in the peace talks on the Syria conflict. Above all, however, in the West, the attitude was becoming more widespread that peace in Syria could only be achieved by working with the Assad regime (albeit without Bashar al-Assad himself) and not against it, since the prospects for its removal have clearly disintegrated following the military intervention of Russia and the Shiite allies of the regime.

Since, however, calls continued in both the West and Saudi Arabia for ground troops to be sent to Syria to fight IS and the Assad regime, the prime minister of Russia, Dmitri Medvedev, warned shortly before the Munich Security Conference that: "All sides must be forced to take a seat at the negotiating table, instead of unleashing a new world war."[42] With strong words such as these,[43] the Russian leadership is attempting to force the West to accept the Assad regime, the "legally elected president", and to take joint action against IS.[44] From Russia's perspective, the USA and the West have played a disastrous role in facilitating Islamist terrorism throughout the world, including in the former Soviet republics, through their interventionist policies in Afghanistan, Iraq, Libya and Yemen.[45]

---

[41] For details on the Russian military activities in Syria, see Malek (2015).

[42] dpa (2016).

[43] In Munich itself, Medwedew (2016) claimed that: "Speaking bluntly, we are rapidly rolling into a period of a new cold war. Russia has been presented as well-nigh the biggest threat to NATO, or to Europe, America and other countries" in: full speech by Dmitry Medvedev at MSC 2016, https://www.voltairenet.org/article190255.html

[44] Malek (2015, p. 20).

[45] Souleimanov (2015, p. 25). However, in the author's view, Moscow does not feel threatened by the terrorists returning from IS, and also has no interest in weakening IS too severely, which deflects western attention away from Russia's policies in Ukraine and in relation to the toppling of Assad (pp. 26–30). Allison (2013) interprets Russia's interests very differently, which are predominantly oriented to the socio-political stance of supporting authoritarian regimes and thus upholding the principle of sovereignty and non-intervention, including with regard to Russia itself, and thus also to preventing Sunni jihadism in the post-Soviet states, as well as to geostrategic alliances against the dominance of the USA.

The question that remains to be answered, therefore, is whether existing Baath regime is sufficiently flexible to survive simply replacing its leading figure, as was the case with the military regimes in Egypt and Yemen. Since the liberal, secular and to some extent democratic forces in Syrian society are clearly unable to find a majority, the question arises for the West as to whether it should not give preference, together with Russia, to a reformed, secular dictatorship dominated by the Alawites over an Islamist, Sunni-dominated dictatorship with a radical outlook that remains to be clarified. However, this could trigger a severe conflict between the western powers with Saudi Arabia and the Gulf states, while Turkey may perhaps fall into line if the Kurdish autonomist forces again came under the rule of a centralist Syrian government. However, such a scenario is rendered unlikely by the fact that the major Sunni population of Syria will no longer be willing to subjugate itself to Alawite-dominated military rule—with or without Assad—so that for a long time, it may be that there will be no peace in Syria. Other aspects of the Syrian conflict must therefore be taken into consideration.

9.5 Creating a National Balance Through Ethnic-Confessional Federalisation

How might it be possible to bring the internationalised civil war in Syria to an end? It is rather unlikely that the states allied to the civil warring parties will reach agreement at a major peace conference in Vienna regarding peace in Syria, and force it onto Syria, as occurred in Sèvres (in August 1920) and in the League of Nations mandate in 1922. Even if all states withdraw their troops and militias and cease deliveries of armaments, it is likely that the civil war will continue for some time. The key to finding peace therefore lies with the Syrians themselves. Either they will continue fighting until one of the warring parties finally achieves victory in a country that has suffered massive destruction and depopulation, which today looks less likely than it did several years ago, or they will one day agree to a compromise peace, as has happened in many other wars in recent decades, when finally war fatigue dominates over confidence of victory in the minds of the population.[46] However, to date, no significant peace movement can be identified in Syria,[47] not even among the refugees.

There is no doubt, however, that agreement among the states involved in the war is an important precondition for ensuring that none of the two sides can count on victory as a result of a gross imbalance in military support for either the Assad regime or the opposition. Currently, it appears that the purpose of the massive

---

[46] "Civil wars are not brought to an end through negotiations without a certain balance of weakness, without a mutual 'painful checkmate' (William Zartman)", Perthes (2013, p. 16).

[47] On the concepts of the Syrian opposition for the future of the country, see Mahmoud and Rosiny (2015).

military intervention by Russia in favour of the Assad regime has been to prevent a victory by the Sunni Islamists, and to persuade the USA to abandon its course of enforcing a victory by the opposition come what may. If this approach succeeds, it would lead to a significant increase in Russia's prestige on the global political stage. There is some chance of this happening, since there is no doubt that the illusion harboured in the USA, that a secular, liberal-democratic opposition in Syria could come to power through elections, has been shattered. The political developments in Iraq, Egypt and Libya in recent years years must surely have destroyed such illusions about the Arab Spring for a very long time to come. The only issue that is open to debate is therefore whether the two major powers will be able to agree on a modified, secular dictatorship such as the one in Egypt, while retaining key power positions among the established military elite (as would be Russia's preference, and probably also that of Iran), or find a way of also offering moderate Sunni Islamist forces a share of the power (which would mainly be in the interest of the alliance partners of the USA, i.e. Turkey, Saudi Arabia and the Gulf states). Neither can afford an open conflict between the alliance partners and the USA. On the other hand, the USA no longer has the power to force its alliance partners to forge a peace, which is why a policy of procrastination over a longer period of time can be expected, unless this is abandoned due to domestic pressures (a Turkish civil war against the Kurds in Turkey, or unrest among the Shiites in Saudi Arabia and Bahrain). However, it is hard to imagine even in theory what such an Alawite-Sunni dual rule in Syria, which is more autocratic than electoral-democratic in nature, might look like. With a compromise peace, a full disarmament of the parties fighting the civil war is rather unlikely. A more realistic scenario is the prospect of regionally separated hegemonial spheres under the civil war armies, as is the case in Iraq and Bosnia-Herzegovina, which are overarched by a formal, federalist overall structure of the state of Syria,[48] even if this would lead to the displacement of people on an ethnic-confessional basis.[49] A division of Syria and Iraq, "the Frankenstein creations of European colonialism" into "Sunnistan", "Shiistan", Kurdistan and an Alawite state, as has been proposed, is almost inconceivable.[50]

Since no state has any real interest in a victory by IS or the al-Nusra Front, and they are at best covertly supported for tactical reasons in the fight against the other sides participating in the civil war, it is likely that peace can only be brought about in two stages: first through a compromise peace between the Assad regime and the opposition, and then as peace through victory over IS (and probably also over the al-Nusra Front). After all, there is currently no indication whatsoever that these two Islamist parties could ever be willing to participate in peace negotiations in order to

---

[48]Somewhat woodenly, albeit generally convincingly, Wolffsohn (2015) suggests for Syria and a very large number of other states a territorial federalisation and also in most cases federalisation of personnel, as a condition for the continued existence of these states.

[49]Rosiny recommends a division of power between the ethnic-confessional communities without territorialisation, Rosiny (2014, p. 7), see also: Rosiny (2013a, b, pp. 14–15).

[50]Bauer (2015).

achieve a political compromise. However, any political shift that may arise within these two warring parties towards a peace compromise should be closely monitored.

Should the Assad regime and the opposition agree to a federalist overall structure, which grants the Alawites, the Kurds, the Sunnis and perhaps also the Druze, their own partial states in a loose umbrella state of Syria, this would increase the chances of releasing the Sunni tribal leaders from their alliance with the IS ideologies or their successors. This would require a corresponding strengthening of the Sunnis in Iraq, so that the Syrian peace process can only move forward in very close correlation with the peace process in Iraq. In Iraq, too, a division of influence between the Sunni Gulf states and Iran is essential, as is a change in Turkey's policy towards the Kurds. As long as the Turkish government remains fixated on subjugating the Kurds in all three post-Ottoman states, it will retain an interest in continuing the Syrian war and in preventing an effective federalisation of Iraq. It is only through a resumption of the policy of attempting to achieve a settlement with the Kurds in Turkey that Turkey will succeed in preventing a scenario in which a federalisation of Iraq and Syria has a destabilising effect on Turkey. Although the Kurds are militarily weaker than the Arabs in both Iraq and Syria, they benefit from the fact that for now, it is highly unlikely that the potential will arise for subjugation under an entirely Arab regime, as was still the case with Alawite rule led by Assad, or Sunni rule led by Saddam Hussein. A prudent approach by the Kurds in Iraq and Syria alike would be satisfied with wide-ranging autonomy and de-facto statehood, and would avoid provoking resistance by all states, as well as purely anti-Kurdish Arabism, through declarations of independence.

9.6 Limited Prospects for a Russian-Western and Sunni-Shiite Peace for the Purpose of Presenting a Common Front Against Islamic State

The terror attacks by the Islamist forces of Islamic State, al-Qaida and associated groups in Europe, Russia and North America created some prospect of cooperation between the West and Russia with a gradual peace-building process in the Middle East, as has already been the case with the Iran nuclear deal. This could also have a positive impact on the chances of a cooperative, peace-oriented policy regarding the Donbas and Crimea conflict. Such a gradual peace-building process also probably requires the joint military destruction of Islamic State, however, yet at the same time a strengthening of the Sunni political positions in Iraq and Syria. After all, it will be almost impossible to bring an end to Islamic State through an Alawite-Shiite and Kurdish conquest of the Sunni settlement areas. A joint Russian-US ground war against IS, supported by Saudi Arabian and Jordanian troops, is also rather unlikely, while the chances are greater of a continuation of the collaborative aerial war. Currently, there are not even vague indications that such a policy is being considered. The prospects for such a policy are rather limited, since achieving peace in Syria (and in Iraq) depends very fundamentally on the level of willingness to enter peace among both the Sunni and Shiite-Alawite Arabs and the Kurdish warring parties in both states themselves, their Sunni neighbouring states and Iran, which to date appears to be very low. It is also impossible to ignore the fact that as it rages on, the Syrian civil war is spilling over into Lebanon. Peace in the Middle East is possible, but realistically speaking, it is rather unlikely in the years to come, and perhaps even for longer. Europe must therefore adjust to the prospect of an influx of further millions of people, above all Sunnis, among whom the jihadis also exert an influence.

References

Allison R (2013) Unheilige Allianz. Rußlands Unterstützung für das Assad-Regime. Osteuropa 63(9):17–43
Bauer W (2015) Gebt den Sunniten einen Staat! Der Nahe Osten braucht eine neue Ordnung, um den Hass zu besiegen, Die Zeit, 3 December, p 3
Bawey B (2016) Assads Kampf um die Macht. Eine Einführung zum Syrienkonflikt, 2nd edn. VS Springer, Wiesbaden
Böhm A et al (2015) Ein bisschen Krieg, Die Zeit, 8 October, p 8
Brauns N (2015) Die Kurden in Syrien und die Selbstverwaltung in Rojava. In: Edlinger F, Kraitt T (eds) Syrien. Ein Land im Krieg. Hintergründe, Analysen, Berichte. Promedia, Wien, pp 139–156
Brinkbäumer K, Bednarz D (2013) Blut und Seele, Der Spiegel No. 41, 7 October, p 87
Buchta W (2015) Terror vor Europas Toren. Der Islamische Staat. Iraks Zerfall und Amerikas Ohnmacht. Campus, Frankfurt am Main
Cockburn P (2015) The rise of Islamic State. ISIS and the new Sunni revolution. Verso, London/Brooklyn
Doppelt so viele Tote wie bisher angenommen (2016). https://www.zeit.de/gesellschaft/zeitgeschehen/2016-02/syrien-krieg-bilanz-bericht-tote-bevoelkerung-verletzte
dpa (2016) Medwedew warnt bei Bodentruppen in Syrien vor "Weltkrieg", Handelsblatt 11 February. http://www.handelsblatt.com/politik-medwedew-warnt-bei-bodentruppen-in-syrien-vor-weltkrieg/12947958.html
Gerlach D (2015) Herrschaft über Syrien. Macht und Manipulation unter Assad. Bundeszentrale für Politische Bildung, Bonn
Gerlach D (2016) Was in Syrien geschieht, Aus Politik und Zeitgeschichte No. 8, pp 6–14
Günther C (2014) Ein zweiter Staat im Zweistromland? Genese und Ideologie des "Islamischen Staates Irak". Ergon, Würzburg
Gutschker T (2016) Syrien nach fünf Jahren Krieg, Frankfurter Allgemeine, 19 January. http://www.faz.net/aktuell/politik/ausland/naher-osten/lage-in-syrien-nach-fuenf-jahren-buergerkrieg-unuebersichtlich-14037420.html
Halm H (2015) Die Araber. Von der islamischen Zeit bis zur Gegenwart, 4th edn. Beck, Munich
Helberg K (2014) Brennpunkt Syrien. Einblick in ein verschlossenes Land, 2nd edn. Herder, Freiburg
Hermann R (2015) Endstation Islamischer Staat? Staatsversagen und Religionskrieg in der arabischen Welt. DTV, Munich
Hermann R (2016) Bürgerkrieg in Syrien. Schlachtfeld der muslimischen Völker, FAZ-Net 15 March. http://www.faz.net/aktuell/politik/ausland/buergerkrieg-in-syrien-schlachtfeld-der-muslimischen-voelker-14115332-p2.html?printPagedArticle=true#pageIndex_2
Heydemann S (2013) Syria and the future of authoritarianism. J Democr 244(4):59–73
Jahn E (2015a) Democratisation or the restoration of dictatorship as the outcome of the Arab Rebellion. In: Jahn E (ed) World political challenges. Political issues under debate, vol 3. Springer, Heidelberg, pp 171–186

References

Jahn E (2015b) Kosovo and elsewhere. Military interventions in defence of human rights ('Humanitarian interventions'). In: Jahn E (ed) World political challenges. Political issues under debate, vol 3. Springer, Heidelberg, pp 43–57

Jahn E (2015c) On the way to two, three, or four Kurdistans. In: Jahn E (ed) International politics. Political issues under debate, vol 1. Springer, Heidelberg

Leonhard J (2014) Die Büchse der Pandora. Geschichte des Ersten Weltkriegs. Beck, Munich

Löchel C (ed) (2015) Der neue Fischer Weltalmanach 2016. Fischer, Frankfurt

Mahmoud R, Rosiny S (2015) Opposition visions for preserving Syria's ethnic-sectarian mosaic, GIGA Working Papers No. 279, Hamburg

Malek M (2015) Kampf dem Terror? Russlands Militärintervention in Syrien. Osteuropa 65 (11/12):3–21

Medwedew D (2016) Full speech at MSC 2016. https://www.voltairenet.org/article190255.html

Meier O (2013) Chemiewaffen in Syrien. Wie sich die Bedrohung verringern läßt, SWP-Aktuell No. 35

Meier O (2014) Mission unaccomplished. Syrien und die Chemiewaffen-Abrüstung, Vereinte Nationen 62(1):15

Musharbash Y (2015) Wo der Terror Staat macht, Die Zeit, 19 November, p 5

Napoleoni L (2015) Die Rückkehr des Kalifats. Der Islamische Staat und die Neuordnung des Nahen Ostens. Rotpunktverlag, Zurich

Neumann PR (2015) Die neuen Dschihadisten. IS, Europa und die nächste Welle des Terrorismus, 3rd edn. Econ, Berlin

Perthes V (1990) Staat und Gesellschaft in Syrien 1970-1989. Deutsches Orientinstitut, Hamburg

Perthes V (2013) Modell vom Zerfall. Warum es uns nicht gleichgültig sein darf, was in Syrien geschieht. Internationale Politik 6:8–16

Reuter C, Stark H (2013) Von roten Linien, Der Spiegel No. 36, 2 September

Rosiny S (2013a) Power sharing in Syria: lessons from Lebanon's Taif experience. Middle East Policy 20(3):41–55

Rosiny S (2013b) Ausweg aus dem Bürgerkrieg. Machtteilung in Syrien. Osteuropa 63(9):3–15

Rosiny S (2014) 'Des Kalifen neue Kleider': Der Islamische Staat in Irak und Syrien, GIGA focus No. 6, Hamburg

Schmidinger T (2014) Krieg und revolution in Syrisch-Kurdistan. Analysen und Stimmen aus Rojava. Mandelbaum, Vienna

Schulte von Drach MC (2015) Wer gegen den IS kämpft. Anti-IS-Koalitionen, Süddeutsche Zeitung, 16 November. http://www.sueddeutsche.de/politik/anti-is-koalitionen-wer-gegen-den-islamischen-staat-kaempft-1.2739217

Souleimanov EA (2015) Ein umkämpftes Dreieck. Russland, der Westen und der, Islamische Staat. Osteuropa 65(11/12):23–33

Syrische Beobachtungsstelle für Menschenrechte (2015) Kämpfe seit fünf Jahren. http://www.faz.net/aktuell/politik/kampf-gegen-den-terror/kaempfe-seit-fuenf-jahren-55-000-tote-durch-terror-und-krieg-in-syrien-13992437.html#/elections

The Soufan Group 2015: Foreign Fighters. An Updated Assessment of the Flow of Foreign Fighters into Syria and Iraq, http://soufangroup.com/wp-content/uploads/2015/12/TSG_ForeignFightersUpdate4.pdf, p 5

Todenhöfer J (2015) Inside IS – 10 Tage im 'Islamischen Staat'. Bertelsmann, Munich

Total Registered Syrian Refugees 2018. https://data2.unhcr.org/en/situations/syria

UNO-Flüchtlingshilfe Syrien 2018. https://www.uno-fluechtlingshilfe.de/spenden-syrien-nothilfe/

Warrick J (2015) Black flags: the rise of ISIS. Doubleday, New York

Wolffsohn M (2015) Zum Weltfrieden. Ein politischer Entwurf, 2nd edn. DTV, Munich

We Will (Not) Succeed! The Helplessness of German and European Refugee Policy

10

Abstract

When the mass flight of refugees to Germany via the Balkans began, Federal Chancellor Angela Merkel proclaimed on 31 August 2015 that "We will succeed!". Tens of thousands of refugees were forced to remain in Hungary under terrible conditions, and Germany declared itself willing to take in most of them. This statement, made in the context of images of German railway stations, where friendly citizens welcomed thousands of refugees with gifts and signs saying "Refugees welcome!", was understood worldwide as being an invitation to hundreds of thousands of refugees from Syria and other countries in which people are suffering from civil war and violent persecution to come to Germany. Immediately, vehement protest arose among parts of the German population against the "welcome policy" of the Merkel-Gabriel government, but also in many European countries in particular, where this policy is being made partly responsible for the increase in the number of refugees coming to Europe and the levering out of internationally recognised agreements such as the Dublin Regulation, as well as for the catastrophic conditions along the routes taken by the refugees. Demands are being made for a strict limit on the number of refugees being received, or even for them to be sent back to Turkey or to their countries of origin, since Europe will not succeed in integrating all the refugees who are arriving there.

Germany in particular has since then begun to urge the other EU countries to also take in refugees, but has met with a high level of resistance, particularly in East Central Europe and Britain. Almost everywhere in Europe, radical rejection of any acceptance of refugees on a mass scale among right-wing nationalist groups and within the EU in general rapidly gained support and expressed itself in acts of violence against refugee homes and refugees. This, together with the growing difficulties in accommodating, feeding and clothing the refugees, also motivated the established parties to seek ways to limit the sudden mass influx of

---

Lectures given on 2 and 16.11.2015.

© Springer Nature Switzerland AG 2020
E. Jahn, *War and Compromise Between Nations and States*,
https://doi.org/10.1007/978-3-030-34131-2_10

people. These included tackling the reasons for refugees fleeing their country, e.g. through diplomatic initiatives to end the war in Syria, as well as support for the war against the Islamic State, the stabilisation of Afghanistan and larger-scale financial support for the refugee camps in southern Turkey, northern Jordan and in Lebanon. A further measure was to establish reception camps in Greece and Italy for the purpose of registering and distributing the refugees in accordance with an allocation quota for the EU which was to be jointly agreed.

Many of these measures will be successful to a certain degree in the long term. However, the mass flight to Europe will not come to an end in the coming decades, with the result that far more fundamental questions regarding the future European refugee policy and the ethno-religious structure of the EU should be considered. Several recommendations will be presented here for discussion.

10.1 The Increase in the Number of Refugees Arriving in Europe

When the mass influx of refugees to Germany via the Balkans began, Federal Chancellor Angela Merkel declared on 31 August 2015 that "We will succeed!".[1] By this she meant that Germany was in a position to accept tens of thousands of refugees fleeing from Syria, as well as from civil wars and torture in other countries, who had been forced to remain in Hungary, and who were demanding to be allowed to continue their journey to Germany. This was Merkel's reaction to the xenophobia which was increasingly being expressed in the form of arson attacks on buildings intended for use as refugee shelters.[2] And with her repeated statement, she reflected the sincere empathy felt by millions of Germans for refugees, in stark contrast to the widespread defensiveness in many other countries of Europe.

On 15 September, the Chancellor used strong words to reject the criticism of her refugee policy: "If we now still need to apologise for the fact that we are showing a friendly face in an emergency situation, then this is not my country."[3] Merkel's statements, and probably to an even greater degree the images of German railway stations where friendly citizens welcomed thousands of refugees with gifts and signs reading "Refugees welcome!", were understood the world over as being an invitation for hundreds of thousands of refugees to come to Germany. News of the German *Willkommenskultur* ("welcome culture") for refugees spread quickly via social media. While many in the media had criticised Angela Merkel as being a cold-

---

[1] Video in Altenbockum (2015a).

[2] During the first half of 2015, 202 attacks on refugee homes were recorded; the same number as in 2014, and three times as many as in 2013, https://www.tagesschau.de/inland/fremdenfeindliche-uebergriffe-103.html

[3] Fried (2015) and Schmid (2015).

hearted Nazi commander[4] during the Greek crisis, she was now portrayed as Mama Merkel and a new Mother Theresa[5] for the suffering refugees, albeit sometimes with an ironic undertone.

What was intended as a reaction to the direct emergency suffered by several tens of thousands of refugees in Hungary, who were not welcome there and who often had to camp out in miserable conditions, was perceived not only in the mass camps in Turkey, Jordan and Lebanon, but also in many regions in the Near East, in South-East Asia and in Africa from which people were fleeing, as being a sign that Germany was willing to receive refugees. With the space of a few weeks, the tens of thousands of refugees streaming into Germany, who were joined by large numbers of unemployed and impoverished refugees from South-Eastern Europe and other continents, swelled to hundreds of thousands. Soon, the figure will reach over a million people, and while many of them will not be granted the right to remain, a very large number will be offered asylum, subsidiary protection or another form of right of residence. In the coming years, they could be followed by further millions of refugees, who after becoming officially entitled to receive asylum will have the right to additionally bring millions of family members to Germany. It depends on the uncertain duration of the wars in Syria (over 4 years to date) and in Afghanistan (almost 40 years) and in other countries whether and when many of those entitled to asylum will return voluntarily or by force to their homeland. Currently, war is being waged in around 25 countries (including wars close to Europe in Libya, Sudan, South Sudan and Somalia), while others are the scene of armed conflicts. And dozens of states are dictatorships where political persecution is being conducted on a massive scale.

In many European countries, protest was already voiced at an early stage against the generous acceptance of refugees in Germany, to a particularly extreme degree in Hungary,[6] but also in Germany itself, where it took on three different forms. Many countries, such as Britain, Canada, the US and Australia, are demanding fixed quotas, and thus an upper limit for the number of refugees received into their own country as well as in the EU overall. Some already regard such an upper limit as having been long exceeded, and are demanding the immediate expulsion of many refugees, in particular those who are unemployed and suffering from economic hardship, who have no prospect of being granted the right to asylum. They counter Merkel's statement by claiming "We will not succeed!". They emphasise the argument that Germany cannot accept all the refugees in the world, and that the ever increasing flow of people to the country must be stopped at some point.

Recently, all German parties have with a single voice propagated the idea that all EU states should in an act of solidarity play their part in accepting refugees to an

---

[4] See the cover image on Der Spiegel, 21 March 2015, see also: http://www.focus.de/finanzen/news/staatsverschuldung/krankhafte-fantasien-der-deutschen-griechische-zeitung-zeigt-kanzlerin-merkel-in-nazi-uniform_aid_712449.html
[5] See the cover image of Der Spiegel, 19 September 2015.
[6] Engels (2015).

extent that corresponds to the size of their respective population, economic power and rate of unemployment, in accordance with a quota yet to be agreed, or which was already agreed in September. They have done so even though until 2013, Germany acted in an entirely unsolidaric manner and refused to receive refugees from Greece and Italy, insisting instead on upholding the Dublin Regulation,[7] which was designed to almost fully seal off the northern EU states from refugees. However, a distribution of all refugees throughout the EU according to mutual agreement, of which there is currently (as of November 2015) no prospect, would only bring a temporary reprieve in the refugee crisis in those countries which are bearing the brunt of the influx, such as Greece, Italy, Malta, Hungary, Sweden, Austria and Germany. In the long term, it would do nothing to change the only limited willingness among the population of the EU to receive refugees. There are almost no objective limits to the acceptance of refugees. After 1945, western and central Germany, which had suffered severely from bombing, received 12 million refugees and displaced persons from the east of the country and from Eastern Europe, although by no means voluntarily and not without massive encroachment on private property. And yet even so, there are very concrete political boundaries when it comes to the will of those members of the electorate in the European states, who want to either close the EU borders or, if necessary, the borders of their own countries, against any further mass influx of refugees. This will is expressed either in the election of xenophobic parties or in a change of policy among the established parties in favour of a drastic limitation of the number of refugees accepted.

Within just a few weeks, an entirely new situation has emerged throughout Europe, unlike during previous months, when the refugee problem was regarded as being a matter only for the Greeks, Italians and Maltese. It was only when the main refugee route changed from the central Mediterranean to the Balkans that the issue became a prime subject of dispute in Germany and throughout the EU, after the death of well over a thousand refugees who had undertaken the journey by sea to Lampedusa had already made the headlines for several days in April 2015. It appears that 23,000 refugees have lost their lives in the Mediterranean since the year 2000 without arousing much interest.[8] It was not until the image of the drowned Syrian boy on the beach at Bodrum in Turkey appeared that the drama of the perilous flight across the Mediterranean became clear to the general public in Europe. It is not only the problems related to receiving and integrating refugees that leave so many European politicians and citizens at a loss, but also above all their far-reaching political consequences (changes in the ethno-religious population structure and cultures, and the attitudes among native citizens and the immigrants towards democracy, the rule of law and the established political élites and parties). Somewhere in

---

[7]Probably the Dublin Regulation was only passed because the EU neighbouring countries on the Mediterranean falsely assumed that the number of refugees arriving across the Mediterranean would remain extremely limited. I was unable to find any academic study that examined how this regulation came to be passed.

[8]Palet (2015).

the middle, between tens of thousands of committed "welcome activists" and a growing number of verbal and in some cases also violent individuals who are against the refugees, a broad layer of tens of millions is emerging who fluctuate between sceptical tolerance of the welcome policy and diffuse discomfort at the idea that this policy could bring about the ruin of Germany and Europe, both socially and above all in terms of democratic politics.

The six terrorist attacks in Paris 3 days ago (on 13.11.2015) will exacerbate the polarisation in society with regard to the refugees. Out of fear that the terrorist acts might nurture resistance among the population against receiving refugees and provoke acts of violence against the refugee homes, as well as against refugees and Muslims in general, leading politicians have been misled into making opportunistic changes to their argument as to the reasons why the refugees have fled. If up to 3 days ago, the bombing of Syrian towns and cities by the Assad regime and Russian fighter jets were given as being the cause, while the acts of violence committed by the anti-Assad opposition were ignored, now Martin Schulz, Sigmar Gabriel, Julia Klöckner, Jean-Claude Juncker and others are claiming that the Syrians and Iraqis coming to Europe are in fact fleeing from IS terror, which now poses an increasing threat to Europe.

10.2 Unlimited or Limited Acceptance of Refugees

The claim "We will succeed" and its negation in all parties, from the Greens through to the radical right-wing parties,[9] are dividing society in Germany and Europe into two parts which now find themselves in vehement dispute and who frequently use offensive language to attack each other, with a rapidly fluctuating degree of quantitative and political strength. The German federal president, Joachim Gauck, probably contributed to the polarisation of society by speaking of a light and a dark Germany.[10] At the beginning of September, only 57% of those polled in the ZDF political barometer and the "Der Tagesspiegel" newspaper supported the government's refugee policy.[11] Later, the level of scepticism and disapproval increased. Fifty-one percent of respondents did not believe that Germany would be able to cope with the large number of refugees.[12] Naturally, however, it is in general not clear when it comes to the statement "We will succeed" ("Wir schaffen das"), as well as its negation, what it actually is that ("das") we will succeed in doing. This could mean, for example, that immediately after the arrival of the refugees, sufficient solid accommodation can be found for them, and they will not be forced to camp out in the open air or in tents, and that they will be given enough to eat and provided with

---

[9]Meiritz (2015), Lachmann (2015), Rau (2015) and Paulwitz (2015).

[10]vek (2015). Der Spiegel intensified the polarisation in its edition of 29 August with two front pages for "Light" and "Dark" Germany.

[11]Lemkemeyer (2015).

[12]Forschungsgruppe Wahlen (2015a).

the necessary medical care, which is often not the case in Greece or in several Balkan countries. However, the phrase could also refer to the longer-term integration of the refugees into the employment market by teaching them German and giving them vocational training, as well as into the social welfare, healthcare and education system. Other people refer to the socio-political integration of the refugees into the religiously secularised, liberal-democratic legal system and into the established pluralistic party system, which is entirely alien to the refugees in their countries of origin.

There is no doubt that the terrorist attacks in Paris on 13 November have reinforced fears that Islamist terrorists may be hidden among the millions of refugees, or that a new generation of terrorists could be raised among the refugee children if they do not become integrated into European society as is expected.

An agreement with "We will succeed" indicates a political attitude in favour of continuing to keep Germany's doors open to all refugees who arrive at the borders of Germany or the EU, while its rejection signalises a demand for a limitation on the number of refugees received. However, attitudes towards the degree and the form of refusal to accept refugees vary widely, and as a result, a series of different positions with several different variants has emerged.

While the Bündnis 90/Die Grünen and Die Linke opposition parties, together with Chancellor Merkel, stress the fact that according to the asylum law and the Geneva Convention on Refugees, there are no limits to the number of refugees who can be accepted, others are demanding a clear limitation. Even the Swedish migration minister Morgan Johansson has now requested that the refugees remain in Germany, since Sweden has no more capacity to receive any more.[13] In the dispute surrounding refugee policy, the means of implementing these positions is also an issue, from generous aid to refugees through to the exertion of force in order either to accommodate and feed them, or to keep them out of Germany and Europe altogether.

10.2.1 Various Welcome Positions

The first of these, *Merkel's welcome position*, demands the unlimited acceptance of all refugees who arrive at the borders of Germany or the EU, or who are saved from drowning in the Mediterranean, whereby the other EU countries should accept a considerable portion of the refugees in accordance with a quota agreed in September or another quota for a small share of the refugees. The problem with this approach is that in Europe it is shared by almost no other government. In Germany, it is supported above all by the Bündnis 90/Die Grünen and Die Linke parties, and in the particularly humanitarian wing of the governing parties. The supporters of an extended welcome culture (*extended welcome position*) want those refugees who arrive on the west coast of Turkey or the coast of Libya and who wish to come to Europe to be collected there by ferries. Others even want to fetch refugees from the

---

[13] Apr/dpa (2015).

mass camps in Jordan, Lebanon and southern Turkey by aeroplane. However, the advocates of this approach ignore the refugee camps located further away in South-East Asia and in sub-Saharan Africa. The demands being made by the Pro Asyl group to completely change the Dublin Regulation in order to enable every refugee to migrate to any country they choose is also extreme.[14] This would make refugees the first ever citizens of the world, who would enjoy global free movement. This third position can thus be specified as a *global citizen position*. Another extreme demand sets those migrants fleeing from economic hardship, severe environmental destruction, poverty and unemployment on a par with those fleeing war, political persecution, the death penalty and torture; in other words, it hugely extends the currently valid refugee law. This is a fourth position, or a *welcome position also for migrants*. It aims to convert most migrants into refugees, as the commonly used terms "economic refugee" or "environmental refugee" have already been doing for some time. However, international law does not recognise such refugees, just as it does not recognise the "tax refugees" referred to in common parlance.

10.2.2 Numerous Positions Designed to Limit the Number of Refugees Accepted

Of these, a first approach demands quota-based regulation (*quota position*), which is designed to distribute all refugees to the EU according to a ratio system, which takes into account population size, economic strength and levels of unemployment among the EU countries as well as characteristics of the refugees such as knowledge of languages, professional qualifications, social situation, state of health and, where possible, domestic preferences (relations with family members or friends) for individual host countries. To date, however, it appears that no-one has been able to develop a practical procedure for distributing the refugees, which regulates who is permitted to draw the major lot of Sweden, Luxembourg or Germany, and who will have to make do with the small lot of Bulgaria, Hungary or Greece. In September 2015, EU interior ministers determined a distribution ratio for 120,000 refugees from Greece, Italy, and—as was originally planned—from Hungary. They had also agreed beforehand to voluntarily accept 40,000 refugees. However, of the planned 160,000 refugees, firm commitments have to date only been made for 1180.[15] According to the quota ratio, Germany should only have to accept 26% of all refugees arriving in the EU.

A second position demands intensified financial support for the refugee camps on the other side of the border of the countries ravaged by civil war and political persecution, in order to considerably reduce the incentive to flee to Europe (*distancing position*). This had to come above all from the EU, which has the greatest level of interest in stopping the movement of refugees to Europe and in particular in

---

[14]Cf. Gertheiss (2014, p. 7).

[15]Stabenow (2015). According to other reports, the figure is even much lower.

persuading the Syrians to stay put in the refugee camps in Lebanon, Jordan and Turkey. The EU would also like to see Saudi Arabia, the gulf states, Iran, the US and many other UN members becoming involved as far as possible. The second and third positions are above all advocated by the conservative and social democrat parties in Europe. Within the CDU/CSU, Horst Seehofer, the Bavarian Minister-President has in particular sharply challenged Angela Merkel's policy towards refugees. He is demanding drastic limitations in the number of refugees being accepted, as well as a legal definition of further safe countries of origin in the western Balkans to which asylum seekers should be returned after just a few days of examination and following rejection of their application, if possible even before they have left a transit zone on the state border. Since the end of the summer of 2015 Seehofer has gained in popularity within the Union parties and among the population, while Angela Merkel's standing has fallen.[16] In October 2015, he was already able to push through some of his demands.

A third approach advocates accommodating refugees who continue to flee from their countries of origin in refugee camps where the living conditions are only slightly better than the minimum UNHCR standard beyond the borders of the EU, in order to avoid creating incentives to leave refugee camps close to the countries of origin or even within the countries of origin themselves (*deterrent position*). This position is held only in the margins of the established conservative and social democratic parties, and is more strongly represented in specifically xenophobic parties. It is likely that a combination of the aforementioned positions runs right through all the established parties, and be met with approval among some business owners.

A fourth approach simply wishes to promote the integration of refugees, who are welcome as workers and potential democratic citizens, in other words, refugees who are not Muslim Brothers being persecuted in Egypt or Islamist opponents of the Assad regime in Syria (*selective position*).

A fifth approach wishes to bring an end to the mass flight to Europe purely through closure of the borders by the police and military, either of one's own country or of the entire European Union, in some cases even by means of border fences according to the Hungarian model (*border closure position*), while at the same time bringing refugees who manage to get through back to where they came from, or imprisoning them as illegal immigrants.

A sixth approach even proposes that refugees who have been allowed to enter Europe so far should be forcibly removed from European territory (*expulsion position*). After that, boats containing refugees who approach the European coastline should be sent back to the open sea after being supplied with water, food and fuel. This approach is already being implemented in parts of South East Asia and in Australia. After these measures have been completed, those protecting Europe's borders are then no longer required to bother themselves with the further fate of the refugees. In some cases, they could also be brought to the coast of Libya. In the case

---

[16]Forschungsgruppe Wahlen e.V. (2015b).

of Turkey, this would certainly not be possible, since the Turkish navy would prevent such a move. The expulsion position is occasionally propagated by radical right-wing nationalist or European extremist groups, who even in individual cases talk of taking refugees to concentration camps or gas chambers. At the PEGIDA demonstration in Dresden on 19 October 2015, the Turkish German main speaker, Akif Pirinçci,[17] made a sarcastic reference to alternatives offered for the approach taken by the established politicians, who advise critics of the current refugee policy to leave Germany: "But unfortunately, the concentration camps are currently not in operation".[18] At first, this statement was interpreted as being a recommendation for how to deal with the refugees themselves.[19]

A seventh hypothetical position, which to date has it seems not yet been publicly proffered by anybody, but which is likely to be put forward in the near future, would be to bring almost three-quarters of the refugees from the Austrian border directly to the borders of the other eight neighbouring states of Germany, and to set them down there in order to transfer them onwards in this way, as the countries on the Balkan route have done so far (*onward transfer position*).

An eighth position is propagated by the Turkish military and politicians: the establishment of a security zone in Syria, which is militarily shielded by the United Nations, NATO or Turkey, to where Syrian refugees should be taken (*security zone position*). A similar model could also be implemented for other civil war countries.

In a week-long dispute over "transit zones" on the southern border of Germany according to a recommendation made by the CSU and later also the CDU, or over "reception centres" distributed throughout the entire Federal Republic according to a recommendation made by the SPD, the subject of debate was nothing more than a marginal matter in relation to the real problems surrounding the issue of the refugees. The dispute also centred around a precise definition of the *Willkommenskultur*, which the Austrian foreign minister Sebastian Kurz recently referred to as *Einladungskultur*[20] ("invitation culture"). In a survey conducted by the *Politbarometer* national television programme, 71% of respondents spoke out in favour of the establishment of transit zones, while 25% said they were against them.[21] Finally, the grand coalition decided on 5 November to create Orwellian-sounding "acceptance facilities". In effect, they will be non-acceptance, or returning facilities, since the whole purpose of the planned facilities is simply to separate migrants from South East Europe, who are to be sent back as quickly as possible, from the real refugees who are to be rapidly and fairly distributed among the German

---

[17] The writer Akif Pirinçci is also the author of the bestseller "Deutschland von Sinnen. Der irre Kult um Frauen, Homosexuelle und Zuwanderer", Manuscriptum, Waltrop 2014.
[18] Willeke (2014).
[19] Eklat bei Pegida-Demo (2015).
[20] von Altenbockum (2015b).
[21] Politbarometer (2015).

federal states in accordance with the 'Königsteiner Schlüssel'[22] the distribution quotas agreed in 1949. There, they will be given the opportunity to begin the lengthy process of applying for asylum.

10.3 The Globalisation of Refugee Movements

Since the history of humankind, people have fled from war or violence inflicted by other people within areas of rule and beyond their borders. And it is also quite certain that in a 100 years and beyond, there will still be refugees. "Removing the reasons for refugees to flee" might sound convincing, but in reality, it is nothing more than a leaden phrase, since the willingness and ability to bring an end to the circumstances that cause people to flee are currently only extremely limited, and will remain so in the future. In the best case scenario, some of these circumstances can be rectified, although the means for doing so are highly contentious.

The military NATO intervention in the Federal Republic of Yugoslavia in 1999 certainly brought an abrupt end to the civil war and the stream of refugees leaving the country, and enabled hundreds of thousands of Albanian refugees to return to Kosovo. Despite widespread poverty and unemployment, Kosovo is now regarded as being a "safe country", whose citizens no longer have the right to asylum in the EU. A not insignificant number of commentators are of the opinion that the current refugee crisis was triggered above all by the refusal of the UN Security Council and NATO to topple the Assad regime after the outbreak of the civil war in Syria in the spring of 2011. Other contemporary observers are of the opposite view, seeing the main root of the problem as being support for the Syrian civil war parties through the delivery of weapons and foreign fighters, and, recently, through the deployment of western and Russian fighter jets. Furthermore, they say, the wars conducted by western powers in Iraq, Afghanistan, Libya, Mali and many other countries, with or without the mandate of the United Nations, are also an important factor in triggering the refugee crisis. In the meantime, other commentators do not make the wars themselves responsible—which must be separately classified in each individual case as offensive, defensive, interventionist or civil wars—but instead the misguided post-war and peace consolidation policies, such as in Iraq and Libya.

In the broader sense, the issue of why refugees leave their countries of origin is linked to the issue of the causes of war and dictatorship, as well as to the issue of responsibility for the global economic order, the anthropogenic climate change and other factors which have led to the enormous degree of poverty and suffering which trigger war. However, the refugees and thus also the refugee policy cannot wait for the emergence of a just world social order. Be that as it may: no power on earth is in a position to bring an end to the mass flight of refugees in the coming months and

---

[22]The Königsteiner Schlüssel of 1949 regulated the distribution of financial burdens between the German federal states, which are calculated on the basis of two-thirds of tax revenue and one third of the population.

10.3 The Globalisation of Refugee Movements

years. A long-term refugee policy must therefore be adopted by all states, i.e. including the EU countries and EU institutions. For Europe, the issue is no longer fixed-term European refugee movements, such as in 1956 during the Hungarian war, or in 1992/1993 and 1999 during the Yugoslav wars, but is rather a global mass flight phenomenon that is likely to last for a long time, and which has a global reach.

The right to asylum and the right of refugees to be accepted into other countries have only been in existence for a few decades. However, since early antiquity there has been a divine right to asylum grounded in religious and magical tradition, and later asylum agreements between rulers who were unwilling to hand over victims of political persecution.[23] It was not until the nineteenth century that states developed the institution of individually assigned state citizenship, which was certified by a document (an identification certificate or passport). The purpose of this was to be able to refuse entry to people from other countries who sought refuge from danger or persecution. Some states even formally agreed to mutually hand over individuals who were the subject of political persecution by them. For common criminals, the same principle applies today. As a result, some states describe individuals being persecuted by them on political grounds as terrorists and common criminals in order to have them extradited by another state, even in cases when those individuals have done nothing more than assert their civic rights in a non-violent manner.

For thousands of years, the journeys taken by refugees were extraordinarily limited in their geographical scope, since there were very few modes of transport available. In order to flee, they usually had to travel on foot, and were only rarely able to use animals to ride or pull carts for greater speed. The radius of travel was increased only by boats and ships, although they were very expensive to use. When during the first half of the twentieth century many millions of people died during the Russian and Chinese civil wars, only a few hundreds of thousands succeeded in fleeing to other countries.[24] Today, motor vehicles, trains, ships, motor-driven dinghies, and in some cases also planes are used to flee over large distances. The seas of the Mediterranean no longer present a significant barrier to flight. Only the oceans and deserts remain a natural obstacle. Modern means of communication such as mobile phones and smartphones are also an extremely important tool in planning individual and family journeys, as well as the coordination of the route over thousands of kilometres. For these reasons, the tendency is for refugee movements to take on a continental, even global dimension. Modern civil war methods are also contributing to mass flight, in which civilians in particular are threatened and driven from their homes, towns and villages are devastated and at the same time, volunteers are attracted from the world over to join in the fight.

Two types of flight abroad can be defined: flight to a nearby country and flight to a remote country (author's own terminology). Most refugees who leave their country of origin remain in neighbouring countries, often in huge refugee camps just on the

---

[23] Kimminich (1978, pp. 23–32).
[24] Zu den Zahlen in der Zwischenkriegszeit siehe Kimminich (1978, pp. 48–49).

other side of the state border. External, "objective" reasons for this are a lack of material resources to flee, as well as the fact that food and health care are provided solely within the confines of the refugee camps. A further reason can be a legal ban on working in the guest country. More rarely, they remain due to barrier fences around the camp and persecution by the police if the refugees leave the camp. A lack of funds which would enable them to make use of other means of fleeing, the risk of injury and death en route and a lack of willingness to accept them in most countries also restrict the possibilities for flight. "Subjective" reasons, which are firmly anchored in their consciousness, are the hope that they will soon be able to return to their homes after the war or violent rule has come to an end, and the fear of not being able to live in an environment with an alien culture, language and ethnic group. Usually, only relatively well-off refugees can afford to flee long distances, who are able to pay the thousands of Euros required in order to use modes of transport, and frequently also to pay people smugglers to enable them to cross borders illegally. Long-distance refugees are usually also comparatively young, healthy, male and willing to take risks.

10.4 The Current Mass Movement of Refugees

Europe has been entirely unprepared for the current mass movement of refugees. Warnings had been made earlier that millions of people would flee from Africa, particularly for environmental reasons, which many chose to ignore as entirely exaggerated alarmism.[25] There are two preferred routes used by people fleeing to Europe: via Libya to Lampedusa, Sicily and Malta, and then further northwards, and via Turkey to Greece and then along the Balkan route to central and northern Europe. Initially, flight was only possible using expensive people smuggler organisations, not infrequently with a high level of danger to life and at the risk of being robbed. After thousands of refugees drowned in the Mediterranean,[26] while others died in terrible circumstances on land—the most spectacular case was the death by suffocation of 71 refugees in a lorry travelling from Hungary to Austria at the end of August 2015[27]—many states have taken on the task of transporting refugees through their territory themselves, sending people from one border to the next. They search the Mediterranean for refugee boats and instead of returning the people brought onto their lifeboats to Libya or Turkey, transport them on to southern Europe. What caused the mass flight to Europe to begin in the spring of 2015? Why did it occur

---

[25] Thus in 1990, the British film The March, directed by David Wheatley based on a script by William Nicholson, was shown by the BBC, and portrayed a mass exodus from Africa as the result of years of drought caused by climate change, which will overwhelm all the border protection of Europe via the Straits of Gibraltar, the Mediterranean islands of Sicily and Malta and across the Bosporus.

[26] According to the UNHCR (2015b), the figure was 3500 in 2014. In April 2015, over 1300 people drowned in the Mediterranean.

[27] Odehnal (2015).

then, and not much earlier or much later? Is there a prospect of refugee numbers returning to the "normal scale" in the decades before 2015? And what would need to be done to ensure that this happens?

Alongside the structural, transport-related reasons why intercontinental mass flight has now become possible, individual political events are also responsible for the current mass flight to Europe. Several of these can be listed here in brief: (1) The war of aggression waged by the US, Britain and other states against Iraq led to the destruction of the established political order in large parts of the Near and Middle East. (2) The misguided post-war policy of the western powers in Iraq stimulated the creation of the "Islamic State" in Iraq and then also in Syria. (3) The formation of international Shia and Sunni military alliances, and then also the renewed competition for superpower status between the US and Russia, have both stoked the civil war in Syria. (4) The Arab Spring was followed by a period in which autocratic regimes either attempted to retain their hold on power by force (in Syria) or to restore it (in Egypt and Yemen). (5) In the main, all warring parties in Syria aspire to peace through victory, and are not willing to seek peace through compromise. (6) The toppling of the Gaddafi regime, which had prevented refugees from Africa from reaching Europe, including with financial support from Europe, opened up refugee routes to the northern coast of Libya from the civil war countries in Africa such as Somalia, Sudan, South Sudan, Nigeria, Mali, Libya and from the extremely repressive state of Eritrea, while Morocco and Spain continued to block the refugee route across the Strait of Gibraltar. (7) The resumption of the civil war in Turkey by the AKP government against the Kurdish PKK, which has already cost between 30,000 and 40,000 human lives, contributed to a situation in which the Erdoğan regime, which is experiencing greater stability, probably not only permitted the flight of Syrians, Afghans, Pakistanis and others to the Greek islands, but even encouraged it. The Balkan route begins in Turkey. (8) The drastic reduction in food rations provided by the UNHCR in the camps around Syria during recent months has caused further tens of thousands of people to flee to Europe.

The mass movement of refugees to Europe is highly unlikely to abate in the years to come. In fact, the opposite will probably occur: the friendly acceptance of millions of refugees in Europe will motivate further millions of internal refugees, who until now have been afraid of the appalling living conditions in the refugee camps close to the border, to flee abroad. Worse still: it will also serve as an incentive for some radical-national regimes to force unwanted ethnic and religious minorities to flee. For many years, anti-Semitism and anti-ziganism in the east of Europe have acted as a means of persuading Jews and Roma to move westwards in disgust. The pro-greater Israel, annexationist politicians who systematically attempt to take possession of the West Bank by building new Jewish settlements and to prevent the creation of a Palestinian state could be tempted by a third Intifada and another Gaza war to secretly provide those Palestinians who are willing to flee with boats for their journey to Europe. The Israeli prime minister, Netanyahu, has already exploited the anti-Semitic terrorist attacks by Muslims in France in the spring of 2015 to invite the Jews living in France to come and live in Israel. If the Turkish government under state president Recep Tayyip Erdoğan intensifies its suppression of the Kurds, the war already begun against the PKK could cause further tens of thousands of Kurds to flee to Europe. Sri Lanka will make attempts to trigger the flight of a large share of its Tamils, while Sudan will do the same with the Darfur peoples, as well Myanmar with its Rohingya. In other words, the danger is that the generous acceptance of refugees in Europe will generate more and more refugees throughout the world, and will encourage religious-ethnic "cleansing" operations in many countries.

10.5 The Legal Status of Refugees

It was not until 1833 that Belgium, as the first liberal national state, began to regard subjects of political persecution as being anything other than criminals, and to grant them asylum.[28] It was only after the experience of the world wars and the National Socialist tyranny that an international convention on refugees could be agreed in Geneva in 1951, and that the right to asylum could be anchored in some constitutions.[29] The convention by no means grants refugees the right to find refuge in any country, nor does it oblige states to accept refuges.[30]

Certainly, neither the UN General Declaration of Human Rights of 10 December 1948,[31] the Geneva Convention on Refugees of 1951,[32] the Basic Law of the Federal Republic of Germany (Art. 16a) nor the corresponding implementation laws set any quantitative upper limit for the right to asylum.[33] According to these regulations, the influx could only be restricted by balancing the rights of the refugees against other rights of the state and its citizens. The original extensive basic right[34] to asylum was restricted in 1993. According to Art. 16a, Para. 1, "subjects of political persecution" enjoy the right to asylum. However, no-one has the right to claim this right "who enters the country from a member state of the European Communities (i.e. today, the EU, E.J.), or from another third state in which the implementation of the agreement regarding the legal status of refugees and the convention on the protection of human

---

[28] Tiedemann (2015, p. 4), see also Oltmer (2010, p. 122).

[29] UNHCR (2005).

[30] Frings, Tießler-Marenda (2012, pp. 15 and 21). On asylum law, see specifically Hong (2008, p. 59), Kimminich (1978, pp. 58–65) and Hailbronner (2014).

[31] Universal Declaration of Human Rights.

[32] The "Convention relating to the status of refugees" which was passed in Geneva at a special conference of the United Nations on 28 July 1951 has been in force since 22 April 1954, and was signed by 145 states. It was supplemented by a "Protocol relating to the status of refugees", which came into force on 4 October 1967. Convention and protocol relating to the status of refugees, http://www.unhcr.org/3b66c2aa10.html

[33] How the other democracies legitimise their drastically limited acceptance of refugees through legislation cannot be described in greater detail here.

[34] On the insertion into the Basic Law of this fundamental right as the right of the persecuted in relation to the state, with reference to the National Socialist past, see Hong (2008, p. 54 and pp. 21–62) passim. General international law had only constituted the right of the state not to deliver politically persecuted individuals to a persecutor state. The right of the state to grant asylum thus became an obligation on the part of the state to grant asylum.

rights and fundamental freedoms is ensured." Those countries which qualify as third states must be classified as such by law. In constitutional terms, therefore, Germany is hardly required to accept any refugees (except those who have arrived directly by plane), and could potentially order all refugees to return to its borders. Other EU states could act in a similar manner and send all refugees on the Balkan route back to Greece or even Turkey. Accordingly, the refugees would have to return to Italy and Malta via the Mediterranean. However, politically, this option is not feasible in most EU countries. Furthermore, in logistical terms, preventing the refugees from entering would mean that a border fence would have to be erected, which would be protected by police and military force, as is the case in Hungary, the USA and Israel, and which is already in existence along land borders of the EU (Greece, Bulgaria, Ceuta and Melilla). Refugee boats would also have to be turned back by the navy if the EU neighbour states cannot be persuaded to provide for the refugees on their territory with the offer of billions of Euros of aid.

The EU countries have since 1997[35] repeatedly concluded agreements with each other which specify the rights of refugees. After the Dublin III Regulation, which has in principle been valid since 1 January 2014,[36] the EU member state (as well as Switzerland, Norway, Iceland and Liechtenstein) which a person seeking asylum first enters is responsible for their asylum application process. The decision made by that state is then valid for all participating states. Officially recognised asylum seekers are allowed to travel within the EU, but for many years are banned from taking up employment in other European countries and receive no social benefits there.

The Qualification Directive determines more precisely the procedure for officially recognising refugees for the EU (with the exception of Britain, Ireland and Denmark).[37] According to these rules, Germany is hardly required to accept any refugees at all, only those who arrive directly by plane from their country of origin. In legal terms, Germany could prevent all other refugees from crossing its border, and could send all those who have managed to do so back to Greece and Italy. However, in logistical, moral and political terms, this is impossible. The mass movement of refugees across the Mediterranean has caused the existing legal framework surrounding immigration to collapse, and has made it necessary to adapt the law to real-life conditions, since neither Germany nor Europe is prepared to implement the existing law using barbaric, violent means.

For some time, Italy has already been allowing refugees to leave the country to the north without completing the asylum application procedure, and in some cases even without registering. Greece regards itself as being unable to provide for the huge numbers of refugees on its East Aegean islands, to register them in an orderly fashion or to conduct an asylum application procedure in accordance with the law. The country is therefore transporting refugees to the mainland and allowing them to

---

[35]Convention determining the State responsible for examining applications for asylum.
[36]Regulation (EU) No 604/2013.
[37]Directive 2011/95/EU.

move northwards from there along the Balkan route. Neither the individual EU states on the Mediterranean nor the EU as a whole are currently in a position to accept or reject refugees in accordance with the legislative regulations. In this way, all states along the Balkan route, from Greece to Austria, have reverted to transit and people smuggling policies, and are illegally allowing hundreds of thousands of refugees to reach the border of Germany at the expense of the state (and while doing so, are incidentally also taking away the commercial profit from the private people smuggling gangs). In so doing, they are exerting moral pressure on Germany to allow the refugees to enter the country, and not to propel them onwards to its other eight borders, as France is to some extent attempting to do on its northern border (Calais). As a result, for the refugees, "Europe" has essentially come to mean "Germany", a phenomenon which has increased the level of Germany's responsibility for the future and cohesion of the EU to a far greater extent than the financial crisis and the Greek debts of previous years.

In connection with the Geneva Convention on Refugees of 1951, the office of the United Nations High Commissioner for Refugees[38] (UNHCR) was created, which at the beginning of 2015 had over 9300 employees.[39] Even though on repeated occasions this office saves the lives of hundreds of thousands of people, it is woefully underfunded by the UN member states, as a result of which it is frequently unable to satisfy even minimal basic human needs. According to the Convention on Refuges, any individual is classified as being a refugee who "owing to well-founded fear of being persecuted for reasons of race, religion, nationality, membership of a particular social group or political opinion, is outside the country of his nationality and is unable or, owing to such fear, is unwilling to avail himself of the protection of that country...".[40] People who are refugees within their own country, who according to UN statistics make up the largest share of all refugees in the world, are therefore not refugees in the legal sense, and are referred to in UN jargon as "IDPs", or Internally Displaced Persons.[41] In 2014, according to UNHCR estimates, the number of refugees in the world was far higher than it had ever been before, totalling 59.5 million. Of these, 19.5 were refugees in the legal sense (i.e. people who had fled abroad), while 38.2 million were IDPs and 1.8 million were seeking asylum.[42] According to the predominant view, flight from poverty, unemployment or the threat of starvation does not provide grounds for asylum or refugee status. This applies primarily to people who flee abroad due to the threat of loss of their entire livelihood through drought or flooding. To date, the only internationally recognised reasons to

---

[38] Such a body had already been created by the League of Nations in 1921. The first High Commissioner for Refugees was Fridtjof Nansen.

[39] UNHCR (2015c).

[40] Art. 1, para. 2 of the Geneva Convention on Refugees.

[41] At the end of 2011, according to estimates made by the UNHCR, there were 26.4 million IDPs, of whom 15.5 million received assistance from this international refugee agency in 26 countries, UNHCR (2015a).

[42] UNHCR (2015d).

flee are war, political persecution and torture and other forms of mass-scale violence perpetrated or tolerated by a state.

10.6 Refugees in Germany and Other European Countries

Before 1967, less than 5000 people per year applied for asylum in Germany. The only exception was in 1956, when the number came to over 16,000 following the revolution and war in Hungary. By 1975, the annual figure for asylum seekers remained below 10,000 with hardly any exception. After that, it increased steadily, and in 1980 exceeded the 100,000 mark for the first time, although it subsequently remained in the tens of thousands. From 1988 to 2000, the figure remained constantly over 100,000, reaching its peak of 438,000 in 1992 during the Yugoslav wars. From 2001 to 2012, it decreased back to the tens of thousands, before increasing rapidly again. In 2013, 127,000 people applied for asylum, with 203,000 applications registered in 2014. The total for 2015 is likely to be many hundreds of thousands, if not up to a million.[43] While the maximum total number of asylum seekers in Germany was registered in 2013, in relation to the population size, there were far more asylum applications in Switzerland, Norway, Austria, Luxembourg, Hungary and Belgium.[44] In Sweden and Malta, the relative figure was even three times higher than in Germany.[45]

In Germany, only between one and two percent of asylum applications between 2006 and 2015 were officially recognised as such.[46] However, during the asylum application process, a decision is not only made as to who has the right to apply for asylum as a "subject of political persecution", but also who is covered by the area of protection according to the Geneva Convention on Refugees of 1951, as well as who is eligible for so-called "subsidiary protection",[47] and who may not be extradited for other legal reasons. This results in an "overall protection share" of just under 40% of those applying for asylum.[48]

---

[43] Die aktuellen Zahlen finden sich unter Bundesamt für Migration und Flüchtlinge (2015a).

[44] In 2013, 66% of all asylum applications in the EU were rejected. In Germany, the official recognition rate is almost 50%, if you add up all forms of right to remain (asylum recipients in the narrower sense, refugees in the sense of the Refugee Convention, persons authorised to receive subsidiary protection and other prohibitions on extradition), which are examined during the asylum application process, see Pro Asyl (2014).

[45] Deutlicher Anstieg (2014, p. 3).

[46] Bundesamt für Migration und Flüchtlinge (2015a, p. 9).

[47] A foreigner has the right to claim "subsidiary protection" who is threatened with a severe degree of suffering such as "the sentencing with or carrying out of the death penalty, torture, inhuman or degrading treatment or punishment or an individual serious threat to life or health of a civilian resulting from arbitrary violence within the scope of an international or inner-state conflict", Bundesamt für Migration und Flüchtlinge (2015b).

[48] Bundesamt für Migration und Flüchtlinge (2015a, p. 9).

10.7 The Increase in Right-Wing Nationalism Following the Large-Scale Acceptance of Refugees from Other Cultures

Politicians should not only be analysed and judged according to what they wish to achieve, but also primarily with regard to their actions and the effect that they have. The surprisingly friendly acceptance of the refugees arriving in Germany in growing numbers from August 2015 and the enormous willingness among tens of thousands of highly committed Germans to help their fellow human beings, which was supported by the majority opinion among the population and the words of welcome offered by Angela Merkel, her government and all Bundestag parties, is perhaps—from a humane political perspective—one of the most gratifying results of the many years' democratic learning process in Germany, which in many countries, at least among a minority of the population, is being regarded with a mixture of approval and awe. This phenomenon was made easier by the currently strong economy, low level of unemployment and lack of personnel in certain industrial sectors in Germany. In countries with a high rate of unemployment and a weak economy, the level of willingness to accept refugees is understandably far lower. There are also other reasons for this which cannot be discussed in greater detail here. The demand for a "fairer" distribution throughout the EU will probably only enjoy limited success. However, even if this were to occur, it would only bring temporary relief to the refugee crisis, and would do nothing to alter the feeling among the majority of Europeans of being overwhelmed by the mass of people arriving on the continent. National state sovereignty, which is still one of the foundations and fundamental principles of the European Union, grants every nation the right to decide how to act with regard to immigration and the acceptance of refugees, as well as which wars it should send its soldiers to fight in. This national state sovereignty will not allow itself to be replaced by appeals to solidarity among Europeans. To this extent, the current complaints by German politicians regarding a lack of solidarity being shown by many other European states is misplaced. Even more dangerous are the attempts to enforce European solidarity through threats to withdraw German money from the European structural fund. The "moral imperialism" shown by the Germans has rekindled a great deal of anti-German sentiment in Europe.

The fact cannot be ignored that the mass flight to Europe has not only been met with sympathy and a willingness to take in people who are suffering, but has also triggered verbal, and occasionally violent, forms of aggression. The acts of violence initially present a challenge to the police and the judiciary. Of far greater political relevance is the growing right-wing radicalism in the attitudes and voting behaviour among certain groups, and perhaps even more so, the sense of unease felt among a broad middle swathe of the population. Those belonging to the latter category regard the continued influx of refugees with fear and concern, but do not yet know how to demand a change in the refugee policy. Should the parties they have supported to date change tack, should they refuse to vote for the democratic parties, or should they vote in protest for new extremist or moderately right-wing radical ("right-wing populist") parties? The mass murder committed by Anders Behring Breivik in Oslo and on Utøya on 22 July 2014, and recently the attack on the Cologne mayoral candidate Henriette Reker on 17 October 2015 could be harbingers of a modern form of violent right-wing extremism. The fact is frequently overlooked that alongside the traditional national right-wing radicalism, a coordinated European right-wing radicalism (of the "European patriots") has also emerged.

From a political sciences perspective, there is no getting around the bitter conclusion that the greater the welcome given to refugees through policies, the greater the extent of right-wing radicalism that is engendered. Here, there is nothing that any democratic defence strategies can do to remedy the situation, be it patient education and campaigning in favour of accepting refugees on the one hand, or on the other, demagogic warnings of a revival of National Socialism and the denunciation of millions of worried citizens who wish to see a limit set on the number of refugees received as closet Neo-Nazis, racists, xenophobes, Islamophobes, and so on. Some radical refugee welcomers are now even inclined to use the term "concerned citizen" as a synonym for Neo-Nazi. The hatred shown by some right-wing extremists is countered by no less hatred against the right-wing populists. All this contributes towards political polarisation, which not only puts peace within society and democracy at risk, but also contributes towards a growing aversion towards European integration. Programmes to integrate foreign refugees must therefore be linked to programmes to integrate those many local citizens who are tending towards right-wing radicalism. These people cannot be excluded from society, either through ostracism or through imprisonment. If this is the correct response, the "European patriots" should not be subject to verbal attack. Instead, painstaking work should be done to persuade them to support democracy and the rule of law, while at the same time taking decisive legal action to sanction the physical violence perpetrated by some of them.

It is quite clear that the refugee crisis has facilitated a national swing to the right among established parties throughout Europe, and has led to huge electoral successes for right-wing populist and right-wing extremist parties. This has been reflected in the most recent elections in Poland, Austria, Denmark, Switzerland, Turkey, and so on. Finally, it has also given new impetus to those proposing that Britain exit the EU. The doors to the EU open to Syrians and Afghans, while Britain, Hungary, and perhaps even France, leave? The bitter question raised by the refugee policy of the European democratic governments, whether they are more social-liberal or conservative, is therefore: how much right-wing radicalism and how much nationalist right-wing populist, anti-European election successes are they willing to generate among the population and during the next round of elections? As a result of its decisive rejection of its National Socialist past and its economic prosperity, Germany is for now not yet in the same fatal position as many other European countries. However, there is much to suggest that the "Alternative für Deutschland" party (or AfD), having rid itself of its liberal-nationalist founding members and reorganised itself into an unambiguously right-wing populist party, could in September 2017 become the third-largest party in the German Bundestag.

10.8 Fundamental Traits of a Global-Humane Refugee Policy

What refugee policy is advisable under the new conditions in Germany and Europe? There is no way out of the current refugee crisis, which in some cases has entailed high human and material costs for all the peoples involved, which is free of contradiction. In 2015, Europe received over a million refugees. However, a far greater number of people are attempting to reach Europe than the European states are willing to accept and integrate into their societies. Since the European Union is a union of nation states, refugee policies are primarily national policies, which can only be made European policy when the national governments and parliaments also reach agreement on this issue. Refugee policy cannot be usurped by the EU Commission or the EU parliament. The existing European asylum legislation and European law is without doubt inadequate in order to tackle the challenges posed by the refugee crisis.[49] Currently, any change made to the European asylum and refugee legislation has only led to a tightening of this legislation, and to the adaptation of German law to that of the other states. It can be assumed that to a large degree, the reaction throughout Europe to David Cameron's slogan, "We need less Europe", has been positive.

First, the fact must be recognised that for most refugees, fleeing to Europe means fleeing to Germany, not only in terms of their intended destination, but also in reality. Germany as a key target country for refugees does not have the options which other states have decided to pursue, or could do in the future. If Germany were to build a fence along its border with Austria, all the other states along the Balkan route would be forced to do the same. Greece would have to prevent refugee boats from landing by force. This would be an absurd "solution" to the refugee problem. Unlike the states along the Balkan route from Greece to Austria, Germany also cannot declare itself a transit country for refugees, and simply transport them onward from its border with Austria to its eight other borders. This would only work if the refugees were to be just as badly treated as they were along the Balkan route, and affluent and democratic Germany is neither politically nor morally in a position to implement such a measure. And a mainland Europe which by driving people from one country to another, either out of helplessness or malice, until they finally end up in Calais in front of the Eurotunnel, cannot then decide 1 day to rent a flotilla of cruise ships to take hundreds of thousands of refugees to Britain, the US, Canada and Australia, where the boats are likely to be barred from entering the ports.

Germany also lacks the political influence needed to push through a distribution of all refugees arriving in Europe in accordance with the quotas agreed by the European interior ministers for the small figure of 120,000 refugees, either through friendly persuasion or even enforcement. The Hungarian prime minister Viktor Orban is therefore correct when he claims that the refugee problem—at least primarily, E.J.—is a German problem, not only in practical terms, but also because

---

[49]On the beginnings of a European asylum and refugee law, and the institutions responsible, see Gertheiss (2014, pp. 2–6), and Haase and Jugl (2007).

German asylum law is extraordinarily generous as a result of its National Socialist past.

It is highly likely that next year, a further one million refugees will travel to Germany, and the prospect cannot be ruled out that in 2017, the year of the Bundestag election, there will be one million more if the current government policy is continued. Technically, Germany could receive all of the current 19.5 million refugees in the world over the next 2 years, and could at least feed and build barracks for them as it did after the Second World War. Germany would "only" have to be prepared to take on a debt of several billions of Euros (and in so doing, to further burden future generations), and to impose control over housing management (of the 1.7 million empty flats and "excessive" living space occupied by current flat owners), and so on. It is out of the question that a willingness to adopt such measures will emerge. An upper limit for the acceptance of refugees is not a technical-economic issue, but an issue of the political will among the majority of society and the degree of tolerance among the opposing minority. This is due not so much to the financial costs, but far more to concerns regarding the longer-term capacity for social and political integration of the refugees and the ethnic-cultural, liberal-democratic nature of German society. This political will is hardly likely to be expanded through humanitarian education measures, but will instead probably decrease over the coming months.

The Europeans and Germans must come to terms with the fact that some wars will last for a long time, and an increasing number of refugees will want to come to Germany. This would increasingly turn Germany into a polyethnic, multireligious country with a large number of social and political problems. The first consequence will be that for years, funding for social services will be severely strained until many refugees find employment. For the large mass of illiterate refugees with a low level of education in terms of linguistic competence or professional skills, it will be difficult to find work, and if they do, this could entail taking jobs away from the local lower strata of society. Certainly, the creation of ethnosocial strata is unavoidable. Unemployment among those refugees granted the right to remain will be higher than among the local population, and will generate a sense of discrimination. Currently, the estimated cost of accepting the refugees is calculated at 10 billion Euros.[50] Soon, this figure will rise considerably. The long-term resident poor and low paid workers in particular will ask why it is that more money is available for each refugee than for them. They will also wonder why it is that jobs can suddenly be found for thousands of new teachers and police officers while they are fighting in vain for fair pay for childcare workers and those caring for the elderly. How is it, they will ask, that solid accommodation can be quickly found for refugees while many German homeless people are still sleeping on the streets, and will probably again die of cold this winter?

This not only encourages xenophobia among the local population, but also hatred against Germans among those frustrated refugees who are today relieved and happy

---

[50]Weingartner and Plickert (2015).

to have been received with such a welcome, but who will tomorrow realise that they will remain socially excluded. Even more immigrant districts will be created, in which German is hardly spoken at all and from which the local German residents will move away. The laws of the market economy inevitably lead to ethnosocial segregation. The capacity to integrate immigrants depends heavily on the ratio between the local population and the immigrants in the place in question, and not solely on the national average.

There are a few reasons why Germany will in general develop a better capacity for integration than the traditional western democracies. After 200 years, the US has still not fully integrated all Afro-Americans, while France, Britain and the Netherlands are still a long way from assimilating the immigrants from their former colonies. What is there in Germany to prevent racial unrest from emerging among the socially discriminated, or pogrom-style attacks being perpetrated against immigrants, as was the case in Rostock, for example? What is there to stop some urban districts from deteriorating to such a degree that not even the police feel safe to enter them? How can the German police force avoid becoming just as brutal as the police forces of other western democracies? What is there, in the longer term, to prevent individuals from arming themselves with private guns? Can the fact be overlooked that the Muslim refugees will dramatically increase the potential level of anti-Semitism in Germany? Or that among the millions of refugees who arrive here that a few dozen may either already be, or may perhaps become, Islamic extremists, who will aggravate the potential for terrorism among German citizens, be they migrants or converts to Islam from long-term resident Christian families? Will not the number of "honorary killings" of Muslim girls increase, who in the eyes of their families are far too willing to integrate? From a neutral standpoint, it can be assumed that the number of cases of murder, rape, robbery and theft will be "normal", despite their difficult social situation, in relation to the corresponding crime rates among the local population, taking into account the fact that most of the refugees are young and male. Across Germany, the crime rate will therefore increase in tandem with the level of immigration.

Not every immigrant will become a fully integrated Cem Özdemir or Yasmin Fahimi.[51] It is likely that efforts to integrate large numbers of migrants and refugees will fail, even if one assumes that Germany will learn fundamental lessons from the mistakes of the integration policies of the other western democracies. A rational response to the question of whether Germany will be able to accommodate and feed those refugees who will not return to their country of origin, first in emergency accommodation facilities and then in apartments, can only be that yes, it will. However, the question of whether Germany will successfully integrate the remaining refugees socially and politically prompts a very different answer: yes, a very large share will be excellently or adequately integrated, but a considerable portion will not. An insufficient level of openness towards integration among a large section of the

---

[51] These are prominent politicians of the Green and the Social Democratic parties with a migration background.

local population coupled with insufficient willingness to integrate among large numbers of refugees (and also migrants) will act in parallel to prevent the real integration of many immigrants. Thus, the response to the above question is: we will largely succeed, but to a far too great extent, we will not. Since it is easier to integrate a small number of refugees than a large influx, it can be concluded that the more refugees arrive, and furthermore within a short period of time, the more likely it is that integration will fail. In other words: a limitation and deceleration of the acceptance of refugees should urgently be considered. The open invitation to all refugees who wish to come to Germany (and Europe) is utterly irresponsible both socially and politically.

All these considerations are not intended as arguments against *the Willkommenskultur*. Quite the opposite. Only such a welcome culture could, alongside the undoubted positive effects arising from the changes in ethnoreligious population structure, prevent or reduce some extremely negative consequences, and help overcome the new challenges faced in the German domestic political arena. A clear, unequivocal differentiation must be made between the *Willkommenskultur* (in relation to the refugees who have arrived in Germany) and the continued policy of inviting additional millions of refugees to make the journey here. A halfway adequate integration of the migrants and refugees is only possible by limiting and decelerating the acceptance of further immigrants.

Furthermore, a clear differentiation should be made between immigration or migration policy and refugee policy. One could even talk of a shameless misuse of the refugees as a substitute for children in Germany by those who wish to see comprehensive immigration as an answer to the insufficient number of workers and to finance future pensions as a compensation for the low birth rate in German society, and who wish to integrate and "Germanise" the refugees as quickly as possible. Many refugees are not interested in such a prospect, but rather wish to live and work in Germany only temporarily. Their main interest is in socialising their children in their native language and in their own culture. Their motivation to learn German to a sufficient standard to enable them to find work themselves and have a better life in exile is only secondary.

Refugees from autocratic countries without a democratic tradition will not become democrats on crossing the border into Europe, but will have to be won over to liberal-democratic attitudes in a decades-long process of socialisation. In the recent parliamentary elections in Turkey, a greater share of the Turks who have been living in Germany for many years voted in favour of Erdoğan's Party for Justice and Development, the AKP than their compatriots at home. In Egypt, members of the Muslim Brotherhood, who are being persecuted and threatened with the death penalty, and who themselves had harassed the Copts, will not automatically become enlightened, secular humanists on arriving in Europe. Undemocratic, right-wing radical views are not a phenomenon unique to a considerable proportion of the longstanding German population, but are also prevalent among the migrants and refugees. The fight against right-wing radical xenophobia among Germans must not make us blind to the hostile, right-wing radical attitudes among some refugees and migrants who do not agree with the social and political way of life of the Germans. The terrorists are just the tip of the iceberg of millions of peaceful immigrants who have not been successfully politically and socially integrated, and who have found no political channel to express their dissatisfaction.

From the above analysis, it follows that the refugees from outside Europe who have already travelled across hundreds of kilometres to reach the EU must remain there, at least until the wars in Syria, Iraq, Somalia etc. have come to an end. A very different question is whether and how Germany and the European states who have no interest in seeing Germany become an overburdened refugee country are able and willing to allow further millions of refugees to come to Europe. On principle, this is not a matter for the EU alone, but also for NATO, since the refugee crisis is expanding to become a crisis for domestic security and stability in Europe, and because Turkey is a NATO member. Germany, the foremost destination for the refugee movement, which can neither close its borders nor transfer the refugees onwards without threatening the existence of the EU, has no other choice but to urge and work towards a closure of the EU borders against an uncontrolled, unlimited influx. In other words: unlike other EU member states, Germany does not have the option of implementing a purely national refugee policy. Securing the outer EU borders might be feasible against a country such as Libya, which has no functioning state organs, but is unthinkable against Turkey. On the other hand, Turkey could at just a small expense confiscate all people smuggler boats along the coast in the interest of national security, and prevent them from leaving Turkish waters in cooperation with the Greek navy and using several boats from other EU countries.

Turkey will only be prepared to abandon its current policy of facilitating the through-transit and smuggling of refugees if the EU and NATO states are willing to pay a large sum to resolve the problem of the refugees in Turkey.[52] Here, the following options are available: (1) The Turkish military (or, alternatively, NATO), with the agreement of the UN Security Council, establishes protection zones for refugees in the north of Syria and Iraq, where people are provided for by the UNHCR until the internationalised civil wars are brought to an end. The same protection zones could be established in Afghanistan and other countries where war is being waged. (2) Turkey declares itself willing to organise refugee settlements within border areas of its own country, which are financed by the EU and NATO states, and as far as possible by the wealthy Arab states. (3) If no agreement with Turkey is possible, the EU could rent an island in Europe and establish settlements there under EU administration where the refugees can remain until their return to their country of origin when peace has been restored. These options will be discussed in greater detail in the excursus below.

The admirable *Willkommenskultur* in Germany, Sweden and other countries with regard to the way the refugees have been treated, which is surprisingly broadly anchored among the general population, can only be maintained if at the same time, there is a drastic limitation set for the number of refugees accepted.

---

[52]The link to other issues such as visa freedom or the resumption of EU accession negotiations is an extremely dubious blackmailing tactic being pursued by Turkey, who can afford to do so because the EU is unwilling to protect the Greek islands from the people smugglers' boats.

10.9 A Recommendation to the German Government

What would I therefore advise Federal Chancellor Angela Merkel or her minister Peter Altmaier to do? First of all, to make a clear political statement such as this:

"The authorities and above all civil society in Germany have in recent months actively supported a very large number of refugees arriving in Europe in their difficulty, and have made them welcome. This was a correct response, and we are very happy at the emergence of the German and European Willkommenskultur in the spirit of the humane and democratic values which we consistently promote. However, in the years to come, we cannot take on unlimited further millions of refugees, and integrate them economically, socially and politically. We will therefore do everything we can in order to restrict the number of refugees accepted in Germany in 2016 (this is my own random figure, E.J.) to 500,000, and in 2017 to 300,000. And we hope that most refugees will soon be able to return home. For this reason, we will intensify our diplomatic efforts in order to achieve a rapid compromise peace between the civil war parties in Syria, Iraq, Afghanistan and the states which are militarily involved in these wars. In recent years, German diplomacy has made some achievements, and has made an important contribution to the signing of the Minsk Agreement on ending the war in Ukraine and on the agreement regarding the prevention of Iran's nuclear armament. We will apply the same dedication in our work towards finding a peaceful solution in the war regions. At the same time, we will support the targeted battle against the terrorist "Islamic State", which endangers both the state and domestic order of many countries. In doing so we will employ means which we regard as being suitable and which have been agreed internationally.

In order to make it easier for the refugees to return home, we will undertake to ensure that they receive professional training in their native language in order to be able to rebuild their country with our help after the destruction caused by the war. We will also teach the refugees German during their stay in our country and give them access to professional training so that they can provide for themselves through their own work while they are living here.

We are neither willing nor able to send back refugees arriving in central Europe over the coming months and years as long as the conditions from which they are fleeing continue. We will integrate some of them into our society in the long term. For this reason, we must prevent too many refugees from coming to Europe. In our view, there are four ways of doing so: (1) To try and persuade some EU member states who to date have only accepted a small number of refugees, or none at all, to relieve the burden on others who have already allowed many to enter their country. Germany is willing and able to apply economic pressure to its European partner countries to act in a similar manner to Germany itself, or according to the model presented by Sweden, Malta and other EU states in their generous acceptance of refugees; (2) To establish and finance safe zones to where refugees can flee, if possible under a UN mandate, in the civil war countries themselves; (3) A large German and European financial contribution to support the refugee camps in the neighbouring countries of the civil war region, i.e. in particular Lebanon, Jordan and Turkey. We will request and urge the US, the wealthy Arab countries and other UN member states to support us in this effort; (4) To establish and finance large refugee settlements on the borders of the European Union using funds from the EU and the EU member states.

We are aware that the refugee crisis presents a Herculean task. This is true not only for Germany, but is also a test of strength of the European Union. We also know that we will not succeed in limiting the flight to Germany and Europe within just a few days. However, we ask the citizens of our country not to let up in their willingness to help the refugees arriving here, and to trust in the fact that we are doing our best to stem the flow of refugees to Germany." After such a declaration has been made, fundamental changes to the Germany refugee policy should then be made.

10.10 The Establishment of European Refugee Settlements: "Refuges" (Refugium)

It is becoming increasingly urgent that international protection zones and settlements, which I here call "refuges" for a growing number of millions of refugees from all over the world, should be established. There are numerous reasons for this. The first is that humanity and international politics will not remain willing or able for much longer to sustainably remove all causes of flight. Due to contradictory national interests, the United Nations Security Council is only able to a very limited degree to guarantee world peace and international security. There will therefore continue to be wars for the indefinite future (currently, around 25 wars are being waged), as well as countless repressive regimes which use torture, and which create the conditions from which people wish to flee. A second reason is that the three large regions of the earth in which people enjoy a high level of security, social peace and prosperity have increasingly become the destination for global refugee movements. These regions are western and central Europe, north America and Oceania (Australia, New Zealand). The states in these three regions are however not willing to accept all refugees and to integrate them socially and make those among them who wish to become so citizens in the longer term. On the basis of state sovereignty, each state ultimately decides itself how many refugees it should accept by legal means, and to what extent it tolerates illegal immigration. The third reason is that the liberal-democratic, affluent states are however not willing to leave the refugees solely to their fate and there wish to contribute to their survival, safety and as far as possible also to ensuring that they live in decent human conditions on the borders of or beyond their ruling country. To date, such intentions have, however, only been implemented to an entirely inadequate degree through the refugee agency of the United Nations, the UNHCR, which is given far too little financial support. The more the suffering of the refugees is withheld from the eyes of the western general public, the lower the level of humanitarian commitment on the part of that public. It was not until millions of people fled across the Mediterranean and across the borders of Europe that an entirely new historical challenge was presented to the EU, and to a certain degree also to north America and Oceania.

The contradiction between the limited willingness among the liberal-democratic states to accept refugees and concern of securing the safety of millions of refugees

10.10 The Establishment of European Refugee Settlements: "Refuges" (Refugium)

can only be resolved by establishing refugee settlements on the borders of the liberal-democratic world or beyond its boundaries. Europe bears a particularly high level of responsibility for the refugees who arrive on its territory or in its waters, or who are saved by European countries on the open seas. Common membership of NATO and the European neighbourhood policy also demand that countries such as Turkey, Lebanon and Jordan be relieved of the burden of accepting refugees. For this reason, the EU and its neighbouring European states, in close cooperation with the UNHCR, should establish numerous refuges of a quasi-ex-territorial nature under the jurisdiction of the EU, either outside EU territory or close to the border of EU territory. These would then cater for, let us say, 40,000–200,000 refugees.

There is already agreement over the fact that all refugees who reach EU territory will be first registered in a European database and identified at initial reception centres on the borders of the EU, where they also undergo health and security checks. Each individual refugee is given a provisional refugee identification card. Then, as many refugees as possible will be distributed across the individual European countries according to an as yet to be developed distribution system designed to take into account both subjective preferences among the refugees for certain countries due to relatives and friends living there, as well as objective factors such as their linguistic and professional skills, whereby these countries determine themselves how many refugees they are willing to accept on the basis of mutual agreement between themselves.

The refuges should accept those refugees who cannot be distributed to the states. They should be established and administered either by the UNHCR or by an EU body which is to be newly created, the EUREF (European Refuges) headed by a High Representative of the EU. The territory required to establish the refuges could be purchased or rented by the EU if it is not donated for the purpose. Here, the most advantageous location would be the islands on the edge of Europe, in order to avoid creating the illusion that the refugees had de facto immigrated to Europe. However, almost unpopulated stretches of terrain in some countries of Europe would also be possible sites for the refugee settlements. The refuges could be funded either from the EU budget, from contributions made by EU member states, or by means of an EU refuge tax, the level of which would need to be agreed (e.g. in the form of a Tobin tax, a solidarity supplement to income, wage and capital earnings tax of e.g. one percent). If not all EU members are prepared to contribute to funding the EU refuges, EUREF should initially be set up by a sub-group of EU states according to the Euro or Schengen group model, while remaining open to entry by other members.

Another possibility is a combination of private and public funds. There are a large number of millionaires and billionaires, but above all also millions of normal EU citizens, who are willing to make a one-off or regular financial contribution in support of the refugees. A civic initiative could begin here and now to establish model refugee settlements through a private association and a private foundation, and in doing so prepare public opinion in Europe for comprehending the decisions that need to be made by the states and EU institutions, which will not be reached overnight.

A refuge should fulfil three objectives: (1) To guarantee protection and safety, decent humanitarian living conditions, food, health services and education facilities; (2) To prepare refugees for returning to their homes after the reasons for fleeing have been remedied; (3) To organise the transfer of long-term refugees to countries which are willing to take them.

Regarding the first objective: the external and internal protection provided by a refuge should be guaranteed by a European police unit which is able to draw on experience from EUPOL and which recruits suitable auxiliary police officers from among the refugees themselves. A European justice service, which includes judges, state attorneys and solicitors, should implement legal order in the refuge in accordance with European law and with the help and cooperation of legal professionals among the refugees. For this purpose, a brief set of fundamental rules should be drawn up which applies to the refuge and which is understandable to everyone, and which should be communicated to the refugees in a brief introductory course. Afterwards, every refugee who wishes to remain in the refuge rather than being sent back to their country of origin should agree to abide by the rules set out in the fundamental rules. They will then be given the status of a fixed-term refuge citizen, and will be given a refuge identification certificate with which they will be able to apply for a visa or gain visa-free access to the EU states in accordance with their legal stipulations.

The issue of the spatial distribution of the refugees in a large settlement the size of a town or city is a difficult challenge. Mixing up the location of accommodation for the refugees on a random basis or following the principle of a consciously designed inter-ethnic neighbourhood could easily lead to conflict, and provide sustenance for individual fears of isolation in an alien environment, since in most cases, there is no common language of communication or experience in dealing with other cultures. Furthermore, it cannot be expected that refugees should be willing to live in direct proximity to supporters of the civil war party from which they have fled, and which has been the cause of traumatic experiences of war and persecution. For this reason, it may be advisable to divide the settlement according to political communities. These should preferably be state communities, and in cases where the refugees come from mutually hostile civil war parties and their sympathiser groups, a separation on the basis of voluntary association could be the best option, which would probably follow according to primarily political-linguistic-ethnic-religious criteria. At the same time, however, voluntary and mandatory intercultural events should also be organised with the aim of promoting peaceful coexistence among refugees in a large settlement who have very different origins and reasons for fleeing. If this succeeds, the refugee settlements could become schools for global tolerance and understanding among people from different countries and cultures.

The refuges should not become hermetically sealed settlements. Children and young people could for example be invited to spend their holidays in the European states. A school exchange could help increase understanding for the refugees through personal experience of the refuges. Mandatory civic education events for all refugees could teach them fundamental values of the European political culture which they have to thank for being allowed to settle the refuges in a manner that respects their human dignity.

10.10 The Establishment of European Refugee Settlements: "Refuges" (Refugium)

European legal and societal standards, such as those relating to relations between the sexes, should not simply be octroyed onto refugees from other continents, but should be explained to them in cultural education centres. Possible compromises should also be sought with their own cultural norms, particularly when the issue under debate is not fundamental human rights, but merely cultural habits which can be changed or tolerated.

To the largest possible degree, the refuges should promote the individual responsibility, motivation and self-organisation of the refugees. Following their recognition as citizens of the refuge, the refugees can participate in the construction and extension and maintenance of solid apartment buildings as soon as building materials, tools and machinery are provided for the purpose. As far as possible, they should be given small plots of land to grow fruit and vegetables. In the longer term, craft enterprises, IT companies and other businesses which only require a small amount of space could be established in the refuges. In the nursery schools and schools, as well as in further education institutions, specialist personnel could be used who would be mainly recruited from among the refugees, particularly since in these institutions, the respective native language should be used. Language courses in English as the global language of communication as the official refuge language could make communication possible between the heterogeneous refugee groups. The construction of mosques and other places of worship would be a clear sign of a tolerant religious culture in the refuges. The rapid mobilisation of workers in the refuges under EU management would make these institutions considerably cheaper to run than the extremely expensive German administration of refugees, which condemns the refugees to months of inactivity which engenders frustration and aggression.

The self-administration organs should be elected in the respective political communities. A federation of these would represent common interests in the refuge. In this way, the refuges can become places where communal, inter-ethnic, inter-cultural democracy and the peaceful settlement of conflicts are experienced, particularly for people who have never had the opportunity in their lives to take responsibility for their own public interests.

Regarding the second objective: the refugees should not be sent back home abruptly after the war has ended or there is a regime change in their countries of origin. To a far greater degree, the resettlement activities should be staggered in terms of their timing and quantity. However, the refugees who are not invited to immigrate to an EU country should then return and become involved in rebuilding their country, even if as a result, their personal living situation initially becomes worse than it was in the EU or a refugee settlement.

Regarding the third objective: refugees should not stay in the refuge for their entire lives, even if the reasons for their flight continue to exists for decades on end. For this reason, refuge citizens of many years should be given a certain degree of preferential treatment when it comes to accepting immigrants into the states who permit limited immigration. States who decide to take on more refugees after all could undertake to ensure that applications for an immigration permit learn the local language while still living in the refugee settlement, in order to be able to take up work on a par with their qualifications as soon as they move to their new home. In this way, they would fill the social security benefits coffers, rather than depleting them. For this purpose, language courses, probably for all European languages, would have to be provided in the refuges, which could be organised and funded either by state cultural institutions or by private refugee associations. Those states willing to accept refugees could also provide access to the desired specialist training in the refuges, or invite refugees to take part in training programmes in the country itself. Refugees would in this way develop the opportunity to immigrate through their own efforts, and would not receive permission to do so simply as a result of their status as victims.

10.11 The Simultaneous Nature of National and European Refusal to Accept Refugees

It is unlikely that a clear, commonly agreed European policy on refugees will be developed for some time. Instead, modest efforts towards this aim are more likely. As a result, a large number of different national refugee policies will compete with each other, and with Brussels, and will continue to trade insults and accusations of blame. Viktor Orban and many others will denigrate Germany with its moral imperialism as being the cause of the refugee chaos in Europe. Conversely, German, Swedish and other politicians will accuse those countries who take in only a small number of refugees, or none at all, as lacking in European solidarity. The people who bear the brunt of the difficulties arising from this situation will be the refugees themselves, who will be shunted from one country to another. However, Europe may further tighten its borders against the refugees in the months to come without really ensuring that the living conditions in the countries neighbouring the civil war region become more compatible with human dignity.

Tens of thousands of Islamist extremists from 80 countries have managed, at least for a time, to create a barbaric Islamic State and to spread fear of terrorist attacks across the world. Why should not tens of millions of people with humane, cosmopolitan attitudes, even if they find themselves in the minority in society, not at last manage to create humane refugee settlements along the lines of the model described above, even if—and precisely because—social majorities are in some cases forcing their governments to seal off their country and the EU against the influx of refugees?

References

Apr/dpa (2015) Schwedischer Minister zu Flüchtlingen: "Bleibt in Deutschland". In: Spiegel online Politik vom 5. November, http://www.spiegel.de/politik/ausland/schweden-kann-fluechtlinge-laut-minister-nicht-mehr-unterbringen-a-1061378.html#ref=nl-dertag

Bundesamt für Migration und Flüchtlinge (2015a) Aktuelle Zahlen zu Asyl, Ausgabe September 2015, http://www.bamf.de/SharedDocs/Anlagen/DE/Downloads/Infothek/Statistik/Asyl/statistik-anlage-teil-4-aktuelle-zahlen-zu-asyl.pdf?__blob=publicationFile

Bundesamt für Migration und Flüchtlinge (2015b) Subsidiärer Schutz, http://www.bamf.de/DE/Migration/AsylFluechtlinge/Subsidiaer/subsidiaer-node.html.Deutlicher. Anstieg der registrierten Asylbewerber auf nahezu 435.000 in der EU28 im Jahr 2013, http://ec.europa.eu/eurostat/documents/2995521/5181442/3-24032014-AP-DE.PDF/c97fa5ca-cf80-4322-9a44-ef5759e037e2?version=1.0

Convention determining the State responsible for examining applications for asylum lodged in one of the Member States of the European Communities. https://eur-lex.europa.eu/legal-content/EN/ALL/?uri=CELEX%3A41997A0819(01)&from=EN

Deutlicher Anstieg (2014) Deutlicher Anstieg der registrierten Asylbewerber auf nahezu 435.000 in der EU28 im Jahr 2013. http://ec.europa.eu/eurostat/documents/2995521/5181442/3-24032014-AP-DE.PDF/c97fa5ca-cf80-4322-9a44-ef5759e037e2?version=1.0

Directive 2011/95/EU of the European Parliament and of the Council of 13 December 2011 on standards for the qualification of third-country nationals or stateless persons as beneficiaries of international protection, for a uniform status for refugees or for persons eligible for subsidiary protection, and for the content of the protection granted, http://eur-lex.europa.eu/legal-content/EN/TXT/?uri=CELEX:32011L0095&from=EN

Eklat bei Pegida-Demo (2015) "Die KZs sind ja leider derzeit außer Betrieb". In: Spiegel online Politik vom 20. Oktober, http://www.spiegel.de/politik/deutschland/akif-pirincci-rede-bei-pegida-in-dresden-abgebrochen-a-1058589.html

Engels JN (2015) Populistisch oder weitsichtig? Die Haltung Ungarns in der europäischen Flüchtlingsfrage, Friedrich-Ebert-Stiftung Perspektive, http://library.fes.de/pdf-files/id-moe/12018.pdf

Forschungsgruppe Wahlen e. V. (2015a) Politbarometer Oktober II, 23 October, http://www.forschungsgruppe.de/Aktuelles/Politbarometer/

Forschungsgruppe Wahlen e. V. (2015b) Bewertung von Politikern nach Sympathie und Leistung bis Oktober 2015, http://www.forschungsgruppe.de/Umfragen/Politbarometer/Langzeitentwicklung_-Themen_im_Ueberblick/Politik_II/8_Sympathiewerte.pdf

Fried N (2015) "... dann ist das nicht mein Land", Süddeutsche Zeitung, 15 September, http://www.sueddeutsche.de/politik/merkel-zu-fluechtlingspolitik-dann-ist-das-nicht-mein-land-1.2648819

Frings D, Tießler-Marenda E (2012) Ausländerrecht für Studium und Beratung. Fachhochschulverlag, Frankfurt

Gertheiss S (2014) Schutz von oder vor Flüchtlingen? Europäische Migrations- und Flüchtlingspolitik ein Jahr nach der Katastrophe von Lampedusa, HSFK-Standpunkte No. 5

Haase M, Jugl JC (2007) Asyl- und Flüchtlingspolitik der EU, http://www.bpb.de/gesellschaft/migration/dossier-migration/56551/asyl-fluechtlingspolitik?p=all

Hailbronner K (2014) Asyl- und Ausländerrecht. Lehrbuch, 3rd edn. Kohlhammer, Stuttgart

Hong M (2008) Asylgrundrecht und Refoulementverbot. Nomos, Baden-Baden

Kimminich O (1978) Die Geschichte des Asylrechts. In: Deutsch O et al (eds) Bewährungsprobe für ein Grundrecht. Art. 16, Abs. 2, Satz 2 Grundgesetz 'Politisch Verfolgte genießen Asylrecht'. Nomos, Baden-Baden, pp 19–65

Lachmann G (2015) "Mir wurde nahegelegt, meine Meinung nicht zu sagen", Die Welt, 17 October, http://www.welt.de/politik/deutschland/article147704582/Mir-wurde-nahegelegt-meine-Meinung-nicht-zu-sagen.html

Lemkemeyer S (2015) Mehrheit mit Flüchtlingspolitik einverstanden, Der Tagesspiegel, 11 September, http://www.tagesspiegel.de/politik/politbarometer-mehrheit-mit-fluechtlingspolitik-einverstanden/12308936.html

Meiritz A (2015) Flüchtlingspolitik: Grüner Palmer auf Linie – mit der CSU. In: Spiegel online Politik, http://www.spiegel.de/politik/deutschland/gruene-boris-palmer-will-fluechtlingszahlen-begrenzen-a-1058657.html

Odehnal B (2015) Polizei jagt ungarisch-bulgarische Schlepperbande, Die Welt, 28 August, http://www.welt.de/politik/ausland/article145763378/Polizei-jagt-ungarisch-ungarische-Schlepperbande.html

Oltmer J (2010) Migration im 19. und 20. Jahrhundert. Oldenbourg, München

Palet LS (2015) Der aussichtslose Kampf der Türsteherin Europas, Die Welt, 23 August, http://www.welt.de/politik/ausland/article142882627/Der-aussichtslose-Kampf-der-Tuersteherin-Europas.html

Paulwitz T (2015) Wir schaffen das - nicht, Junge Freiheit, 30 September, https://jungefreiheit.de/debatte/kommentar/2015/wir-schaffen-das-nicht/

Politbarometer (2015) Deutliche Mehrheit für Transitzonen, Politbarometer, 23 October, http://www.heute.de/deutliche-mehrheit-fuer-transitzonen-cducsu-im-minus-fdp-bei-fuenf-prozent-seehofer-mit-verlusten-40678036.html

Pro Asyl (2014) Zahlen und Fakten, http://www.proasyl.de/de/themen/zahlen-und-fakten/

Rau JP (2015) "Wir schaffen das nicht": Landrat Frank Hämmerle spricht im Interview Klartext zum Thema Flüchtlinge, http://www.suedkurier.de/region/kreis-konstanz/kreis-konstanz/Wir-schaffen-das-nicht-Landrat-Frank-Haemmerle-spricht-im-Interview-Klartext-zum-Thema-Fluechtlinge;art372432,8195222

Regulation (EU) No 604/2013 of the European Parliament and of the Council of 26 June 2013 establishing the criteria and mechanisms for determining the Member State responsible for examining an application for international protection lodged in one of the Member States by a third-country national or a stateless person, http://eur-lex.europa.eu/legal-content/EN/TXT/?uri=CELEX:32013R0604

Schmid T (2015) Wir schaffen das, aber es schafft auch uns, Die Welt, 27 September, http://www.welt.de/debatte/kommentare/article146892410/Wir-schaffen-das-aber-es-schafft-auch-uns.html

Stabenow M (2015) Europas Flüchtlingstektonik, Frankfurter Allgemeine Zeitung, 2 November, p 12

Tiedemann P (2015) Flüchtlingsrecht. Die materiellen und verfahrensrechtlichen Grundlagen. Springer, Berlin

UNHCR (2005) Geschichte des Asyls, http://www.lastexitflucht.org/againstallodds/factualweb/de/2.3/articles/2_3_3_Geschichte_des_Asyls.html; Bundeszentrale für Politische Bildung 2015: Asylrecht, http://www.bpb.de/nachschlagen/lexika/recht-a-z/21849/asylrecht

UNHCR (2015a) Internally displaced people, http://www.unhcr.org/pages/49c3646c146.html

UNHCR (2015b) Mittelmeer: Rekordzahl an Flüchtlingen und Migranten, http://www.unhcr.de/home/artikel/435da63ac57f3eaee63d95d2e4f7eb9b/mittelmeer-rekordzahl-von-fluechtlingen-und-migranten.html

UNHCR (2015c) Staff figures, http://www.unhcr.org/pages/49c3646c17.html

UNHCR (2015d) Zahlen und Statistiken, http://www.unhcr.de/service/zahlen-und-statistiken.html

Universal Declaration of Human Rights (1951). http://www2.ohchr.org/english/issues/education/training/docs/UNYearbook.pdf, pp 14–16

vek (2015) Bundespräsident Gauck bei Flüchtlingen: "Es gibt ein helles Deutschland". In: Spiegel online Politik, 26 August, http://www.spiegel.de/politik/deutschland/joachim-gauck-bei-fluechtlingen-es-gibt-ein-helles-deutschland-a-1049850.html

von Altenbockum J (2015a) Wir schaffen das! Frankfurter Allgemeine Zeitung, 1 September, http://www.faz.net/aktuell/politik/inland/fluechtlingskrise-eu-laender-verweigern-fluechtlingsaufnahme-13778593.html (alle Internetquellen am 26.11.2015 abgerufen)

von Altenbockum J (2015b) In der Transitzone, Frankfurter Allgemeine Zeitung, 2 November, p 1

Weingartner M, Plickert P (2015) Asylbewerber kosten bis zu 10 Milliarden Euro, http://www.faz.net/aktuell/wirtschaft/wirtschaftspolitik/asylbewerber-kosten-bis-zu-10-milliarden-euro-13758770.html

Willeke S (2014) Wir Dummschwätzer?, Die Zeit, 24 April, http://www.zeit.de/2014/18/akif-pirincci-verteidiger/

11 Brexit: A Preliminary Step Towards the Exit, or the Harbinger of Deeper Integration Within the European Union?

Abstract

On 29 March 2017, the United Kingdom of Great Britain and Northern Ireland (the UK) announced to the European Council that it intended to leave the European Union after 51.9% of Britons voted in favour of doing so in a referendum on 23 June 2016, and the British parliament had acquiesced to the will of the majority of those participating in the vote. This then triggered the start of negotiations to be held over the next 2 years, aimed at producing a deal designed to regulate the manner in which the UK should exit and the future relations between the EU and the UK. After 2 years at the latest, the exit of the UK will become legally binding, if the European Council and the UK do not mutually agree to extend the negotiation period. The government of the UK has stated multiple times that it is aiming for a "hard" exit, in other words, an exit from the European single market, the customs union and its obligation to abide by the decisions of the European Court of Justice. Regaining full British control over the immigration of EU citizens and its limitation was a central theme of the proponents of exiting the European Union. Here, the UK is attempting to adopt a more distanced relationship with the EU than Switzerland and Norway. The UK aims to achieve a free trade agreement with the EU, which it only wants to negotiate after the exit has been regulated.

To a large extent, it is expected that both sides will suffer considerable economic disadvantages after Brexit, which are likely to be far more severe for the UK than for the remaining EU members. For the UK, the risk that Scotland, the majority of whose population voted in favour of remaining in the EU, might leave the UK after more than 300 years has also increased. In 2014, just 55.3% of Scots voted to remain a part of the UK.

Brexit, which was welcomed by US president Donald Trump, has given impetus to sentiments and political parties in many EU countries who also wish to see their country leave the EU, and who even desire a complete dissolution of

---

Lecture given on 24.4.2017.

© Springer Nature Switzerland AG 2020
E. Jahn, *War and Compromise Between Nations and States*,
https://doi.org/10.1007/978-3-030-34131-2_11

this union of states. However, it also provides grounds for making greater effort to strengthen identification with the European community among EU citizens, and to make reforms to the Union. However, ideas as to the direction that these reforms should take are highly controversial. Should there be "more Europe" (an expansion of the competencies of the EU Commission and the EU Parliament), "less Europe" (a return of EU competencies to the nation-states) or greater integration in different groups of countries? It would be advisable to adapt the intensity of EU integration to the wishes of the EU citizens, which can be influenced by intensified information campaigns. Only a deceleration of the process of integration can consolidate the legitimacy of the EU.

11.1 The Uncertain Consequences of Brexit

On 29 March 2017, the United Kingdom of Great Britain and Northern Ireland (UK) announced to the European Council that it intended to leave the European Union after 51.9% of Britons, with 72.2% of the electorate participating, voted in favour of doing so in a referendum on 23 June 2016. On 1 February 2017, the British parliament, voted by a large majority (albeit without the Scottish National Party and with just 47 of the 232 Labour members) to acquiesce to the will of the majority of the population, although prior to the referendum, most members of parliament had been against exiting the EU. This then triggered the start of negotiations to be held over the next 2 years, aimed at producing a deal designed to regulate the manner in which the UK should exit and the future relations between the EU and the UK. After 2 years at the latest, the exit of the UK will become legally binding, if the European Council and the UK do not mutually agree to extend the negotiation period. This has meanwhile occurred three times. The treaty regulating the exit from the EU requires the approval of the British and European parliaments, and a qualified majority of the European Council, i.e. of 72% of the EU countries—or 20 of the 27 member states who are eligible to vote. These states must also represent at least 65% of the population of the European Union (without the British). If the treaty fails to garner the necessary support, the United Kingdom will exit without a deal. If Britain really does not wish to bend to the principle of freedom of movement within the European single market, it must also terminate its membership of the European Economic Area, an issue which to date has been almost entirely ignored in political debate.[1]

The British government has clearly stated that it wants a "hard Brexit",[2] in other words, not such a close association with the EU as that of Norway, a member of the European Economic Area, in other words, of an intensified free trade zone, and of

---

[1] Neuhäuser (2017, p. 18).

[2] For a brief overview of the options available to the British government after Brexit—the Norwegian, Swiss, Canadian and Turkish model, and the WTO option—see Hosp (2016).

the Schengen area, or of Switzerland, which is not a member of the EEA, but which is within the Schengen area. Both countries are obliged through bilateral agreements to comply with important EU regulations, such as freedom of movement of goods, services and capital, as well as people. However, following a referendum on 9 February 2014, Switzerland wishes to restrict freedom of movement of people, although this poses a risk to its two bilateral agreements with the EU.

The British House of Lords has attempted to secure in the exit deal the right to remain in the UK of the EU citizens who are living and working there, although it failed to do so when the government under Theresa May and the House of Commons voted against it. The restoration of British sovereignty over immigration into the country was a central theme within the movement in favour of exiting the EU. It is directed not so much against immigration from non-EU countries as against that of EU citizens, particularly from Poland, Bulgaria and Romania. Following pressure from the business sector, when the ten eastern and central European countries joined the EU in 2004 and 2007, Britain, unlike Germany and other countries, decided not to wait for 7 years before allowing freedom of movement for workers. Ultimately, the extent should not be underestimated to which Germany's acceptance of nearly a million refugees in 2015 and its pressuring of the other EU countries to do the same may have contributed towards the decision to leave the EU.[3]

In the coming months, topics of contention will be the conditions under which the UK leaves the EU, such as its financial obligations (on the basis of the applicable EU budget plans, civil servants' pensions, etc.) the country will have to continue to meet even after it has exited. A far more difficult process will be shaping the future economic relations between the EU and Britain, in which both sides have an eminent interest. However, the EU, to the extent that its 27 remaining members will continue their support for the Brexit policy, appears to be in a stronger negotiating position, since in 2015, Britain sent 44% of its exports to the EU, while the reverse figure was just 6.5%.[4] Here, Germany has a particularly strong interest in finding a mutually beneficial solution, since the UK is its third-largest export market. For this reasons, the British government is counting on the fact that Germany will be responsive to British demands during the exit negotiations. Britain wishes to retain free access to the European single market. However, the single market not only means freedom of movement of goods, services and capital, but also of workers, and Brussels (i.e. the European Commission, the European Parliament and the European Council) and the remaining 27 EU members are unwilling to tamper with this principle. Any willingness to compromise on this issue could easily persuade other EU members to exit the Union. Currently, 3.3 million EU citizens live and work in the UK, and are of key importance to numerous British companies, while 1.2 million Britons live on the continent.

---

[3]This was already foreseen as being likely in 2015 Stuart (2015, p. 86). See also Niedermeier and Ridder (2017, pp. 17–18).

[4]Neuhäuser (2017, p. 22).

In April 2017, there was widespread scepticism as to how it will be possible to successfully negotiate a joint exit treaty within the next 17 months (by October 2018), which could still be ratified before the European parliamentary elections in May 2019. In fact, on 14 November 2018, the British government and the EU succeeded in agreeing a treaty text that was 585 pages long, although it was not approved by the British parliament after being put to the vote three times. The problem is that Britain needs to amend thousands of laws and dozens of international treaties that it had already signed in accordance with the Brussels *aquis communitaire*. Britain will need to employ 30,000 staff in its newly created Brexit Ministry.[5]

11.2 Brexit as a Driver for Hopes for an End to—or Reform of—the EU

There is a whole series of varying positions with regard to Brexit. The proponents of Brexit in the UK (the 'brexiteers' or 'leavers') saw in Brexit the promise of an economic upturn with a reduction in unemployment among Britons, the restoration of national sovereignty over decision-making regarding the influx of migrants of all types, the liberation from legislation and jurisdiction originating from Brussels that is (allegedly) in the interest of other countries, and a restoration of British sovereignty and major power status in the world. For US president Donald Trump, Brexit holds the promise of a weakening of European trading power vis-à-vis the USA.[6] The right-wing nationalist, populist parties throughout Europe have been encouraged by Brexit to follow the British example and work towards achieving an exit of their country from the EU, or even the dissolution of the EU overall. They, too, hope to see an increase in national power and an economic upturn, as well as a decrease in unemployment. In many countries, this means above all an increase in power in relation to Germany, whose economic and political clout is regarded by these parties as being oppressive.

However, those who support Brexit outside of the UK also have their political reasons for doing so. Some see the EU after Brexit as being liberated from the constant brakes imposed by the UK on the process of European political integration, with repeated demands, which were then granted, for special national treatment.[7] They hope that Brexit will bring about a new impetus for the process of creating an very closer Union.

---

[5]Neuhäuser (2017, p. 18).

[6]In Russia, too, there are figures who welcome Brexit, e.g. Narochnitskaya (2016) (Brexit has become a slap in the face for the EU), https://izborsk-club.ru/10220. (All Internet sources retrieved on 18 April 2017).

[7]"No country voted so frequently against EU initiatives and legislative proposals as Britain", Schult (2016, p. 32).

On the part of the opponents of Brexit in Britain (the 'remainers', who wish to remain in the EU), there is concern about economic decline, and in some cases also regarding foreign policy isolation and a marginalisation of the country, whose strength on the global political stage has, in their view, been entirely overestimated by the supporters of Brexit. Opponents of Brexit in other countries harbour very different concerns. Some see the exit of the first country from the EU as an extremely dangerous precedent case, which could be imitated by other countries.[8] To date, the continuous expansion and, as a result, deepening, of European integration appeared to be an irreversible success story. Following the initial regression, severe doubts have now taken hold over the optimistic historical image of the continuous progress of supranational integration and the obsolete nature of nationalism in Europe. Put in positive terms, this means that the supporters of the EU see themselves as being called upon to legitimise the project of European integration as a project for peace—in 2012, the EU had been awarded the Nobel Peace Prize—among EU citizens by making a renewed political effort, since the memory of the two world wars and the many bilateral, national wars appears to be fading. In the eyes of EU supporters, the European project also needs to be justified through broad public communication, but also with regard to providing evidence of successful new social and economic achievements, since the crises in the European economy, which are having widely ranging impact at national level, are also providing sustenance for desires, however illusory they may be, for a re-nationalised prosperity policy—be it of a neoliberal or social-state interventionist nature.

Some opponents of Brexit regard Britain's exit from the EU as a weakening of the liberal economic policy of the northern EU countries in relation to the state interventionist policy of most southern EU states, which is regarded as being socially illusory and economically catastrophic. Henceforth, Germany can be overruled by these countries if they wish to bring an end to the austerity policy in the EU or create joint banking liability in order to protect deposits.

Others again see the exit from the EU as being a weakening of the power political balance within the EU, which to date has been based on the balance between the three greater powers of France, Britain and Germany (due to its continuous government crises, Italy has only rarely been able to assert its demographic-economic weight), a few medium-sized countries and a large number of small ones. Thus, there was no single hegemonial power within the Union, which doubtless contributed to its success. As a result of Britain's exit, the clout and responsibility held by Germany within the EU will increase enormously, which could be damaging to the Union. At the same time, the influence of the EU with regard to security and global policy will also be severely reduced following the exit of Britain as an atomic power and as a permanent member of the Security Council.

---

[8]"The exit of Britain from the EU would probably mark the start of a Europe-wide chain reaction" according to Scheuermann (2016).

Some people also regard Brexit as a welcome or unavoidable stimulus for reform within the EU. There can be no more "continuation as before".[9] However, the direction that any reform should take remains a highly contentious issue. Some argue in favour of "more Europe" i.e. greater competencies for Brussels (the European Commission and the European Parliament), in order to achieve the most uniform possible, better coordinated economic, financial and taxation policy, and also to guarantee cooperation in the fight against terrorism, the securing of EU borders and an effective European climate policy.[10] The EU should also be in a position to implement a joint foreign and military policy. With this in mind, the old proposal of taking European integration at different speeds was again presented for debate by the president of the European Commission, Jean-Claude Juncker.[11] This is designed to enable EU members who are particularly in favour of integration to create institutions for a joint policy in further policy areas.[12] For others, EU reform should mean "less Europe". They wish to give some EU competencies back to the national parliaments with a view to enhanced subsidiarity, or even to reassign them to regional authorities. For them, the maxim is decentralisation in place of consistently forging ahead with centralisation.

11.3 Britain's Half-Hearted Membership of the EU

As a former global power, the UK has always had a changing and ambivalent relationship towards European integration.[13] Shortly after the Second World War, the former British prime minister, Winston Churchill, in his famous speech at the University of Zurich on 19 September 1946, proclaimed that "We must build a kind of United States of Europe". He continued: "The first step in the re-creation of the European family must be a partnership between France and Germany. In this way only can France recover the moral and cultural leadership of Europe. There can be no revival of Europe without a spiritually great France and a spiritually great Germany... Small nations will count as much as large ones and gain their honour by their contribution to the common cause". Churchill did not want to see Britain incorporated into the United States of Europe, since: "We British have our own Commonwealth of Nations".[14] At that time, India, whose emperor was the king of the United Kingdom, and large parts of the Middle East, were still ruled by the British.

---

[9]Niebler (2017, p. 14). Niebler is the Chairman of the CSU Europe group and Co-Chairman of the CDU/CSU faction in the European Parliament.

[10]Beach (2016).

[11]Kurbjuweit (2016).

[12]However, there are those in Poland who regard this as posing a potential disadvantage to those countries who will not belong to the core of the EU, see Buras (2017).

[13]See the brief overview by Smith (2016).

[14]Churchill (1946).

A few years after Churchill's speech in Zurich, the process of integration began on the European continent, with the foundation of the European Coal and Steel Community (ECSC) in 1952 and the European Atomic Energy Community (EURATOM) and above all, the European Economic Community (EEC) in 1957, through the six "Carolingian" core states of France, Germany, Italy, Belgium, the Netherlands and Luxembourg.

At around the same time, the final decline of British global power became clear, when in 1947, India and shortly afterwards, the Middle East, were lost to the British Empire. In 1956, Egypt nationalised the Suez Canal under Gamal Abdel Nasser. Britain and France, in cooperation with Israel, attempted to annul this by means of a military invasion, and to topple the Nasser regime. However, through joint diplomatic activity, and with the threat of military force, the USA and the Soviet Union succeeded in preventing this. The process of decolonisation, which was accelerated in 1960, ultimately triggered the end of the European colonial powers. As a result, Britain's influence in the Commonwealth also declined.[15] Additionally, the growing economic importance of the EEC, also for the British economy, which was in crisis,[16] awakened British interest in becoming involved in the process of European integration. The consolidation of Soviet power in central and eastern Europe, with the foundation of the Council for Mutual Economic Assistance (COMECON) and the Warsaw Treaty Organisation, which was reinforced when the uprisings in the GDR in 1953, and in Poland and Hungary in 1956, were put down, created an additional security-related reason for Britain to seek closer ties to western continental Europe.[17] Thus, in 1963, the UK submitted an application for membership of the EEC, which was rejected following a veto by France under President Charles de Gaulle, however. In his view, British membership of the EEC posed a risk to French dominance in western Europe. The second application by the UK in 1967 was also not successful. It was only when de Gaulle stepped down in 1969 that Britain was able to enter the EEC on 1 January 1973. The British public welcomed this step in a referendum in 1975, when 67% of the votes cast were in favour of membership. In numerous opinion surveys in the decades that followed, there were also clear majorities in favour of membership of the European (Economic) Community.

The predominantly economically motivated interest in the formation of a community of European states always contrasted with a lack of interest in closer political

---

[15]However, the association with the Commonwealth still plays an extremely important role, see Kielinger (2014).

[16]By contrast, in 2016, "in the United Kingdom, Europe, which was racked by crisis, with its Euro crisis at the centre, was seen as posing a risk to the now booming national economy in the UK, which in 2014 was the fastest growing economy among the G7, and which was regarded as protecting it against infection and covetousness from the continent." Niedermeier and Ridder (2017, p. 15).

[17]On the extremely divergent attitudes in Britain, France and Germany towards European integration after 1945 on the basis of their history, see a very brief overview by Windsor (1994). Above all, he discusses the British aversion towards a federalisation of Europe.

union, however. Even early on, the long-term prospect of a Federal State of Europe, the United States of Europe, was sharply rejected. Even so, in the decades that followed, the UK agreed to all decisions regarding a deepening of the European integration process, and even to the Constitutional Treaty of 29 October 2004. As is well known, this treaty already failed to be ratified following its rejection in referenda in France and the Netherlands in May/June 2005, so that no British referendum was called.

Britain's half-hearted attitude was expressed in the form of a series of special regulations, which were forced through in Brussels by the British government. Thus, in 1984, prime minister Margaret Thatcher succeeded in reducing British contribution payments to the European budget, although Britain continued to pay the second-largest net amount.[18] Britain, like Denmark, only signed the Maastricht Treaty of 1992 on the creation of the European Union and a common currency when a clause was added that permitted it not to join the Euro zone, to which all other countries are committed as soon as they fulfil certain conditions. Britain and Ireland did not join the Schengen Agreement on the abolition of identity checks at borders within the Schengen area, unlike non-EU members Switzerland, Norway, Iceland and Liechtenstein. When the Lisbon Treaty was signed, the UK ensured that for it (like Poland), the Charter of Fundamental Rights of the European Union, which came into force in 2009, would not be binding. The UK also failed to participate in the Agreement on Social Policy of 1999 relating to the regulation of work-related issues at European level.

The British government also wrung out these concessions because there was a large minority in Britain who were in favour of an exit from the EU. Thus, during the 1970s and 1980s, it was mainly politicians from the Labour Party and trade unionists who were opposed to the European communities, whom left-wing Europeans regarded for decades as being a capitalist organisation, and not as an organisation promoting peace and understanding among European nations. It was not until the 1990s that political opinions were reversed in Britain. The EU gained increasing acceptance within the Labour Party, albeit reticently, while among Conservatives, the level of rejection grew. There was always a minority among them who criticised European integration as a German project, which aimed to realise National Socialist claims for dominance over Europe in a different guise. Following the establishment of the United Kingdom Independence Party (UKIP) in 1993, the Conservative Party came under particular pressure to respond to the growing mood in favour of exiting the EU among the population and within the Party. The decision mentioned earlier by the British government under Tony Blair not to restrict the immigration of workers from the new EU countries for 7 years, as did Germany and several other states, turned out to be fatal. In the parliamentary elections of May 2015, UKIP under Nigel Farage won 12.6% of the vote, although just one seat in the parliament, due to

---

[18] In 2015, the UK paid a net amount of 11.5 billion euros towards the EU budget. The figure for Germany was 14.3 billion and for France, 5.5 billion euros. Kafsack (2016).

the first-past-the-post system. In the European elections in 2014, it even won 26.6% of the vote, making it the largest British party in the European Parliament.

Probably with the primary aim of consolidating party unity and to improve the chances of the Conservative Party in the election of 2015 by de-escalating the debate over Europe (and for 2 years, this strategy certainly proved to be successful),[19] David Cameron promised in January 2013 that there would be a referendum on EU membership, clearly in the hope that prior to this, he would be able to negotiate EU reforms in Brussels that would promote British interests and then succeed in winning a solid majority among the British population in favour of the EU. Above all, he hoped to limit immigration by EU citizens, which he succeeded in doing to the extent that now, a country may submit an application to the EU Commission for a "state of immigration emergency", which is intended to ensure that over a period of 7 years, newly arriving EU citizens are only entitled to receive limited social contribution payments for 4 years. He also attempted to stop the Eurozone countries from discriminating against EU countries that had retained their own currency, to secure a reduction in Brussels bureaucracy and to make the goal of the Lisbon Treaty—"ever closer union"—non-binding for Britain. The modest success of these negotiations made no significant impact on the strength of the exit campaign being fought by the opponents of British EU membership.

Of decisive importance for the result of the referendum on Brexit was probably not only the fact that a large portion of the tabloid press traditionally propagated Eurosceptic views, but above all, that in recent years, the socially disadvantaged layers of society regarded the influx of EU citizens and other foreigners as posing a threat to their own opportunities for employment, and above all, a fundamental mistrust had taken hold of the socio-political elites, which in some cases were entangled in corruption scandals. As a result, they perceived their warnings regarding the economic risks posed by an exit as being motivated by a desire within the establishment to retain its privileges. The driving force of the exit campaign, Boris Johnson, was seen by many in Britain as being far more trustworthy than the prime minister, David Cameron, from the same Conservative Party.[20]

11.4 Possible Economic and Political Consequences of Brexit

Brexit has deeply divided British society. The forces that lost the referendum have been unwilling to come to terms with the largely unexpected result after 23 June 2016 and the planned exit from the EU by the UK. Instead, they are attempting to prevent Brexit through mass demonstrations and a petition, signed by millions of citizens, calling for a second referendum. They consist in large part of young British people, only a few of whom voted in the referendum, and who voted by a large

---

[19]Oppermann (2016, p. 518) and von Ondarza (2016).
[20]Oppermann (2016, pp. 525–529). On the role of the leading figures and agitation during the Brexit campaign, see Niedermeier and Ridder (2017, pp. 23–32).

majority to remain in the EU.[21] There have also been appeals to parliamentarians to at least ensure a softer Brexit. Of greater significance than the social rift between the generations and social strata—the majority of the more highly educated among the population, business people, banks and large companies were in favour of remaining in the EU, while many blue-collar workers and those marginalised in society were against—is probably the regional division between London, Scotland and Northern Ireland on the one hand, and large parts of the rest of England and Wales on the other. This could certainly yet have severe consequences.[22]

There is largely only speculation regarding the economic consequence of Brexit for Britain and the EU 27, since even economists are unable to issue reliable forecasts. Attempts to play down the impact of Brexit by arguing that only one country is leaving the EU, while the other 27 have firmly decided to remain loyal, is misleading. According to another perspective on Brexit: "The economy of the United Kingdom is exactly the same size as that of 20 of the smallest EU countries put together. It is as though 20 of the 28 countries were exiting simultaneously."[23] While the relative economic power of Germany increases as a result of Brexit, and thus its political influence in the EU with regard to a wide range of issues, its specific economic, neoliberal clout on the Council of Ministers will be severely weakened, since now, "those countries bordering the Mediterranean than pin their faith in the state" (Werner Sinn) are in a position to outvote the "Deutschmark block" (Germany, the Netherlands, Austria and Finland). They could respond to the protectionism announced by Donald Trump with EU protectionism led by France. "They can and will be in control, and will turn Europe into a trade fortress." ... According to Sinn, Germany will "become an appendage and a paymaster of a new Latin Monetary Union" led by France, which under President Emmanuel Macron wants to usher in "a joint Eurobudget, Eurobonds, joint deposit protection and joint unemployment security", in other words, a financial redistribution from Germany and the other northern countries to the southern member states of the EU.[24] The creation of new institutions within the Euro zone with state competencies will, he claims, divide the EU in a dangerous way, and will threaten its existence. Even before Brexit, other observers already saw an undermining of the existing EU treaties and the democratic, political support for the European integration project in the European nations with heterogeneous political cultures through the increased tendency towards majority decisions instead of consensus decisions, and towards the expansion of power and change in functions of the European Central Bank (ECB) and the European

---

[21]"It emerges that the cohort of 18–24-year-olds voted in favour of remaining in the EU by a majority of 75%. Among 25–49-year-olds and 50–64-year-olds, the desire to remain within the EU decreased rapidly, with just 56% or even only 44% in favour. Among voters aged over 65, just 39% were in favour of remaining within the EU." However, it was "clear that just 36% of 18–24-year-olds who were eligible to vote in the referendum actually did so, in contrast to 83% of the over-65s." Niedermeier and Ridder (2017, p. 34). However, see also Yeung (2016).

[22]Cf. Sturm (2016).

[23]Sinn (2017).

[24]Sinn (2017).

Stability Mechanism (ESM), neither of which has been democratically legitimised.[25] By contrast, some authors promote more intensive socio-economic integration as a means for removing the asymmetries between the EU nations.[26]

After the referendum, the value of the British pound decreased by 8%, and fell further until 11 October 2016, before partially recovering.[27] This facilitated a rise in British share prices. In the longer term, many observers are forecasting a weakening of the British domestic economy following an exit from the European single market and the introduction of customs barriers.[28] Above all, banks and financial institutions will leave the country—taking between 70,000 and 100,000 jobs with them[29]—and relocate from London to Dublin, Paris and Frankfurt. In those cities, an influx of thousands of bankers is expected, although there are also fears of a significant rise in property prices and rents.

For several reasons, Brexit puts at risk not only the prosperity, but also the unity of the United Kingdom of Great Britain and Northern Ireland, often referred to in short form as Britain or England, while its citizens are known as Britons. In precise terms, Great Britain consists only of England, Wales and Scotland. The four parts of the state are also known as nations, which participate in international football tournaments, for example, with their own teams, and under their own national flags. The kernel of the UK is England, which covers more than half of the total area of the country,[30] and which also has the most inhabitants of the four parts of the UK, namely 54.3 million of the 64.6 million total population (2014). England, which during the early Middle Ages consisted of seven kingdoms, has been united under a single king since Egbert of Wessex (802–839).

The three non-English parts of the UK are politically, culturally and linguistically linked to England with differing degrees of intensity, depending largely on the point in time at which they were conquered by the English. First, in numerous wars from the eleventh to thirteenth century, England conquered the Welsh principalities, which had previously only been briefly brought under common rule, although for a long time afterwards, there were uprisings against England by the Welsh. From 1301 onwards, the English heir to the throne bore the title "Prince of Wales". In 1542, Wales was finally incorporated into the English legal system. It was not until 1988, with the establishment of a National Assembly for Wales, that it achieved a very limited degree of autonomy.

Scotland had been a kingdom since 843, which was at war with England over many centuries, and which at times was a vassal of the English crown. However, under the Scottish royal dynasty, the Stuarts, England became joined with Scotland

---

[25]Kielmansegg (2015, pp. 28–29, 98–110).

[26]Platzer (2014).

[27]Euro/British Pound (2018).

[28]Rhodes (2016). Sked (2016) takes a different view.

[29]Hesse (2016, p. 18).

[30]130,000 of a total 243,000 square km. By comparison: the Federal Republic of Germany covers an area of 357,000 square km.

in 1603 in the form of a personal union. After several civil wars, including wars begun for religious-confessional reasons, and the economic bankruptcy of Scotland, the Scottish parliament, that was formed from just a few thousand people, agreed in 1707 to the unification of the two countries to form the Kingdom of Great Britain (Act of Union), while preserving important Scottish institutions, above all the Presbyterian Church.

Scotland covers nearly a third of the territory of the UK, with an area of 130,000 square km. However, it has a population of just 5.5 million, or 8.3% of the total population of the country. Sixty-two percent of Scots voted to remain in the EU. This led First Minister Nicola Sturgeon of the Scottish National Party (SNP) to again call for a referendum on Scottish independence, so that the country could remain in the EU. In a first referendum on 18 September 2014, just 55.3% of Scots voted to remain in the UK—with a voter participation of 84.6%. However, the EU quickly made it clear that Scotland could not remain in the EU after Brexit, but would first have to go through a lengthy acceptance procedure in order to enter the EU as an independent state. That aside, Scotland cannot simply hold a referendum on exiting the UK as it sees fit, but requires approval to do so from London. Even if a majority were to vote to leave the UK, the British parliament would have to permit Scotland to do so. At any rate, prime minister Theresa May made it clear that a new referendum in Scotland was out of the question until Brexit had been brought to a final conclusion.

The vote in Northern Ireland of 55.8% against Brexit, which right through the confessional boundaries, has clearly also intensified separatist sentiments there, albeit only to a low degree.[31] The island of Ireland used to be known occasionally as Little Britain, as was Bretagne (Brittany), where Britons had emigrated since the fourth century. The conquest of Ireland by England began in the eleventh century and extended over several centuries. In 1541, Henry VIII, through a statute of the Irish parliament of nobles created the Kingdom of Ireland in a personal union with the Kingdom of England. The expropriation of Irish property and the settlement of English, Welsh and Scots, particularly in Northern Ireland, was intended to underscore English rule. However, the rebellions continued in the centuries that followed, and in 1801, the English finally abolished the Irish government institutions and dissolved the Irish parliament, forcing the creation of the United Kingdom of Great Britain and Ireland.

As a result of the partial success of the Irish Home Rule movement with the founding of the Irish Free State, the Kingdom was reduced in 1922 to the United Kingdom of Great Britain and Northern Ireland, which was not named as such until 1927. The question is whether the process of disintegration of the UK will continue in the twenty-first century. While it was possible to end the civil war in Northern Ireland with the Good Friday Agreement signed on 10 April 1998[32] between the UK, Ireland and the Northern Irish conflicting parties, this could reignite if a new customs

---

[31]Federl (2016).
[32]The Agreement (1998).

border is established with Ireland.[33] The Agreement permitted the formation of a Northern Ireland Assembly, after earlier Northern Irish parliaments had been repeatedly disbanded by London.[34] Today, too, the regional parliaments in the UK can be suspended by the British parliament in London (as was the case in Northern Ireland from 2002 to 2007). In constitutional terms, therefore, they have little security. The Agreement precludes not a later, peaceful, union between Northern Ireland and the Republic of Ireland following the emergence of a demographic majority of Catholics, who are generally Irish nationalist in outlook, and who have a higher birth rate. The majority of Northern Irish, like the majority of Scots, voted in favour of retaining their membership of the EU, also because this enables open economic borders with Ireland that facilitate communication. It remains unclear whether Scottish and Northern Irish national separatism will mutually support each other, and what position the Northern Irish Protestants, many of whose forefathers originally came from Scotland, will take in the complex new political situation.

One other area of interest, away from the centre stage, is the potential isolation of Gibraltar from the labour and sales market in Spain, even though 95.9% of its population voted to remain in the EU. Gibraltar has been ruled by the British since 1713. Spain has now renewed its old claim to annexation of this small territory (6.5 square km, with 33,000 inhabitants).

11.5 The Need to Adapt European Integration to the Changeable Willingness to Integrate Among EU Citizens

From a peace policy perspective, the decision by the UK to exit the EU is highly regrettable, even though common membership of NATO will continue. The power of the EU, the impact on international politics of which has to date been mainly to de-escalate conflicts and balance interests (for example in the Ukraine conflict and in the dispute over the atomic industry in Iran), will be significantly weakened vis-à-vis the USA and Russia. The role and responsibility of Germany in the EU will increase, in many situations by no means to Germany's advantage. The tendency towards increased state debts, with an uneven distribution of the burden throughout the EU, will grow. In the long term, this is likely to strengthen national-populist figures in all member states, who assign the blame for the economic and social woes to countries other than their own.

What is advisable in this situation? In recent decades, European integration in all countries has mainly been a matter for the political and social elites and their understanding of the national benefits of an ever closer interconnection between the economy and many areas of politics. They regard new tasks as being: a reduction in youth unemployment through European funds, the introduction of European taxes

---

[33] Cf. Moltmann (2017).
[34] Moltmann (2013, 2015).

for financial transactions,[35] the facilitation of programmes to combat transnational criminality and terrorism, migration and refugee movements, controlling climate change, and better coordination of foreign and security policy. By contrast, the wider population views integration with scepticism and disapproval, and as a result, it's legitimacy is only very limited. Thus far, only smaller minorities have put up political opposition to European integration. This discrepancy between the political views of the elites and the wider population does not appear to many contemporaries as being dangerous. Instead, they regard it as an advantage that the elitist element in the parliamentary democracy lends far greater weight to the will of the parliamentary people's representatives when it comes to making most specific political decisions than to the will of the voters. Only in certain democracies is this discrepancy modified by referenda and plebiscites. Furthermore, the elitist constitution of the media landscape occasionally masks the contradictions between the views that are predominantly published and the actual views among the majority of the population, which in parliamentary democracies are clearly expressed in unexpected ways, at least occasionally, in referenda and elections.

The dilemma of the gross discrepancy between an understanding of the necessity and benefits of European integration and globalisation, and the illusory notions of a renationalisation of the economy and national political power and decision-making competencies is impossible to resolve, but can be significantly mitigated. On the one hand, European integration can in many cases be adapted more strongly to the will of the citizens. Many decisions do not need to be taken in Brussels, and can be made at national or even regional level, even if this will certainly entail certain disadvantages. To this extent, British policy in recent decades has often incorporated the weaker European identity among Britons in an expedient way. It was merely that the opening up of the British employment market to citizens of the new EU countries—which occurred too early, and which was not at all necessary—was a fatal error that had devastating political consequences.

On the other hand, European integration must take into account the slow growth of a sense of shared European identity, which is by all means reflected empirically.[36] The majority of young Britons, like those who were better educated and better off in society, voted for the UK to remain in the EU. They have the opportunity, if they retain and expand on their pro-European attitude, to represent the majority of the British people in a few years' time, and to reverse Brexit.[37] However, current demands to revoke the Brexit decision are of little help. During the forthcoming negotiations, it would be far better to urge a rejection, both within and outside parliament of the "hard Brexit" policy proposed by Theresa May's government and

---

[35]Ponzano (2016, p. 46).

[36]Liebert (2016). The opposite position is presented by White (2016).

[37]73% of Britons under 25 voted in favour of remaining, while 60% of the over-65s voted to leave. However, young people voted in far fewer numbers than the older population, Oppermann (2016, pp. 517, 528). According to later studies, far more young people voted that had initially been assumed. A higher participation among young people would probably have led to a closer result, but would not have overturned it, Yeung (2016).

its supporters in the Conservative Party, and to insist on a "soft Brexit" along the lines of the Norway model (without Schengen membership). This requires a public debate and intensive education measures regarding the role that Poles and other EU citizens play in the British economy, which also appears to benefit socially worse-off Britons far more than it harms them. Political will is not static, even if prejudices are sometimes deeply entrenched. Thus, political education and social learning processes have an opportunity to forge a new desire for British EU membership among the majority population in several years' time.

Since the Labour Party is clearly currently unable to present a serious, pro-European inspired opposition to the Conservatives, and there is no foreseeable prospect of the Liberal Democratic Party experiencing an upswing in support, hopes for a revision of the "hard Brexit" policy must be directed towards changing public opinion, which alone can exert pressure on Conservative parliamentarians by urging them to change their policy if they wish to be re-elected. The possibility of a radical shift of opinion among the population, and a withdrawal in due time of the application to exit the EU before March 2019 or at a later point in time, if the negotiating period is extended by mutual agreement, cannot be entirely excluded. The chances of achieving a "soft Brexit" as the result of a cleverly calculated pro-European policy are therefore probably greater.

The 27 EU members should firmly persist in upholding the conditions that the UK must meet if it wishes to remain in the European single market, although at the same time, they should remain open to the possibility of a "soft Brexit". They should by no means play the "Scottish card"[38] and put pressure on London by supporting Scottish aspirations for a "retention" of membership of the EU in accordance with the inverse Denmark-Greenland model of 1985.[39] At the same time, Brussels should calmly point out that an independent Scotland would enjoy the same right to apply for EU membership as Slovakia or Slovenia did, which were accepted as members of the EU not long after declaring independence.

Within the EU, it is advisable that the subsidiarity principle, i.e. the relocation of several Brussels competencies to national or regional parliaments, should be reinforced, although at the same time, public opinion among EU citizens should be informed through both successful policy and better education regarding the benefits of EU integration, while not overlooking the disadvantages that this also brings. At the same time, Brussels institutions must tackle the issues to which the majority of EU citizens expect them to find a solution. While these do not include a uniform refugee policy, they do cover effective security for the EU's external borders against illegal immigration and better Europe-wide coordination of the fight against terrorism, and perhaps even the establishment of a European police

---

[38] However, this option is not available by any means as a common EU option, since several states, particularly Spain, are combating separatist movements.

[39] At that time, the Autonomous Territory of Greenland exited the EEC, while Denmark, to whom it still belongs, remained a member. Thus, in the Scottish mindset, England and Wales could exit the EU without this impacting Scotland's membership.

force. The development of a European sense of identity is less a task of the Brussels institutions than of the political parties and social institutions in the EU countries. Above all, however, for must be created for exchanging European political views, which is certainly an extremely costly enterprise, given the number of languages currently spoken by EU citizens. In the long term, the EU states will not be able to avoid the introduction of English as a binding second language for all EU citizens, in order to make it easier to establish a genuinely European public opinion. Currently, there are only national public opinions, which differ widely, with an added European element. From this perspective, the exit of the UK even presents a slight advantage,[40] since the social privileges of being able to speak the EU language as their mother tongue will now only be held by the few Irish citizens.

11.6 The Fatal Strengthening of German Influence in the EU as a Result of Brexit

What is likely to happen with regard to Brexit? It is rather unlikely that Britain will already no longer be a member of the EU in March 2019. During the exit negotiations, both sides, the EU 27 and the UK, will play poker with maximum positions. Britain will place its hopes on a fracturing of the negotiation position among the EU 27. However, both sides have no interest in having a bad relationship with each other in the future. For this reason, the negotiating period will probably be extended. As a result, the likelihood increases of events happening that are almost impossible to predict today, which could significantly change the course of the negotiations and public opinion in Europe. Thus, further victories by parties wanting to leave the EU in other EU countries, the escalation of the socio-economic crisis in Greece and other Mediterranean EU states, as well as dramatic external events such as a renewed escalation of the war in Ukraine, the confrontation between Russia and the USA in the Middle East or elsewhere, and several other scenarios, will also determine the fate of the Brexit negotiations. It is therefore impossible to offer reliable prognoses regarding the outcome of the exit negotiations. It is improbable, however, that in the coming decades the EU will disintegrate, or that significant progress will be made towards European integration. Rather, the process of "muddling along" is likely to continue.

---

[40]In the administrative apparatus in Brussels, the exit of many Britons from the translation and interpreting services is causing significant damage, however, to the extent that they are unable or unwilling to become citizens of the remaining EU countries.

References

Beach D (2016) A stronger, more supranational Union. In: Zimmermann, Dür (2016), pp 46–54
Buras P (2017) Prepare for a New Europe, Warschau, http://emerging-europe.com/voices/voices-intl-relations/prepare-for-a-new-europe/
Churchill W (1946) Speech delivered at the University of Zurich, 19 September, Churchill_Zurich_Speech_19091946.docx, and https://www.youtube.com/watch?v=5k5KuXTL8hc&feature=youtu.be
Euro/British Pound (2018). http://fxtop.com/en/historical-exchange-rates.php?C1=GBP&C2=EUR&A=1&DD1=16&MM1=10&YYYY1=2013&DD2=16&MM2=10&YYYY2=2018&MA=1&YA=1&LANG=de&CJ=0
Federl F (2016) Unmut in Nordirland nach Brexit wächst. Der Tagesspiegel, 25 June, http://www.tagesspiegel.de/politik/nach-eu-referendum-unmut-in-nordirland-nach-brexit-waechst/13788224.html
Hesse M et al. (2016) Schwarzer Donnerstag. Der Spiegel 26:14–19
Hosp G (2016) Alternativen zur EU-Mitgliedschaft, https://www.bpb.de/internationales/europa/brexit/228813/alternativen-zur-eu
Kafsack H (2016) Deutschland überweist das meiste Geld an Brüssel, FAZNET, 8 August, http://www.faz.net/aktuell/wirtschaft/eurokrise/deutschland-zahlt-am-meisten-in-den-eu-haushalt-14378202.html
Kielinger T (2014) Großbritannien: Am Rande Europas, im Zentrum der Debatte. Politische Studien 449 (May/June):6–18
Kielmansegg PG (2015) Wohin des Wegs, Europa? Beiträge zu einer überfälligen Debatte. Nomos, Baden-Baden
Kurbjuweit D (2016) Willige und Fähige. Der Spiegel 26:20–21
Liebert U (2016) European identity formation in (the crisis). In: Zimmermann, Dür (2016), pp 98–106
Moltmann B (2013) Ein verquerer Frieden. Nordirland fünfzehn Jahre nach dem Belfast-Abkommen von 1998, HSFK-Report No. 5
Moltmann B (2015) Innerstaatliche Konflikte. Nordirland, http://www.bpb.de/internationales/weltweit/innerstaatliche-konflikte/54664/nordirland
Moltmann B (2017) Nordirland: Das Ende vom Lied? Der Friedensprozeß und der Brexit, HSFK-Report No. 4
Narochnitskaya N (2016) Brexit stal poshchechinoy Evrosoyuzu (The Brexit became a slap in the face of the EU), https://izborsk-club.ru/10220
Neuhäuser A (2017) Goodbye Europe. Politische Studien 472(March/April):16–25
Niebler A (2017) Großbritannien sagt, no! Politische Studien 472(March/April):10–15
Niedermeier A, Ridder W (2017) Das Brexit-Referendum. Hintergründe, Streitthemen, Perspektiven. Springer, Wiesbaden
Oppermann K (2016) Das gespaltene Königreich. Die politischen Hintergründe und Ursachen des, 'Brexit'-Referendums. Politische Vierteljahresschrift 57(4):516–533
Platzer HW (2014) Rolling back or expanding European integration? Barriers and paths to deepening democratic and social integration. International Policy Analysis of the Friedrich-Ebert-Stiftung, Berlin, library.fes.de/pdf-files/id/ipa/10527.pdf
Ponzano P (2016) After Brexit. What should the European Union do? The Federalist Debate 3:44–47
Rhodes M (2016) Brexit – a disaster for Britain and for the European Union. In: Zimmermann, Dür (2016), pp 252–257
Scheuermann C (2016) Das Projekt Angst. Der Spiegel 9:91
Schult C (2016) So geht doch! Der Spiegel 24:32–35
Sinn HW (2017) Die Bedeutung des Brexit für Deutschland und Europa. Frankfurter Allgemeine Zeitung, 16 March, p 19

Sked A (2016) The case for Brexit: why Britain should leave the EU. In: Zimmermann, Dür (2016), pp 258–264

Smith J (2016) Europa und das Vereinigte Königreich. Kleine Geschichte der Beziehungen seit 1945. Aus Politik und Zeitgeschichte (49–50):11–16

Stuart G (2015) Der Weg Großbritanniens mit oder ohne Europäische Union. Politische Studien 66 (2):86–91

Sturm R (2016) Uneiniges Königreich? Großbritannien nach dem Brexit-Votum. Aus Politik und Zeitgeschichte (49/50):17–23

The Agreement 1998 Agreement reached in the multi-party-negotiations, http://cain.ulst.ac.uk/events/peace/docs/agreement.htm

von Ondarza N (2016) Die verlorene Wette. Entstehung und Verlauf des britischen EU-Referendums. Aus Politik und Zeitgeschichte (49/50):4–10

White J (2016) A common European identity is an illusion. In: Zimmermann, Dür (2016), pp 107–114

Windsor P (1994) Großbritannien und die europäische Integration. Europäische Rundschau 1:39–49

Yeung P (2016) Turnout among young voters 'Almost double' initial report. In: Independent, 10 July, https://www.independent.co.uk/news/uk/politics/eu-referendum-brexit-turnout-young-voters-youth-vote-double-a7129181.html

Zimmermann H, Dür A (eds) (2016) Key controversies in European integration, 2nd edn. Macmillan, Basingstoke

The Catalan Independence Movement: A Challenge That Spain and the EU Have Chosen to Suppress

Abstract

On 27 October 2017, the Catalan regional parliament declared Catalan independence. This declaration was in turn pronounced unconstitutional by the Spanish constitutional court. The Senate, the second parliamentary chamber, then gave the Spanish government the authority to dissolve the regional parliament, dismiss and imprison the regional government and set new elections for 21 December. The head of the Catalan government, Carles Puigdemont, and four of his ministers, fled to Belgium to avoid imprisonment. During these elections, the parties attempting to attain independence for the region again won a majority of representative seats, but not of the vote. The dispute surrounding the independence of Catalonia is weakening the economy of the region and the entire country, and is endangering Spain's political stability. The EU is not willing to mediate in the dispute, since it regards it as being a domestic matter for Spain to deal with.

The huge increase in support for the Catalan independence movement was triggered in 2010 by the rejection of important clauses in the Catalan Statute of Autonomy by the Spanish People's Party and the constitutional court, and by the property and banking crisis of 2008. A stabilisation of Spain's political system appears only to be achievable through fundamental reform, including constitutional reform. For this purpose, a change of attitude is required in the concept of the nation, which accepts that nations in multi-ethnic states such as Spain can be a part of more comprehensive nations, and that the Castilian language is just one language spoken in Spain, but not the Spanish language.

When the Madrid-based politicians and the majority of Spanish society fail to integrate the linguistic-cultural and regional Catalan nation on an equal basis in Spain, where four, or multiple, languages are spoken, be it through extended autonomy or federalisation, a clear majority can emerge in Catalan society that demands the state separation of the region from Spain. In such a case, it would be beneficial if a democratic right of separation and unification were to be created for

---

Lecture given on 23.4.2018.

© Springer Nature Switzerland AG 2020
E. Jahn, *War and Compromise Between Nations and States*,
https://doi.org/10.1007/978-3-030-34131-2_12

states and the European Union, which requires a qualified majority (such as the 55% in the case of Montenegro in 2006) in referenda on the entry and exit of states. Proposals to this aim will be put forward in this essay. Democracy cannot be limited to the self-regulation of the governed by their representatives in historically determined states, many of which have only been created as a result of force through war. Instead, the democratic decision-making process should also cover state formation, and independent, federative or autonomous statehood—in other words, the separation and unification of states.

12.1 The Speechless Political Stalemate Between the Central Spanish Government and the Catalan Independence Movement

Since the end of the Franco dictatorship in November 1975, there have, as in former times, been strong attempts to strengthen Catalan self-reliance and its position as a separate state, which on 27 October 2017 culminated in the declaration of independence and sovereignty of the Catalan Republic. Seventy-two of the 135 delegates to the regional parliament in Barcelona voted in favour, while ten voted against, and two submitted empty voting cards after the opposition had left the assembly hall.[1] On 1 October, a referendum held on independence, which was declared unconstitutional by the Spanish constitutional court, and which was in part hindered by the Spanish authorities, had already demanded that this step be taken. In this referendum, in which 42.5% of the population eligible to vote participated, 90.1% voted in favour of independence.[2]

Already on 27 October, after the Spanish constitutional court declared the Catalan declaration of independence to be illegal, the Spanish Senate, the second parliamentary chamber, authorised the government in Madrid headed by Mariano Rajoy, invoking Art. 155 of the constitution,[3] to dissolve the Catalan parliament and to depose and arrest the Catalan government. In addition, the Catalan police force, the *Mossos d'Esquadra*, were to be subordinated to the Interior Ministry in Madrid and

---

[1] Rößler (2017b).

[2] Rößler (2017a).

[3] Article 155 "(1) If an Autonomous Community does not fulfil the obligations imposed upon it by the Constitution or other laws, or acts in a way seriously prejudicing the general interests of Spain, the Government, after lodging a complaint with the President of the Autonomous Community and failing to receive satisfaction therefore, may, following approval granted by an absolute majority of the Senate, take the measures necessary in order to compel the latter forcibly to meet said obligations, or in order to protect the above-mentioned general interests. (2) With a view to implementing the measures provided in the foregoing clause, the Government may issue instructions to all the authorities of the Autonomous Communities." Spanish constitution (1978). (All websites retrieved on 3.10.2018).

new elections were to be set for 21 December. The central government showed no willingness at all to even talk to the regional government about its desire for independence. Carles Puigdemont, the president of the Catalan government, the *Generalitat de Catalunya*, and four of his ministers, fled to Brussels[4] and asked the European Union to mediate with the government in Madrid. However, this request was rejected by the EU Commission on the grounds that this was a domestic matter for Spain, which had nothing to do with the Commission.[5] The Catalan vice-president, Oriol Junqueras, and eight ministers, as well as members of the parliamentary presidium, were interned in Madrid. However, with the exception of Junqueras and the interior minister, and two former leaders of the independence movement who had previously been arrested, all those who had been accused of "rebellion, insurrection against the state authority and misappropriation of public funds" (during the organisation of the banned independence referendum) were released on bail a few days later.

On 21 December, with a high level of voter participation of 79.1%,[6] the Catalan parliamentary elections did not deliver the result expected by prime minister Rajoy. His party, the "People's Party" (*Partido Popular*), won just 4.2% of the vote. The parties that came out in favour of Catalan independence received only 47.5% of the total number of votes, but again held a majority of delegate seats (70 of 135)[7] after winning in the rural areas, where, in accordance with the voting laws, votes carry more weight. In the meantime, in the major cities, where migrants from southern Spain (mainly from Andalusia and Extremadura) are concentrated, more votes were given to those who opposed independence. While it would appear that mainly Catalans with deep roots in the region, who speak Catalan as their mother tongue—the Catalophones[8]—voted for independence, while migrants from other regions in Spain and Latin America who are Castilian native speakers voted against, there is no evidence that research has been conducted into these connections.

---

[4] A European arrest warrant issued by the Spanish Supreme Court for the extradition of Puigdemont was withdrawn prior to the election in December, but renewed on 23 March 2018 when Puigdemont was in Finland. During his return journey to Belgium by car, he was arrested in Schleswig-Holstein, shortly after crossing the border with Denmark, and on 5 April was released on condition that he did not leave Germany until a final court judgement had been issued regarding the Spanish extradition request.

[5] Stabenow (2017).

[6] Eleccions katalanes (2017).

[7] For a long time, the parties that had a parliamentary majority considered re-electing Carles Puigdemont, which would, however, have required his presence in the parliament in Barcelona. Finally, on 14 May, the lawyer and writer Quim Torra was elected in order to pre-empt a dissolution of parliament.

[8] In statistical surveys in Catalonia, the majority of the population stated that their mother tongue was Castilian, although in 2001, 94.5% said that they understood Catalan, with 74.5% saying that they spoke it, 74.4% that they could read it and 49.8% that they could write it, Bernecker et al. (2007, p. 211). In the world of work and in the public sphere, the main language is Castilian. For more recent figures, see: Generalitat de Catalunya (2015).

Prior to the escalation of the conflict between the central government and the central parliament in Madrid and the regional government and regional parliament in Barcelona, the Catalan efforts to attain independence had been expressed in very different ways. These included support for initiatives for further democratic decentralisation for the whole of Spain, in the form of greater autonomisation of the regions or even federalisation of the entire state, or a desire to achieve exclusive Catalan autonomy with special rights, in contrast to other parts of Spain, or even full state independence for Catalonia as part of the European Union. Another facet were cultural policy efforts to promote the Catalan language (*Català*) and culture, not just in Catalonia but also in the other "Catalan countries" (*Països Catalans*),[9] particularly in the Valencia region and on the Balearic islands. Extremely modest efforts towards the establishment of an overarching Catalan political nationalism[10] aiming at uniting all Catalan countries, can be ignored here, since they have gained only little traction within Catalonia, and almost none at all outside the region.

Overall, Catalan linguistic-cultural awareness and the Catalan national political efforts to attain some form of statehood (autonomy with differing degrees of competence, federative member state, confederative state in a close association of states, independent state within or outside the European Union),[11] referred to here collectively as Catalan nationalism,[12] presents a considerable challenge to Spanish nationalism, in other words, to the sense of national identity among the large majority of citizens of Spain that supports the Spanish state. However, to a certain extent, it also presents a challenge to the European Union, since the Catalan government approached the Union with a request to mediate with the central government in Madrid, and pro-European Catalans hope for support from Europe in their desire for freedom. Until now, however, the EU has been unable to develop a

---

[9]These include: the autonomous communities of Catalonia, Valencia and the Balearic Islands, as well as the corridors in the east of Aragonia, a small area in Murcia and the independent state of Andorra, "North Catalonia" in France (Roussillon, Cerdagne) and the town of Alghero on Sardinia. See: Marí i Mayans (2016).

[10]Thus, some authors talk of a nation of Catalan countries, Joan i Marí (2007, p. 77).

[11]For the phases of predominance of the one or other form of Catalan independence, see Puhle (2014).

[12]In contrast to the widespread understanding of nationalism as a potentially violent, aggressive, intolerant, xenophobic ideology and form of behaviour, which is more accurately termed "chauvinism", here, as is predominantly the case in nationalism research, nationalism is regarded as being the concept of the nation state, in other words, the will of a large group to maintain, restore or newly create shared statehood. In contrast to most literature on nationalism, nation statehood is understood as being not only an independent state, but also a federative state and an autonomous territorial or personal-corporate state form. For more detail, see three texts on nationalism in Jahn (2015b, pp. 1–53). In this way, the fluctuation of national movements between independentism, federalism and autonomism can be better understood. The oddities of common political language use in the western world include the fact that usually, only a people organised in the form of a state is termed "nation", the majority of whom do not regard themselves as being nationalistic, while a stateless ethnic group is not known or recognised as a nation, even though their nationalist political activists are accused of nationalism in the pejorative sense. Non-nations are accordingly nationalistic, while nations are non-nationalistic.

common nationalities policy in its dealings with demands made by national minorities in its member states, even though it already demonstrated early attempts to do so with regard to national minorities in the non-member states of Czechoslovakia and Yugoslavia, and later Bosnia-Herzegovina and Serbia.

The national whole and the linguistic-national parts are not as relatively clear in Spain, however, and cannot be clearly differentiated from each other, as is the case in Belgium, Canada or the United Kingdom, for example, where there is also tension between state nationalism and particular nationalism. In the latter three states, inner-state particularism has far clearer contours and structures than in Spain. Belgium and Canada are federations in which the linguistic-national parts of the overall state have strong positions that are anchored in the constitution; Great Britain officially consists of four nations within the overall British nation.

Even so, the linguistic unity of the multinational United Kingdom is far less contentious than that of Spain, which is officially monolingual, where even the name of the predominant language fluctuates between affiliation with a particular and an overall state identity, namely between Castilian (*castellano*) and Spanish (*espagñol*). For several reasons, the strongly centralist policy that unfolded over three- respectively five hundred years does not have the same power of language assimilation as the French or English language, so that alongside the dominant Castilian language, Catalan, Basque, Galician and several other regional languages[13] and dialects also play a considerable role.[14]

The escalation of the conflict between Madrid and Barcelona throws up several questions. What positions are taken by which political parties? What are the power relations between them? Why, unlike the many bloody conflicts surrounding the independence of Catalonia in the past and the numerous national disputes elsewhere, is there apparently no risk at present of an escalation in the fight for and against Catalan independence, and the outbreak of civil war? In particular, I will discuss what options are available for a peaceful regulation of, or even resolution to, this conflict.

12.2 The Dispute Surrounding the Legal and Political Concept of the Nation as the Intellectual Core of the Differences Between Spanish and Catalan Nationalism

Catalonia is one of the 17 regions of Spain officially known as autonomous communities (*Comunidades Autónomas*), with an area of 32,000 km^2 and a population of 7.6 (in 2017) in its four provinces. It therefore covers an area larger than

---

[13] In Catalonia, for example, the official language is also Aranese, alongside Catalan and Castilian. Aranese is a variant of Gascon and Occitan, and is spoken by just 5000 or so people in the Val d'Aran on the border with France.

[14] There is no unequivocal data about the regional languages spoken in Spain, since the differentiation between language, variant and dialect is disputed. Löchel (2017, p. 426) for example lists the following languages, aside from Spanish (Castellano): Catalan, Galician, Valencian, Basque, Aranese, Asturian, Berber, Aragonese, Portuguese, Arabic, Caló and Romani.

Belgium, and has a population far higher than that of Denmark. Spain has an area of 506,000 km² and a population of 47 million (in 2011). The area covered by Catalonia is therefore 6.3% of the total, although it is home to 15.9% of the population. The region contributes overproportionately to Spain's GDP, with 18.8%.[15]

The peaceful transition from the Franco dictatorship made it easier when drawing up the constitution for the new parliamentary democracy in 1978, with a monarch as head of state, to find a compromise between traditional state centralism and elements of autonomy for the regions.[16] Spain is thus both divided into the numerous provinces (now 52) formed along the lines of the French *départements* and in 17 autonomous communities, which were created on the basis of the historical power structures. With the bureaucratic-centralist administered provinces, the historical regional authorities of the kingdoms (reinos), with their corporative-parliamentary privileges, of which only residual elements remained in the Basque Country and in Navarra, were to be abolished. Catalonia was divided into four provinces.[17] Of the 17 regions, the "historical territories", the Basque Country, Navarra, Galicia and Catalonia, play a separate role, with their own legal traditions and languages.

The second parliamentary chamber, alongside the Congress of Deputies (*Congreso de los Diputados*), the Senate (Senado), only plays a subordinate role in the legislative process.[18] It also hardly represents the autonomous communities at all, since only a small number of senators (58 in 2016) are elected from the parliaments of the regions according to the parties' proportional representation, while most (208) are elected directly in the provinces. Accordingly, the regions are not involved in the legislative procedure of the state as a whole, as is the case in a federation, but merely have limited self-regulation and self-administration rights. These rights are not the same for all 17 regions, but were negotiated separately between the individual governments and parliaments of the regions and the central organ when the autonomy statutes were drafted. Thus, for example, the Basque Country, Navarra and Catalonia obtained more extensive rights than most regions with a population that spoke Castilian, such as those pertaining to the proportion of taxes determined and collected solely by the central state.

It was in the historically trained awareness of the potentially endangered entity of the Spanish state, which could be threatened by the nationalist movements of many Catalans and Basques,[19] and to a lesser degree also some Galicians, or by autonomous movements on the Canary Islands, the Balearic Islands and in Asturia and

---

[15]Paluzie i Hernández (2015, p. 195). In 2005, the figure was 19%, Bernecker et al. (2007, p. 223).

[16]Kraus (1996).

[17]The Catalans want to replace them with the seven bailiwicks (*veguerías*). While this is provided for in the Statute of Autonomy of 2006, it has not yet been implemented by a corresponding Spanish law. Also, the region has been divided into traditional districts (*comarques*) as before the Franco dictatorship, of which there are currently 42.

[18]Barrios (1999).

[19]For a comparison between the Catalan and Basque national movements under the influence of globalisation and Europeanisation, see Eser (2013).

12.2 The Dispute Surrounding the Legal and Political Concept of the Nation as... 231

Andalusia, that the political bearers of this state and of Spanish nationalism anchored their concept of the nation in the constitution of 29 December 1978. Accordingly, the "Spanish people", who ratified the constitution, and on whom, according to Art. 1, all state power rests, and the "Spanish nation", which is the subject of the Preamble, are identical. At the same time, the Preamble also mentions the "peoples of Spain", but not the "nation of Spain". Art. 2 states that: "The Constitution is based on the indissoluble unity of the Spanish Nation (*nación*), the common and indivisible homeland of all Spaniards; it recognizes and guarantees the right to self-government of the nationalities (*nacionalidades*) and regions of which it is composed and the solidarity among them all."[20] Here, the nation is not a collective of people, but a country, a territorial-legal entity. The same territorial concept is contained in the acknowledgement and guarantee of the right to autonomy for the nationalities and regions as components of the nation. Accordingly, the Catalans are also not a nationality, but the country of Catalonia is.

In the same way, in the language of Catalan nationalism, territorial and social terms get mixed up. Here, sometimes the country of Catalonia and sometimes the Catalan people is a nation. Accordingly, the nation of Spain lies outside Catalonia, and Catalans and Spanish are only legally unified by the Spanish state. While Catalans belong to the Spanish state, they are not Spanish. According to the radical pro-Catalan view, Spain is occupying Catalonia in contravention of the right to self-determination of the peoples or nations, and has degraded it to the level of a colony.

In addition, the Catalan nation as a collective can mean two things: first the entire population of Catalonia (with Spanish citizenship), and second, however, only the autochthonous, Catalan-speaking Catalans as opposed to the Castilian-speaking "Spanish" who have moved there. However, nationalism based on lineage plays only a minor role in Catalan society, which is traditionally open-minded as a result of intensive trade[21]; to a far greater extent, linguistic and cultural nationalism dominate alongside regional nationalism (all citizens of Catalonia are Catalans), which therefore also regards immigrants from southern Spain and newcomers from all other countries who have learned the Catalan language as being Catalans. Linguistic and cultural national identity is the core of the driving political factor of regional nationalism.[22] The protagonists of linguistic-cultural nationalism are the main proponents of inclusive territorial nationalism, which also includes people loyal to the country who speak Castilian or another language as their mother tongue.[23]

---

[20] Spanish constitution (1978).

[21] In the view of the former president of Catalonia, Artur Mas, 30–40% of the Catalan population are of Catalan origin, Mas i Gavarró (2015, p. 78).

[22] The study by Mose (2014) in the spirit of "critical geopolitics" overlooks the important differences between territorial and personal (linguistic-cultural) concepts of the nation.

[23] Catalan politicians emphasise that Catalonia is a multi-lingual and essential bi-lingual country, but do not say in detail which status the Castilian language would attain in an independent Catalonia, see e.g. Forcadell i Lluís (2015, pp. 34–35) and Mas i Gavarró (2015, pp. 88–89). A judge at the court of justice in Barcelona who was suspended for his involvement in drafting a Catalan constitution supports the idea of all citizens being able to continue using Spanish in all public institutions, although in his view, Catalan should be the only official language, Vidal i Marsal (2015, p. 165).

The efforts by many Catalans to gain recognition not just as a people but also as a nation, which does not necessarily imply recognition of an independent Catalan state, achieved a minor success in 2006 when at least in the preamble of the Statute of Autonomy of 18 June, which had to be accepted not just by the Catalan parliament, but also the parliament of Spain as a whole (as well as in a Catalan referendum), it is stated that "the parliament of Catalonia ... defines Catalonia as a nation".

By contrast, in the moderate Catalan mindset, Spain is considered to be a multinational, plural state. Accordingly, the Catalan nation is a part of the Spanish nation. The problem with this attitude, however, is that it has no separate name for Castilian-speaking Spain. A term such as "Great Castilia" would surely not be acceptable in the Castilian-speaking regions beyond the two autonomous communities of Castilia-Léon and Castilia-La Mancha.

12.3 Stricter Legalism and Status Quo, More Autonomy, Federalisation in Spain or an Independent Catalonia

The different ways in the word is used reflects the dispute surrounding Spanish and Catalan statehood, whereby here, statehood is understood as being all forms of state-territorial order, alongside that of an independent and a confederative state, and that of the federative member state and autonomous territory, as well as of the association of states and international organisation.[24]

In the dispute between the proponents of Spanish and Catalan nationalism, five main positions are taken. The first advocates the constitutional status quo and demands the strict observance of constitutional law and the constitutional prosecution of the leading representatives of the Catalan independence parties and organisations, as well as the suspension of the autonomous Catalan organs, as long as they do not abide by the Spanish constitution in its present form. Its supporters, particularly the ruling conservative "People's Party" with prime minister Rajoy,[25] also reject all dialogue with the advocates of Catalan independence. They were also opposed to the passing of the reformed Statute of Autonomy by Catalonia in 2006, which was only made possible due to the simultaneous socialist governments in Madrid and Barcelona. This "People's Party" has its roots in the political forces that supported the Franco dictatorship. The right-wing liberal opposition party, which was only founded

---

[24] More broadly, statehood can also be spoken of in a non-territorial, corporative sense, when groups of people take on state functions, such as in Belgium and in the political concepts of personal-cultural autonomy. However, despite the strong traditions of anarchism and social self-organisation, strangely enough, it appears that this form of statehood is not debated in Catalonia and Spain.

[25] In the last Spanish parliamentary elections in June 2016, the "People's Party" received 33.0% of the vote, and 137 parliamentary seats (of the 350 seats in the *Congreso de los Diputados*).

in 2006, the "Citizens—Party of the Citizenry" (*Ciutadans—Partit de la Ciutadania,* C's) is a Spanish-centralist party.[26]

The second position is represented by those who demand more autonomous competencies for all regions, particularly a higher proportion of tax income.[27] They wish to continue the process of ongoing decentralisation in Spain, which in recent decades has led several times to an extension of the autonomous competencies in bilateral and multilateral reforms of the legal order. This position is held in particular by the numerous regional parties in the Basque Country, Galicia, Andalusia, on the Canary Islands, etc. and until very recently also in Catalonia and is supported or tolerated at the central level primarily by the Spanish Socialist Worker's Party (*Partido Socialista Obrero Español,* PSOE). The regional parties currently hold 25 seats in the Spanish parliament. It appears that the party founded in the spring of 2014, "We can" (Podemos)[28] sympathises with this position. Podemos came out in support for the right by Catalonia to hold a referendum on independence, although the party itself favours the unity of Spain. However, it should be noted that the solidarity among the various autonomist parties is very limited, and that most regional-autonomist parties wish to negotiate special rights for their region with the central government in Madrid.

A third position is in practice only held in Catalonia. It is oriented solely to the reinforcement of the autonomy of Catalonia within Spain, and feels legitimised and privileged, compared to the Basque Country, Galicia and Andalusia, for example, due to the historical personal union in the past between the Kingdom of Aragon-Catalonia (under the Catalan ruling dynasty and with Catalan as the predominant language) and the Kingdom of Castilia, and on the other by the great importance of the Catalan language and culture. From this perspective, Spain is essentially a dual state. Radical variants of this position formerly demanded a transformation of Spain along the lines of the Austro-Hungarian Compromise of 1867 or the formation of an Iberian confederation between Spain, Catalonia and Portugal.

In Catalonia, the party alliance that existed until June 2015, *Convergència i Unió* (CiU), consisting of the *Convergència Democràtica de Catalunya* (CDC) and the Christian Democrat *Unió Democràtica de Catalunya* (UDC) under Jordi Pujol, ruled from 1980 to 2003.[29] It very cleverly pursued a strategy that gradually expanded the privileged Catalan autonomy by means of the traditional Catalan *pactismo,* the compromise negotiated with the Spanish holders of power. Thus, during the course of time, Catalonia received an ever-increasing proportion of the income tax raised in the region: first 15%, then 30%, and finally, 33%, as well as the entire property tax.

---

[26]It first participated in the regional elections of 2006 and in 2015 became the second-largest party in Catalonia. In December 2017, it received 25.4% of the vote and 36 parliamentary seats. It also participated in the Spanish elections of 2015 and 2016 as *Ciudadanos—Partido de la Ciudadanía* and most recently won 13.1% of the vote and 32 parliamentary seats.

[27]This position is often characterised by the derogatory phrase *café para todos* (coffee for all).

[28]In the Spanish parliamentary election of 2016, in an alliance with the Communist Party and other left-wing parties, it received 21.1% of the vote, and 71 parliamentary seats.

[29]See in detail Marí i Mayans (2007).

However, Catalonia must participate in the inter-regional financial compensation, which is considerably more extensive than the financial compensation between the federal states in Germany.[30]

These successes were facilitated by the fact that the CiU, with the mandates achieved through the Spanish parliamentary elections, was frequently able to be the party that tipped the balance when the government was formed in Madrid. The strategy of doggedly expanding Catalan autonomy was also pursued from 2003 to 2010 by a left-wing coalition of the Socialists (PSC), the Republican Left of Catalonia (*Esquerra Republicana de Catalunya*, ERC) and the "Initiative for Catalan Greens" (*Iniciativa per Catalunya Verds*, ICV) that emerged from the former Communist Party and the Green Party. In 2005, together with the CiU, it presented the draft of a new Statute of Autonomy, which described Catalonia as an independent nation, which was due extensive competencies. However, this draft was rejected by the Spanish People's Party PP and by parts of the PSOE in particular as being unconstitutional. Finally, the parliaments in Madrid and Barcelona, despite the opposition of the PP and ERC respectively, for whom the concessions made by Madrid appeared inadequate, agreed on the new autonomy statute for Catalonia of 18 June 2006, which replaced that of 1979 and which is still valid today. After a constitutional complaint was submitted by the PP, the constitutional court[31] declared several articles of the statute to be unconstitutional, and that others may only be interpreted in the spirit of the constitution. This extreme, centralist policy of the PP stimulated the desire for independence in Catalonia.[32] A core component of the success of the radical autonomist policy, alongside the better tax position of the region, lay in securing the use of the Catalan language, which had been entirely prohibited for decades under Franco.[33]

A fourth position demands a fundamental reform of the Spanish constitution in the sense of a transformation of the country to create a federation. This would require a fundamental change in the nature of the second parliamentary chamber, the Senate, to become a representative body for the regions. Within the Spanish socialist party, the PSOE,[34] which is currently in opposition, which maintains cooperation of varying intensity with its independent sister party in Catalonia (*Partit dels*

---

[30]Catalonia complains above all that the state investment by Madrid in the infrastructure of the region, which is important for economic prosperity, is disproportionately low, see Paluzie i Hernández (2015, pp. 189–190).

[31]For a critical discussion of the role of the constitutional court in Spain, see Bubrowski (2017).

[32]They are perceived as having provided the decisive impetus for the emergence of the independence movement by Mas i Gavarró (2015, pp. 67–68) and Casals i Couturier (2015, p. 125).

[33]Article 6 "(1) Catalonia's own language is Catalan. As such, Catalan is the language of normal and preferential use in Public Administration bodies and in the public media of Catalonia, and is also the language of normal use for teaching and learning in the education system. (2) Catalan is the official language of Catalonia, together with Castilian, the official language of the Spanish State. All persons have the right to use the two official languages and citizens of Catalonia have the right and the duty to know them..." Statute of Autonomy (2006).

[34]In June 2016, it won 22.7% of the vote and 85 parliamentary seats.

Socialistes de Catalunya, PSC), there is sympathy for this position, although it is hard to discern how strongly this position is represented in the party, which ruled in Spain from 1982 to 1996 and from 2004 to 2011 without really taking steps towards federalisation. While during the nineteenth century, there were those who advocated federalism, today, there is little support for the idea, either in the regions or at the central state level.

The fifth position is that of nation state independence, which was advocated in former decades, particularly in the Basque Country, in part also with terrorist means.[35] Since 2012, the demand for an independent state has increasingly been raised in Catalan politics at mass demonstrations.[36] This demand is advocated most clearly by the ERC and also by the new left-wing radical socialist-environment party, the "Popular Unity Candidacy" (*Candidatura d'Unitat Popular*, CUP). The latter even expressed its support for the independence of all Catalan countries (i.e. also the Balearic Islands and Valencia in particular).[37]

In 2010, the CiU, headed by Artur Mas from the CDC, again took over government business in Catalonia, and at the initiative of the "People's Party", following the rejection of important articles of the Statute of Autonomy by the constitutional court, shifted from a radical-autonomistic course to one of independence. On 8.4.2014, the Spanish Congress of Deputies rejected an application by Catalonia for a referendum on independence by 299 votes to 347. Mas was forced to bow to pressure from the left-wing radical CUP due to his austerity measures. In January 2016, he was succeeded by the journalist and mayor of Girona, Carles Puigdemont of the CDC[38]—in the interim, the CiU party alliance had disintegrated. On being sworn in on 12.1.2016, Puigdemont refrained from swearing allegiance to the Spanish constitution and the king, and instead pledged his loyalty to the Catalan people. On 7.10.2016, the Catalan parliament approved the referendum on independence mentioned above, which the constitutional court immediately declared to be illegal. It was not until a year later, on 8.10.2017, that a major demonstration was held in Barcelona in favour of the preservation of the unity of Spain, clearly reflecting the split in Catalan society.

Many advocates of an independent nation state in Catalonia are, like their counterparts in the Basque Country, Quebec, Flanders and Scotland, frequently willing to pragmatically accept radical-autonomist or federative reforms in the

---

[35] On terrorism in the Basque Country, see Waldmann (1989).

[36] On 11.9.2012, the Catalan national holiday, hundreds of thousands demonstrated in Barcelona for "a new state in Europe"; a year later, 1.6 million Catalans took part in a 400 km-long human chain to demand Catalan independence; and 1 year later again, 1.8 million demonstrated in Barcelona in support of this political goal. In an informal survey, many millions of Catalans voiced their support for independence. For detailed interviews with advocates of Catalan independence, see Schreiber (2015).

[37] In 2015, it received ten mandates, and four in 2016, thus securing the now secessionist majority in the regional parliament.

[38] The party broke up in July 2016 following corruption scandals, and reformed under the name the Catalan European Democratic Party (*Partit Demòcrata Europeu Català*, PDeCAT).

hope of building up power positions for full national independence in the later future. The national independence movements in Europe are all pro-European and wish to remain in the European Union and the Eurozone. The EU itself rejects fast-track membership of new nation states on principle,[39] although it remains silent on the retention of the euro and continued membership of the single market.[40]

12.4 Historical Reference Points for Catalan Independence

The advocates of a Catalan nation invoke a long history of independent Catalan statehood and Catalan efforts to attain independence after the Arab conquest, which with the aid of North African Berber tribes extended over almost the entire Iberian peninsula and parts of southern France during the eighth century.[41] After the Arabs and the Moors (Berbers who had been Islamised by the Arabs) had been pushed back to the Pyrenees in 759, the Christian reconquest (*reconquista*) of the Iberian peninsula began in the north from 795 onwards. This process was not completed until 1492 with the destruction of the Emirate of Granada.[42] In the north-east, the Carolingian county of Barcelona was first created, which in 1148 extended to the mouth of the Ebro river. In 1137, the rule of the counts of Barcelona was expanded through marriage to the Kingdom of Aragon; Catalan was the official language and Barcelona was the capital city. For the county of Barcelona, the term Principality of Catalonia (*Principat de Catalunya*) came into use at the start of the twelfth century. The economic centre of the kingdom were the coastal towns of Catalonia with their trade in a large network of trading sites through the Mediterranean region, where they competed with Genoa, Pisa and Venice. The Catalan bourgeois traders and the meetings of the estates of the nobility, the clergy and the city patricians limited the power of the king in Catalonia-Aragon, while in Castilia, the king was able to retain far more authority.

During the thirteenth century, Catalonia succeeded in expanding east- and southwards following the conquest of Valencia and the Balearic Islands, which led to the creation of the Catalan-speaking region as it is today, with its Valencian variety. In 1282, the king of Aragon became the king of Sicily (until 1713), in 1324 the king of Sardinia (until 1718) and in 1442, the king of Naples (until 1713). During the fourteenth century, Athens and central Greece also came under Catalan-Aragonese rule.

In a contract with the Kingdom of Castilia in 1244, Aragon was forced to leave the conquest of the south of the peninsula to the Kingdom of Castilia, while Portugal

---

[39] The question as to whether the Catalans could be excluded from the EU without infringing their EU citizens' rights is discussed by Fassbender (2017).

[40] In a future discussion of this issue, one argument that is likely to play a role is that already in the past, non-EU members (such as Montenegro) have adopted the euro as their currency.

[41] On the earlier history of Catalonia, see Matthée (1988, pp. 21–40), Bernecker et al. (2007), Collado Seidel (2007) and Stegmann (2018).

[42] See the map Reconquista.

already took control of the Algarve in 1251. The attempts to expand Catalan rule to the Occitan regions in southern France through to the Alps (the Catalan language is closely related to Occitan) failed in 1213. In 1639, Catalonia was forced to cede its territories north of the Pyrenees (North Catalonia, or Cerdagne and Roussillon) to France.

Through the marriage between Isabella I of Castilia and Ferdinand II of Aragon in 1469, a dynastic tie was created between the two kingdoms, which was broken again after the death of Isabella, before they were permanently united in 1516 under her grandson, the Habsburg Karl I (as the Holy Roman Emperor Karl V). His son, Philipp II, did not inherit Karl's entire empire, which was divided in 1556 between the Spanish and Austrian Habsburgs. The two Spanish halves of the Empire did however retain their traditional legal order for a long time afterwards, even though Philipp II and his successors called themselves the king of Spain and formally remained the kings of Castilia and Aragon.

Ferdinand II prohibited the Catalan port cities from trading with Latin America, granting the sole right to do so to the Andalusian ports in Seville, Cadiz and Huelva. The prohibition was not revoked until 1778, which had a beneficial effect on Catalonia's industrial development. After the Ottomans penetrated through to the Mediterranean region, the importance of trade in the Mediterranean declined in comparison with Atlantic trade, and with it, the degree of power held by Catalonia in Spain.

From 1640 to 1659, the lower Catalan nobility tried in vain to ally with France and to form a free republic under French protection. After the death of the childless great grandson of Philipp II, Karl II, Louis XIV of France succeeded in making his grandson King Philipp V of Spain during the War of the Spanish Succession of 1701–1714. However, most Catalans supported the pretender to the Habsburg throne, Archduke Karl, who later became emperor as Karl VI. After the conquest of Barcelona on 11 September 1714—the date was first commemorated in 1901, and has been a national holiday in Catalonia since 1980—the Spanish king dissolved the Catalan self-administration institutions, thus founding the centralised statehood of Spain. During the same year, he legitimised the Spanish Academy, which had been established the previous year, making it the Royal Spanish Academy, the purpose of which, among other things, was to standardise Castilian as the Spanish language.

After 1714, too, there were attempts to separate Catalonia from the main part of Spain. After the French Revolution, Catalonia briefly (1812–1814) became part of the Napoleonic Empire before returning to Spain. In the political conflicts and civil wars of nineteenth century Spain, many Catalans supported the arch-conservative, clerical, absolutist-monarchist forces that hoped to attain or restore their old regional rights in their battle against the liberal forces, which aimed to achieve a unitarian, centralist state. In the brief First Spanish Republic of 1873/74, the moderate liberals considered drafting a federal constitution for the first time, however. Five years previously, liberal representatives from the Catalan regions had joined forces to create the Tortosa Pact, in which they demanded a federative restructuring of Spain. In the decade that followed, drafts were made for the constitution of a Catalan state. With the emergence of the labour movement, the concept of Catalan independence was adopted by the left wing of the radical republicans, the socialists and anarchists, as was reflected for the first time in the brief uprising of Barcelona in 1909, while the middle classes tended to seek support from Madrid for a protectionist economic policy.

In the Second Spanish Republic, Catalonia briefly attained autonomy in 1931. The leading Catalan politicians attempted to found a Catalan state as a component of a Federative Spanish Republic. Anarchist organisations attained strong positions of power for a time, although after the victory of Francisco Franco in the Spanish Civil War (1936–1939), these powers were removed.[43] During this war, the Catalans held out for the longest in their resistance against Franco's troops, which fought for a conservative, clerical, fascist Spain against both "the Reds" (the Republicans) and "the separatists" (of Catalonia in particular).

12.5 Concepts of a Federalisation of Spain and of a European Unification and Separation Law

What Spanish, Catalan and European policies are advisable in order to peacefully regulate or even resolve the present conflict between the proponents of Spanish and Catalan nationalism? While the likelihood of an escalation in the Spanish-Catalan conflict to the level of civil war is very low, dragging out the dispute surrounding the declaration of independence by the Catalan parliament over months or even years threatens to do considerable damage to the economy of the region and to the country as a whole. A civil war is unlikely due to the traumatic memory of the war of 1936–1939 and of the Franco dictatorship. Catalonia's police force is not heavily armed, and Catalans are hardly represented at all among the officer corps. As a result, the region has no opportunity to put up a successful armed fight, and also has no powerful foreign backers on which it can rely.

The defenders of the Spanish nation state could present good political, social and cultural arguments in favour of a full acceptance of the Spanish state by a large majority of Catalans, Basques and all other regional populations, in other words, a maintenance or development of a sense of Spanish national identity. The granting of further autonomous competencies would also probably strengthen the Spanish state, since Catalan independence would then hold almost no promise of additional linguistic and cultural policy and economic gains. Madrid already has no need to fear a referendum on Catalonian independence. It could tolerate it, while at the same time making it clear that it will not automatically accept the result. The chances of a majority acceptance of the state of Spain in a referendum in Catalonia are not slim, since as a result of the electoral laws, the separatist parties received a majority of

---

[43] Bernecker (1978) and Brinkmann (2007).

delegate seats, but not of the vote. Opinion polls have also never shown a clear majority in favour of Catalonian independence.[44]

It would be helpful for a stabilisation of Spain if there were a change of political mindset in Madrid that abandons a centralist, unitarian, Castilian-dominated nation state and which builds on the plural elements of the constitution that are already in existence, which acknowledge the fact that Spain is a multi-lingual, multi-ethnic state. This would be made easier if the term "Spanish" were to be removed from the official vocabulary to denote the Castilian language, which is already not used by the entire population today. There is no Canadian, Belgian, Cypriot or Swiss language, and it follows that in a state with several languages that in principle have equal rights, there should be no privileged "Spanish". This includes the willingness to allow non-Castilian languages to take priority in different areas of society and in certain regions, which is negotiated under constitutional law. In this way, the concept of the nation could be released from its connection with independent statehood. Today, Canada no longer has any problem with the fact that for many of its citizens, there is a Quebec nation alongside the Canadian one, which can be represented by a National Assembly of Quebec. This does not mean that Anglo-Canadians have to regard themselves as an independent nation. The Castilian-Spanish or Castilophone Spanish (a term created by the author of this essay) would also not have to define themselves as a separate nation. Since there are states (territorial-state bodies) within states, there can certainly also be nations within nations. And the more the European Union develops as a citizens' union, and not just as a union of states, the more likely there will also be a European (Union) nation that consists of many individual nations.

In the longer term, Spain, like Canada, and above all like Belgium in recent decades, could gradually and cautiously transform into a federal state, in other words, drive forward federalisation and thus the self-reliance of the regions, as well as strengthen regional involvement in decision-making with regard to common nation state matters. Without federalisation, states such as Switzerland,[45] Canada[46] or Belgium[47] would hardly be able to survive, or would at least have had to give up their democratic character. In Spain, there have been several important advocates of federalisation since the early nineteenth century, but to date, they have not succeeded in asserting their demands. The consolidation of democracy in Spain since 1978 is likely to have reduced the traditional fear among the primarily Castilian holders of state authority, the church, and above all the military, of a dissolution of Spain as a result of granting limited, federative self-reliance to Catalonia, the Basque Country,

---

[44]In the autumn of 2011, according to a survey, 28.2% of the Catalan population supported independence, while 30.4% were for a federal state, and 30.3% were for retaining the status quo of autonomy. According to another survey in 2010, 48.1% of those questioned were in favour of independence (far more than 3 years previously), and 35.3% were against, Eser (2013, pp. 15–16).

[45]For a more detailed discussion, see Jahn (2008).

[46]For a more detailed discussion, see Jahn (2015c).

[47]For a more detailed discussion, see Jahn (2015a).

Navarra and other regions. Furthermore, the political role of the military as protectors of a Castilian concept of unity and the historical major power mission of Spain is also likely to have declined, so that a modernising, reformist Spain could gradually and carefully set out on the path to extended decentralisation and finally, federalisation.

In Catalonia, enthusiasm for federalisation has been very limited so far. Most Catalanists have assumed to date that due to its culture,[48] its social structure and its economic superiority, as well as its political past of statist pluralism in the Spanish dual kingdom of Castilia and Aragon-Catalonia, Catalonia deserves to be treated better than other regions. For this reason, it is likely that it will depend more on other regions, such as Andalusia, the Canary Islands, the Balearic Islands and Asturia, whether the regions will become member states of a federal state of Spain and whether the Senate will become a real, federative, second parliamentary chamber. Here, like Quebec, Catalonia could certainly retain certain privileges or gain new ones due to its special historical role and its own large linguistic culture. However, as a result of federalisation, Catalonia would obtain formal involvement in the decision-making process with regard to matters that pertain to Spain as a whole, which would go beyond the informal influence obtained through "pactism" in the Congress of Deputies.

Only when the inclusion of the majority of the population in marginal regions inclined to separation does not succeed should a peaceful separation be considered.[49] Examples of successful, peaceful, national separatism are the creation of Norway, Slovakia and Montenegro. The strong desire for independence in some regions in western democracies should be cause for a general legalisation of the partition or unification of states and federal states, and of state unions such as the EU. Such a partition or unification of states and state unions is a far more serious decision, with more far-reaching consequences, than the appointment of a new government or confirmation of an existing one through elections. For this reason, it should not depend on the decision with an absolute or relative majority in a referendum, since it is far too dependent on momentary political moods, which can change within a short space of time. There are a wide range of options worldwide for making democratic decisions dependent on qualified majorities and high-level participation in a referendum. For example, the EU made a majority of 55% of those eligible to vote in a

---

[48]The Catalan pro-national movement began in the nineteenth century, and like many other movements was initially a linguistic-cultural "rebirth" movement (*renaixença*) without political aspirations, and only became politicised as a national movement with autonomist, federative and indpendentist goals towards the end of the nineteenth century, first as a middle class, and then also as a workers' movement. Here, the loss of the colonies following the military defeat against the USA in 1898 played an important role, see Eser (2013, pp. 133–141).

[49]The rejection on principle of the secession of marginal areas from existing states as being undemocratic when the existing state people reject a secession is not convincing. The self-constitution of a population of an area as a demos and thus as a nation is in itself the fundamental prerequisite for democracy. To date, since the US-American secession from the British Empire, it has led to the secession of 32 states from others in Europe alone. Almost all states throughout the world have been created as a result of secession.

referendum on independence a condition for the separation of Montenegro from the Federal Republic of Yugoslavia.[50] The rule could also be introduced that a decision to divide or unify states may only become valid after a referendum is held 4 or 5 years later, with the same result.[51] Thus, it would certainly be better for the EU when decisions such as British accession and then exit from the EU would have to be made twice, with a qualified majority. It was not very convincing that just 51.9% of the vote on 23 June 2016 was sufficient to cause Britain to leave the EU.

12.6 Spanish and European Indecision in the Fatal Process of "Muddling Through"

The danger in the current political relationship between Spain and Europe is that there is no willingness to forge a well thought-through, common nationalities policy. The central government in Madrid, as long as it was led by the conservative People's Party and was strongly influenced by former Franquist elites, firmly held on to the inflexible, legalistic position of rigid implementation of the existing constitution, and was not willing to consider reforming the constitution in any way. After June 2018, there may be a greater chance of compromise under the new government of Pedro Sánchez with the social democratic party, the PSOE; however, to date, there has been almost no sign of such a development. Therefore, attention must turn to the new parties, Podemos and Ciudadanos/Ciutadans, which are supported by the younger generations, which are less in thrall to intellectual concepts of Spanish-Catalan history, and which are strongly influenced by cultural Europeanisation and globalisation. However, it appears that their ideas have hardly been analysed at all to date.

Currently, there is even less hope when it comes to European learning processes. Many EU member states have been repeatedly willing to tolerate national-separatist movements in post-communist countries, as long as they advocated liberal-

---

[50] A two-thirds majority is certainly too high a barrier, since in regions with a tendency towards separation, large numbers of people are always eligible to vote who come from other regions. For this reason, the requirements of a 55% threshold for national separation is more appropriate, since it still demands a 10% advantage over the political opponent. However, a 60% threshold would also be worth considering. In 2014, 44.7% voted in favour of independence in Scotland, with 49.4% in Quebec in 1995 (with an unclear referendum question), 55.5% in Montenegro in 2006, 74% in Latvia in 1991, 78% in Estonia in 1991, 88.2% in Slovenia in 1990, over 90% in Kosovo in 1991 (only among Kosovo Albanians), 90.5% in Lithuania in 1991, 92.3% in Ukraine in 1991, 94.7% in Croatia in 1991, over 95% in Georgia in 1991, 97.9% in Moldova in 1994, 99.5% in Armenia in 1991, and 99.8% in Azerbaijan in 1991.

[51] This would dramatically reduce dependency on a momentary political mood, and put the seriousness of the desire to separate to a further test. Without doubt, the disadvantage of holding a second referendum is that the uncertainty regarding the future of the overall state and the region wishing to separate brings significant disadvantages to the economic development of both spaces, and would demand that measures be taken against manipulation of the second referendum through targeted voter resettlement.

democratic tendencies as opposed to autocratic structures, particularly in the Soviet Union and Yugoslavia, and in their successor states. For example, they most recently supported the attainment of independence for Montenegro and Kosovo. However, at the same time, they are entirely restrictive with regard to national-emancipatory efforts in the established member states, regardless of whether these are left- or right-wing in socio-political terms. Accordingly, in each case, they support the governments that embody the political and constitutional status quo—in Britain with regard to the Northern Ireland and Scotland issue, in Belgium with respect to Flanders, and in France with regard to Corsica—and do almost nothing to facilitate feasible political and legal compromises. The same applies to the question of the Turks in Cyprus and the Kurds in the NATO member state of Turkey. In the European Parliament, critical voices can be heard, but these have no power to change the situation on the ground. Thus, the Catalonia conflict will continue for a long time to come.

References

Barrios H (1999) Das politische System Spaniens. In: Ismayr W (ed) Die politischen Systeme Westeuropas, 2nd edn. Leske + Budrich, Opladen, pp 563–603

Bernecker WL (1978) Anarchismus und Bürgerkrieg. Zur Geschichte der Sozialen Revolution in Spanien 1936–1939. Hoffmann und Campe, Hamburg

Bernecker WL, Eßer T, Kraus PA (2007) Eine kleine Geschichte Kataloniens. Suhrkamp, Frankfurt a. M

Brinkmann S (2007) Katalonien und der Spanische Bürgerkrieg. Geschichte und Erinnerung, Walter Frey, Berlin

Bubrowski H (2017) Autoritätsverlust. Katalonien nimmt das spanische Verfassungsgericht als verlängerten Arm der Regierung wahr, Frankfurter Allgemeine Zeitung 21 October, p 10

Casals i Couturier M (2015) Die Wirtschaftskultur. In: Schreiber (2015), pp 117–132

Collado Seidel C (2007) Kleine Geschichte Kataloniens. Beck, Munich

Eleccions katalanes (2017). https://cat.elpais.com/resultats/eleccions/2017/autonomiques/09/index.html

Eser P (2013) Fragmentierte Nation – globalisierte Region? Der baskische und katalanische Nationalismus im Kontext von Globalisierung und europäischer Integration. transcript, Bielefeld

Fassbender B (2017) Brüchige Fassade. In der Katalonien-Krise wird die EU ihrem Anspruch, eine, Union der Bürger' zu sein nicht gerecht, Frankfurter Allgemeine Zeitung 26 October

Forcadell i Lluís C (2015) Die Kraft der Zivilgesellschaft. In: Schreiber (2015), pp 21–41

Generalitat de Catalunya. Institut d'Esdadística de Catalunya (2015) Enquesta d'usos lingüístics de la poblaciò, https://www.idescat.cat/serveis/biblioteca/docs/cat/eulp2013.pdf

Jahn E (2008) The Swiss state-nation and self-willed nation: a model for the regulation of relations between ethnic and national groups in the East European States? In: Jahn E (ed) Nationalism in late and post-communist Europe, vol 3. pp 291–343

Jahn E (2015a) Federalisation: a first step towards the division of Belgium? In: Idem international politics. Political issues under debate, vol 1. Springer, Heidelberg, pp 75–89

Jahn E (2015b) World political challenges. Political issues under debate, vol 3. Springer, Heidelberg

Jahn E (2015c) Canada: has it passed the tests as a multicultural nation, or has the democratic secession of Quebec been postponed? In: Jahn E (2015b), pp 257–284

References

Joan i Marí B (2007) Eine europäische Perspektive für die Katalanischen Länder. In: Eßer T, Stegmann TD (eds) Kataloniens Rückkehr nach Europa 1976-2006. Geschichte, Politik, Kultur und Wirtschaft. LIT, Münster, pp 75–82

Kraus PA (1996) Nationalismus und Demokratie. Politik im spanischen Staat der Autonomen Gemeinschaften. Deutscher Universitätsverlag, Wiesbaden

Löchel C (2017) Der neue Fischer Weltalmanach 2018. Fischer, Frankfurt a. M

Marí i Mayans I (2007) Kataloniens Rückkehr auf die politische Bühne (1976-2006). In: Eßer, Stegmann (2007), pp 31–50

Marí i Mayans I (2016) Die Katalanischen Länder. Geschichte und Gegenwart einer europäischen Kultur, 2nd edn. transvia Walter Frey, Berlin

Mas i Gavarró A (2015) Die Politik im Dienst der Zukunft. In: Schreiber (2015), pp 61–93

Matthée U (1988) Katalanische Frage und spanische Autonomie. Schöningh, Paderborn

Mose J (2014) Katalonien zwischen Separatismus und Transnationalisierung. Zur Konstruktion und Dynamik raumbezogener Identitäten. LIT, Berlin

Paluzie i Hernández E (2015) Das Potenzial eines eigenständigen Kataloniens. In: Schreiber (2015), pp 185–202

Puhle HJ (2014) Trajectories and functions of Catalan nationalism since the 19th century. Studies on National Movements 2:1–27. http://snm.nise.eu/index.php/studies/article/view/0203a

Reconquista, https://de.wikipedia.org/wiki/Reconquista

Rößler HC (2017a) Erste Tränen in der Revolution des Lächelns, Frankfurter Allgemeine Zeitung 7 October, p 3

Rößler HC (2017b) Katalonien erklärt Unabhängigkeit, Frankfurter Allgemeine Zeitung 28 October, p 1

Schreiber K (2015) Die Übersetzung der Unabhängigkeit. Wie die Katalanen es erklären, wie wir es verstehen. Hille, Dresden

Spanish constitution (1978). http://www.senado.es/web/conocersenado/normas/constitucion/index.html?lang=en

Stabenow M (2017) Auch in Brüssel alles beim Alten. Die EU-Kommission bleibt dabei, dass der Katalonien-Konflikt eine innere spanische Angelegenheit ist, Frankfurter Allgemeine Zeitung 7 October, p 2

Statute of Autonomy of Catalonia approved on 19 July 2006 (2006). https://web.gencat.cat/en/generalitat/estatut/estatut2006/

Stegmann TD (2018) Geschichte Kataloniens und der Katalanischen Länder, https://www.uni-frankfurt.de/44860046/Texte_zu_Katalonien

Vidal i Marsal S (2015) Eine Verfassung der Bürger. In: Schreiber (2015), pp 151–174

Waldmann P (1989) Ethnischer Radikalismus. Ursachen und Folgen gewaltsamer Minderheitenkonflikte am Beispiel des Baskenlandes, Nordirlands und Quebecs. Westdeutscher Verlag, Opladen

13. Switzerland: A Model for the Regulation of Relations Between Ethnic and National Groups in Multilingual States?

Abstract

Over a long period, Switzerland has time and again been held up as a model when new states have been formed or existing ones reformed. However, there are other commentators who regard Switzerland as being a special case that cannot be emulated in the search for a solution to nationality conflicts in linguistically, ethnically or nationally heterogeneous states.

Switzerland is no multinational or polyethnic, but a multilingual, polyglott country, in which four autochthonous languages are recognised as national or state languages. The country has the advantage that three of its languages are highly regarded culture languages in its large neighbouring states, which make it considerably for it to access the global market. The language groups of differing sizes (63.6% German, 19.2% French, 7.6% Italian and 0.6% Rhaeto-Romance) are clearly divided territorially, and the language boundaries have remained almost unchanged for centuries. The language difference has never been seriously politicised by being organised along ethnic or national lines. For the state structures and for constitutional law, it plays only an extremely minor role. Switzerland is a multi-cantonal state (with 26 cantons) and not a multi-national federal state (with four national member states). While most cantons are monolingual, three major cantons are bilingual, and one is even tri-lingual. Within the cantons, highly developed municipal autonomy guarantees the predominance of one language respectively as the language used in schools, churches and by the official authorities. Communication between the language groups is enabled by the fact that the Swiss are conversant in two, sometimes three, and in rare cases also four national languages. However, English is increasingly playing a role in commercial interactions as the first foreign language.

The party system is not oriented to the language groups, but to the differing worldviews and social attitudes of the population. An informal concordance democracy has created a permanent coalition among the four largest parties that

---

Lecture given on 3.12.2018.

© Springer Nature Switzerland AG 2020
E. Jahn, *War and Compromise Between Nations and States*,
https://doi.org/10.1007/978-3-030-34131-2_13

has lasted for many decades, which guarantees proportional representation between the language groups, whereby minorities tend to receive preferential treatment rather than being disadvantaged.

Due to the high degree of politicisation and nationalisation of the language groups that began during the nineteenth century in most other states, it is not possible to emulate the Swiss way of organising peace between the linguistic groups. Large multi-ethnic states require a privileged language as the *lingua franca* for the state as a whole. However, elements of the linguistic peace in Switzerland can be adopted by a cooperative nationalities policy: the federalisation of historic areas and not of language territories, a high degree of municipal autonomy, and the recognition of all autochthonous languages as being equal.

13.1 Switzerland: Model for Multilingual and Polyethnic States or Special Case?

Over a long period, Switzerland has time and again been held up as a model when new states have been formed or existing ones reformed.[1] However, there are a number of quite different political and unpolitical, real or imaginary qualities of Switzerland that have been considered worthy of imitation. The Swiss political system has been seen, for example, as a prime example of a well-governed small rural and urban republic, of a directly elected and plebiscitary democratic order, of the formation of a federal state on the basis of a federation of states, of a peace order, of armed neutrality, of prosperity and social equilibrium, and, most of all, of a country that has "solved its nationality problems".[2] At the same time, however, Switzerland has always been seen as an exception among states, one that differs in fundamental ways from the normal run of monarchies, large states entangled in wars and alliances, societies torn apart by class struggle, representative democracies, and nation-states striving to attain linguistic and ethnic homogeneity. If Switzerland differs so fundamentally, it obviously cannot be imitated. On occasions, comparisons have been made in order to draw attention to Switzerland's "incomparability", i.e. to emphasise the fundamental differences between the language issue in Switzerland and the nationalities question in other countries.[3] How, then, can we

---

[1] For differentiated examinations of what the model is expected to provide, see Schieder (1992) and Schoch (1998).

[2] See the overview of standards of comparison provided in Schoch (1998, pp. 4–5). See also Havlin (2011).

[3] See Sobota (1927), and, on similar comments by Tomáš G. Masaryk and Edvard Beneš, Schieder (1992, pp. 317–324).

13.1 Switzerland: Model for Multilingual and Polyethnic States or Special Case?

best describe Switzerland and the ways in which it has dealt with questions of language and nationalities: model or special case, prime example or exception?

It is noticeable that there is usually something very sweeping about appeals that are made to the Swiss model as a kind of "paradise of the peoples", something to be contrasted with the numerous "prison houses of the peoples", as a prime example of a multilingual "state of many nationalities" or even a "multinational state", which is to be distinguished from the nation-state with its tendency to be monolingual. Rarely is any attempt made to describe in a precise way the actual conditions relating to ethno-demography, language policy, and constitutional law that prevail in Switzerland. In this way Switzerland has been, and still is, usually just held up as an abstract, mythical embodiment of peace between peoples, either for something to which an appeal is made when individual, smaller states like Bosnia-Herzegovina or Cyprus with linguistically, ethnically, or nationally more mixed populations are being founded or reformed, or as for the purposes of future programmes for the creation of federal states or state federations, as in the case of the "United States of Europe"[4] or even the "United Nations" of the entire world, or as.

After the First World War, for example, the founders of the Czechoslovakian Republic announced that their state would be the Switzerland of the East.[5] The Minister for National Minorities in Hungary, which became independent at the same time, also toyed with this term as a label for his country.[6] Before its disintegration along ethno-confessional lines in 1975, the Lebanon was often spoken of as the Switzerland of the Middle East.[7] A number of African states have claimed the title of "Switzerland of Africa", among them Rwanda before the 1994 ethnic massacres[8] and Eritrea after the country gained its independence.[9] After 1992, Kirgizstan liked to refer to itself as the Switzerland of Central Asia. This list of states laying claim to the status of potential Switzerland is certainly far from complete.[10] In many cases the states making this claim have pursued policies towards their linguistic minorities that are as far removed as can be imagined from Switzerland's.

For decades, some quite erroneous conceptions of conditions in Switzerland have become fixed in the minds of various people elsewhere in the world. One of these curious stereotypes is the belief that Switzerland is made up of cantons that are linguistically, ethnically, or even nationally relatively homogeneous. Western politicians referred to Switzerland as a model when they proposed dividing Cyprus into two national cantons and Bosnia-Herzegovina into ten (in the Vance-Owen Plan

---

[4]Cf. Ernst (1998) and Goetz (1996).
[5]For more details see Raschhofer (1938, pp. 100–, 372–). On Edvard Beneš's "promised Switzerland", see also Jaksch (1958, pp. 222–229) and Havlin (2011, pp. 91–182).
[6]Kann (1993, p. 457).
[7]Hanf (1990, p. 62).
[8]Herrmann (1994).
[9]Molt (1994).
[10]Schoch (1998, p. 5) also mentions Cameroon and Uruguay, though without placing these claims in a context explicitly related to nationalities policy. Havlin (2011, p. 63) also mentions Costa Rica.

of 28.10.1992). On 31 May 1994, the Bosnian-Croatian Federation was divided up into six and later eight national and two mixed cantons and the district of Sarajevo. In the case of Kosovo, it was also proposed in 1999 that a Serbian canton should be set up alongside one or more Albanian cantons.

13.2 "Swissification" as a Model or as a Risk for Ethnonational Policies

As long ago as the Paris Peace Conference, the German-Austrian delegation to those talks circulated a proposal to divide Czechoslovakia into nationally-based cantons. The Czechoslovakian government, making its last attempt to preserve the unity of the state in 1938, proposed reordering the country according to the same principle. Faced with the prospect that Germany would annex the German-speaking areas of Czechoslovakia, the government agreed to set up three or four nationally homogeneous German-speaking cantons.[11] It was also suggested on a number of occasions that the Swiss model should be applied in order to save the Habsburg monarchy from disintegration.[12] The Austrian monarchist lawyer Friedrich Tezner, however, took the view in 1905 that the idea of transforming the Habsburg monarchy into a "greater Switzerland", with a "cantonal organisation on a national basis", was a nightmare vision that would amount to the abdication of the centralist monarchy and the abandonment of the country's claim to be a great power.[13] For proponents of the most homogeneous nation state possible in linguistic national terms, "Swissification" is also a highly unpalatable political scenario.

It makes little sense to speak of Switzerland as a model, a state whose political order could be adopted by others. This applies to all states: states are very complex entities, and each of them has a history of its own that has been shaped in numerous specific ways. Strictly speaking, therefore, no state can serve as a model for others. However, it is true that particular political and legal institutions and constitutional provisions are often adopted by one state from another which does, in this sense, serve as a model. If we use the term "model" in this fairly strict sense and restrict its application to the constitutional sphere, there have been very few attempts to imitate Switzerland—at least, not in the field of nationalities law. There is a straightforward explanation for this: The secret of the peaceful co-existence of languages in Switzerland has very little to do with anything in the constitution that is explicitly concerned with "nationalities policy".

The reason for the absence of such constitutional provisions is that Switzerland did not have to regulate any nationality conflicts. As a result of favourable historical conditions, no such conflicts ever arose. Thus, the Swiss model may only be of

---

[11]Cf. Schieder (1992, pp. 316, 322–323).
[12]Advocates of the Swiss model were e.g. Julius Fröbel, Adolf Fischhof, József Eötvös and to a certain extent also Karl Renner, Havlin (2011, pp. 43–53).
[13]Tezner with a book from 1905 cited in Schieder (1992, p. 312).

instructive value in those multilingual regions, which have in the interim already become a rarity, where the original language awareness has not yet been politicised to become linguistic-ethnic national awareness.

The term "fundamental language consciousness" is used here to describe something that has probably existed throughout history, the speaker's awareness of a language or dialect that is shared with others, or distinguishes one from others, in one's immediate environment. This has to be distinguished from a modern, complex, consciousness of language, which is abstracted from the social and regional variations of a language as ethnic and then national movements come into being, and which gives rise to a consciousness of a wider community using a (written) language that can no longer be experienced directly. Only at the point where the notion of a larger linguistic-cultural, ethnic unit is associated with the idea of a political and political state unit does the transition from a linguistic-cultural-ethnic (linguistic-cultural) consciousness to an (ethno-) national one take place, and this type of consciousness is as a rule set in motion and disseminated by a societal movement.

The word "Switzerland" is a territorial and, in linguistic-ethnic terms, neutral term for the state. Although the word comes from the German-Swiss canton of the same name,[14] all Swiss citizens today treat it as a territorial term and its equivalent is accepted without any difficulty in the different languages in which the name of the state can be written (*Schweiz*, *Suisse*, *Svizzera*, *Svizra*, Switzerland). There are only a few other states to which this applies—Belgium, Cyprus, Canada, the United States of America. By contrast, in a very large number of states, the state name relates to a particular linguistic, ethnic or national group among the state citizens, and already confers on them an exclusive linguistic national or ethnonational character in symbolic terms, e.g. Poland, the Czech Republic, Slovakia, Turkey, France or Germany. In such countries, there is no doubt that the formation of a political nation forged by will from the legally constituted state nation is rendered more difficult by the fact that the state name evokes ethnic connotations and that indeed, is intended to do so according to the constitution.[15]

The Swiss themselves consider Switzerland to be a nation-state; it is not a nationalities state, nor is it a multinational state. All citizens of the state make up the Swiss nation. Accordingly, the Swiss people are represented in the National Council, and there is no council of nationalities or council of nations. Furthermore, the Swiss are not just a state-nation in the objective sense deriving from state law,

---

[14] In the fifteenth century, the name of the "most aggressive and democratic" member of the union was adopted and used from then on to refer to the whole confederation; see Im Hof (1991, p. 34).

[15] However, in some cases the ethnic connotation is weakened by, for example, the distinction made between Russians (in the ethnic sense) and citizens of the Russian Federation, and also between Latvians and citizens of Latvia. "Russia" does not therefore just mean the land of the Russians. In the past, some East European minority languages also employed different terms to distinguish between state citizenship and belonging to a people. In German it was possible to speak of the (ethnic) Magyars or alternatively of the Magyar, Slovakian, and German Hungarians, and also of the German and Czech Bohemians.

they are also a self-willed nation[16] in the subjective political sense, as it would probably be hard to find a single Swiss citizen who would want to see the country divided up into a number of different states, or to see the state as a whole or parts of it incorporated into other states. This can be contrasted with the cases of Cyprus, Spain, Belgium, or Canada, where there is little sense of complete congruence between the state-nation and the political self-willed nation. Many citizens of these states who are members of the state-nation consider that they belong to a different self-willed nation, and want a (independent or federal) state of their own. Switzerland can at least serve as an example which shows that it is in principle possible for a multilingual population to be united as one nation. The country also demonstrates that differences in the spoken language must not automatically lead to explosive language conflicts or even to the division of a nation or state along some kind of more or less clearly demarcated language border.

13.3 The Laborious Development of the Multi-lingual Nation State and Multi-cantonal Federal State

With an area of 41,290 square kilometres, Switzerland is smaller than Lower Saxony, while its population equals that of the German federal state at 8.1 million (in 2013).

The Swiss people, as the Swiss nation is often also called, consists of four language groups which are very unequal in size. Each of these groups speaks, as its mother tongue or the language it speaks best, one of the four (national) languages specified in the constitution[17] (German, French, Italian, and Rhaeto-Romanic or Romansh) or one of the dialects of these languages. There are also numerous smaller groups speaking languages that do not enjoy any special legal status. The primary criterion for the recognition of a language as one of the country's languages is that its speakers should have been settled in the country for a period of centuries. The numerical size of the respective groups and their size as a proportion of all Swiss citizens are not relevant. Another important element is the fact that even the two smaller language groups form majorities in a number of communes and in some regions (larger units made up of a number of communes). These groups are therefore not simply diaspora groups forming minorities in every locality. The territory of the Swiss state consists of three language areas that are clearly separated from one

---

[16] For the notions self-willed nation, state-nation and ethnic nation (or linguistic nation) see Jahn (2015, pp. 20–22).

[17] Article 116 of the Swiss constitution that was in force from 1938 to 1999 read: "German, French, Italian, and Romansh are Switzerland's national languages. German, French, and Italian are declared to be the official languages of the federation". In the new federal constitution from 18 April 1999, Article 4 reads: "The country's languages are German, French, Italian, and Romansh". It is noticeable that in the new constitution, the word "nation" and its derivatives appear only in phrases such as "National Council" or "national roads", and have been removed from the preamble and from the characterisation of the languages. The sovereign is referred to as "the Swiss people" or "the people".

another, each of which is inhabited by a linguistic majority. The important thing is that each regional majority is made up exclusively of local majorities, not just of a majority of local minorities. There are, however, many Swiss who live outside their "own" majority language area, in the linguistic diaspora. Neither the language areas nor the language groups have any political or legal status,[18] i.e. they do not have any state bodies of their own to represent them.

The four official Swiss language groups are not organised as such. But they are not called nations, nationalities, peoples, or ethnic groups (*Ethnien, ethnische Gruppen, Volksgruppen*). The reason why language groups in Switzerland are not referred to as ethnic groups is that this term is usually reserved for groups that are able to trace their historical descent back a long way, such as the Germanic Alemannians or the Raetians and Celts.[19] All expressions closely related to the idea of the nation refer to Switzerland and its citizens in their entirety, not to a linguistic or any other kind of smaller societal unit.

In Swiss society, the attribution of greater significance to the "language community" than to "ethnicity" means that the communicative aspects of human existence are prioritised over those related to kinship or to the community from which one is descended. If we want to find a more precise term reflecting Switzerland's own self-perception, however, we cannot call the country a multinational or a polyethnic, but only a multilingual state. In Switzerland, actual or supposed descent groups are considered to have only a very limited societal significance, because the territorial principle that dominates in questions of language assumes that Swiss citizens do not resist and are quite happy with linguistic assimilation.

In Switzerland, the terms "nation" and "national unity" are not charged with the significance that is attached to them in some other western nation-states where the dominant concept of the nation is also a state-based one. A Swiss citizen must not necessarily have a feeling of primary identification with the nation or with the Swiss people; this identification could also be with the people of a canton, i.e. of a constituent state.[20] The word "*Völkerschaft*" (people) as used in Switzerland also

---

[18] Under the influence of Italian fascism and German National Socialism, futile attempts were made to forge a political-legal entity out of the Francophone cantons, Reinhardt (2011, p. 429). At the same time, in 1938, Rhaeto-Romance was recognised as the Swiss national language, in defence against Mussolini's efforts to incorporate the Swiss territories to the south of the central Alpine range, Zala (2014, p. 503, 513).

[19] Ethnic groups are therefore not regarded as being linguistic-cultural units and the family relations of past generations that they usually imply in practice. An official study published by the Swiss Interior Ministry points out that some Germanic groups (the Langobardians, the Burgundians) have adopted Romance languages during the course of history, and some Celtic and Raetian or Romance groups have adopted the German language, Zustand und Zukunft (1989, p. 12). More in detail Morerod and Favrod (2014).

[20] Although Article 1 of the constitution in force up until 1999 spoke of the "united peoples' of the 23 cantons", the expression "people" (Völkerschaft) of a "canton", like "nation" (which appeared in the old preamble) disappeared from the new constitution. In the new Article 1 there is a curiously illogical formulation: "the Swiss people and the cantons" (not, as would make more sense here, the peoples of the cantons, E.J.) are said to form "the Swiss confederation".

lacks the ethnic-linguistic connotations; rather, it refers to the citizens of a constitutionally "sovereign canton" which, as in all federations that have come into existence via a process in which different states fuse together, has entrusted part of its sovereignty to the federal state. The sovereignty of the federation (Eidgenossenschaft) therefore derives from that of its members. Even today, cantonal awareness remains greater in many contexts than awareness of the overall state, so that the state of Switzerland is not divided into cantons, but instead, the cantons are overarched as separate states by a Swiss superstate.

Nor does Switzerland have a capital city. Bern is only the "federal city", and is also the capital city of Bern canton. This symbolic distinction has some very real practical consequences. Bern considers itself a German-speaking city and does very little to accommodate Swiss citizens whose mother tongue is anything other than German.[21] Strictly speaking, Switzerland also has no head of state. The seven-member Federal Council is the highest state body, and the duties of Federal President are performed by each of the Council's members in rotation, for a year at a time. It is customary for at least two members of the Federal Council to come from French-speaking Switzerland, and one member from the Italian-speaking areas is appointed at intervals.

The continuity of the state's, and of its constituent states', existence is the most important prerequisite of Switzerland's strong national consciousness and of the strong consciousness of cantonal unity. This makes it easier for the Swiss to identify both with their own canton and with the state as a whole.

With the exception of the short period in which Swiss territory was annexed by France between 1793 and 1813, the Swiss cantons and cantonal alliances have been independent since 1499 or 1648, ... after the independence of the Confederation of the original cantons had already emerged under the Holy Roman Empire since 1291.[22] Switzerland's territory has been reduced in size on a number of occasions, but there has been no change since 1815. The cantonal boundaries have also remained virtually unchanged since 1833, when Basel canton was divided in two.[23] The only exceptions here came when Jura canton was detached from Bern canton (in 1978) and a few minor adjustments of other boundaries were made. Even the Bern-Jura split had a historical basis.[24] The whole of the Jura had only been part of Bern canton since 1815, and it had been divided along confessional lines since the Reformation as a result of the different territorial alliance policies pursued by the North and the South since the fourteenth century. The eventual consequence of this in 1978 was that the Northern Jura became a separate canton and the Southern Jura remained part of Bern canton.

---

[21] See Zustand und Zukunft (1989, pp. 144–149).

[22] On the creation and development of the Swiss cantons since the thirteenth century, see Wiget (2012), Reinhardt (2011, pp. 31–447), Im Hof (1991, pp. S. 21–105), von Greyerz (1991, pp. 7–119), Luck (1986, pp. 53–342) and Maissen (2010). On the popular presentation of the creation of Switzerland see Schweizerisches Nationalmuseum (2011).

[23] See Im Hof (1991, p. 50, 75).

[24] See Aubert (1987, pp. 52–54) and Ruch (2001).

13.3 The Laborious Development of the Multi-lingual Nation State and Multi...

Switzerland is a federal state made up of 23 constituent states, the cantons. Usually, however, the number of cantons is put at 26[25]; as three former full cantons have each been divided into two half cantons which have only one seat each in the Council of States, the upper chamber of the Swiss parliament. The half cantons enjoy just as much sovereignty as the full cantons, and the half cantons are not associated with each other politically via any overarching cantonal institutions. The full cantons each have two seats in the Council of States, on the model of the US Senate. By comparison with the units making up other federations, Switzerland's constituent states are often very small. Their average size is 1588 square kilometres, and their average population is 264,000 Swiss citizens.[26]

As "sovereign" constituent states[27]; the Swiss cantons enjoy a high degree of self-government and self-administration, and the fields in which they have extensive powers include language policy, education, and culture, areas where the union—even in terms of its legal powers—can only intervene to a very limited extent by means of coordinating and regulatory measures.[28] It is therefore misleading to speak of a Swiss language policy, since language policy is largely in the hands of the cantons, which deal with it in a variety of ways.[29] Swiss school systems, for example, are very heterogeneous, and children start to learn foreign languages at different ages.[30]

Switzerland's constituent states are regional-historical rather than national-historical units, and most of them have a considerable historical pedigree. Switzerland itself as a state, however, is only 150 years old. A prehistory associated with various federations of states on Swiss territory is part of the national consciousness of all Swiss citizens. In 1991, therefore, it was possible to celebrate the 700th anniversary of the founding of the state. Seen in this light, Switzerland is a multiregional rather than a multinational federal state.

Of the 26 Swiss cantons, 22 are almost completely monolingual[31]—17 German-speaking, four French-speaking, and one Italian-speaking. Even so, this means that three large cantons are bilingual, with either a French-speaking majority and a

---

[25] See the striking change in the terminology used in Article 1 of the new constitution.

[26] The smallest canton, the city of Basel, has an area of only 37 square kilometres, and Appenzell-Innerrhoden, the smallest of those that are not simply urban areas, is only 137 square kilometres; this canton also has the smallest population, at 16,003 (in 2016).

[27] Article 3 of the Federal Swiss Constitution of 1999 reads: "The cantons are sovereign insofar as their sovereignty is not limited by the Federal Constitution; they exercise all rights that are not entrusted to the Union".

[28] Cantonal competencies include the school system, the courts, legal measures in force in the communes, taxation, and important elements of civil law. On the relationship between cantonal and federal powers, see Steiner (1971), Gruner (1977, pp. 55–67), Gabriel (1983, pp. 20–24), and Linder (1999, pp. 138–141).

[29] See for example on the canton Bern Werlen (2000).

[30] For more details on this see Gretler (1989).

[31] Sixteen monolingual cantons only adjoin other cantons where the same language is spoken, i.e. there are only six monolingual cantons where a different language is spoken on the other side of the cantonal boundary. Zustand und Zukunft (1989, p. 20).

German-speaking minority (Valais/Wallis, Fribourg/Freiburg) or vice versa (Bern/ Berne). The largest canton in terms of area (Graubünden/ Grischun/Grigioni) is trilingual (German/Romansh/Italian), although the language areas within this canton are clearly separated from one another. The Romansh-speakers therefore do not have a canton of their own, but have two larger islands and some smaller islands in Graubünden, which are separate from one another. In 2016, just under a quarter of the inhabitants of Switzerland lived in the country's four multilingual cantons, which make up almost half the state's territory (1,874,646 or 22.3% out of 8,417,730 inhabitants) living on 19,962 out of 41,285 square kilometres of territory.[32]

The territory of the Swiss state is made up of 2408 communes (2013). These communes enjoy a large degree of autonomy, although this varies to some extent in the different cantons. One of the country's language groups is in the absolute majority in almost every commune.[33] Swiss citizenship is not conferred by the state or the cantons. One becomes a Swiss citizen by being accepted as a member of a commune, and this then has to be confirmed by the canton.[34] In Graubünden, the citizens of a commune can decide to change the language used in schools or for official purposes, and they also decide which textbooks are to be used in schools.

The communal autonomy provides the legal basis for the territorial principle in matters to do with language, and so also for the stability and continuity of the language areas. It is this communal autonomy, rather than cantonal autonomy, that is chiefly responsible for the clear separation of one language area from another and for the stability of the language borders, many of which run through the middle of the cantons.

When the most recent census was carried out in 1990, 5,753,000 Swiss citizens were asked to provide information about their first or main language.[35] The answer they gave was: 73.4% German, 20.5% French, 4.1% Italian, 0.7% Romansh, and 1.3% other languages. In addition to the Swiss citizens themselves, there were a further 1.2 million foreigners living in the country in 1990 (18.1%),[36] and their inclusion makes a considerable difference to the figures. The figures for the various first or main languages are: 63.6% German, 19.2% French, 7.6% Italian, 0.6%

---

[32] Calculated from the figures given in Löchel (2017, p. 402).

[33] There are only three communes at the point where the German-, French-, and Italian-speaking areas meet, where the regional majority is in a local minority, and in the area that used to have a majority of Romansh-speakers there are a number of communes that have been extensively both germanized and italianized; see. In. Eidgenössisches Departement des Innern (1989, maps 1 and 17).

[34] Communal autonomy is much more pronounced in some cantonal constitutions than in others; for details, see Linder (1999, pp. 156–159). It contains, among other things, a provision to safeguard the existence of the commune, while at the same time allowing for associations of municipalities, as well as their own taxes and determination of the rate of taxation, whereby the communal taxes contribute to roughly one third of public expenditures. On the regulation on natuarlisation in the cantons, see Stadlin (1990, Table XX).

[35] The question asked was: "Which language do you think in and speak best?"

[36] Eidgenössische Volkszählung 1990 (1993, pp. 581, 583). In 2011 this amounted to 22.8% of the population, Bundesamt für Statistik (2013, p. 26).

Romansh, and 8.9% other languages.[37] Swiss policy on the naturalisation of foreigners is very restrictive, which means that no significant change in numerical relations between the language groups has come about as a result of very unequal rates of naturalisation of immigrants from the neighbouring countries or as a result of immigration of new language groups from more distant countries.

Within the Swiss population as a whole (citizens plus foreigners), the "non-national languages" Spanish, Portuguese, Serbian, Croatian, Turkish, and English are all more widely spoken as mother tongues than the "national language" Romansh.[38] The foreigners' language groups, like those of naturalised citizens, have, however—as in almost all countries of the world—a quite different status in respect of language policy from those of the long-established citizens. Even so, the language teaching programmes that six other states support for the benefit of their nationals resident in Switzerland are much more extensive than the "Local history and language" instruction supposedly provided in schools for the language groups from within Switzerland living outside their own language areas, which is almost nonexistent. This means, for example, that a Spanish, Portuguese, or Turkish couple living in Geneva (in French-speaking Switzerland) are more likely to be able to find a school where their children can be taught in their mother tongue than a German-speaking Swiss couple. There is therefore a debate in Switzerland about whether Swiss citizens living outside their own majority language areas should have the same language rights as foreign nationals. The current policy of giving foreigners more rights than Swiss citizens from other language areas is conditioned by a desire to ensure that the foreigners will be able to return to their countries of origin if and when there is a rise in unemployment in Switzerland.

13.4 The Non-nationalisation of the Language Groups as the Key to Language Tolerance

If we wanted to treat language groups in Switzerland as "language-national" groups, it would be more justified to speak of Switzerland as a nation-state with a German-Swiss titular nation and three national minorities. Up until 1798 and again between 1815 and 1848, albeit with certain important reservations, the language of the Confederation was exclusively German (after the practice of writing all official documents in Latin had been abandoned). There are nine out of a total of 22 East European states in which the titular nation accounts for less than 74% of the population. It makes much more sense, therefore, to compare Switzerland with hybrid ethno-national states than with the great polyethnic empires (Austria-Hungary, the Ottoman

---

[37]Bundesamt für Statistik (2000, p. 419). At the end of 2010 the corresponding share was 65.6% German, 22.8% French, 8.4% Italian, 4.5% English and 0.6% Romansh, Bundesamt für Statistik (2013, pp. 25–26).

[38]The Romansh-speakers enjoy particularly high esteem in some respects, and are seen as the original inhabitants of Switzerland, a group of people speaking a language that only exists in Switzerland and is given a special lustre by its association with the Roman Empire.

Empire, the Russian Empire) or with multinational states (the Soviet Union, India, the European Union as a potential federal state) in which there was or is no linguistic-ethnic majority, just numerous minorities.[39]

The difference between a polyethnic state and a country like Switzerland, where four languages are spoken, is that this does not require any special *lingua franca* because communication can be conducted flexibly enough in at least two of these languages. A country with dozens of language groups, on the other hand, cannot manage without a shared *lingua franca*. In this respect, Switzerland cannot serve as a model for the EU, Russia, and other state formations where there are numerous territorial languages.

It is only possible to understand Switzerland's complex linguistic diversity if one bears in mind that there are, in addition to the four official national languages, various dialects. The diversity and importance of these dialects varies from one language group to another. If one only learns the standard language, it follows by no means that one can also understand the related dialect—and vice versa. Frequently, either the standard language or the dialect must be learned in adult life, so to speak as a foreign language, and this is obviously difficult. Alongside the fact that there are four national languages, therefore, the situation is complicated by diglossia (the existence of a standard language alongside a very different dialect) within some of these language groups.

Until recently, Romansh only existed in the form of diverse dialects which had come into being in Alpine valleys that were very isolated from each other.[40] This fragmentation of the Romansh-speaking population makes it easier for them to be assimilated, above all by the German-speaking surrounding environment. For this reason, a standardised form of Romansh, Rumansch Grischun, developed by Heinrich Schmid, a professor of Romance languages from Zürich, was introduced in 1982.[41] However, schools and the media have been slow to adopt this standardised version. It may be that this late attempt to standardised the language has actually accelerated the pace at which the Romansh dialects have fallen victim to germanisation. In recent years, the Swiss authorities have done a lot to save Romansh. Romansh is the only exclusively Swiss language.[42]

In the German language group, the traditional practice is for the dialects to dominate the spoken language and for standard German to be used for writing.

---

[39]With these systematic considerations in mind it is necessary to make an analytic, and to some extent also a theoretical, distinction between research on polyethnic and multinational states and work on hybrid ethno-national states Jahn (2008, p. 59).

[40]Five of these dialects exist in written form—Sursilvan, Sutsilvan, Surmiran, Vallader, and Putèr (the last two are known collectively as Ladin).

[41]There were a number of unsuccessful earlier standardisation attempts in the second half of the nineteenth century and again in the 1960s (Leza Uffer's "Interromansh"); see Schläpfer (1982, pp. 284, 300).

[42]It is related only to a limited extent to the Dolomite Ladin and Friaulian languages spoken in Northern Italy. Its relationship to other Romance languages such as French and Italian is even more distant.

The dialects are known collectively as *Schweizerdeutsch* or *Schwyzerdütsch*. "93.3% of all German-speakers use dialect as their everyday language, and 66.4% even say that they do not speak standard German".[43] These (mainly South Alemannian) dialects are locally and regionally extremely diverse, though they are closely enough related for Swiss dialect speakers to be able to understand each other most of the time.[44] On the other hand, people who only speak standard German or a quite different German dialect find it almost impossible to understand *Schwyzerdütsch* without a good deal of practice. This fragmentation of the German language group in Switzerland is one of the main factors strengthening the local character of group consciousness and the spirit of cantonal identity.

In the last two to three decades, there has been an upsurge in the use of dialects throughout Western Europe, and *Schwyzerdütsch* has been part of this. The increase in the use of dialect has been particularly noticeable in the Swiss mass media. It is also possible that as the political distance between Switzerland and the political systems in Germany and Austria has diminished, and economic, social, and touristic interdependence has increased, the need to use dialect more as a way of emphasising their own separateness from the other German-speaking countries.

The increased use of dialect has significant consequences for the language situation in Switzerland.[45] Some Swiss are also concerned about a connection between the preferential treatment being given to dialects and a decline in competence in the standard language, which is vital if the Swiss are to have good prospects of economic and professional success in the German-speaking countries, and works to counter the country's cultural isolation from Germany and Austria. More importantly, the decline in the use of standard German makes communication within Switzerland more difficult. Many Italian- and French-speaking Swiss learn standard German but do not learn *Schwyzerdütsch*, which means that it is even more difficult for them to communicate in German-speaking parts of the country than it is for Germans and Austrians. The upsurge in the use of dialect in the electronic media also has a notable effect on the dialects themselves, which are filtered out and they become standardised, as this makes it easier for them to be understood everywhere.

In French-speaking Switzerland, the dialects (*patois*) have now become almost irrelevant. Ninty-eight per cent of French-speaking Swiss speak standard French. "Only 2.1% speak *patois*, and no more than 0.6% speak *patois* alone."[46] The French-speaking Swiss are also politically, culturally, and regionally self-confident enough

---

[43] Bundesamt für Statistik (2000, p. 418). See also Bundesamt für Statistik (2017).

[44] There are, however, considerable differences between the dialects, even within Bern canton: "It is said that there are German-speaking members of the cantonal parliament who, in order to gain a clearer understanding of what their colleagues from Häslital, Saanenland, or Grindewald are saying, are relieved to be able to rely on the simultaneous translation—into French!" Stadlin (1990, p. 235).

[45] Among the less important of these is the fact that a movement campaigning for the recognition of "*Schwyzertüütsch*" as the fifth national language has been launched. This movement is unlikely to achieve its goal, not least because of competition between different dialects in the struggle for recognition as a new Swiss written language. See Zustand und Zukunft (1989, p. 164).

[46] Bundesamt für Statistik (2000, p. 419).

not to feel any need to prove that their language and culture are different from those of France itself. The most important reason for this is probably the fact that French was standardised in the seventeenth and eighteenth centuries, and this process was at that time associated with a high level of social prestige. Although the French-speaking areas in the Swiss Confederation were subordinate and later relatively weak, they were able to compensate for this in part by using the opportunity to participate in France's language and culture, which at that time dominated Europe. The French Revolution advanced the standardised use of French by extending the norms observed by the elite, in both the spoken and written forms of the language, to the people as a whole.[47] Even today, it is easier for German-Swiss immigrants to assimilate in the French-speaking parts of the country than it is for French-speakers to assimilate in German-speaking Switzerland.

The Italian-speaking Swiss are located statistically somewhere between the two larger language groups. 82.5% of all Italian-speakers use the standard language, 17.4% use dialects, and only 5.4% speak nothing but a dialect.[48] At present standard Italian is establishing itself more strongly, because of the growing numbers of Italian "guest workers" in Switzerland.

One of Switzerland's distinguishing features is the fact that, in addition to the country's four languages, the main languages are also the cultural and national languages of three neighbouring great powers. This gives the country some unique advantages, but also some disadvantages. If the three main languages had, like Romansh, been relatively isolated languages such as Estonian, Albanian, or Basque, Swiss unity would not have developed such a cohesive force, nor would it have been exposed to the special threats it has faced from the neighbouring German, French, and Italian nationalisms.

Every Swiss citizen who learns one or other of the great national languages thereby gains access to the culture and the economic space of an enormous Swiss hinterland: Italy, France, Germany, and Austria, which provide them with a constant flow of cultural services which the endangered ethnic groups elsewhere in Europe can only dream of.

During the age of nationalism, Switzerland's linguistic affinity with Germany and Austria, France, and Italy gave rise to irredentist claims by the neighbouring great powers or by "nationalist" (expansionist) movements in these states.[49] During the French Revolution, "national" claims to Western Switzerland were made on the grounds of linguistic affinity. At the Congress of Vienna in 1815, the idea of assigning Switzerland, along with Liechtenstein and Luxemburg, to the German Confederation was considered and finally rejected. When Italy became united as a state in the 1860s, there were demands for the annexation of Ticino/Tessin and the

---

[47]See Schläpfer (1982, p. 180).

[48]Bundesamt für Statistik (2000, p. 419).

[49]The governments of the three neighbouring states have only supported or made irredentist claims to Swiss territory in certain periods—during and after the French Revolution, during the Fascist period in Italy, and during the Nazi period in Germany.

13.4 The Non-nationalisation of the Language Groups as the Key to...

valleys of Southern Graubünden.[50] In the 1930s and 1940s, Fascist Italy and Nazi Germany claimed parts or the whole of Swiss territory as they pursued their national-imperial foreign policies. However, there was no more than a lukewarm response to these claims on the part of separatist movements within Switzerland.[51] More noteworthy have been occasional inclinations within Switzerland to be influenced by social and political tendencies in whichever of the neighbouring states was most powerful at any given time, or to lean towards the foreign policy of the neighbouring state with which a particular part of Switzerland felt a linguistic and cultural affinity, especially during the First World War.[52] This resulted in a serious test of Switzerland's ability to withstand internal strains, and created what became known as the *"Röstigraben"* between French- and German-speaking Switzerland as a clear line of demarcation between different political cultures.

On the whole, however, Switzerland's neutrality and, to an even greater extent, the constitutional distance between the country's political system and those of the monarchical and dictatorial regimes in the vicinity over the past 200 years, have provided sufficient grounds, and also instruments, for Switzerland to be able to assert itself in the face of all the challenges arising from external irredentism and internal separatism. In this way Switzerland's shared national and state identity has remained more important than the cross-border language communities linking parts.

Switzerland is therefore unusual in that there is a close connection between a certain isolation of the state in respect of its own quadrilingualism and its simultaneous openness to the neighbouring linguistic-cultural spaces; these two idiosyncrasies exist in a relationship of productive tension.

There is one unique respect in which the situation in Switzerland differs from many other countries: The language groups live for the most part in areas that are almost completely self-contained. In Switzerland there are no larger regional and only very few local linguistic enclaves;[53] if one disregards the separation of Italian-speaking Bregaglia/Bergell and of Poschiavo/Puschlav from the rest of Graubünden and of Ticino; these areas, however, have borders with Italy itself and so are not really linguistic enclaves. There are only four Romansh-speaking areas, containing a total of 72 communes, which are genuine enclaves.

This clear spatial separation between the language areas should not be confused with separation between the language groups. There are larger or smaller linguistic

---

[50] Luck (1986, p. 396).

[51] See Wolf (1969) and Dreifuß (1971).

[52] See Im Hof (1991, p. 134).

[53] Of the 2973 communes in Switzerland, there were in 1980 only three German-speaking local enclaves in French-speaking areas and two in Ticino, plus one French-speaking commune in the German-speaking area. In total, then, there were (in addition to many Romansh-speaking communes) only six communes located outside a self-contained language area; see Eidgenössisches Departement des Innern (1989), explanatory notes to Map 1.

minorities in all the language areas,[54] but these minorities enjoy no specific minority rights apart from the right to use their language freely, and they are, in accordance with the established societal conventions, subject to a high level of expectation that they should assimilate in the next generation.

A further peculiarity of the situation in Switzerland is the fact that ever since the late medieval period, and even more so since the period of industrialisation, the boundaries between the language groups have been extremely stable.[55] Since the first census was conducted in 1860, there have been no dramatic changes on the map recording the language spoken by the majority of the population in different areas, nor have there been any major changes in the proportion of citizens belonging to the different language groups; the only changes reflect the decline in the numbers of Romansh-speakers.[56] Five factors account for this, each of them providing a further contrast between Switzerland and Eastern Europe. Firstly, there have been no systematic expulsions of members of other language groups, no mass murders, and no genocide, as in many other countries. Switzerland has not suffered a major war since the Napoleonic period, and the policy of neutrality that has been pursued for the past 200 years has made an important contribution to this.[57] It has therefore been impossible for any kind of hatred or mistrust between language-national groups to arise. Secondly, there is a political taboo forbidding any deliberate, politically motivated attempt to redraw the existing language borders.[58]

Thirdly, the absence of any significant gap in living standards between different groups within Switzerland has prevented any disproportionate growth in the size of any language group as a result of unequal birth-rates. Fourthly, industrialisation and urbanisation have only very rarely contributed to realignments of language borders and of the ratios of representation in towns and villages. Where this has happened, however, there have been heated language conflicts between the established inhabitants and the new arrivals, as happened for example in Fribourg/Freiburg and in Biene/Biel. It was possible to resolve the protracted language conflict in Northern Switzerland in 1978 by setting up a new canton, Jura, which was created by detaching part of Bern canton and transferring some communes from one canton to

---

[54]See for a breakdown of the statistics to the communal level Eidgenössisches Departement des Innern (1989), maps 2–6, and for changes in the makeup of the population between 1950 and 1989 see maps 7–11 (no page numbers). It can be seen from these statistics that there are at least a few German-Swiss living in all but six of the almost 3000 Swiss communes, and that there are French- and Italian-speaking Swiss citizens or foreigners living in the overwhelming majority of the communes.

[55]On the history of the Swiss language borders see Schläpfer (1982, pp. 54–61) and Zustand und Zukunft (1989, pp. 10–36).

[56]For the details see Zustand und Zukunft (1989, pp. 30–35). The proportion of the total population accounted for by the majority language group, i.e. the German-speakers, has declined slightly as the Italian-speakers have increased as a result of the increase in immigration from Italy. There was a slight increase in the proportion of German-speakers, as a proportion of citizens, until 1970.

[57]See Bonjour (1970–1978).

[58]The only exceptions being attempts to reromanise the areas where there was a Romansh-speaking majority until a few decades ago.

another after plebiscites had been conducted. This conflict never seriously threatened the integrity of the state, though politicians from the French-speaking areas have at intervals demanded that the Jura should become part of France.[59] The fifth factor tending to stabilise the language borders that should be mentioned is the fact that long stretches of these borders are not really dividing lines at all, "because extensive uninhabited areas consisting of Alpine peaks separate the German inhabitants of Saanetal from the French-speakers in Wallis, those living in Urn from the inhabitants of Ticino, and the population of Glarn from those living in the Bündner Oberland".[60] Given these geographical conditions, it is hardly possible for gradual realignments of the language borders to come about; the situation on the more densely populated plains is quite different. To sum up: We can see that Switzerland has remained unaffected by numerous developments that provided grounds for the politicisation of linguistic-ethnic difference elsewhere.

The stability of the language areas does not rest on Switzerland's cantonal order alone. In addition to cantonal self-government, the main factor is communal autonomy and self-government. This is responsible for the country's linguistic-territorial stability and for the fact that the language boundaries are more or less permanent—not just those between the cantons, but also those within the three bilingual or trilingual cantons. As a result, new arrivals from other language areas are under social pressure to assimilate by adopting the language spoken in their new place of residence.[61]

In practice, therefore, Switzerland is an association of three or four language territories; these language territories do not have any constitutional status of their own. No group is organised as an individual national unit—neither the citizens of a language territory, nor the cantons, nor the communes, which help to determine the shape of the language territories. The only organisations that can be said to have a language policy are private social associations which devote themselves to the well-being of a language and a language community.[62] However, these associations do not have anything like either the membership or the social and political significance that some language-political organisations have acquired elsewhere as driving forces within national movements, in struggles to form nations and to strengthen the position of particular languages.

The great religious cleavages and differences between Christianity and Islam, Latin Christianity and Orthodoxy, were of no importance in Switzerland. The country has, however, been affected by the confessional cleavages between Catholicism and Protestantism or secularism, which were the cause of a brief Swiss civil war as recently as 1847. Of greater significance for the Swiss language peace is the fact that the boundaries between the religious confessions bear no relation to the language boundaries, so the

---

[59]For more on the creation of Jura canton see Aubert (1987, pp. 51–85). On separatism in Jura canton see Ruch (2001).

[60]Schläpfer (1982, p. 54).

[61]See Tscharner (2000).

[62]See the list of these organisations in Switzerland, along with a characterisation of their political goals, in Eidgenössisches Departement des Innern (1989, pp. 106–108).

confessional and linguistic cleavages cannot mutually strengthen one another, as elsewhere. 43.3% of the Swiss are Roman Catholics, and 47.3% of them belong to the Protestant Reformed Church.[63] Both the German-speaking and the French-speaking Swiss are divided along confessional lines.[64] Jura, Valais/Wallis, and Fribourg/Freiburg cantons are predominantly Catholic, Vaudt (Waadt), Neuchatel (Neuenburg), and the francophone part of Bern are Protestant, and Geneva is biconfessional.[65]

13.5 Astute Language Policy as a Condition for Language Peace

Much more important than the structurally fairly constant elements already mentioned a deliberate policy aiming to promote language peace and the national unity of all Swiss citizens has to be taken into account. To describe Switzerland as a quadrilingual or polyglot country is not to say that all its citizens speak four languages. There are unlikely to be more than a few thousand who speak all four of the national languages fluently. Most Swiss citizens are only genuinely fluent in one of the four,[66] though many of them also speak a second or third national language either well or very well, or speak a non-national language such as English to the same standard.[67] The official study carried out by the Swiss Interior Ministry and mentioned earlier speaks, on the basis of the actual use of language across the

---

[63] Of the total population, 46.1% are Roman Catholics, 40% Protestants, 1% Orthodox, 2.2% Muslims, and 7.4% are members of no church Bundesamt für Statistik (2000, pp. 421–422). At the end of 2010, among permanent residents aged 15 and over, 38.6% were 38.6% Roman Catholics, 28% Protestants, 4.5% Muslims, 0.2% Jews and 20.1% members of no church, Bundesamt für Statistik (2013, p. 25).

[64] The ratio of Protestant to Roman Catholic German-Swiss is 57:43, and that of Protestant to Roman Catholic French-Swiss is 46:54. The Romansh-speakers are also divided along confessional lines, 32:68. The Italian speakers are almost exclusively—95%—Roman Catholic. These ratios are calculated on the basis of figures given in Eidgenössische Volkszählung 1990 (1997, Thematische Tabellen, p. 2).

[65] Eidgenössische Volkszählung (von 1990) (1993, Geographische Tabellen, p. 2).

[66] Responding to a question on this point, the following percentages of the language groups described themselves as monolingual: 65.4% of the German-speakers, 43.4% of the French-speakers, 27% of the Italian-speakers, 20.3% of the Romansh-speakers, and 2.1% of the English-speakers; see Bundesamt für Statistik (2000, p. 419). At the end of 2010, 83.9% of the population defined itself as being monolingual, Bundesamt für Statistik (2013, p. 25).

[67] In their answers to questions asked in the examination taken by all new recruits entering national service in 1984, no more than about one third of all young Swiss men of all social strata said they were reasonably competent in another national language in respect of understanding (understanding the spoken and written forms of the language), writing, and speaking it. Recruits from Ticino and Graubünden had above average competence in foreign languages. 29.4% of the German-speakers were fairly competent in French, and 25.5% of the French-speakers were fairly competent in German; the figures for their competence in English were similar. The Italian-speakers, on the other hand, were distinguished by their high level of competence in French (59.3%) and German (29.9%), though fewer of them (16.8%) spoke English. Of those who had grown up speaking a different mother tongue, the figures for those with a good or at least some level of competence in German, French, and Italian were 67.4%, 79.8%, and 36.8% respectively. See Eidgenössisches Departement des Innern (1989, pp. 20, 35, 36).

whole of the country, of a Switzerland that is somewhere between bi- and trilingual rather than quadrilingual.[68] This means that for the time being at least, many of the Swiss can communicate with each other in German and French, and some can do so in Italian as well.

In 1990, for the first time, a question was asked about each individual's colloquial language, that is to say the language or languages (it was possible to name more than one) "which a person speaks regularly in everyday life". The resident population of Switzerland responded as follows to this question: 72% spoke German in their everyday lives, 33% French, 14.5% Italian, 11.1% English, and 11.2% other languages.[69]

The commission of experts also, however, noted that there had been a significant shift in language use and in the prestige attached to different languages. "Consideration is now being given, all over Switzerland, to an idea that was until recently considered unpatriotic, namely the possibility that English could become Switzerland's preferred second language. The possibility that knowledge of German and French, as something present throughout Swiss society, could be diluted and give way to English may be a future vision, but there are already a number of indications that this vision could become reality".[70]

The commission considered that this tendency towards anglicisation would have serious political consequences: "This will lead inevitably to a weakening of Swiss national cohesion. The behaviour of the language areas would become even more strongly oriented than it already is towards the foreign country or countries speaking the same language. If we give up the use of our national languages as a priority in the teaching and learning of second and third languages, there will be no way of preventing the cultural *anschluss* of the different parts of the country with the neighbouring countries".[71]

This tendency to prefer English as a second language, in spite of all the efforts being made by the Swiss state and the education system to retain one of the other national languages as the second language, is a consequence of the profound economic, social, and everyday cultural integration of Switzerland with Europe and the world that has become a reality for Switzerland in recent years. Although communication between Swiss citizens with different mother tongues has in practice become increasingly anglicised, there is at present only a small minority who would be prepared to see English granted the status of an official fifth Swiss national language.[72]

---

[68]Zustand und Zukunft (1989, p. 299).

[69]Bundesamt für Statistik (2000, p. 418).

[70]Bundesamt für Statistik (2000, p. 301); see also pp. 259ff, where there is mention of the "dismal prospect that English could become the language the Swiss use to communicate with each other". Ebenda, S. 301, vgl. S. 259f, wo von der "düsteren Möglichkeit einer weitgehenden Dominanz des Englischen als Sprache der Schweizer untereinander" gesprochen wird. Indeed, English does not yet appear to play a key role in communication among the Swiss, at least according to Haas (2010, p. 41).

[71]Bundesamt für Statistik (2000, pp. 303–305).

[72]Dürmüller (1989, p. 9).

Switzerland tried for a long time to counter this threat to Swiss national unity by recognising only a second national language, rather than English, as the first foreign language to be taught in schools.[73] However, in 2000, the canton of Zurich was the first canton to introduce English as the first foreign language, which led to heated debates over the national cohesion of Switzerland, particularly in Suisse Romande. Special efforts, now backed up by constitutional provisions, are being made to promote the use of Switzerland's minority languages. In addition, the commission favours an intra-national exchange of young people and civil servants between the Swiss language areas. However, the experts were well aware that these measures would not be sufficient to bring to a halt the increase in the use of English or reverse the growing indifference to the other national languages.

Other authors have argued that there is no reason why the trend towards the use of English as Switzerland's *lingua franca* should be seen as a dangerous development.[74] Urs Dürmüller considers this development to be regrettable but irreversible. He also suggests that there is a positive side to the increasing use of anglicisms in the Swiss national languages, as it makes it easier rather than more difficult for the Swiss to communicate with each other using the national languages, since the creation of a linguistically pure and artificial national specialist vocabulary for use in connection with professional or leisure activities would inevitably be an obstacle to communication.[75]

Switzerland's quadrilingual or polyglot linguistic identity therefore does not really exist at the level of the individual.[76] Rather, it is an interpersonal or associated multilingualism, in other words a situation in which people who are monolingual in their respective mother tongues live alongside one another and need foreign languages in order to communicate. In Switzerland, there have so far been only a few modest attempts to set up schools where two languages enjoy equal status as languages of instruction and the second of them is not taught as a foreign language—so that, for example, physics is taught in one language and chemistry in the other. Those designing censuses would also have to give up the assumption that each individual can only speak one "mother tongue", i.e. one language which he or she considers to be his or her first language, the language they speak best.

---

[73]However, no corresponding provision was added to the language law of 2007, Späti (2015, p. 119).

[74]For example Schoch (1998, p. 53). On the fundamental problem, see Dröschel (2011).

[75]Eidgenössisches Departement des Innern (1989, p. 3).

[76]It is still the case that very few people are completely fluent in two or more languages; such individuals are almost always people whose parents come from different language groups or who moved at an early age from one language area to another. Children of bilingual parents frequently grow up as monoglots, so that there is almost no increase from one generation to the next in the number of bilingual individuals. One should not forget that there are numerous transitional stages between some degree of competence in a foreign language and bilingualism, extending from a limited capacity to understand the spoken and written forms of the language to a word-perfect ability to speak and write the language; on this point see Gretler (1989, pp. 35–36).

13.5 Astute Language Policy as a Condition for Language Peace

Language policy in Switzerland is frequently summed up as resting on two principles, the territorial principle and the principle of the free choice of language. After prolonged discussion, it was agreed that both of them should be stated in the new constitution. The free choice of language appears as Article 18 in the list of basic rights, and the territorial principle is laid down in the longer Article 70, in association with some provisions guaranteeing the special protection of the minority languages, in the section on education, research, and culture (the substance of which had already been agreed in a referendum in 1996). The provisions include: "(1) The official languages of the Union are German, French, and Italian. For purposes of communication with Romansh-speakers, Romansh is also an official language of the Union. (2) The cantons decide which languages they wish to use as official languages. In order to preserve harmony between the language communities, they take due note of the usual linguistic makeup of the area and show consideration for the traditional linguistic minorities".

The free choice of language use is accepted in everyday life, but the processes of language socialisation, as promoted by the state and society, and the state and private schools as well, are dominated by an utterly intolerant linguistic diktat that is widely observed: The territorial language and the principle of *cuius regio, eius lingua*, which requires the assimilation of the linguistic minority in accordance with the tradition of princely and later democratic territorial rule, are dominant.

In other words, no French-speaking individual or group is allowed to set up a French-speaking school in the German-Swiss language area, and vice versa. Children of French-speakers who go to school in Eastern Switzerland are taught exclusively in German, and they can only learn to read and write in French in foreign language classes or at home. The same principle applies in the other language areas.[77] Up until now the societal-territorial pressure to assimilate has been so great, and the level of migration between the different language areas so low, that over the course of the last 200 years there have only been a few very slight readjustments of the language boundaries within the country. Once again, the only exception has been the Romansh-speaking area, which has been considerably reduced in size.

If we leave this aside, Switzerland therefore consists of three monoglot language areas which have no political or administrative organisational unity but which are unified in practice. Within these areas, the majority is clearly privileged with regard to the language policy of the schools and of official bodies, and the minorities are equally clearly discriminated against. This situation rests on a far-reaching societal consensus accepted by both local and cantonal majorities and minorities. The three language areas which coexist with one another, and are governed and administered in language matters as they would be if they were more or less homogeneous ethnic

---

[77]There are only a few towns and rural communes in Switzerland where larger minorities have a chance of being taught in their mother tongue. There is no uniform legal provision specifying the minimum size such a minority would have to reach; the decision is more or less in the hands of the canton or commune.

nation-states. The German-Swiss, the majority in the state as a whole, enjoy no privileges in the cantonal and especially in the communal areas in which they are in the minority. Seen from the perspective of the prevailing conception of the nation-state, it is incomprehensible that a majority should have so few rights in "its own state".

Although an unusually high level of protection is guaranteed to linguistic minorities with a territorial majority in Switzerland, very little protection is given to linguistic groups that form minorities in territories within that state. Even so, because the majority principle is largely a local principle rather than a regional one applying to larger areas and because the linguistic minorities are concentrated in a few areas, Switzerland as a whole is regarded as a model for the protection of linguistic minorities in the whole of Europe and throughout the world.

The main secret of Switzerland's language peace is therefore to be found in the territorial principle, which rests on a societal consensus, is not laid down in law, and has a solid foundation in the high level of communal autonomy and the emphasis placed on cantonal sovereignty.[78] It is this communal autonomy, that is responsible for the fact that even in the bilingual and trilingual cantons, Switzerland's language peace goes largely unchallenged. The principle of free choice of language ensures that Swiss citizens will be able to move within the country and communicate in any national language to the extent that their interlocutor is competent to do so. This second principle also makes allowances wherever possible for whatever is customary in a given language territory. Languages enjoy quite different degrees of prestige in Switzerland. This leads to a complicated hierarchy and pecking order associated with Switzerland's code of linguistic behaviour, which involves standard languages and written languages, customary ways of speaking and writing, preferences for different types of written and spoken material, and the important role of the dialects.

The quantitative dominance of German over French is largely alleviated by the division of the German-speaking area into a number of clearly distinct dialect areas, while the French-speaking area has no such divisions and both the German-speakers' diglossia (simultaneous use of standard language and dialect) and general cultural-political traditions tend to render French more prestigious than standard German.

The lowlier status of Italian, on the other hand, is conditioned not only by the limited number of Italian native speakers among Swiss citizens and citizens who speak Italian as a foreign language, but also by the social status of the Italian-speakers who migrate to Switzerland or within Switzerland to find work, regardless of whether they are citizens of Switzerland or of Italy. Even so, one cannot speak of a clear ethno-social stratification of Swiss society, because the language groups live in accordance with a spatial-horizontal rather than a social-hierarchical division of

---

[78]"Federalism is therefore regarded as one of the fundamental reasons why identification processes tend to run along cantonal or even municipal lines, rather than on the basis of language boundaries", Späti (2015, p. 40).

labour, so that each language group more or less meets the requirements enabling it to be considered a complete society.[79]

In the long term the expectation of assimilation, which becomes central to the western understanding of the nation at the point where it goes beyond the purely legal and state-based concept of the nation, is likely to become more and more unrealistic for Switzerland as well, and this corresponds to a concept of the nation which is largely rooted in an agricultural society. This assumes that the rate of assimilation is more or less the same as the level of immigration, and that in most cases migration only happens once in an individual's lifetime and may sometimes take two or three generations. If assimilation takes place more rapidly than immigration, or at least proceeds at approximately the same speed, it can be guaranteed that the number of immigrants will not exceed the number of those who have assimilated and of emigrants over a long period, so that there is no prospect of any fundamental shifts or of a previous minority language becoming the majority language.

Although the language-territorial consequences of modern horizontal mobility are frequently rendered less dramatic when temporal limits are placed on migration, e.g. by repatriation measures or re-emigration, the new media and the anonymity of life in big cities also make it possible for people to retain long-term roots in their original language communities. The spread of English as the Swiss and European *lingua franca* also makes it easier for recent immigrants to avoid assimilation into the territorial language community of their new place of residence.[80]

The linguistic heterogeneity of some territories, which is often described disparagingly as a relic of the Middle Ages, is probably much more modern, in a different kind of way, than the expectation of linguistic assimilation and the corresponding political assimilation requirement of the western nation-state, which could at best be called early modern. In contemporary society, there is more reason to expect a linguistic mix in the population than the homogenisation of a given language territory. Thus, in Switzerland, too, an interest is emerging in the principle of personal-cultural autonomy propagated before 1914 by the Austromarxists, which is taken up by the catchword "non-territorial" or "corporative" federalism.[81] Gita Steiner-Khamsi has expressed this in a cautious manner: "Retaining one's own language outside one's own territory [i.e. one's country of origin, not the country of residence; E. J.], which is the rule among foreign language minorities, would appear to be a consideration worth taking seriously for domestic language communities as well in a period of increased mobility when more people are prepared to emigrate. What we should be discussing in the current debate about language policy is how, for example, French-speakers can retain their own language when they move to live in the German-speaking part of Switzerland, and how

---

[79] On this aspect of nationalism see the contribution by Hroch (2008).

[80] It appears that there has not yet been any detailed analysis of the available data on the shifts in the size of different language communities within the Swiss communes.

[81] Linder (1999, pp. 354–356).

German-Swiss can do the same when they move out of the German-speaking area".[82]

When we look at the question from this perspective, it could turn out that the language problems of regions in the world in which, different languages continue to be spoken alongside one another, will be a model rather than a nightmare vision for the future development of Switzerland and Europe. In other words, the "solutions" to the language problem found so far in the West, which involve the linguistic assimilation of minorities, will not after all be suitable.

13.6 Concordance Democracy as a Means to the Social Integration of a Linguistically Heterogeneous Society

Another important factor that should also be seen as an expression of Switzerland's language peace is the fact that the party system[83] is not organised along lines corresponding to the language groups. The same is true of the large business associations, the trade unions, the churches, and many other organisations. Switzerland's main parties, the Liberal Democratic Party, the Christian Democratic People's Party (which was originally a conservative Catholic party), the Social Democratic Party, and the Swiss People's Party (originally called the Peasant's, Traders', and Citizens' Party), as well as most of the smaller parties, draw their members and support from all the language groups.[84] Without a doubt, all the parties are very concerned to maintain a certain balance between the languages, alongside cantonal considerations, when making appointments to party posts. There is a tendency for the linguistic minorities to occupy a larger proportion of posts than the majority. Pure majority decisions are only rarely made. The party system is organised along lines that reflect secularist-clerical divisions (Liberal Democrats vs. Christian Democrats) or social divisions (peasants or bourgeoisie vs. workers), rather than language-based differences.

Swiss democracy can be described as concordance democracy,[85] a type that helps to promote peace between the language groups. However, the emergence of Swiss concordance democracy since 1891[86] has been the result of a perceived need for agreement, not between the language groups, but between (at first) the conservative-Catholic and secular-liberal parties in Swiss society and (later) between the bourgeois and social democratic parties. Between 1943 and 1953, and for the whole

---

[82]Steiner-Khamsi (1989, p. 91).

[83]For details see Steiner (1971), Gruner (1977) and Gabriel (1983, 1993). Daum, Pöhner and Teuwsen observe a lesser role among the parties Daum et al. (2014, pp. 27–35). Tsachevsky (2014, pp. 81–97).

[84]The only regional party is the Lega dei Ticinesi, which in 1995 had one MP in the 200-member National Council.

[85]See Steiner (1971, pp. 81–83) and Gabriel (1993, p. 82).

[86]See Im Hof (1991, p. 124).

period since 1959, Switzerland has been ruled by a grand coalition made up of the four largest parties. In the legislative period since 2015, these four large parties held 169 of the 200 seats in parliament.

There are also certain mechanisms in the Swiss political system which provide a counterweight limiting the danger of excessive ossification and corruption of Swiss democracy as a consequence of the fact that the same parties are permanently in office. One of these is the institutionalisation of opinion poll initiatives and referenda.[87] In addition, party discipline is fairly weak.[88]

Both this concordance democracy and Switzerland's language peace function with astonishingly little constitutional regulation, and indeed with very few legal regulations of any sort. They provide for a high degree of flexibility, so that decisions can be made either by a majority or according to the principles of consensus and proportionality. This presupposes a political culture that will, in case of doubt, prefer to make sure the rights of a minority are respected rather than to declare that the will of the majority represents the general will.

A conscious distinction is therefore made between a number of different areas of public life in which the territorial language is respected to different degrees, depending on what appears reasonable in the circumstances—the language of instruction in schools, the language used in church and in the courts, the language used within official bodies, the language used actively and passively by the authorities in their dealings with the citizens, written and spoken languages used for communication between state enterprises and large private businesses, and so on.

In formal terms, Article 107 of the 1874 Federal Constitution states that at least two of the federal judges must be French-speakers. In the new Federal Constitution dating from 1999, Article 188, Paragraph 4, reads as follows: "When appointing judges to the Federal Court, the Federal Assembly shall take into consideration the representation of the official languages". In Wallis canton, where the majority of the population are French-speakers, at least one of the five members of the State Council, i.e. the cantonal government, must come from the German-speaking area of Oberwallis.[89] Customary law requires, as has been mentioned, that Switzerland's seven-member government, the Federal Council, should include at least two representatives of the French-speaking cantons and frequently also one representative of the Italian-speaking canton Ticino. The administrations of the mixed-language communes and cantons also take care to ensure that there is either a

---

[87] Gabriel (1993, p. 154).

[88] It is quite possible for a cantonal party to oppose the policy of the federal party. In some circumstances a federal party can, as a consequence of the principle of the individual responsibility of the federal ministries (departments), attack a minister (a member of the Federal Council) who is a member of another governing party, and so indirectly attack the government of which it is a part. And finally, as the governing coalition is not committed to any joint government programme, there is scope for opposition within the government. Steiner (1971, pp. 82–85).

[89] Stadlin (1990, p. 433). The report published by the Interior Ministry's commission, which has already been mentioned, even proposed that in future there should always be a Romansh-speaker on the bench of the Federal Court.

proportional distribution of posts among the language groups or even an overrepresentation of the minority languages. Democracy in Switzerland is seen in a very limited sense in terms of rule by the majority.

Even though the Swiss are very reluctant to politicise or institutionalise the differences between their language groups, these are ever-present in the country's political consciousness and behaviour. Like the press and the publishing industry, these forms of communication are inseparable from the language groups. Switzerland has almost no institutions responsible for ensuring that the same political content is transmitted to society as a whole in the four national languages; this is only done for a few initiatives and decisions in the sphere of legal policy. This means that almost all public statements (speeches, political articles and books, journalistic contributions in the form of sound material or pictures, films) are addressed exclusively to their own language groups. In addition, television serves to provide the Swiss language groups with a substantial degree of access to the public spheres of the four large neighbouring countries. The broadcasting authorities are organised into three separate regional bodies serving the three large language areas, and the German-speaking organisation is responsible for broadcasting in Romansh. There is no centralised media policy which could ensure that all language groups were provided with access to the same kind of discussion of the same political themes, or even that the same topics would be raised at all. Given these conditions, it is extraordinary that a consensus still emerges on the central questions of Swiss politics. Presumably, this can be explained by a parallel rather than a coordinated homogeneity between the political cultures of the language groups. Another important prerequisite of the maintenance of a minimum political consensus between the language groups is without doubt the fact that some parts of the Swiss population, especially the elites, are able to use their knowledge of another national language to follow the development of public opinion in the other language areas, and also occasionally to intervene actively in the other areas.

The language groups demonstrate different forms of electoral and voting behaviour. The effects of these differences between the language groups are limited by the constitutional provision requiring a cantonal majority as well as a majority of all votes cast before constitutional laws can be passed. This means that it is very unusual for the minorities as whole to be outvoted by a German-Swiss majority. The fear of a dangerous widening of the country's internal "*Röstigraben*",[90] which is frequently referred to, has reappeared at regular intervals.

A new idea intended to strengthen the feeling of collective Swiss identity is the demand that bilingual people should be given some kind of special recognition. Further new ideas include higher salaries for bi- or trilingual civil servants, and intentionally intercultural education. It is also clear that Switzerland is beginning to relax the strict assimilation requirement and so to recognise that there is now much

---

[90]The fact that this "trench" was named after a Swiss way of cooking potatoes can be seen as an attempt to find a linguistically and emotionally milder way of referring to certain social and political confrontations that were in themselves very serious and heated.

greater mobility within the country. Moving to live in another language area can be a temporary move, and this makes the idea that assimilation is necessary for anyone who moves to live somewhere else for 2 or 5 years more and more pointless. It is particularly nonsensical that French- or Italian-speakers should be unable to find schools in the federal city, Bern, that will teach their children in their mother tongue, and should also be forbidden to set up such schools, simply because Bern is located in the German-speaking area.

13.7 Using the Multi-lingual and Multi-cantonal Swiss Structures Not as a Model to Be Emulated, But as an Impulse for Independent Nationalities Policies

The language area principle has had a pacifying effect on Switzerland over a period of many decades and even centuries, and it has prevented any linguistic-national or ethno-national mobilisation and drifting apart of the Swiss people. However, this principle is essentially the product of a peasant society which assumes that migration is both the exception and a step that will be taken only once in a lifetime. The modern economy and modern society, on the other hand, require frequent and, even more importantly, repeated moves from one place of residence to another, in other words a tendency towards neo-nomadism on the part of individuals and nuclear families. This differs radically from traditional collective tribal nomadism. The rate of migration will always be faster than any possible rate of assimilation. It is therefore likely that Switzerland too will have, step by step, to adopt an understanding of language groups based on the individual. In the terms the Swiss themselves use, this means that the liberal-individual principle of the free choice of language will become more important than the territorial principle with its homogenisation requirement.

The transition from the traditional-collective language area principle to the modern-individual principle of the free choice of language will in future cause more language problems, and probably also more intense language conflicts, than in the past. However, it will be possible to mitigate their effects by reaching compromises, for example more generous support for autochthonous languages than for those spoken by new arrivals, and ensuring that the territorial language is established as at least the second language, so that the multilingual principle as the general goal of the state will replace the principle of complete assimilation and monolingualism. The idea and assumption that each individual will be monolingual corresponds to the political principle of the linguistic nation-state, which will usually be homogeneous, a state formation which has the same goal in both its "western-French" and its "eastern-German" (Herder) form: a linguistically homogeneous nation-state.

Even though fully bi- and trilingual individuals will remain the exception for a long time, it is no longer unrealistic and utopian to think that every citizen in modern society could speak one or two foreign languages well or fluently. The first foreign language could be the one spoken in the immediate vicinity, the second the *lingua franca* of the larger region (in most cases English).

Switzerland has a level of multicultural tolerance that is quite exceptional and exemplary in the world and also in Western Europe. However, Switzerland in the twenty-first century will be a multilingual country in which language groups that arrived recently will probably still not have assimilated after three, four, or five generations and will demand the same language rights as the Romansh-speaking citizens. There may still be considerable differences in the long term between the legal status of the newly settled language groups and that of the old-established groups, but the difference will no longer be an absolute one. It will be necessary to find a range of formal—and perhaps more importantly—informal compromises.

The effect of the emphasis placed on communal and cantonal independence is that the expressions "linguistic majority" and "minority" become nothing more than quantitative-functional terms, and whether an individual person belongs to the majority or a minority depends on the spatial or other relevant context. No Swiss citizen, therefore, belongs to a majority in any intrinsic or valuating sense. As a Swiss (native) citizen, no-one is intrinsically a member of a majority or minority, which is connected with legal privileges or discrimination. Accordingly, no-one feels proud of belonging to a "state-carrying" majority or people, or to a titular nation.

There is also a political memory of the fact that there would be no multilingual Switzerland today if the inhabitants of Ticino and the French-speakers had not decided that their loyalties lay with Switzerland at what was probably the most crucial moment in Swiss history, at the time of the French Revolution and the beginning of the reordering of Europe in 1792–1815 into states based on linguistic-national principles. The German-Swiss would not have been able to force Southern and Western Switzerland to remain within a confederation developing towards a federal state if they had not wished to do so.

The Swiss case is only instructive for other countries in instances where what is at stake is how to deal with territorial language, ethnic, or national minorities within the state as a whole. Switzerland can provide no assistance where minorities within subdivisions of the state are concerned, since in this respect Swiss language policy too leaves a lot to be desired. Advocates of the personal-cultural approach to nationalities policy, especially in Austria-Hungary and later in Estonia as well, have made much more interesting suggestions as to how this problem could be dealt with than can be found in Switzerland's prevailing thinking.[91]

In all cases in which linguistic difference is already politicised, i.e. nationalised, what is needed is a nationalities policy (not just a language policy). It might be possible for a policy striving to depoliticise and denationalise linguistic and ethnic difference, the goal of which was to transform (ethno-) nations and nationalities within a state into mere language groups, to seek to reproduce the situation in Switzerland in the very long term, but it would be fruitless to try and institutionalise these conditions directly.

---

[91] See Hanf (1991).

13.8 The Persistence of the Linguistic-Ethnic Assimilatory Nation State Versus Proposals for Decentralisation and Federalisation

One way in which specific large groups could be adequately taken into account in future will be the organisation of states as federations or states containing autonomous areas. After the historical experience of the dissolution of the communist federations federalism is fundamentally discredited for some time to come. Originally, federalism was a way of overcoming political fragmentation into small states to form a larger one (USA, Switzerland, Germany) while retaining part of the individual entities' statehood and sovereignty. The multinational communist states in Eastern Europe were also set up with this unifying aim in mind. In 1991–1993, however, this form of federalism in Eastern Europe proved to be a starting-point for dividing states up along the borders of the federal subjects. Suddenly it lost its value as a peace strategy, in this case as a strategy for peacemaking in nationalities policy, for a long time to come. One could, on the basis of this East European experience, conclude that a federation should be organised as far as possible on lines that are multiregional rather than multinational, and that a federation should consist of as many smaller spatial units as possible (26 in Switzerland rather than only four, which would correspond to the number of language areas). However, it is unlikely that either of these strategies would be able in the long term to meet the objection that federalism can be used as a lever to split the state.[92] In addition to federalism communal autonomy rests of the most effective instruments that could be used to defuse nationality conflicts and at the same time to educate society in the rules of democratic politics and civil citizenship.

It is also be politically possible to recognise the languages of the smaller peoples in the constitution, alongside the titular nation's language, in a way that is clearly stated, mentions them by name, and gives them an equal constitutional status—even though it will for the time being be very difficult to get this generally accepted.

Multilingualism in the population, in the sense of speaking a national language other than one's own mother tongue Multilingualism in the population, in the sense of speaking a national language other than one's own mother tongue, remains a useful means for integrating states with two or three language groups. In state formations with numerous language groups, like Russia or the European Union, a *lingua franca* is indispensable.

A "de-ethno-nationalisation" of the party system can only be the result of a long process of depoliticisation of linguistic-ethnic differences, cannot be the starting-point by force for the integration of a state and a society. In the long term, it is quite possible that this will help to consolidate democracy. If parties, which are in fact ethno-national but whose names do not reveal this, show that they can work

---

[92] In the West European debate on the future of the European Union, on the other hand, federalism is still seen—especially in the UK—as a dubious instrument whose purpose is to create an unwanted concentration of state power and centralized statehood.

constructively over a long period in forming administrations, they could also in time gain voters and eventually also members from other ethnic groups.

The creation of a shared political public sphere made up of different language groups is one of the most difficult problems that have to be addressed if multilingual democracies are to develop. The attempt to democratise the European Union, in other words, to develop a European, multilingual, multinational *demos* from the peoples of Europe, which is able to make decisions regarding common European problems by means of a dual-chamber European parliament and a European government, is faced with the same problem.

Tolerance between the language groups, ethnic groups, or ethno-nations of a state is a precondition of many of the measures contributing to greater state stability and to improved democracy, and it is also the long-term result of such measures. Tolerance can therefore only be propagated as the goal of a modern multilingual state; it cannot be enforced by political decree, and can only to a very limited extent be guaranteed through legislation. Although Switzerland can in no sense serve as a model for a successful nationalities policy in other states, a careful and differentiated comparative examination of Switzerland's language peace can help us to develop a better understanding of the prospects, difficulties, and limitations of a nationalities policy whose goal is peaceful and democratic coexistence between a number of nations/nationalities/ethnic or language groups within one state or one confederation.

References

Aubert JF (1987) So funktioniert die Schweiz, 5th edn. Cosmos, Bern
Bonjour E (1970–1978) Geschichte der schweizerischen Neutralität. Vier Jahrhunderte eidgenössischer Außenpolitik, vol 9, various edn. Helbing & Lichtenhahn, Basel
Bundesamt für Statistik (ed) (2000) Statistisches Jahrbuch der Schweiz 2000. Verlag NZZ, Zurich
Bundesamt für Statistik (ed) (2013) Statistisches Jahrbuch der Schweiz 2013. Verlag NZZ, Zurich
Bundesamt für Statistik (ed) (2017) Schweizerdeutsch und Hochdeutsch in der Schweiz. Statistik der Schweiz, Neuchâtel
Daum M, Pöhner R, Teuwsen P (2014) Wer regiert die Schweiz? Ein Blick hinter die Kulissen der Macht. Verlag Hier und Jetzt, Baden
Dreifuß E (1971) Die Schweiz und das Dritte Reich. Vier deutschschweizerische Zeitungen im Zeitalter des Faschismus 1933–1939. Frauenfeld, Stuttgart
Dröschel Y (2011) Lingua Franca English. The role of simplification and transfer. Peter Lang, Bern et al.
Dürmüller U (1989) Englisch in der Schweiz. In: Eidgenössisches Departement des Innern (1989), pp 1–14
Eidgenössische Volkszählung 1990 (1993) Sprachen und Konfessionen. Bundesamt für Statistik, Bern
Eidgenössische Volkszählung 1990 (1997) Die Sprachenlandschaft. Bundesamt für Statistik, Bern
Eidgenössisches Departement des Innern (ed) (1989) Materialienband zum Schlussbericht der Arbeitsgruppe zur Revision von Artikel 116 der Bundesverfassung, Bern
Ernst A (1998) Wie die Schweiz, so Europa? Vielsprachigkeit, Öffentlichkeit und politische Integration, Neue Zürcher Zeitung 5, December
Gabriel JM (1983) Wie die Schweiz regiert wird, 4th edn. Schweizer Spiegel-Verlag, Zurich
Gabriel JM (1993) Das politische System der Schweiz: eine Staatsbürgerkunde, 4th edn. Haupt, Bern

References

Goetz H (1996) Der Schweizerische Bundesstaat als Vorbild für Europa und die Welt? Eine historisch-politische Betrachtung zum Friedensproblem. Haag & Herchen, Frankfurt

Gretler A (1989) Das schweizerische Bildungswesen unter dem Blickwinkel der Sprachproblematik – Sprachunterricht in der Schweiz. In: Eidgenössisches Departement des Innern (1989), pp 15–44

Gruner E (1977) Die Parteien der Schweiz, 2nd edn. Francke, Bern

Haas W (ed) (2010) Do you speak Swiss? Sprachenvielfalt und Sprachenkompetenz in der Schweiz. Verlag Neue Zürcher Zeitung, Zurich

Hanf T (1990) Koexistenz im Krieg. Libanon, Staatszerfall und Entstehen einer Nation. Nomos, Baden-Baden

Hanf T (1991) Konfliktminderung durch Kulturautonomie. Karl Renners Beitrag zur Frage der Konfliktregelung in multiethnischen Staaten. In: Fröschel E, Mesner M, Ra'anan U (eds) Staat und Nation in multiethnischen Gesellschaften. Passagen, Vienna, pp 61–90

Havlin M (2011) Die Rede von der Schweiz. Ein medial-politischer Nationalitätendiskurs in der Tschechoslowakei 1918–1938. Peter Lang, Frankfurt a.M.

Herrmann B (1994) Eine afrikanische Schweiz? Eritrea nach dem Ende des dreißigjährigen Krieges, Frankfurter Rundschau 5, February

Im Hof U (1991) Geschichte der Schweiz, 5th edn. Frankfurt a.M.

Jahn E (2008) The Swiss state-nation and self-willed nation: a model for the regulation of relations between ethnic and national groups in the East European states? In: Jahn E (ed) Nationalism in late and post-communist Europe, vol 3. Nationalism in National Territorial Units, Nomos, Baden-Baden, pp 291–343

Jahn E (2015) Democracy and nationalism: twin children of the sovereignty of the people. In: Jahn E (ed) World political challenges. Political issues under debate, vol 3. Nomos, Baden-Baden, pp 19–35

Jaksch W (1958) Europas Weg nach Potsdam. Schuld und Schicksal im Donauraum. DTV, Stuttgart

Kann R (1993) Geschichte des Habsburger Reiches 1526 bis 1918. Böhlau, Vienna

Kreis G (ed) (2014) Die Geschichte der Schweiz. Schwabe, Basel

Linder W (1999) Schweizerische Demokratie. Institutionen – Prozesse – Perspektiven. (4th edn. 2017 with Müller J) Haupt, Bern

Löchel C (ed) (2017) Der neue Fischer Weltalmanach 2018. Zahlen, Daten, Fakten. Fischer, Frankfurt a.M.

Luck JM (1986) A history of Switzerland. The first 100,000 years: before the beginnings to the days of the present. Sposs, Palo Alto, CA

Maissen T (2010) Geschichte der Schweiz. hier + jetzt, Baden

Miroslav H (2008) The historical condition of 'nationalism' in Central and East European countries. In: Jahn E (ed) Nationalism in late and post-communist Europe, vol 3. Nationalism in National Territorial Units, Nomos, Baden-Baden, pp 97–109

Molt P (1994) Ein Produkt der Kolonialherrschaft. Wie es in der einstigen "Schweiz Afrikas" zum Bürgerkrieg gekommen ist, Frankfurter Rundschau, 20 January

Morerod JD, Favrod J (2014) Entstehung eines sozialen Raumes (5–13. Jahrhundert). In: Kreis (2014), pp 81–92

Raschhofer H (ed) (1938) Die tschechoslowakischen Denkschriften für die Friedenskonferenz von Paris 1919/1920. Heymann, Berlin

Reinhardt V (2011) Die Geschichte der Schweiz. Von den Anfängen bis heute. Beck, Munich

Ruch C (2001) Struktur und Strukturwandel des jurassischen Separatismus zwischen 1974 und 1994. Haupt, Bern

Schieder T (1992) Die Schweiz als Modell der Nationalitätenpolitik. In: Schieder T Nationalismus und Nationalstaat. Studien zum nationalen Problem im modernen Europa, (first published 1958), 2nd edn. Vandenhoeck & Ruprecht, Göttingen, pp 303–328

Schläpfer R (ed) (1982) Die viersprachige Schweiz. Benziger, Zurich, Cologne

Schoch B (1998) Die Schweiz – ein Modell zur Lösung von Nationalitätenkonflikten? HSFK-Report, No. 2

Schweizerisches Nationalmuseum (ed) (2011) Entstehung Schweiz. Unterwegs vom 12. ins 14. Jahrhundert. hier + jetzt, Baden

Sobota E (1927) Die Schweiz und die tschechoslowakische Republik. Orbis, Prague

Späti C (2015) Sprache als Politikum. Ein Vergleich der Schweiz und Kanadas seit den 1960er Jahren. Wißner, Augsburg

Stadlin P (ed) (1990) Les Parlements des cantons suisses. Die Parlamente der schweizerischen Kantone. I Parlamenti dei cantoni svizzeri. Kalt-Zehnder, Zug

Steiner J (ed) (1971) Das politische System der Schweiz. Piper, Munich

Steiner-Khamsi G (1989) Ausländische sprachliche Minderheiten in der Schweiz. In: Eidgenössisches Departement des Innern (1989), pp 89–100

Tsachevsky V (2014) The Swiss model – the power of democracy. Peter Lang, Frankfurt a.M.

Tscharner B (2000) Sprachkontakt und Gesellschaft. In: Verein für Bündner Kulturforschung (ed) Handbuch der Bündner Geschichte, vol 3. Bündner Monatsblatt, Chur, pp 193–210

von Greyerz H et al. (1991) Geschichte der Schweiz. DTV, München

Werlen I (ed) (2000) Der zweisprachige Kanton Bern. Stuttgart, Bern and Vienna

Wiget J (ed) (2012) Die Entstehung der Schweiz. Vom Bundesbrief 1291 zur nationalen Geschichtskultur des 20. Jahrhunderts. Klio, Zurich

Wolf W (1969) Faschismus in der Schweiz. Die Geschichte der Frontenbewegungen in der deutschen Schweiz, 1930–1945, Flamberg, Zurich

Zala S (2014) Krisen, Konfrontation, Konsens (1914–1949). In: Kreis (2014), pp 490–539

Zustand und Zukunft (1989) Eidgenössisches Departement des Innern (ed) Zustand und Zukunft der viersprachigen Schweiz. Abklärungen, Vorschläge und Empfehlungen einer Arbeitsgruppe des Eidgenössischen Departements des Innern, Bern

Table of Contents for Volumes 1, 2 and 3

Egbert Jahn
International Politics
Political Issues Under Debate, Volume 1
Heidelberg: Springer
ISBN 978-3-662-47684-0

Contents

Foreword

The Structures of Conflict and Cooperation in the East of Europe

Limits on the Future Expansion of the European Union. On the Disputed Membership of Turkey, Ukraine and Other States

Kosovo and Elsewhere. Military Interventions in Defence of Human Rights ("Humanitarian Interventions")

Bosnia and Herzegovina: EU Policy in Deadlock

Federalisation: A First Step Towards the Division of Belgium?

A Temporary or Terminal Failure of the UN Plans for Cyprus

The Castling of Presidential Functions by Vladimir Putin

The Creation of New Fronts Between Russia and the West in the South Caucasus

On the Way to Two, Three, or Four Kurdistans?

The Jewish-Arab Conflict Over State Formation and Consolidation in the Near East

International Aspects of the Permanent Crisis in Iraq

The Iranian Atomic Programme: A Reason for the Deployment of Defensive Missiles in Europe or Another Military Intervention by the USA?

Escalating Conflict in Korea Due to Nuclear Armament? Or Prospects for National Reunification?

Commemoration of Genocide as a Contemporary Political Weapon. The Example of the Ottoman Genocide of the Armenians

The Toleration of Genocide in Africa: From Rwanda to Darfur

The Han Chinese Ethno-nationalisation of China (Tibet, Xingjiang)

Egbert Jahn
German Domestic and Foreign Policy
Political Issues Under Debate, Volume 2
Heidelberg: Springer
ISBN 978-3-662-47928-5

Contents

Foreword

Political Issues Under Debate. On the Meaning and Purpose of a Series of Political Science Lectures on Contemporary History

The Offences and Repudiation of Thilo Sarrazin. Are There Limits to Freedom of Political Opinion in Germany?

The Dispute over the Veil. The Conflict Between Laicism (The Separation of State and Religion) and Religious Tolerance

The Globalisation of the Danish Cartoon Dispute

"Multiculturalism" or German *Leitkultur* as Maxims for the "Integration" of Foreigners

Integration or Assimilation of Ethnic Minorities. On the Future of Danish, Sorbian, Italian, Turkish and Other Germans in the Federal Republic of Germany

The Advantages and Risks of Multiple Citizenship

Denglish Instead of German? The Changing Use of Language in Germany

From the Constitutional Treaty to the Lisbon Treaty: Is the European Union on the Way to Becoming a Federal State?

Once Again: Was Germany Defeated or Liberated on the 8th of May 1945?

From the West European Commemoration of Auschwitz to a Pan-European Commemoration of Auschwitz and the GULag Archipelago: An Inevitable Consequence of the Eastward Extension of the EU for Commemoration Policies

The Expellers and the Expelled. On an Appropriate form of Commemoration

The "Defence of Germany in the Hindu Kush". The German Role in Afghanistan

Should Germany Be a Permanent Member of the UN Security Council? On the Efforts to Reform the United Nations

Egbert Jahn
World Political Challenges
Political Issues Under Debate, Volume 3
Heidelberg: Springer
ISBN 978-3-662-47911-7

Contents

Foreword

The Wondrous Growth of Nation-states in the Age of Globalisation

Democracy and Nationalism: Twin Children of the Sovereignty of the People

A Global-human Perspective: The United Nation States of Europe and the World

The Peace Congress of the Socialist International in Basel, November 24–25, 1912

A Century of Wars and Striving for Peace Since the Peace Congress of Basel

Sarajevo 1914. A Century of Debate About the Guilt for the First World War

On the Saying: There Have Always Been Wars. There Will Always Be Wars as Long as Humanity Exists

The Present Clash of Religious Communities and Regional Civilisations in the Global Civilising Process

Geopolitics: An Ideology for the Legitimising the National Socialist Policy of Conquest or a Scientific and Political Field, That is Unappreciated Today?

Democratization or the Restoration of Dictatorship as the Outcome of the Arab Rebellion

"With What Ink Remains": Stabbing a Pen into the Hornet's Nest of Israeli, Jewish and German Sensitivities

Kashmir: Flashpoint for a Nuclear War or Even a Third World War?

The New Western War of Intervention in Mali

Linguistic Assimilation of all Citizens or Minority Protection: The Precedent Set by the Åland Islands

Canada: Has It Passed the Tests as a Multicultural Nation, or Has the Democratic Secession of Quebec Been Postponed?

The Exacerbation of the Competition Between Brussels and Moscow over the Integration of Ukraine

CPSIA information can be obtained
at www.ICGtesting.com
Printed in the USA
LVHW050842131220
674041LV00006B/58